Bc - A Digest of
the Old Testament

El Paso UMC
Family Resource Center

BC

A Digest of the Old Testament

Paraphrase by Kenneth N. Taylor

Compiled by John Calvin Reid

A Division of G/L Publications
Glendale, California, U.S.A.

Text from The Living Bible
© Copyright 1971 by
Tyndale House, Publishers
Wheaton, Illinois 60187

Additional material and arrangement
© Copyright 1971 John Calvin Reid

Published by
Regal Books Division, G/L Publications
Glendale, California 91209 U.S.A.

Library of Congress Catalog Card No. 74-169589

Hardcover ISBN 0-8307-0195-8
Softcover ISBN 0-8307-0196-6

Originally published under the title
GOD AND HIS WORLD
by Regal Books Division, G/L Publications

Printed in U.S.A.

CONTENTS

PUBLISHER'S FOREWORD

M OST people's knowledge of history is like a string of graduated pearls without a string," a historian is quoted as saying . This statement seems to be especially true concerning people's knowledge of Bible history. Many are familiar with the principal characters and events of the Old Testament, but would be hopelessly lost if they needed to arrange these personalities and episodes in historic sequence.

"The Old Testament should be read by all, for it stands tall among all the books that have ever been published," says Dr. Harold Lindsell, editor of *Christianity Today*. In their search for truth and life's answers many people bypass the Old Testament. They may do this for two simple reasons—the vast extent of its contents, and the less than obvious historical sequence of its books.

God and His World makes available the majestic truths of the Old Testament in a sequential, flowing form the reader can easily understand. The compiler's selected highlights provide Old Testament portions ideal for personal or family reading. And for some readers these selected Scriptures will serve to encourage a full reading of the unabridged Old Testament.

This condensed paraphrase in today's language will make inspiring, exciting reading for youth, for families, for just ordinary people. Like Esther of old, this volume has appeared "for such an hour as this."

In arranging for the publishing of this manuscript we were convinced that *God and His World* would become a classic in our time. More important, we believe it will open to millions the unparalleled account of God's dealings with His world and His ultimate creation—man—in order that man might have a filial relationship with Him. To this end we have published this book.

Cyrus N. Nelson
President, G/L Publications

COMPILER'S PREFACE

F EW people need to be *urged* to pray," someone has said, "but many need to be *helped*." I am persuaded that the same principle applies to Bible reading.

Scholars who have produced new translations and vivid paraphrases of the Scriptures (including Dr. Kenneth N. Taylor, whose text is being used in this volume) have rendered a great service. The Bible has been made more *readable,* with the gratifying result that it is *more widely read.*

A similar purpose has motivated me in the preparation of this book. A lifelong experience in the preaching and pastoral ministry has brought to my attention over and over the difficulties encountered by many who try to read and understand the Old Testament in particular.

There is the matter of its length (three and one-half times longer than the New Testament, 39 books altogether); then its repetitions (in Kings and Chronicles, for example); also its "begats"; and the countless dietary laws in Leviticus.

The simplest and most practical solution to these difficulties, it seems to me, is to be found in the principle of *selectivity.*

Some years ago when Kodak photography was still in its infancy and color photography not yet born, it was my privilege to tour the Holy Land. A trigger-happy amateur with camera in hand, I snapped pictures right and left. Later, financially unable to develop all of my snapshots into slides, I carefully examined the negatives one by one, in each case trying to make a good and wise decision.

The principle used was a simple one: *"Select and preserve the best."* This same principle has guided me during the countless but inspiring hours spent in company with "The Book of Books" in the preparation of this volume.

Personally I reverence the Bible as a whole and agree with the Apostle Paul that "All Scripture is inspired by God and profitable for teaching, for reproof, for correction, and for training in righteousness" (2 Timothy 3:16, *RSV*).

However, some passages, by virtue of their nature and content, provide more profit to the reader than others. Also, the very wealth and variety of material in the Bible discourages many from reading it with understanding and delight.

The majority who read the Scriptures regularly use "a Bible within the Bible" in their personal and family devotions—some passages are read over and over, others seldom or never at all. So, what many already do privately on a small scale, I have undertaken to do publicly on a larger scale by presenting the highlights of the Old Testament.

All along I have kept in mind what might be called, for the lack of a better term, "the person in the street"—the man or woman or youth to whom the Bible is a relatively unknown and seldom-opened book.

To all such, and to all others who read this preface, I would say, "Let me lend you a helping hand. Here in vivid paraphrase are highlights from the Book of Books arranged in such a way that you will find the material in chronological sequence (except in the case of Book III, "Highlights from Poetry"), topically fresh and spiritually significant. Take and read!"

In acknowledging the encouragement I have received from many friends, I presume to gratefully quote the statement of one: "A great idea! If only more people would come to see that God gave us the Bible, not to be *worshiped*, but to be *read!*" It is my hope and prayer that as you read and meditate upon these Scripture highlights, it will not only speak and minister to your heart, but also arouse and intensify your interest in the Bible as a whole.

John Calvin Reid

Book I

HIGHLIGHTS
FROM
HISTORY

Selections from Genesis through Nehemiah

PART 1 How It All Began

Selections from Genesis

1. The Creation

WHEN God began creating the heavens and the earth, the earth was at first a shapeless, chaotic mass with the Spirit of God brooding over the dark vapors. Then God said, "Let there be light." And light appeared. And God was pleased with it and divided the light from the darkness. So He let it shine for awhile, and then there was darkness again. He called the light "daytime" and the darkness "nighttime." Together they formed the first day.

And God said, "Let the vapors separate to form the sky above and the oceans below." So God made the sky, dividing the vapor above from the water below. This all happened on the second day.

Then God said, "Let the water beneath the sky be gathered into oceans so that the dry land will emerge." And so it was. Then God named the dry land "earth," and the water "seas." And God was pleased. And He said, "Let the earth burst forth with every sort of grass and seed-bearing plant and fruit trees with seeds inside the fruit. These seeds will produce the kinds of plants and fruits they came from." And so it was, and God was pleased. This all occurred on the third day.

Then God said, "Let there be bright lights in the sky to give light to the earth and to identify the day and the night; they shall bring about the seasons on the earth and mark the days and years." And so it was. For God made two huge lights, the sun and moon, to shine down upon the earth—the larger one, the sun, to preside over the day and the smaller one, the moon, to preside through the night. He also made the stars. And God set them in the sky to light the earth and to preside over the day and night, and to divide the light from the darkness. And God was pleased. This all happened on the fourth day.

Then God said, "Let the waters teem with fish and other life, and let the skies be filled with birds of every kind." So God created great sea creatures, every sort of fish and every kind of bird. And God looked at them with pleasure and blessed them all. "Multiply and stock the oceans," He told them. To the birds He said, "Let your numbers increase. Fill the earth!" That ended the fifth day.

And God said, "Let the earth bring forth every kind of animal—cattle and reptiles and wildlife of every kind." And so it was. God made all sorts of wild animals and cattle and reptiles. And God was pleased with what He had done. Then God said, "Let Us make a man—someone like Ourselves—to be the master of all life upon the earth and in the skies and in the seas."

So God made man like his Maker.
Like God did God make man;
Man and maid did He make them.

And God blessed them and told them, "Multiply and fill the earth and subdue it; you are masters of the fish and birds and all the animals. And look! I have given you the seed-bearing plants throughout the earth and all the fruit trees for your food. And I've given all the grass and plants to the animals and birds for their food." Then God looked over all that He had made, and it was excellent in every way. This ended the sixth day.

At last the heavens and earth were successfully completed with all that they contained. So on the seventh day, having finished His task, God ceased from this work He had been doing. And God blessed the seventh day and declared it holy because it was the day when He ceased this work of creation.

2. The Garden of Eden

The Lord God placed the man in the Garden of Eden as its gardener to tend and care for it. But the Lord God gave the man this warning: "You may eat any fruit in the garden except fruit from the Tree of Conscience—for its fruit will open your eyes to make you aware of right and wrong, good and bad. If you eat its fruit, you will be doomed to die."

And the Lord God said, "It isn't good for man to be alone; I will make a companion for him, a helper suited to his needs." Then the Lord God caused the man to fall into a deep sleep, took one of his ribs and closed up the place from which He had removed it. He made the rib into a woman and brought her to the man.

"This is it!" Adam exclaimed. "She is part of my own bone and flesh! Her name is 'woman' because she was taken out of a man." This explains why a man leaves his father and mother and is joined to his wife in such a way that the two become one person.

3. The Fall

The serpent was the craftiest of all the creatures the Lord God had made. So the serpent came to the woman. "Really?" he asked. *"None* of the fruit in the garden? God says you mustn't eat *any* of it?"

"Of course we may eat it," the woman told him. "It's only the fruit from the tree at the *center* of the garden that we are not to eat. God says we mustn't eat it or even touch it, or we will die."

"That's a lie!" the serpent hissed. "You'll not die! God knows very well that the instant you eat it you will become like Him, for your eyes will be opened—you will be able to distinguish good from evil!" The woman was convinced. How lovely and fresh looking it was! and it would make her so wise! So she ate some of the fruit and gave some to her husband, and he ate it too.

That evening they heard the sound of the Lord God walking in the garden; and they hid themselves among the trees. The Lord God called to Adam, "Why are you hiding?"

And Adam replied, "I heard You coming and didn't want You to see me naked. So I hid."

"Who told you you were naked?" the Lord God asked.

"Have you eaten fruit from the tree I warned you about?"

"Yes," Adam admitted, "but it was the woman You gave me who brought me some, and I ate it."

Then the Lord God asked the woman, "How could you do such a thing?"

"The serpent tricked me," she replied.

So the Lord God said to the serpent, "This is your punishment: you are singled out from among all the domestic and wild animals of the whole earth—to be cursed. You shall grovel in the dust as long as you live, crawling along on your belly. From now on you and the woman will be enemies, as will all of your offspring and hers. And I will put the fear of you into the woman, and between your offspring and hers. He shall strike you on your head while you will strike at his heel."

Then God said to the woman, "You shall bear children in intense pain and suffering; yet even so, you shall welcome your husband's affections, and he shall be your master."

And to Adam, God said, "Because you listened to your wife and ate the fruit when I told you not to, I have placed a curse upon the soil. All your life you will struggle to extract a living from it. It will grow thorns and thistles for you, and you shall eat its grasses. All your life you will sweat to master it, until your dying day. Then you will return to the ground from which you came. For you were made from the ground, and to the ground you will return." So the Lord God banished him forever from the Garden of Eden and sent him out to farm the ground from which he had been taken. Thus God expelled him and placed mighty angels at the east of the Garden of Eden, with a flaming sword to guard the entrance to the Tree of Life.

4. The First Murder

Then Adam had sexual intercourse with Eve his wife, and she conceived and gave birth to a son, Cain (meaning "I have created"). For as she said, "With God's help, I have created a man!" Her next child was his brother Abel. Abel became a shepherd, while Cain was a farmer.

At harvest time Cain brought the Lord a gift of his farm produce. Abel brought the fatty cuts of meat from his best lambs and presented them to the Lord. And the Lord accepted Abel's offering, but not Cain's. This made Cain both dejected and very angry. His face grew dark with fury.

"Why are you angry?" the Lord asked him. "Why is your face so dark with rage? It can be bright with joy if you will do what you should! But if you refuse to obey, watch out. Sin is waiting to attack you, longing to destroy you. But you can conquer it!"

One day Cain suggested to his brother, "Let's go out into the fields." And while they were together there, Cain attacked and killed his brother.

But afterwards the Lord asked Cain, "Where is your brother? Where is Abel?"

"How should I know?" Cain retorted. "Am I supposed to keep track of him wherever he goes?"

But the Lord said, "Your brother's blood calls to Me from the ground. What have you done? You are hereby banished from this ground which you have defiled with your brother's blood. No longer will it yield crops for you, even if you toil on it forever! From now on you will be a fugitive and a tramp upon the earth, wandering from place to place."

Cain replied to the Lord, "My punishment is greater than I can bear. For You have banished me from my farm and from You, and made me a fugitive and a tramp. Everyone who sees me will try to kill me."

The Lord replied, "They won't kill you, for I will give seven times your punishment to anyone who does." Then the Lord put an identifying mark on Cain as a warning not to kill him. So Cain went out from the presence of the Lord and settled in the land of Nod, east of Eden.

5. The Flood

As the population increased decadence set in. When the Lord saw the extent of human wickedness and that the trend and direction of men's lives were only towards evil, He was sorry that He had made them. And He said, "I will blot out from the face of the earth all mankind that I created. Yes, and the animals too, and the reptiles and the birds. For I am sorry I made them." But Noah was a pleasure to the Lord. Here is the story of Noah:

He was the only truly righteous man living on the earth at that time. He tried always to conduct his affairs according to God's will. And he had three sons—Shem, Ham and Japheth. Meanwhile the crime rate was rising rapidly across the earth and, as seen by God, the world was rotten to the core.

As God observed how bad it was and saw that all mankind was vicious and depraved, He said to Noah, "I have decided to destroy all mankind; for the earth is filled with crime because of man. Yes, I will destroy mankind from the earth. Make a boat from resinous wood, sealing it with tar. Construct decks and stalls throughout the ship. Make it four hundred fifty feet long, seventy-five feet wide and forty-five feet high. Construct a skylight all the way around the ship, eighteen inches below the roof. Make three decks inside the boat—a bottom, middle and upper deck—and put a door in the side.

"Look! I am going to cover the earth with a flood and destroy every living being—everything in which there is the breath of life. All will die. But I promise to keep you safe in the ship, with your wife and your sons and their wives. Bring a pair of every animal—a male and a female—into the boat with you, to keep them alive through the flood. Bring in a pair of each kind of bird and animal and reptile. Store away in the boat all the food that they and you will need."

And Noah did everything as God commanded him.

Finally the day came when the Lord said to Noah, "Go into the boat with all your family, for among all the people of the earth, I consider you alone to be righteous." One week later, when Noah was 600 years, two months and 17 days old, the rain came down in mighty torrents from the sky. Subterranean waters burst forth upon the earth for forty days and nights. But Noah had gone into the boat with his wife and his sons, Shem, Ham and Japheth, and their wives. With them in the boat were pairs of every kind of animal—domestic and wild—and reptiles and birds of every sort.

As the water rose higher and higher above the ground, the boat floated safely upon it, until finally the water covered all the high mountains under the whole heaven, standing 22 feet and more above the highest peaks.

All existence on the earth was blotted out—man and animals alike, and reptiles and birds. God destroyed them all, leaving only Noah alive, and those with him in the boat. And the water covered the earth 150 days.

God didn't forget about Noah and all the animals in the boat! He sent a wind to blow across the waters, and the floods began to disappear, for the subterranean water sources ceased their gushing, and the torrential rains subsided. So the flood gradually receded until the boat came to rest upon the mountains of Ararat.

Meanwhile Noah sent out a dove to see if it could find dry ground. But the dove found no place to light, and returned to Noah, for the water was still too high. So Noah held out his hand and drew the dove back into the boat. Seven days later Noah released the dove again, and this time, towards evening, the bird returned to him with an olive leaf in her beak. So Noah knew that the water was almost gone.

Then at last the earth was dry. God told Noah, "You may all go out." The boat was soon empty. Noah, his wife, his sons and their wives all disembarked, along with all the animals, reptiles and birds—all left the ark in pairs and groups.

Then Noah built an altar and sacrificed on it some of the animals and birds God had designated for that purpose. And Jehovah was pleased with the sacrifice and said to Himself, "I will never do it again—I will never again curse the earth, destroying all living things, even though man's bent is always toward evil from his earliest youth, and even though he does such wicked things. As long as the earth remains, there will be springtime and harvest, cold and heat, winter and summer, day and night. And I seal this promise with this sign: I have placed My rainbow in the clouds as a sign of My promise until the end of time, to you and to all the earth. When I send clouds over the earth, the rainbow will be seen in the clouds, and I will remember My promise to you and to every being that never again will the floods come and destroy all life."

6. The Tower of Babel

In time, many generations of men descended from Noah and his sons. These all spoke a single, simple language. As the population grew and spread eastward, a plain discovered in the land of Babylon was soon thickly populated.

The people who lived there began to talk about building a great city with a temple-tower reaching to the skies—a proud, eternal monument to themselves. "This will weld us together," they said, "and keep us from scattering all over the world." So they made great piles of hard-burned brick and collected bitumen to use as mortar.

But when God came down to see the city and the tower mankind was making, He said, "Look! If they are able to accomplish all this when they have just *begun* to exploit their linguistic and political unity, just think of what they will do later! Nothing will be unattainable for them! Come, let us go down and give them different languages so that they won't understand each other's words!" So, in that way, God scattered them all over the earth, and that ended the building of the city. That is why the city was called Babel (meaning "confusion"), because it was there that Jehovah confused them by giving them many languages, thus widely scattering them across the face of the earth.

7. Abram's Call

Among the later descendants of Shem (one of the sons of Noah) was a man named Terah who had three sons: Abram, Nahor and Haran. And Haran had a son named Lot, but Haran died young in the land where he was born (in Ur of the Chaldeans) and was survived by his father. Meanwhile, Abram had married his half-sister Sarai. But she was barren.

Then Terah took his son Abram, his grandson Lot (his son Haran's child) and his daughter-in-law Sarai. They left Ur of the Chaldeans to go to the land of Canaan, but they stopped instead at the city of Haran and settled there. Terah died there at the age of 205.

After the death of Abram's father, God told him, "Leave your own country behind you, and your own people, and go to the land I will guide you to. If you do, I will cause you to become the father of a great nation; I will bless you and make your name famous, and you will be a blessing to many others. I will bless those who bless you and curse those who curse you; and the entire world will be blessed because of you."

So Abram departed as the Lord had instructed him. Lot went too. Abram was 75 years old at that time. He took his wife Sarai, his nephew Lot, and all his wealth—the cattle and slaves he had gotten in Haran—and finally arrived in Canaan. Traveling through Canaan they came to a place near Shechem, and set up camp beside the oak at Moreh. (This area was inhabited by Canaanites at that time.)

Then Jehovah appeared to Abram and said, "I am going to give this land to your descendants." And Abram built an altar there to commemorate Jehovah's visit. Afterwards Abram left that place and traveled southward to the hilly country between Bethel on the west and Ai on the east. There he made an altar to the Lord and prayed to Him.

8. Lot's Choice

Abram was very rich in livestock, silver and gold. Lot too was very wealthy with sheep and cattle and many servants. But the land could not support both Abram and Lot with all their flocks and herds. There were too many animals for the available pasture. So fights broke out between the herdsmen of Abram and Lot, despite the danger they all faced from the tribes of Canaanites and Perizzites present in the land.

Then Abram talked it over with Lot. "This fighting between our men has got to stop," he said. "We can't afford to let a rift develop between our clans. Close relatives such as we are must present a united front! I'll tell you what we'll do. Take your choice of any section of the land you want, and we will separate. If you want that part over there to the east, then I'll stay here in the western section. Or, if you want the west, then I'll go over there to the east."

Lot took a long look at the fertile plains of the Jordan River, well watered everywhere (this was before Jehovah destroyed Sodom and Gomorrah): the whole section was like the Garden of Eden, or like the beautiful countryside around Zoar in Egypt. So that is what Lot chose—the Jordan Valley to the east of them. He went there with his flocks and servants, and thus he and Abram parted company. For Abram stayed in the land of Canaan, while Lot lived among the cities of the plain, settling at a place near the city of Sodom. The men of this area were unusually wicked and sinned greatly against Jehovah.

After Lot was gone, the Lord said to Abram, "Look as far as you can see in every direction, for I am going to give it all to you and your descendants."

9. God's Promise to Abraham

Afterwards Jehovah spoke to Abram in a vision. This is what He told him: "Don't be fearful, Abram, for I will defend you. And I will give you great blessings."

But Abram replied, "O Lord Jehovah, what good are all Your blessings when I have no son? For without a son, some other member of my household will inherit all my wealth."

Then Jehovah told him, "No, no one else will be your heir, for you will have a son to inherit everything you own." Then God brought Abram outside beneath the nighttime sky and told him, "Look up into the heavens and count the stars if you can. Your descendants will be like that—too many to count!"

And Abram believed God; then God considered him righteous on account of his faith. And when he was ninety-nine years old, God appeared to him and told him, "I am the Almighty; obey Me and live as you should. I will prepare a contract between us, guaranteeing to make you into a mighty nation. In fact you shall be the father of not only one nation, but a multitude of nations!" Abram fell face downward in the dust as God talked with him.

"What's more," God told him, "I am changing your name.

It is no longer Abram ('Exalted Father'), but Abraham ('Father of Nations')—for that is what you will be. I have declared it. I will give you millions of descendants who will form many nations! Kings shall be among your descendants! And I will continue this agreement between us generation after generation, forever, for it shall be between Me and your children as well. It is a contract that I shall be your God and the God of your posterity. And I will give all this land of Canaan to you and them forever. And I will be your God. Your part of the contract," God told him, "is to obey its terms. You personally and all your posterity have this continual responsibility: that every male among you shall be circumcised; the foreskin of his penis shall be cut off. This will be the proof that you and they accept this covenant. Every male shall be circumcised on the eighth day after birth."

Then God added, "Regarding Sarai your wife—her name is no longer Sarai but Sarah ('Princess'). And I will bless her and give you a son from her! Yes, I will bless her richly, and make her the mother of nations! Many kings shall be among your posterity."

10. Abraham's Urgent Plea

The Lord appeared again to Abraham while he was living in the oak grove at Mamre. This the way it happened: One hot summer afternoon as he was sitting in the opening of his tent, he suddenly noticed three men coming toward him. He sprang up and ran to meet them and welcomed them.

"Sirs," he said, "please don't go any further. Stop awhile and rest here in the shade of this tree while I get water to refresh your feet and a bite to eat to strengthen you. Do stay awhile before continuing your journey."

"All right," they said, "do as you have said."

Then Abraham ran back to the tent and said to Sarah, "Quick! Mix up some pancakes! Use your best flour, and make enough for the three of them!" Then he ran out to the herd and selected a fat calf and told a servant to hurry and butcher it. Soon, taking them cheese and milk and the roast veal, he set it before the men and stood beneath the tree beside them as they ate. Then the men stood up from their meal and started on toward Sodom, and Abraham went with them part of the way.

The Lord said to Abraham, "I have heard that the people of Sodom and Gomorrah are utterly evil and that everything they do is wicked. I am going down to see whether these reports are true or not. Then I will know." So the other two went on toward Sodom, but the Lord remained with Abraham awhile. Then Abraham approached Him and said, "Will You kill good and bad alike? Suppose You find 50 godly people there within the city—will You destroy it, and not spare it for their sakes? That wouldn't be right! Surely You wouldn't do such a thing, to kill the godly with the wicked! Why, You would be treating godly and wicked exactly the same! Surely You wouldn't do that! Should not the Judge of all the earth be fair?"

And God replied, "If I find 50 godly people there, I will spare the entire city for their sake."

Then Abraham spoke again. "Since I have begun, let me go on and speak further to the Lord, though I am but dust and ashes. *Suppose there are only 45?* Will You destroy the city for lack of five?"

And God said, "I will not destroy it if I find 45."

Then Abraham went further with his request. *"Suppose there are only 40?"*

And God replied, "I won't destroy it if there are 40."

"Please don't be angry," Abraham pleaded. "Let me speak: *Suppose only 30 are found there?*"

And God replied, "I won't do it if there are 30 there."

Then Abraham said, "Since I have dared to speak to God, let me continue—*Suppose there are only 20?*"

And God said, "Then I won't destroy it for the sake of the 20."

Finally, Abraham said, "Oh, let not the Lord be angry; I will speak but this once more! *Suppose only ten are found?*"

And God said, "Then for the sake of the ten, I won't destroy it." And the Lord went on His way when He had finished

His conversation with Abraham. And Abraham returned to his tent.

11. The Destruction of Sodom

That evening the two angels came to the entrance of the city of Sodom, where Lot was sitting. When he saw them he stood up to meet them and welcomed them. "Sirs," he said, "come to my home as my guests for the night. You can get up as early as you like and be on your way again."

"What relatives do you have here in the city?" the men asked. "Get them out of this place—sons-in-law, sons, daughters, or anyone else. For we will destroy the city completely. The stench of the place has reached to heaven and God has sent us to destroy it."

So Lot rushed out to tell his daughter's fiancés, "Quick, get out of the city, for the Lord is going to destroy it." But the young men looked at him as though he had lost his senses.

At dawn the next morning the angels became urgent. "Hurry," they said to Lot, "take your wife and your two daughters who are here and get out while you can, or you will be caught in the destruction of the city." When Lot still hesitated, the angels seized his hand and the hands of his wife and two daughters and rushed them to safety outside the city, for the Lord was merciful. "Flee for your lives," the angels told him. "And don't look back. Escape to the mountains. Don't stay down here on the plain or you will die."

Then the Lord rained down fire and flaming tar from heaven upon Sodom and Gomorrah and utterly destroyed them, along with the other cities and villages of the plain, eliminating all life—people, plants, and animals alike. But Lot's wife looked back as she was following along behind him, and she became a pillar of salt.

That morning Abraham was up early and hurried out to the place where he had stood before the Lord. He looked out across the plain to Sodom and Gomorrah and saw columns of smoke and fumes as from a furnace rising from the cities there. So God heeded Abraham's plea and kept Lot safe, removing him from the maelstrom of death that engulfed the cities.

12. The Birth of Isaac

Then God did as He had promised, and Sarah became pregnant and gave Abraham a baby son in his old age, at the time God had said; and Abraham named him Isaac (meaning "Laughter!"). Eight days after he was born, Abraham circumcised him, as God required. (Abraham was 100 years old at that time.)

And Sarah declared, "God has brought me laughter! All who hear about this shall rejoice with me. For who would have dreamed that I would ever have a baby? Yet I have given Abraham a child in his old age!" Time went by and the child grew and was weaned; and Abraham threw a big party to celebrate the happy occasion.

13. Abraham's Offering

Later on, God tested Abraham. "Abraham!" God called. "Yes, Lord?" he replied.

"Take with you your only son—yes, Isaac whom you love so much—and go to the land of Moriah and sacrifice him there as a burnt offering upon one of the mountains which I'll point out to you!" The next morning Abraham got up early, chopped wood for a fire upon the altar and saddled his donkey. Then he took with him his son Isaac and two young men who were his servants and started off to the place where God had told him to go. On the third day of the journey Abraham saw the place in the distance.

"Stay here with the donkey," Abraham told the young men, "and the lad and I will travel yonder and worship, and then come right back." Abraham placed the wood for the burnt offering upon Isaac's shoulders, while he himself carried the knife and the flint for striking a fire. So the two of them went on together.

"Father!" Isaac asked, "we have the wood and the flint to make the fire, but where is the lamb for the sacrifice?"

"God will see to it, my son," Abraham replied. And they went on. When they arrived at the place where God had told Abraham to go, he built an altar and placed the wood in order, ready for the fire. Then he tied Isaac and laid him on the altar over the wood. And Abraham took the knife and lifted it up to plunge it into his son, to slay him.

At that moment the Angel of God shouted to him from heaven, "Abraham! Abraham!"

"Yes, Lord!" he answered.

"Lay down the knife; don't hurt the lad in any way," the Angel said, "for I know that God is first in your life—you have not withheld even your beloved son from Me." Then Abraham noticed a ram caught by its horns in a bush. So he took the ram and sacrificed it, instead of his son, as a burnt offering on the altar. Abraham named the place "Jehovah Sees"—and it still goes by that name to this day.

Then the Angel of God called again to Abraham from heaven. "I, the Lord, have sworn by Myself that because you have obeyed Me and have not withheld even your beloved son from Me, I will bless you with incredible blessings and multiply your descendants into countless thousands and millions, like the stars above you in the sky, and like the sands along the seashore. These descendants of yours will conquer their enemies and be a blessing to all the nations of the earth—all because you have obeyed Me."

So they returned to his young men and traveled home again to Beer-sheba.

14. The Death and Burial of Sarah

When Sarah was 127 years old she died in Hebron in the land of Canaan; there Abraham mourned and wept for her. Then, standing beside her body, he said to the men of Heth: "Here I am, a visitor in a foreign land, with no place to bury my wife. Please sell me a piece of ground for this purpose."

"Certainly," the men replied, "for you are an honored

prince of God among us; it will be a privilege to have you choose the finest of our sepulchers, so that you can bury her there."

This is the land he bought: Ephron's field at Mach-pelah near Mamre, the cave at the end of the field and all the trees in the field. They became his permanent possession, by agreement in the presence of the men of Heth at the city gate. So Abraham buried Sarah there in the field and cave deeded to him by the men of Heth as a burial plot.

15. Isaac's Betrothal

Abraham was now a very old man, and God blessed him in every way. One day Abraham said to his household administrator, who was his oldest servant, "Swear by Jehovah, the God of heaven and earth, that you will not let my son marry one of these local girls, these Canaanites. Go instead to my homeland, to my relatives, and find a wife for him there."

So the servant vowed to follow Abraham's instructions. He took with him ten of Abraham's camels loaded with samples of the best of everything his master owned. He journeyed to Iraq, to Nahor's village. There he made the camels kneel down outside the town, beside a spring. It was evening and the women of the village were coming to draw water.

"O Jehovah, the God of my master," he prayed, "show kindness to my master Abraham and help me to accomplish the purpose of my journey. See, here I am, standing beside this spring, and the girls of the village are coming out to draw water. This is my request: when I ask one of them for a drink and she says, 'Yes, certainly, and I will water your camels too!'—let her be the one You have appointed as Isaac's wife. That is how I will know."

As he was still speaking to the Lord about this, a beautiful young girl named Rebekah arrived with a water jug on her shoulder and filled it at the spring. (Her father was Bethuel the son of Nahor and his wife Milcah.) Running over to her, the servant asked her for a drink.

"Certainly, sir," she said, and quickly lowered the jug for

him to drink. Then she said, "I'll draw water for your camels, too, until they have enough!" So she emptied the jug into the watering trough and ran down to the spring again and kept carrying water to the camels until they had enough. The servant said no more, but watched her carefully to see if she would finish the job, so that he would know whether she was the one.

Then at last, when the camels had finished drinking, he produced a quarter-ounce gold earring and two five-ounce golden bracelets for her wrists. "Whose daughter are you, miss?" he asked. "Would your father have any room to put us up for the night?"

"My father is Bethuel, the son of Milcah, the wife of Nahor," she replied. "Yes, we have a guest room and plenty of straw and food for the camels."

The man stood there a moment with head bowed, worshiping Jehovah. "Thank You, Lord God of my master Abraham," he prayed. "Thank You for being so kind and true to him, and for leading me straight to the family of my master's relatives."

The girl ran home to tell her folks.

And when her brother Laban saw the earring, also the bracelets on his sister's wrists, and heard her story, he rushed out to the spring where the man was still standing beside his camels. Laban said to him, "Come and stay with us, friend; why stand here outside the city when we have a room all ready for you and a place prepared for the camels!" So the man went home with Laban, and Laban gave him straw to bed down the camels, feed for them and water for the camel drivers to wash their feet.

Then supper was served. But the old man said, "I don't want to eat until I have told you why I am here."

"All right," Laban said, "tell us your errand."

"I am Abraham's servant," he explained. "And Jehovah has overwhelmed my master with blessings so that he is a great man among the people of his land. God has given him flocks of sheep and herds of cattle, and a fortune in silver and gold, and many slaves and camels and donkeys. Now when Sarah, my master's wife, was very old, she gave birth to my master's son, and my master has given him everything he owns. And my master made me promise not to let Isaac marry one of the local girls, but to come to his relatives here in this far-off land, to his brother's family, and to bring back a girl from here to marry his son. Well, this afternoon when I came to the spring I prayed this prayer: 'O Jehovah, the God of my master Abraham, if You are planning to make my mission a success, please guide me in this way: Here I am, standing beside this spring. I will say to some girl who comes to draw water, "Please give me a drink of water!" And she will reply, "Certainly! And I'll water your camels too!" Let that girl be the one You have selected to be the wife of my master's son.'

"And this is exactly what happened!

"God had led me along just the right path to find a girl from the family of my master's brother. So tell me yes or no. Will you or won't you be kind to my master and do what is right? When you tell me, then I'll know what my next step should be, whether to move this way or that."

Then Laban and Bethuel replied, "The Lord has obviously brought you here, so what can we say? Take her and go! Yes, let her be the wife of your master's son, as Jehovah has directed."

At this reply, Abraham's servant fell to his knees before Jehovah. Then he brought out jewels set in solid gold and silver for Rebekah, and lovely clothing; and he gave many valuable presents to her mother and brother. Then they called Rebekah. "Are you willing to go with this man?" they asked her.

And she replied, "Yes, I will go." So Rebekah and her servant girls mounted the camels and went with him.

Meanwhile, Isaac, whose home was in the Negeb, had returned to Beer-lahai-roi. One evening as he was taking a walk out in the fields, meditating, he looked up and saw the camels coming. Rebekah noticed him and quickly dismounted. "Who is that man walking through the fields to meet us?" she asked the servant.

And he replied, "It is my master's son!" So she covered her face with her veil. Then the servant told Isaac the whole story, and Isaac brought Rebekah into his mother's tent and she became his wife. He loved her very much, and she was a special comfort to him after the loss of his mother.

Abraham deeded everything he owned to Isaac; however,

he gave gifts to the sons of his concubines and sent them off into the east, away from Isaac. Then Abraham died at the ripe old age of 175. And his sons Isaac and Ishmael buried him in the cave of Mach-pelah near Mamre, in the field Abraham had purchased from Ephron, the son of Zohar the Hethite, where Sarah (Abraham's wife) was buried.

16. The Birth of Esau and Jacob

This is the story of Isaac's children: Isaac was forty years old when he married Rebekah, the daughter of Bethuel the Aramean from Padan-aram, and the sister of Laban. He pleaded with Jehovah to give Rebekah a child, for even after many years of marriage she had no children. Then at last she became pregnant. And it seemed as though children were fighting each other inside her! "I can't endure this," she exclaimed. So she asked the Lord about it.

And He told her, "The sons in your womb shall become two rival nations. One will be stronger than the other; and the older shall be a servant of the younger!" And sure enough, she had twins. The first was born so covered with reddish hair that one would think he was wearing a fur coat! So they called him Esau. Then the other twin was born with his hand on Esau's heel! So they called him Jacob (meaning "He grabs heels!"). Isaac was 60 years old when the twins were born.

17. The Birthright Traded

As the boys grew, Esau became a skillful hunter, while Jacob was a quiet sort who liked to stay at home. Isaac's favorite was Esau because of the venison he brought home, and Rebekah's favorite was Jacob.

One day Jacob was cooking stew when Esau arrived home exhausted from the hunt. Esau said, "Boy, am I starved! Give me a bite of that red stuff there!" (From this came his nickname "Edom," which means "Red Stuff.")

Jacob answered, "All right, trade me your birthright for it!"

"When a man is dying of starvation, what good is his birthright?" asked Esau.

"Well then, vow to God that it is mine!" said Jacob.

And Esau vowed, thereby selling all his eldest-son rights to his younger brother. Then Jacob gave Esau bread, peas and stew. So he ate and drank and went on about his business, indifferent to the loss of the rights he had thrown away.

18. The Wells Restored

Now a severe famine overshadowed the land, as had happened in Abraham's time, and so Isaac moved to the city of Gerar where Abimelech, king of the Philistines, lived. And Isaac redug the wells of his father Abraham, the ones the Philistines had filled after his father's death, and gave them the same names they had had before when his father had named them. His shepherds also dug a new well in Gerar Valley and found a gushing underground spring.

When he went to Beer-sheba, Jehovah appeared to him on the night of his arrival. "I am the God of Abraham your father," He said. "Fear not, for I am with you and will bless you, and will give you so many descendants that they will become a great nation—because of My promise to Abraham, who obeyed Me." Then Isaac built an altar and worshiped Jehovah. He settled there, and his servants dug a well.

19. Jacob the Deceiver

One day, in Isaac's old age when he was half-blind, he called for Esau his oldest son. He said, "My son?"

"Yes, father?" Esau answered him.

Isaac said, "I am an old man now and expect to die 'most any day. Take your bow and arrows out into the fields and get me some venison. Prepare it just the way I like it—savory and good—and bring it here for me to eat. Then I will give you the blessings that belong to you, my firstborn son, before I die."

But Rebekah overheard the conversation. So when Esau left for the field to hunt the venison, she called her son Jacob and told him what his father had said to his brother. "Now do exactly as I tell you," she said. "Go out to the flocks and bring me two young goats, and I'll prepare your father's favorite dish from them. Then take it to your father, and after he has enjoyed it he will bless *you* before his death, instead of Esau!"

"But mother!" Jacob said, "he won't be fooled that easily. Think of how hairy Esau is, and how smooth my skin is! What if my father feels me? He'll think I'm making a fool of him, and curse me instead of blessing me!"

Rebekah answered, "Let his curses be on me, dear son. Just do what I tell you. Go out and get the goats." So Jacob followed his mother's instructions, bringing the dressed kids, which she prepared in his father's favorite way. Then she took Esau's best clothes—they were there in the house—and instructed Jacob to put them on. And she made him a pair of gloves from the hairy skin of the young goats and fastened a strip of hide around his neck. Then she gave him the meat with its rich aroma and some fresh-baked bread. Jacob carried the platter of food into the room where his father was lying. "Father?" Jacob said.

Isaac asked, "Yes? Who is it, my son—Esau or Jacob?"

"It's Esau, your oldest son," said Jacob. "I've done as you told me to do. Here is the delicious venison you wanted. Sit up and eat it, so that you will bless me with all your heart!"

And Isaac said, "How were you able to find it so quickly, my son?"

"Because Jehovah your God put it in my path!" answered Jacob.

Then Isaac said, "Come over here. I want to feel you, and be sure it really is Esau!" Jacob went over to his father. He felt him. Isaac said to himself, "The voice is Jacob's, but the hands are Esau's!" The ruse convinced him and he gave Jacob his blessings. But Isaac again asked, "Are you really Esau?"

"Yes, of course," Jacob answered.

"Then bring me the venison," said Isaac, "and I will eat it and bless you with all my heart." Jacob took it over to him and

Isaac ate; he also drank the wine Jacob brought him.

Then Isaac said, "Come here and kiss me, my son!" Jacob went over and kissed him on the cheek. Isaac sniffed his clothes and finally seemed convinced. "The smell of my son is the good smell of the earth and fields that Jehovah has blessed. May God always give you plenty of rain for your crops, good harvests of grain and new wine. May the nations be your slaves. Be the master of your brothers. May all your relatives bow low before you. Cursed are all who curse you, and blessed are all who bless you."

As soon as Isaac had blessed Jacob, and almost before Jacob left the room, Esau arrived, coming in from his hunting. He also had prepared his father's favorite dish and brought it to him. He said, "Here I am, father, with venison. Sit up and eat it so that you can give me your finest blessings!"

But Isaac asked him, "Who is it?"

"Why, it's me, of course! Esau, your oldest son!" Isaac began to tremble noticeably.

"Then who was just here with venison, and I have already eaten it and blessed him with irrevocable blessing?" Now Esau began to sob with deep and bitter sobs.

"O my father, bless me, bless me too!" he cried.

"Your brother was here and tricked me," said Isaac, "and has carried away your blessing."

Esau said bitterly, "No wonder they call him 'the Cheater,' for he took my birthright and now he has stolen my blessing. Oh, haven't you saved even one blessing for me?"

Isaac replied, "I have made him your master, and have given him yourself and all of his relatives as his servants. I have guaranteed him abundance of grain and wine—what is there left to give?"

But Esau pleaded, "Not one blessing left for me? O my father, bless me too."

Hearing Esau's weeping, Isaac said, "Yours will be no life of ease and luxury, but you shall hew your way with your sword. For a time you will serve your brother, but you will finally shake loose from him and be free."

So Esau hated Jacob because of what he had done to him. He said to himself, "My father will soon be gone, and then I will kill Jacob." But someone got wind of what he was planning and reported it to Rebekah. She sent for Jacob and told him that his life was being threatened by Esau.

"This is what to do," she said. "Flee to your Uncle Laban in Haran. Stay there with him awhile until your brother's fury is spent and he forgets what you have done. Then I will send for you. For why should I be bereaved of both of you in one day?"

Then Rebekah said to Isaac, "I'm sick and tired of these local girls. I'd rather die than see Jacob marry one of them."

So Isaac called for Jacob and blessed him and said to him, "Don't marry one of these Canaanite girls. Instead, go at once to Padan-aram, to the house of your grandfather Bethuel, and marry one of your cousins—your Uncle Laban's daughters. God Almighty bless you and give you many children; may you become a great nation of many tribes! May God pass on to you and to your descendants the mighty blessings promised to Abraham. May you own this land where we now are foreigners, for God has given it to Abraham."

20. Jacob's Dream

So Jacob left Beer-sheba and journeyed toward Haran. One night when he stopped to camp at sundown, he found a rock for a headrest. He lay down to sleep and dreamed that a staircase reached from earth to heaven. He saw the angels of God going up and down upon it. At the top of the stairs stood the Lord. "I am Jehovah," He said, "the God of Abraham, and of your father Isaac. The ground you are lying on is yours! I will give it to you and to your descendants. For you will have descendants as many as dust! They will cover the land from east to west and from north to south; and all the nations of the earth will be blessed through you and your descendants. What's more, I am with you, and will protect you wherever you go, and will bring you back safely to this land; I will be with you constantly until I have finished giving you all I am promising."

Then Jacob woke up. "God lives here!" he exclaimed in

terror. "I've stumbled into His home! This is the awesome entrance to heaven!" The next morning he got up very early and set his stone headrest upright as a memorial pillar and poured olive oil over it. He named the place Bethel ("House of God"), though the previous name of the nearest village was Luz. And Jacob vowed this to God: "If God will help and protect me on this journey and give me food and clothes, and will bring me back safely to my father, then I will choose Jehovah as my God! And this memorial pillar shall become a place for worship; and I will give You back a tenth of everything You give me!"

21. Jacob's Marriages

Jacob traveled on, finally arriving in the land of the East. He saw in the distance three flocks of sheep waiting to be watered, lying beside a well in an open field. But a heavy stone covered the mouth of the well. (The custom was that the stone was not removed until all the flocks were there. After watering them, the stone was rolled back over the mouth of the well again.)

Jacob went over to the shepherds and asked them where they lived. "At Haran," they said.

"Do you know a fellow there named Laban the son of Nahor?"

"We sure do."

"How is he?"

"He's well and prosperous. Look, there comes his daughter Rachel with the sheep."

"Why don't you water the flocks so they can get back to grazing?" Jacob asked. "They'll be hungry if you stop so early in the day!"

"We don't roll away the stone and begin the watering until all the flocks and shepherds are here," they replied.

As this conversation was going on Rachel arrived with her father's sheep, for she was a shepherdess. And because she was his cousin—the daughter of his mother's brother—and because the sheep were his uncle's, Jacob went over to the well and rolled away the stone and watered his uncle's flock. Then

Jacob kissed Rachel and started crying! He explained about being her cousin on her father's side, and that he was her Aunt Rebekah's son. She quickly ran and told her father, Laban, and as soon as he heard of Jacob's arrival, he rushed out to meet him and greeted him warmly and brought him home. Then Jacob told him his story.

"Just think, my very own flesh and blood!" Laban exclaimed.

After Jacob had been there about a month, Laban said to him one day, "Just because we are relatives is no reason for you to work for me without pay. How much do you want?" Now Laban had two daughters, Leah, the older, and her younger sister, Rachel. Leah had lovely eyes, but Rachel was shapely and in every way a beauty.

Well, Jacob was in love with Rachel. So he told her father, "I'll work seven years if you'll give me Rachel as my wife."

"Agreed!" Laban replied. "I'd rather give her to you than to someone outside the family." So Jacob spent the next seven years working to pay for Rachel. But they seemed to him but a few days, he was so much in love.

Finally the time came for him to marry her. "I have fulfilled my contract," Jacob said to Laban. "Now give me my wife, so that I can sleep with her." So Laban invited all the men of the settlement to celebrate with Jacob at a big party. Afterwards, that night, when it was dark, Laban took Leah to Jacob, and he slept with her. (And Laban gave to Leah a servant girl, Zilpah, to be her maid.) But in the morning—it was Leah!

"What sort of trick is this?" Jacob raged at Laban. "I worked for seven years for Rachel. What do you mean by this trickery?"

"It's not our custom to marry off a younger daughter ahead of her older sister," Laban replied smoothly. "Wait until the bridal week is over and you can have Rachel too—if you promise to work for me another seven years!" So Jacob agreed to work seven more years. Then Laban gave him Rachel too. And Laban gave to Rachel a servant girl, Bilhah, to be her maid.

So Jacob slept with Rachel, too, and he loved her more than Leah, and stayed and worked the additional seven years.

22. Covenant Between Laban and Jacob

Some years later Jehovah spoke to Jacob and said, "Return to the land of your fathers and to your relatives there, and I will be with you." By this time Jacob had 11 sons and one daughter. He had also become very wealthy; he had many servants, flocks, herds, camels and donkeys.

"I am the God you met at Bethel," Jehovah continued, "the place where you anointed the pillar and made a vow to serve me. Now leave this country and return to the land of your birth."

So one day while Laban was out shearing sheep, Jacob set his wives and sons on camels and fled without telling Laban his intentions. He drove the flocks before him—Jacob's flocks he had gotten there at Padan-aram—and took everything he owned and started out to return to his father Isaac in Canaan.

Laban didn't learn of their flight for three days. Then, taking several men with him, he set out in hot pursuit. Seven days later God appeared to Laban in a dream. "Watch out what you say to Jacob," he was told. "Don't give him your blessing and don't curse him." Laban finally caught up with Jacob as he was camped at the top of a ridge; Laban meanwhile camped below him in the mountains. "What do you mean by sneaking off like this?" Laban demanded. "Are my daughters prisoners, captured in a battle, that you have rushed them away like this? Why didn't you give me a chance to have a farewell party with singing and orchestra and harp? Why didn't you let me kiss my grandchildren and tell them good-bye? This is a strange way to act."

"I sneaked away because I was afraid," Jacob answered. "I said to myself, 'He'll take his daughters from me by force.' "

Laban replied, "These women are my daughters, and these children are mine, and these flocks and all that you have—all are mine. So how could I harm my own daughters and grandchildren? Come now and we will sign a peace pact, you and I, and will live by its terms."

So Jacob took a stone and set it up as a monument, and told his men to gather stones and make a heap. And Jacob and Laban ate together beside the pile of rocks.

"This heap," Laban said, "stands between us as a witness of our vows that I will not cross this line to attack you and you will not cross it to attack me. I call upon the God of Abraham and Nahor, and of their father, to destroy either one of us who does." So Jacob took oath before the mighty God of his father Isaac to respect the boundary line. Then Jacob presented a sacrifice to God there at the top of the mountain and invited his companions to a feast. Afterwards he spent the night with them on the mountain. Laban was up early the next morning, kissed his daughters and grandchildren, blessed them and returned home.

23. Jacob the Wrestler

So Jacob and his household started on again. And the angels of God came to meet him. When he saw them he exclaimed, "God lives here!" So he named the place "God's territory!" Jacob now sent messengers to his brother Esau in Edom, in the land of Seir, with this message: "Hello from Jacob! I have been living with Uncle Laban until recently. Now I own oxen, donkeys, sheep and many servants, both men and women. I have sent these messengers to inform you of my coming, hoping that you will be friendly to us."

The messengers returned with the news that Esau was on the way to meet Jacob—with an army of 400 men! Jacob was frantic with fear. He divided his household, along with the flocks and herds and camels, into two groups; for he said, "If Esau attacks one group, perhaps the other can escape."

Then Jacob prayed, "O God of Abraham my grandfather, and of my father Isaac—O Jehovah who told me to return to the land of my relatives and said that You would do me good—I am not worthy of the least of all Your loving kindnesses shown me again and again just as You promised me. For when I left home I owned nothing except a walking stick! And now I am two armies! O Lord, please deliver me from destruction at the hand of my brother Esau, for I am frightened —terribly afraid that he is coming to kill me and these mothers and my children."

Jacob stayed where he was for the night and prepared a present for his brother Esau. His strategy was to appease Esau with the presents before meeting him face-to-face! "Perhaps," Jacob hoped, "he will be friendly to us." So the presents were sent on ahead, and Jacob spent that night in the camp. But during the night he got up and wakened his two wives and his two concubines and his 11 children, and took them across the Jordan River at the Jabbok ford. Then he returned again to the camp and was there alone; and a Man wrestled with him until dawn.

And when the Man saw that he couldn't win the match, He struck Jacob's hip and knocked it out of joint at the socket. Then the Man said, "Let me go, for it is dawn."

But Jacob panted, "I will not let you go until you bless me."

"What is your name?" the Man asked.

"Jacob," was the reply.

"It isn't anymore!" the Man told him. "It is Israel—one who has power with God. Because you have been strong with God, you shall prevail with men."

What is *your* name?" Jacob asked Him.

"No, you mustn't ask," the Man told him. And He blessed him there.

Jacob named the place Peniel ("The Face of God"), for he said, "I have seen God face-to-face, and yet my life is spared." The sun rose as he started on, and he was limping because of his hip.

24. Forgiveness for Jacob

Then far in the distance Jacob saw Esau coming with his 400 men. Jacob now arranged his family into a column, with his two concubines and their children at the head, Leah and her children next, and Rachel and Joseph last. Then Jacob went on ahead.

As he approached his brother he bowed low seven times before him. And then Esau ran to meet him and embraced him affectionately and kissed him; and both of them were in tears! Esau looked at the women and children and asked, "Who are these people with you?"

"My children," Jacob replied.

"And what were all the flocks and herds I met as I came?" Esau asked.

And Jacob replied, "They are my gifts to curry your favor!"

"Brother, I have plenty," Esau laughed. "Keep what you have."

"No, but please accept them," Jacob said, "for what a relief it is to see your friendly smile! I was as frightened of you as though approaching God! Please take my gifts. For God has been very generous to me and I have enough." So Jacob insisted, and finally Esau accepted them. So Esau started back to Seir that same day.

Meanwhile Jacob and his household went as far as Succoth. There he built himself a camp with pens for his flocks and herds. (That is why the place is called Succoth, meaning "huts.") Then they arrived safely at Shechem, in Canaan, and camped outside the city.

25. Rachel's Death

"Move on to Bethel now and settle there," God said to Jacob, "and build an altar to worship the God who appeared to you when you fled from your brother Esau." So Jacob instructed all those in his household to destroy the idols they had brought with them, and to wash themselves and to put on fresh clothing.

"For we are going to Bethel," he told them, "and I will build an altar there to the God who answered my prayers in the day of my distress and was with me on my journey." Finally they arrived at Luz (also called Bethel) in Canaan. And Jacob erected an altar there and named it "The altar of the God who met me here at Bethel" because it was there at Bethel that God appeared to him when he was fleeing from Esau. And God said to him, "You shall no longer be called Jacob ('Cheater') but Israel ('One who prevails with God')."

Leaving Bethel he and his household traveled on toward Ephrath (Bethlehem). But Rachel's pains of childbirth began while they were still a long way away. After a very hard delivery, the midwife finally exclaimed, "Wonderful—another boy!" And with Rachel's last breath (for she died) she named him Ben-oni ("Son of my sorrow"); but his father called him Benjamin ("Son of my right hand"). So Rachel died and was buried near the road to Ephrath (also called Bethlehem). And Jacob set up a monument of stones upon her grave, and it is there to this day.

Here are the names of the twelve sons of Jacob:

The sons of Leah:
    Reuben, Jacob's oldest child
    Simeon
    Levi
    Judah
    Issachar
    Zebulun
The sons of Rachel:
    Joseph
    Benjamin
The sons of Bilhah, Rachel's servant-girl:
    Dan
    Naphtali
The sons of Zilpah, Leah's servant-girl:
    Gad
    Asher
All these were born to him at Padan-aram.

So Jacob came at last to Isaac his father at Mamre in Kiriath-arba (now called Hebron), where Abraham too had lived. Isaac died soon afterwards at the ripe old age of 180. And his sons Esau and Jacob buried him.

26. The Selling of Joseph

So Jacob settled again in the land of Canaan where his father had lived.

Jacob's son Joseph was now 17 years old. His job, along with his half-brothers, the sons of his father's wives Bilhah and Zilpah, was to shepherd his father's flocks. But Joseph tattled to his father about some of the things they were doing.

Now as it happened, Israel loved Joseph more than any of his other children, because Joseph was born to him in his old age. So one day Jacob gave him a special gift—a brightly colored coat. His brothers of course noticed their father's partiality and consequently hated Joseph; they couldn't say a kind word to him.

One night Joseph had a dream and promptly reported the details to his brothers, causing even deeper hatred.

"Listen to this," he proudly announced. "We were out in the field binding sheaves. My sheaf stood up, and your sheaves all gathered around it and bowed low before it!"

"So you want to be our king, do you?" his brothers derided. And they hated him both for the dream and for his cocky attitude.

Then he had another dream and told it to his brothers. "Listen to my latest dream," he boasted. "The sun, moon and eleven stars bowed low before me!"

This time he told his father as well as his brothers; but his father rebuked him. "What is this?" he asked. "Shall I indeed, and your mother and brothers come and bow before you?" His brothers were fit to be tied concerning this affair, but his father gave it quite a bit of thought and wondered what it all meant.

One day Joseph's brothers took their father's flocks to Shechem to graze them there. A few days later Israel called for Joseph and told him, "Your brothers are over in Shechem grazing the flocks. Go and see how they are getting along, and how it is with the flocks and bring me word."

"Very good," Joseph replied. So he traveled to Shechem from his home at Hebron Valley.

A man noticed him wandering in the fields. "Who are you looking for?" he asked.

"For my brothers and their flocks," Joseph replied. "Have you seen them?"

"Yes," the man told him, "they are no longer here. I heard your brothers say they were going to Dothan." So Joseph followed them to Dothan and found them there. But when they saw him coming, recognizing him in the distance, they decided to kill him!

"Here comes that master dreamer," they exclaimed. "Come on, let's kill him and toss him into a well and tell father that a wild animal has eaten him. Then we'll see what will become of all his dreams!"

But Reuben hoped to spare Joseph's life. "Let's not kill him," he said; "we'll shed no blood—let's throw him alive into this well here; that way he'll die without our touching him!" (Reuben was planning to get him out later and return him to his father.)

So when Joseph got there, they pulled off his brightly colored robe, and threw him into an empty well—there was no water in it. Then they sat down for supper. Suddenly they noticed a string of camels coming towards them in the distance, probably Ishmaelite traders who were taking gum, spices and herbs from Gilead to Egypt.

"Look there," Judah said to the others. "Here come some Ishmaelites. Let's sell Joseph to them! Why kill him and have a guilty conscience? Let's not be responsible for his death, for, after all, he is our brother!" And his brothers agreed. So when the traders came by, his brothers pulled Joseph out of the well and sold him to them for 20 pieces of silver. And the traders took him along to Egypt.

Some time later, Reuben (who was away when the traders came by) returned to get Joseph out of the well. When Joseph wasn't there, he ripped at his clothes in anguish and frustration. "The child is gone; and I, where shall I go now?" he wept to his brothers.

Then the brothers killed a goat and spattered its blood on Joseph's coat. They took the coat to their father and asked him to identify it. "We found this in the field," they told him. "Is it Joseph's coat or not?"

Their father recognized it at once. "Yes," he sobbed, "it is my son's coat. A wild animal has eaten him. Joseph is without doubt torn in pieces." Then Israel tore his garments and put on sackcloth and mourned for his son in deepest mourning for many weeks. His family all tried to comfort him, but it was no use. "I will die in mourning for my son," he would say, and then break down and cry.

27. Joseph's Temptation

When Joseph arrived in Egypt as a captive of the Ishmaelite traders, he was purchased from them by Potiphar, a member of the personal staff of Pharaoh, the king of Egypt. Now this man Potiphar was the captain of the king's bodyguard and his chief executioner.

The Lord greatly blessed Joseph there in the home of his master, so that everything he did succeeded. Potiphar noticed this and realized that the Lord was with Joseph in a very special way. So Potiphar gave Joseph the complete administrative responsibility over everything he owned. He hadn't a worry in the world with Joseph there, except to decide what he wanted to eat! Joseph, by the way, was a very handsome young man.

One day at about this time Potiphar's wife began making eyes at Joseph and suggested that he come and sleep with her. Joseph refused. "Look," he told her, "my master trusts me with everything in the entire household; he himself has no more authority here than I have! He has held back nothing from me except you yourself because you are his wife. How can I do such a wicked thing as this? It would be a great sin against God."

But she kept on with her suggestions day after day, even though he refused to listen and kept out of her way as much as possible. Then one day as he was in the house going about his work—as it happened, no one else was around at the time—she came and grabbed him by the sleeve demanding, "Sleep with me." He tore himself away, but as he did, his jacket slipped off and she was left holding it as he fled from the house.

When she saw that she had his jacket and that he had fled, she began screaming. When the other men around the place came running in to see what had happened, she was crying hysterically. "My husband had to bring in this Hebrew slave to insult us!" she sobbed. "He tried to rape me, but when I screamed, he ran, and forgot to take his jacket!"

She kept the jacket, and when her husband came home that night, she told him her story. "That Hebrew slave you've had around here tried to rape me, and I was only saved by my screams. He fled, leaving his jacket behind!"

Well, when her husband heard his wife's story, he was furious. He threw Joseph into prison where the king's prisoners were kept in chains.

But the Lord was with Joseph there, too, and was kind to him by granting him a favor with the chief jailer. In fact, the jailer soon handed over the entire prison administration to Joseph, so that all the other prisoners were responsible to him. The chief jailer had no more worries after that, for Joseph took care of everything, and the Lord was with him so that everything ran smoothly and well.

28. Joseph in Prison

Some time later it so happened that the king of Egypt became angry with his chief baker and his wine taster, so he jailed them both in the prison where Joseph was, in the castle of Potiphar, the captain of the guard, who was the chief executioner. They remained under arrest there for quite some time, and Potiphar assigned Joseph to wait on them.

One night each of them had a dream. The next morning Joseph noticed that they looked dejected and sad. "What in the world is the matter?" he asked.

And they replied, "We both had dreams last night, but there is no one here to tell us what they mean."

"Interpreting dreams is God's business," Joseph replied. "Tell me what you saw."

The wine taster told his dream first. "In my dream," he said, "I saw a vine with three branches that began to bud and blossom, and soon there were clusters of ripe grapes. I was holding Pharaoh's wine cup in my hand, so I took the grapes and squeezed the juice into it, and gave it to him to drink."

"I know what the dream means," Joseph said. "The three branches mean three days! Within three days Pharaoh is going to take you out of prison and give you back your job as his wine taster. And please have some pity on me when you are back in his favor. Mention me to Pharaoh, and ask him to let me out of here. For I was kidnapped from my homeland among the Hebrews, and now this—here I am in jail when I did nothing to deserve it."

When the chief baker saw that the first dream had such a good meaning, he told his dream to Joseph, too. "In my dream," he said, "there were three baskets of pastries on my head. In the top basket were all kinds of bakery goods for Pharaoh, but the birds came and ate them."

"The three baskets mean three days," Joseph told him. "Three days from now Pharaoh will take off your head and impale your body on a pole, and the birds will come and pick off your flesh!"

Pharaoh's birthday came three days later, and he gave a big party for all of his officials and household staff. He sent for his wine taster and chief baker, and they were brought to him from prison. Then he restored the wine taster to his former position; but he sentenced the chief baker to be impaled, just as Joseph had predicted.

Pharaoh's wine taster, however, promptly forgot all about Joseph, never giving him a thought.

29. Joseph the Governor of Egypt

One night two years later, Pharaoh dreamed that he was standing on the bank of the Nile River, when suddenly, seven sleek, fat cows came up out of the river and began grazing in the grass. Then seven other cows came up from the river, but they were very skinny and all their ribs stood out. They went over and stood beside the fat cows. Then the skinny cows ate the fat ones! At which point Pharaoh woke up!

Soon he fell asleep again and had a second dream. This time he saw seven heads of grain on one stalk, with every kernel well formed and plump. Then suddenly seven more heads appeared on the stalk, but these were shrivelled and withered by the east wind. And these thin heads swallowed up the seven plump, well-formed heads! Then Pharaoh woke up again and realized it was all a dream.

Next morning, as he thought about it, he became very concerned as to what the dreams might mean; he called for all the magicians and sages of Egypt and told them about it, but not one of them could suggest what his dreams meant.

Then the king's wine taster spoke up. "Today I remember my sin!" he said. "Some time ago when you were angry with a couple of us and put me and the chief baker in jail in the castle of the captain of the guard, the chief baker and I each had a dream one night. We told the dreams to a young Hebrew fellow there who was a slave of the captain of the guard, and he told us what our dreams meant. And everything happened just as he said: I was restored to my position of wine taster, and the chief baker was executed and impaled on a pole."

Pharaoh sent at once for Joseph. He was brought hastily from the dungeon. After a quick shave and change of clothes, he came in before Pharaoh. "I had a dream last night," Pharaoh told him, "and none of these men can tell me what it means. But I have heard that you can interpret dreams, and that is why I have called for you."

"I can't do it by myself," Joseph replied, "but God will tell you what it means!" So Pharaoh told him the dreams. "Both dreams mean the same thing," Joseph told Pharaoh. "God was telling you what He is going to do here in the land of Egypt. The seven fat cows (and also the seven fat, well-formed heads of grain) mean that there are seven years of prosperity ahead. The seven skinny cows (and also the seven thin and withered heads of grain) indicate that there will be seven years of famine following the seven years of prosperity. So God has showed you what He is about to do.

"My suggestion is that you find the wisest man in Egypt and put him in charge of administering a nationwide farm program. Let Pharaoh divide Egypt into five administrative districts, and let the officials of these districts gather into the royal storehouses all the excess crops of the next seven years, so that there will be enough to eat when the seven years of famine come. Otherwise, disaster will surely strike."

Turning to Joseph, Pharaoh said to him, "Since God has revealed the meaning of the dreams to you, you are the wisest man in the country! I am hereby appointing you to be in charge of this entire project. What you say goes, throughout all the land of Egypt. I alone will outrank you." Then Pharaoh placed his own signet ring on Joseph's finger as a token of his authority, and dressed him in beautiful clothing and placed the royal golden chain about his neck and declared, "See, I have placed you in charge of all the land of Egypt."

Pharaoh also gave Joseph the chariot of his second-in-command, and wherever he went the shout arose, "Kneel down!" And Pharaoh declared to Joseph, "I, the king of Egypt, swear that you shall have charge over all the land of Egppt."

Joseph went out from the presence of Pharaoh and began traveling all across the land. And sure enough, for the next seven years there were bumper crops everywhere. During those years, Joseph requisitioned for the government a portion of all the crops grown throughout Egypt, storing them in nearby cities. After seven years of this, the granaries were full to overflowing, and there was so much that no one kept track of the amount.

Then the seven years of famine began, just as Joseph had predicted. There were crop failures in all the surrounding countries too, but in Egypt there was plenty of grain in the storehouses. The people began to starve. They pleaded with Pharaoh for food, and he sent them to Joseph. "Do whatever he tells you to," he instructed them. So now, with severe famine all over the world, Joseph opened up the storehouses and sold grain to the Egyptians and to those from other lands who came to Egypt to buy grain from him.

30. An Encounter with Brothers

When Jacob heard that there was grain available in Egypt he said to his sons, "Why are you standing around looking at one another? I have heard that there is grain available in Egypt. Go down and buy some for us before we all starve to death." So Joseph's ten older brothers went down to Egypt to buy grain. However, Jacob wouldn't let Joseph's younger brother Benjamin go with them, for fear some harm might happen to him (as it had to his brother Joseph).

So it was that Israel's sons arrived in Egypt along with many others from many lands to buy food, for the famine was as severe in Canaan as it was everywhere else. Since Joseph was governor of Egypt and in charge of the sale of the grain, it was to him that his brothers came and bowed low before him with their faces to the earth. Joseph recognized them instantly, but pretended he didn't. "Where are you from?" he demanded roughly.

"From the land of Canaan," they replied. "We have come to buy grain."

Then Joseph remembered the dreams of long ago! But he said to them, "You are spies. You have come to see how destitute the famine has made our land."

"No, no," they exclaimed. "We have come to buy food. We are all brothers and honest men, sir! We are not spies!"

"Yes, you are," he insisted. "You have come to see how weak we are."

"Sir," they said, "there are twelve of us brothers, and our father is in the land of Canaan. Our youngest brother is there with our father and one of our brothers is dead."

"So?" Joseph asked. "What does that prove? You are spies! This is the way I will test your story: I swear by the life of Pharaoh that you are not going to leave Egypt until this youngest brother comes here. One of you go and get your brother! I'll keep the rest of you here, bound in prison. Then we'll find out whether your story is true or not. If it turns out that you don't have a younger brother, then I'll know you are spies."

So he threw them all into jail for three days.

The third day Joseph said to them, "I am a God-fearing man and I'm going to give you an opportunity to prove yourselves. I'm going to take a chance that you are honorable: only one of you shall remain in chains in jail, and the rest of you may go on home with grain for your families; but bring your youngest brother back to me. In this way I will know whether you are telling me the truth; and if you are, I will spare you." To this they agreed.

Speaking among themselves, they said, "This has all happened because of what we did to Joseph long ago. We saw his terror and anguish and heard his pleadings, but we wouldn't listen."

"Didn't I tell you not to do it?" Reuben asked. "But you wouldn't listen. And now we are going to die because we murdered him." Of course they didn't know that Joseph understood them as he was standing there, for he had been speaking to them through an interpreter. Now he left the room and found a place where he could weep.

Returning, he selected Simeon from among them and had him bound before their eyes. Joseph then ordered his servants to fill the men's sacks with grain, but also gave secret instructions to put each brother's payment at the top of his sack! He also gave them provisions for their journey.

So they loaded up their donkeys with the grain and started for home. But when they stopped for the night and one of them opened his sack to get some grain to feed the donkeys, there was his money in the mouth of the sack! "Look," he exclaimed to his brothers, "my money is here in my sack." They were filled with terror. Trembling, they exclaimed to each other, "What is this God has done to us?"

When they came to their father Jacob in the land of Canaan they told him all that had happened. "The king's chief assistant spoke very roughly to us," they told him, "and took us for spies. 'No, no,' we said, 'we are honest men, not spies. We are 12 brothers, sons of one father; one is dead, and the youngest is with our father in the land of Canaan.'

"Then the man told us, 'This is the way I will find out if you are what you claim to be. Leave one of your brothers here with me and take grain for your families and go on home, but bring your youngest brother back to me. Then I shall know whether you are spies or honest men; if you prove to be what you say, then I will give you back your brother and you can come as often as you like to purchase grain.'"

As they emptied out the sacks, there at the top of each was the money paid for the grain! Terror gripped them, as it did their father. Then Jacob exclaimed, "You have bereaved me of my children—Joseph didn't come back, Simeon is gone, and now you want to take Benjamin too! Everything has been against me."

Then Reuben said to his father, "Kill my two sons if I don't bring Benjamin back to you. I'll be responsible for him."

But Jacob replied, "My son shall not go down with you, for his brother Joseph is dead and he alone is left of his mother's children. If anything should happen to him, I would die."

31. Return for Supplies

But there was no relief from the terrible famine throughout the land. When the grain they had brought from Egypt was almost gone, their father said to them, "Go again and buy us a little food."

But Judah told him, "The man wasn't fooling one bit when he said, 'Don't ever come back again unless your brother is with you.' We cannot go unless you let Benjamin go with us."

"Why did you ever tell him you had another brother?" Israel moaned. "Why did you have to treat me like that?"

But the man specifically asked us about our family," they told him. "He wanted to know whether our father was still living and he asked us if we had another brother, so we told him. How could we know that he was going to say, 'Bring me your brother'?"

Judah said to his father, "Send the lad with me and we will be on our way; otherwise we will all die of starvation—and not only we, but you and all our little ones. I guarantee his safety. If I don't bring him back to you, then let me bear the blame forever. For we could have gone and returned by this time if you had let him come."

So their father Israel finally said to them, "If it can't be avoided, then at least do this. Load your donkeys with the best products of the land. Take them to the man as gifts—balm, honey, spices, myrrh, pistachio nuts and almonds. Take double money so that you can pay back what was in the mouths of your sacks, as it was probably someone's mistake, and take your brother and go. May God Almighty give you mercy before the man, so that he will release Simeon and return Benjamin. And if I must bear the anguish of their deaths, then so be it."

So they took the gifts and double money and went to Egypt and stood before Joseph. When Joseph saw that Benjamin was with them he said to the manager of his household, "These men will eat with me this noon. Take them home and prepare a big feast." So the man did as he was told and took them to Joseph's palace.

They were badly frightened when they saw where they were being taken. "It's because of the money returned to us in our sacks," they said. "He wants to pretend we stole it and seize us as slaves, with our donkeys." As they arrived at the entrance to the palace, they went over to Joseph's household manager, and said to him, "O sir, after our first trip to Egypt to buy food, as we were returning home, we stopped for the night and opened our sacks and the money was there that we had paid for the grain. Here it is; we have brought it back again, along with additional money to buy more grain. We have no idea how the money got into our sacks."

"Don't worry about it," the household manager told them; "your God, even the God of your fathers, must have put it there, for we collected your money all right." Then he released Simeon and brought him out to them. They were then conducted into the palace and given water to refresh their feet; and their donkeys were fed. Then they got their presents ready for Joseph's arrival at noon, for they were told that they would be eating there.

When Joseph came home they gave him their presents, bowing low before him. He asked how they had been getting along. "And how is your father—the old man you spoke about? Is he still alive?" Looking at his brother Benjamin, he asked, "Is this your youngest brother, the one you told me about? How are you, my son? God be gracious to you."

Then Joseph made a hasty exit, for he was overcome with love for his brother and had to go out and cry. Going into his bedroom, he wept there. Then he washed his face and came out, keeping himself under control. "Let's eat," he said.

Joseph ate by himself; his brothers were served at a separate table and the Egyptians at still another, for Egyptians despise Hebrews and never eat with them. He told each of them where to sit, and seated them in the order of their ages, from the oldest to the youngest, much to their amazement! Their food was served to them from his own table. He gave the largest serving to Benjamin—five times as much as to any of the others! They had a wonderful time bantering back and forth, and the wine flowed freely!

32. The Cup in Benjamin's Sack

When his brothers were ready to leave, Joseph ordered his household manager to fill each of their sacks with as much grain as they could carry—and to put into the mouth of each man's sack the money he had paid! He was also told to put Joseph's own silver cup at the top of Benjamin's sack, along with the grain money. So the household manager did as he was told. The brothers were up at dawn and on their way with their loaded donkeys.

But when they were barely out of the city Joseph said to his household manager, "Chase after them and stop them and ask them why they are acting like this when their benefactor has been so kind to them? Ask them, 'What do you mean by stealing my lord's personal silver drinking cup, which he uses for fortune-telling? What a wicked thing you have done!' " So he caught up with them and spoke to them along the lines he had been instructed.

"What in the world are you talking about?" they demanded. "What kind of people do you think we are, that you accuse us of such a terrible thing as that? Didn't we bring back the money we found in the mouth of our sacks? Why would we steal silver or gold from your master's house? If you find his cup with any one of us, let that one die. And all the rest of us will be slaves forever to your master."

"Fair enough," the man replied, "except that only the one who stole it will be a slave. The rest of you can go free." They quickly took down their sacks from the backs of their donkeys and opened them. He began searching the oldest brother's sack, going on down the line to the youngest. And the cup was found in Benjamin's!

They ripped their clothing in despair, loaded the donkeys again, and returned to the city. Joseph was still home when Judah and his brothers arrived, and they fell to the ground before him. "What were you trying to do?" Joseph demanded. "Didn't you know such a man as I would know who stole it?"

And Judah said, "Oh, what shall we say to my lord? How can we plead? How can we prove our innocence? God is punishing us for our sins. Sir, we have all returned to be your slaves, both we and he in whose sack the cup was found."

"No," Joseph said, "Only the man who stole the cup, he shall be my slave. The rest of you can go on home to your father."

Then Judah stepped forward and said, "O sir, let me say just this one word to you. Be patient with me for a moment, for I know you can doom me in an instant, as though you were Pharaoh himself. Sir, you asked us if we had a father or a brother, and we said, 'Yes, we have a father, an old man, and a child of his old age, a little one. And his brother is dead, and he alone is left of his mother's children, and his father loves him very much.' And now, sir, if I go back to my father and the lad is not with us—seeing that our father's life is bound up in the lad's life—when he sees that the boy is not with us, our father will die; and we will be responsible for bringing down his gray hairs with sorrow to the grave.

"Sir, I pledged my father that I would take care of the lad. I told him, 'If I don't bring him back to you, I shall bear the blame forever.' Please sir, let me stay here as a slave instead of the lad, and let the lad return with his brothers. For how shall I return to my father if the lad is not with me? I cannot bear to see what this would do to him."

33. Joseph Makes Himself Known

Joseph could stand it no longer. "Out, all of you," he cried out to his attendants, and he was left alone with his brothers. Then he wept aloud. His sobs could be heard throughout the palace, and the news was quickly carried to Pharaoh's palace.

"I am Joseph!" he said to his brothers. "Is my father still alive?" But his brothers couldn't say a word, they were so stunned with surprise. "Come over here," he said. So they came closer. And he said again, "I am Joseph, your brother whom you sold into Egypt! But don't be angry with yourselves that you did this to me, for God did it! He sent me here ahead of you to preserve your lives. These two years of famine will grow to seven, during which there will be neither plowing nor harvest. God has sent me here to keep you and your families alive, so that you will become a great nation. Yes, it was God who sent me here, not you! And He has made me a counselor to Pharaoh, and manager of this entire nation, ruler of all the land of Egypt. Hurry, return to my father and tell him that his son Joseph says, 'God has made me chief of all the land of Egypt. Come down to me right away!' "

Then weeping with joy, he embraced Benjamin. And Benjamin began weeping too. And he did the same with each of his brothers, who finally found their tongues!

The news soon reached Pharaoh—"Joseph's brothers have come"; and Pharaoh was very happy to hear it, as were his officials. Then Pharaoh said to Joseph, "Tell your brothers to load their pack animals and return quickly to their homes in Canaan. Bring your father and all of your families and come here to Egypt to live."

So Joseph gave them wagons, as Pharaoh had commanded, and provisions for the journey. They returned to the land of Canaan, to Jacob their father. "Joseph is alive," they shouted to him. "And he is ruler over all the land of Egypt!"

But Jacob's heart was like a stone; he couldn't take it in. However, when they had given him Joseph's messages, and when he saw the wagons filled with food that Joseph had sent him, his spirit revived. And he said, "It must be true! Joseph my son is alive! I will go and see him before I die."

So Jacob left Beer-sheba, and his sons brought him to Egypt, along with their little ones and their wives, in the wagons Pharaoh had provided for them. They brought their livestock too, and all their belongings accumulated in the land of Canaan, and came to Egypt—Jacob and all his children, sons and daughters, grandsons and granddaughters—all his loved ones.

Jacob sent Judah on ahead to tell Joseph that they were on the way and would soon arrive in Goshen—which they did. Joseph jumped into his chariot and journeyed to Goshen to meet his father and they fell into each other's arms and wept a long while. Then Israel said to Joseph, "Now let me die, for I have seen you again and know you are alive."

After their arrival, Joseph went in to see Pharaoh. "My father and my brothers are here from Canaan," he reported, "with all their flocks and herbs and possessions. They wish to settle in the land of Goshen."

And Pharaoh said to Joseph, "Choose anywhere you like for them to live. Give them the best land of Egypt. The land of Goshen will be fine. And if any of them are capable, put them in charge of my flocks, too."

Then Joseph brought his father Jacob to Pharaoh. And Jacob blessed Pharaoh.

"How old are you?" Pharaoh asked him.

Jacob replied, "I have lived 130 long, hard years, and I am not nearly as old as many of my forebears." Then Jacob blessed Pharaoh again before he left.

So Joseph assigned the best land of Egypt—the land of Rameses—to his father and brothers, just as Pharaoh had commanded. And Joseph furnished food to them in accordance with the number of their dependents.

So Israel lived in the land of Goshen in Egypt. Soon the people of Israel began to prosper, and there was a veritable population explosion among them.

Jacob lived 17 years after his arrival, so that he was 147 years old at the time of his death. As the time drew near for him to die, he called for his son Joseph and said to him, "Swear to me most solemnly that you will honor this, my last request: do not bury me in Egypt. But when I am dead, take me out of Egypt and bury me beside my ancestors." And Joseph promised. "Swear that you will do it," Jacob insisted. And Joseph did. Soon afterwards Jacob took to his bed.

35. Jacob's Death

One day not long after this, word came to Joseph that his father was failing rapidly. So, taking with him his two sons, Manasseh and Ephraim, he went to visit him. When Jacob heard that Joseph had arrived, he gathered his strength and sat up on the bed to greet him, and said to him, "I never thought that I would see you again, but now God has let me see your children too."

Then he blessed Joseph with this blessing: "May God, the God of my fathers Abraham and Isaac, the God who has shepherded me all my life, wonderfully bless these boys. He is the Angel who has kept me from all harm. May these boys be an honor to my name and to the names of my fathers Abraham and Isaac; and may they become a mighty nation."

But Joseph was upset and displeased when he saw that his father had laid his right hand on Ephraim's head; so he lifted it to place it on Manasseh's head instead. "No, father," he said. "You've got your right hand on the wrong head! This one over here is the older. Put your right hand on him!"

But his father refused. "I know what I'm doing, my son," he said. "Manasseh too shall become a great nation, but his younger brother shall be greater than he; he shall become many nations." Then Israel said to Joseph, "I am about to die, but God will be with you and will bring you again to Canaan, the land of your fathers. And I have given the choice land of Shechem to you instead of to your brothers, as your portion of that land which I took from the Amorites with my sword and with my bow."

Later Jacob called together all his sons and, having blessed them one by one, he told them, "Soon I will die. You must bury me with my fathers in the land of Canaan, in the cave in the field of Mach-pelah, facing Mamre—the field Abraham bought from Ephron the Hethite for a burial ground. There they buried Abraham and Sarah his wife; there they buried Isaac and Rebekah his wife; and there I buried Leah. It is the cave which my grandfather Abraham purchased from the sons of Heth." Then when Jacob had finished his prophecies to his sons, he lay back in the bed, breathed his last and died.

Joseph threw himself upon his father's body and wept over him and kissed him. Afterwards he commanded his morticians to embalm the body. The embalming process required 40 days with a period of national mourning of 70 days.

So his sons did as Israel commanded them and carried his body into the land of Canaan and buried it there in the cave of Mach-pelah—the cave Abraham had bought in the field of Ephron the Hethite, close to Mamre. Then Joseph returned to Egypt with his brothers and all who had accompanied him to the funeral of his father.

36. Comfort for the Brothers

Now that their father was dead, Joseph's brothers were frightened. "Now Joseph will pay us back for all the evil we did to him," they said. So they sent him this message: "Before he died, your father instructed us to tell you to forgive us for the great evil we did to you. We servants of the God of your father beg you to forgive us." When Joseph read the message, he broke down and cried.

Then his brothers came and fell down before him and said, "We are your slaves."

But Joseph told them, "Don't be afraid of me. Am I God, to judge and punish you? As far as I am concerned, God turned into good what you meant for evil, for He brought me to this high position I have today so that I could save the lives of many people. No, don't be afraid. Indeed, I myself will take care of you and your families." And he spoke very kindly to them, reassuring them.

So Joseph and his brothers and their families continued to live in Egypt. Joseph was 110 years old when he died. He lived to see the birth of his son Ephraim's children, and the children of Machir, Manasseh's son, who played at his feet.

"Soon I will die," Joseph told his brothers, "but God will surely come and get you, and bring you out of this land of Egypt and take you back to the land He promised to the descendants of Abraham, Isaac and Jacob." Then Joseph made his brothers promise with an oath that they would take his body back with them when they returned to Canaan. So Joseph died at the age of 110. They embalmed him and his body was placed in a coffin in Egypt.

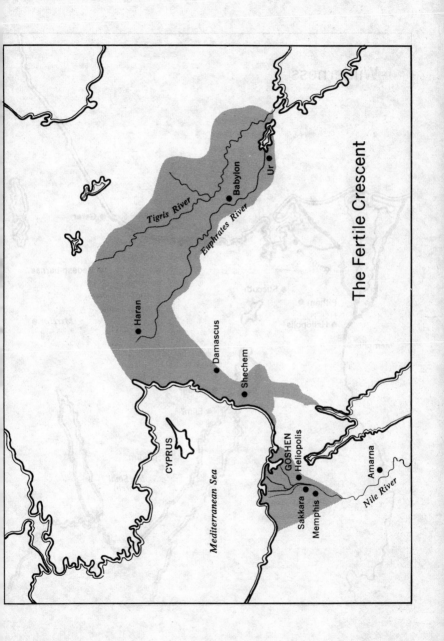

The Fertile Crescent

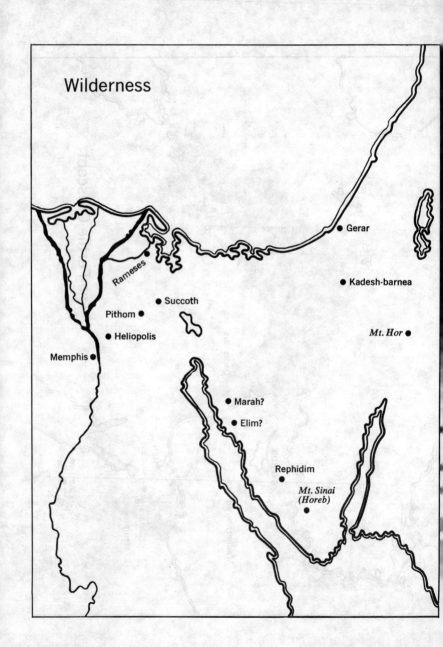

Wilderness

● Gerar

● Kadesh-barnea

Rameses

● Succoth

Pithom ●

Heliopolis ●

Memphis ●

Mt. Hor ●

● Marah?

● Elim?

Rephidim

Mt. Sinai (Horeb) ●

PART 2 Israel's First Encounter with Egypt

1. Oppression Under the Egyptians

EVENTUALLY a new king came to the throne of Egypt who felt no obligation to the descendants of Joseph. He told his people, "These Israeli are becoming dangerous to us because there are so many of them. Let's figure out a way to put an end to this. If we don't and war breaks out, they will join our enemies and fight against us and escape out of the country."

So the Egyptians made slaves of them and put brutal taskmasters over them to wear them down under heavy burdens while building the store-cities Pithom and Ra-amses. But the more the Egyptians mistreated and oppressed them, the more the Israeli seemed to multiply! Then Pharaoh commanded all his people to throw the newborn Hebrew boys into the Nile River. But the girls, he said, could live.

2. The Birth of Moses

There were at this time a Hebrew fellow and girl of the tribe of Levi who married and had a family, and a baby son was born to them. When the baby's mother saw that he was an unusually beautiful baby, she hid him at home for three months.

Then when she could no longer hide him, she made a little boat from papyrus reeds, waterproofed it with tar, put the baby in it, and laid it among the reeds along the river's edge. The baby's sister watched from a distance to see what would happen to him. Well, this is what happened: a princess, one of

53

Pharaoh's daughters, came down to bathe in the river, and as she and her maids were walking along the river bank, she spied the little boat among the reeds and sent one of the maids to bring it to her. When she opened it, there was a baby! And he was crying. This touched her heart. "He must be one of the Hebrew children!" she said.

Then the baby's sister approached the princess and asked her, "Shall I go and find one of the Hebrew women to nurse the baby for you?"

"Yes, do!" the princess replied. So the little girl rushed home and called her mother!

"Take this child home and nurse him for me," the princess instructed the baby's mother, "and I will pay you well!" So she took him home and nursed him. When he was older, she brought him back to the princess and he became her son. She named him Moses (meaning "to draw out") because she had drawn him out of the water.

3. Moses' Flight to Midian

One day many years later when Moses had grown up and become a man, he went out to visit his fellow Hebrews and saw the terrible conditions they were under. During his visit he saw an Egyptian knock a Hebrew to the ground—one of his own Hebrew brothers! Moses looked this way and that to be sure no one was watching, then killed the Egyptian and hid his body in the sand.

The next day as he was out visiting among the Hebrews again, he saw two of them fighting. "What are you doing, hitting your own Hebrew brother like that?" he said to the one in the wrong.

"And who are you?" the man demanded. "I suppose you think you are *our* prince and judge! And do you plan to kill me as you did that Egyptian yesterday?" When Moses realized that his deed was known, he was frightened. And sure enough, when Pharaoh heard about it he ordered Moses arrested and executed. But Moses ran away into the land of Midian.

As he was sitting there beside a well, seven girls who were daughters of the priest of Midian came to draw water and fill the water troughs for their father's flocks. But the shepherds chased the girls away. Moses then came to their aid and rescued them from the shepherds and watered their flocks.

When they returned to their father Reuel he asked, "How did you get the flocks watered so quickly today?"

"An Egyptian defended us against the shepherds," they told him; "he drew water for us and watered the flocks."

"Well, where is he?" their father demanded. "Did you just leave him there? Invite him home for supper."

Moses eventually decided to accept Reuel's invitation to live with them, and Reuel gave him one of the girls, Zipporah, as his wife. They had a baby named Gershom (meaning "foreigner"), for he said, "I am a stranger in a foreign land."

4. Moses at the Burning Bush

One day as Moses was tending the flock of his father-in-law Jethro, the priest of Midian, out at the edge of the desert near Horeb, the mountain of God, suddenly the Angel of Jehovah appeared to him as a flame of fire in a bush. When Moses saw that the bush was on fire and that it didn't burn up, he went over to investigate. Then God called out to him, "Moses! Moses!"

"Who is it?" Moses asked.

"Don't come any closer," God told him. "Take off your shoes, for you are standing on holy ground. I am the God of your fathers—the God of Abraham, Isaac and Jacob." (Moses covered his face with his hands, for he was afraid to look at God.) Then the Lord told him, "I have seen the deep sorrows of My people in Egypt, and have heard their pleas for freedom from their harsh taskmasters. Now I am going to send you to Pharaoh, to demand that he let you lead My people out of Egypt."

"But I'm not the person for a job like that!" Moses exclaimed.

Then God told him, "I will certainly be with you, and this is the proof that I am the one who is sending you: when you have led the people out of Egypt, you shall worship God here upon this mountain!"

But Moses asked, "If I go to the people of Israel and tell them that their fathers' God has sent me, they will ask, 'Which God are you talking about?' What shall I tell them,"

"The Sovereign God" was the reply. "Just say, 'I AM has sent me!' Yes, tell them, 'Jehovah, the God of your ancestors Abraham, Isaac and Jacob has sent me to you.' This is My eternal name to be used throughout all generations."

But Moses pleaded, "O Lord, I'm just not a good speaker. I never have been, and I'm not now, even after You have spoken to me, for I have a speech impediment."

"Who makes mouths?" Jehovah asked him. "Isn't it I, the Lord? Who makes a man so that he can speak or not speak, see or not see, hear or not hear? Now go ahead and do as I tell you, for I will help you to speak well, and I will tell you what to say."

But Moses said, "Lord, please! Send someone else."

Then the Lord became angry. "All right," He said, "your brother Aaron is a good speaker. And he is coming here to look for you, and will be very happy when he finds you. So I will tell you what to tell him, and I will help both of you to speak well, and I will tell you what to do. He will be your spokesman to the people. And you will be as God to him, telling him what to say. And be sure to take your rod along so that you can perform the miracles I have shown you."

Now Jehovah said to Aaron, "Go into the wilderness to meet Moses!" So Aaron traveled to Mount Horeb, the mountain of God, and met Moses there. They greeted each other warmly. Moses told Aaron what God had said they must do and what they were to say. Moses told him about the miracles they must do before Pharaoh.

So Moses and Aaron returned to Egypt and summoned the elders of the people of Israel to a council meeting. Aaron told them what Jehovah had said to Moses, and Moses performed the miracles as they watched. Then the elders believed that

God had sent them. And when they heard that Jehovah had visited them and had seen their sorrows and had decided to rescue them, they rejoiced, bowed their heads and worshiped.

5. Pharaoh's Heart Hardened

After this presentation to the elders, Moses and Aaron went to see Pharaoh. They told him, "We bring you a message from Jehovah, the God of Israel. He says, 'Let My people go, for they must make a holy pilgrimage out into the wilderness, for a religious feast, to worship Me there.'"

"Is that so?" retorted Pharaoh. "And who is Jehovah, that I should listen to Him and let Israel go? I don't know Jehovah and I will not let Israel go." That same day Pharaoh sent this order to the taskmasters and officers he had set over the people of Israel: "Don't give the people any more straw for making bricks! However, don't reduce their production quotas by a single brick, for they obviously don't have enough to do or else they wouldn't be talking about going out into the wilderness and sacrificing to their God. Load them with work and make them sweat; that will teach them to listen to Moses and Aaron's lies!"

So the taskmasters and officers informed the people: "Pharaoh has given orders to furnish you with no more straw. Go and find it wherever you can; but you must produce just as many bricks as before!" So the people scattered everywhere to gather straw. The taskmasters were brutal. "Fulfill your daily quota just as before," they kept demanding.

Then Moses went back to the Lord. "Lord," he protested, "How can You mistreat Your own people like this? Why did You ever send me, if You were going to do this to them? Ever since I gave Pharaoh Your message, he has only been more and more brutal to them. You have not delivered them at all!"

"Now you will see what I shall do to Pharaoh," the Lord told Moses, "for he must be forced to let My people go; he will not only let them go, but will *drive them out of his land!* Therefore tell the descendants of Israel that I will use My mighty power and perform great miracles to deliver them from slavery and make them free and I will accept them as My people and be their God and they shall know that I am Jehovah their God who has rescued them from the Egyptians. I will bring them into the land I promised to give to Abraham, Isaac and Jacob. It shall belong to My people."

So Moses told the people what God had said, but they wouldn't listen anymore because they were too dispirited after the tragic consequence of what he had said before.

Now the Lord spoke to Moses again and told him, "Go back again to Pharaoh and tell him that he *must* let the people of Israel go." So Moses and Aaron did as the Lord commanded them. Moses was 80 years old and Aaron eighty-three at this time of their confrontation with Pharaoh.

Then the Lord said to Moses and Aaron, "Pharaoh will demand that you show him a miracle to prove that God has sent you; when he does, Aaron is to throw down his rod, and it will become a serpent." So Moses and Aaron went in to see Pharaoh and performed the miracle as Jehovah had instructed them—Aaron threw down his rod before Pharaoh and his court and it became a serpent. Then Pharaoh called in his sorcerers—the magicians of Egypt—and they were able to do the same thing with their magical arts! Their rods became serpents too! But Aaron's serpent swallowed their serpents!

Pharaoh's heart was still hard and stubborn, and he wouldn't listen, just as the Lord had predicted.

6. Plagues in Egypt

Then the Lord instructed Moses: "Tell Aaron to point his rod toward the waters of Egypt and all its rivers, canals, marshes and reservoirs, and even the water stored in bowls and pots in the homes will turn to blood."

So Moses and Aaron did as the Lord commanded them. As Pharaoh and all of his officials watched, Aaron hit the surface of the Nile with the rod and the river turned to blood. The fish died and the water became so foul that the Egyptians couldn't drink it; and there was blood throughout the land of Egypt. But then the magicians of Egypt used their secret arts and they, too, turned water into blood; so Pharaoh's heart remained hard and stubborn, and he wouldn't listen to Moses and Aaron, just as the Lord had predicted.

The following week the Lord said to Moses, "Go in again to Pharaoh and tell him that Jehovah says, 'Let My people go and worship Me. If you refuse, I will send vast hordes of frogs across your land from one border to the other. The Nile River will swarm with them, and they will come out into your houses, even into your bedrooms and right into your beds! Every home in Egypt will be filled with them. They will fill your ovens and your kneading bowls; you and your people will be immersed in them!' "

Then the Lord said to Moses, "Instruct Aaron to point the rod toward all the rivers, streams and pools of Egypt, so that there will be frogs in every corner of the land." Aaron did, and frogs covered the nation. But the magicians did the same with their secret arts, and they, too, caused frogs to come up upon the land.

Then Pharaoh summoned Moses and Aaron and begged, "Plead with God to take the frogs away, and I will let the people go and sacrifice to Him." So Moses and Aaron went out from the presence of Pharaoh, and Moses pleaded with the Lord concerning the frogs He had sent. And the Lord did as Moses promised—dead frogs covered the countryside and filled the nation's homes. They were piled into great heaps, making a terrible stench throughout the land.

But when Pharaoh saw that the frogs were gone, he hardened his heart and refused to let the people go, just as the Lord had predicted.

Then the Lord said to Moses, "Tell Aaron to strike the dust with his rod, and it will become lice, throughout all the land of Egypt." So Moses and Aaron did as God commanded, and suddenly lice infested the entire nation, covering the Egyptians and their animals.

Then the magicians tried to do the same thing with their secret arts, but this time they failed. "This is the finger of God," they exclaimed to Pharaoh. But Pharaoh's heart was hard and stubborn, and he wouldn't listen to them, just as the Lord had predicted.

Then God sent other plagues, each one more severe, but Pharaoh continued to harden his heart. After the first three plagues, God by the hand of Moses sent:

4. Flies.
5. Disease among Egypt's cattle but not among Israel's.
6. Boils.
7. A severe hailstorm in Egypt but not in the land of Goshen.
8. Locusts.
9. Deep darkness in Egypt, but Israel had light as usual.

During the plague of darkness, Pharaoh called for Moses and said, "Go and worship Jehovah—but let your flocks and herds stay here; you can even take your children with you."

"No," Moses said, "we must take our flocks and herds for sacrifices and burnt offerings to Jehovah our God. Not a hoof shall be left behind; for we must have sacrifices for the Lord our God, and we do not know what He will choose until we get there."

Again the Lord hardened Pharaoh's heart and he would not let them go. "Get out of here and don't let me ever see you again," Pharaoh shouted at Moses. "The day you do you shall die."

"Very well," Moses replied. "I will never see you again."

Then the Lord said to Moses, "I will send just one more disaster on Pharaoh and his land, and after that he will let you go; in fact, he will be so anxious to get rid of you that he will practically throw you out of the country. Tell all the men and women of Israel to prepare to ask their Egyptian neighbors for costly gold and silver jewelry." (For God caused the Egyptians to be very favorable to the people of Israel, and Moses was a very great man in the land of Egypt and was revered by Pharaoh's officials and the Egyptian people alike.)

Now Moses announced to Pharaoh, "Jehovah says, 'About midnight I will pass through Egypt. And all the oldest sons shall die in every family in Egypt, from the oldest child of

Pharaoh, heir to his throne, to the oldest child of his lowliest slave; and even the firstborn of the animals. The wail of death will resound throughout the entire land of Egypt; never before has there been such anguish, and it will never be again. But not a dog shall move his tongue against any of the people of Israel, nor shall any of their animals die. Then you will know that Jehovah makes a distinction between Egyptians and Israeli.' All these officials of yours will come running to me, bowing low and begging, 'Please leave at once, and take all your people with you.' Only then will I go!" Then, red-faced with anger, Moses stomped from the palace.

7. The Passover

Then the Lord said to Moses and Aaron, "From now on, this month will be the first and most important month of the Jewish calendar. Annually, on the tenth day of this month (announce this to all the people of Israel), each family shall get a lamb (or, if a family is small, let it share the lamb with another small family in the neighborhood; whether to share in this way depends on the size of the families). This animal shall be a year-old male, either a sheep or a goat, without any defects.

"On the evening of the fourteenth day of this month, all these lambs shall be killed, and their blood shall be placed on the two side-frames of the door of every home and on the panel above the door. Use the blood of the lamb eaten in that home. Everyone shall eat roast lamb that night with unleavened bread and bitter herbs. The meat must not be eaten raw or boiled, but roasted, including the head, legs, heart and liver. Don't eat any of it the next day; if all is not eaten that night, burn what is left.

"Eat it with your traveling clothes on, prepared for a long journey, wearing your walking shoes and carrying your walking sticks in your hands; eat it hurriedly. This observance shall be called the Lord's Passover.

"For I will pass through the land of Egypt tonight and kill all the oldest sons and firstborn male animals in all the land of

Egypt, and execute judgment upon all the gods of Egypt—for I am Jehovah. The blood you have placed on the doorposts will be proof that you obey Me, and when I see the blood I will pass over you and I will not destroy your firstborn children when I smite the land of Egypt.

"You shall celebrate this event each year (this is a permanent law) to remind you of this fatal night. The celebration shall last seven days. For that entire period you are to eat only bread made without yeast. Anyone who disobeys this rule at any time during the seven days of the celebration shall be excommunicated from Israel.

"On the first day of the celebration, and again on the seventh day, there will be special religious services for the entire congregation, and no work of any kind may be done on those days except the preparation of food. This annual 'Celebration with Unleavened Bread' will cause you always to remember today as the day when I brought you out of the land of Egypt; so it is a law that you must celebrate this day annually, generation after generation. Again I repeat, during those days you must not eat anything made with yeast; serve only yeastless bread."

Then Moses called for all the elders of Israel and said to them, "Go and get lambs from your flocks, a lamb for one or more families depending upon the number of persons in the families, and kill the lamb so that God will pass over you and not destroy you. Drain the lamb's blood into a basin, and then take a cluster of hyssop branches and dip them into the lamb's blood. Strike the hyssop against the lintel above the door and against the two side panels, so that there will be blood upon them. None of you shall go outside all night. For Jehovah will pass through the land and kill the Egyptians; but when He sees the blood upon the panel at the top of the door and on the two side pieces, He will pass over that home and not permit the Destroyer to enter and kill your firstborn.

"And remember, this is a permanent law for you and your posterity. And when you come into the land that the Lord will give you just as He promised and you celebrate the Passover, and your children ask, 'What does all this mean? What is this ceremony about?' You will reply, 'It is the celebration of Jehovah's passing over us, for He passed over the homes of the people of Israel, though He killed the Egyptians; He passed over our houses and did not come in to destroy us.' " And all the people bowed their heads and worshiped.

So the people of Israel did as Moses and Aaron had commanded. And that night, at midnight, Jehovah killed all the firstborn sons in the land of Egypt, from Pharaoh's oldest son to the oldest son of the captive in the dungeon; also all the firstborn of the cattle. Then Pharaoh and his officials and all the people of Egypt got up in the night; and there was bitter crying throughout all the land of Egypt, for there was not a house where there was not one dead.

And Pharaoh summoned Moses and Aaron during the night and said, "Leave us; please go away, all of you; go and serve Jehovah as you said. Take your flocks and herds and be gone; and oh, give me a blessing as you go."

And the Egyptians were urgent upon the people of Israel, to get them out of the land as quickly as possible. For they said, "We are as good as dead."

The Israeli took with them their bread dough without yeast, and bound their kneading troughs into their spare clothes, and carried them on their shoulders. And the people of Israel did as Moses said and asked the Egyptians for silver and gold jewelry, and for clothing. And the Lord gave the Israeli favor with the Egyptians, so that they gave them whatever they wanted. And the Egyptians were practically stripped of everything they owned!

The sons of Jacob and their descendants had lived in Egypt 430 years, and it was on the last day of the four-hundred and thirtieth year that all of Jehovah's people left the land. That very day the Lord brought out the people of Israel from the land of Egypt, wave after wave of them crossing the border.

Then Moses said to the people, "This is a day to remember forever—the day of leaving Egypt and your slavery; for the Lord has brought you out with mighty miracles. Now remember, during the annual celebration of this event you are to use no yeast; don't even have any in your homes. During those celebration days each year you must explain to your children why you are celebrating—it is a celebration of what the Lord did for you when you left Egypt. This annual memorial week will brand you as His own unique people, just as though He had branded His mark of ownership upon your hands or your forehead. And in the future, when your children ask you, 'What is this all about?' you shall tell them 'With mighty miracles Jehovah brought us out of Egypt from our slavery.' "

God did not lead them through the land of the Philistines, although that was the most direct route from Egypt to the Promised Land. The reason was that God felt the people might become discouraged by having to fight their way through, even though they had left Egypt armed; He thought they might return to Egypt. Instead, God led them along a route through the Red Sea wilderness.

Moses took the bones of Joseph with them, for Joseph had made the sons of Israel vow before God that they would take his bones with them when God led them out of Egypt—as he was sure God would.

Leaving Succoth, they camped in Etham at the edge of the wilderness. The Lord guided them by a pillar of cloud during the daytime and by a pillar of fire at night. So they could travel either by day or night. The cloud and fire were never out of sight.

8. Crossing the Red Sea

When word reached the king of Egypt that the Israeli were not planning to return to Egypt after three days but to keep on going, Pharaoh and his staff became bold again. "What is this we have done, letting all these slaves get away?" they asked. So Pharaoh led the chase in his chariot, followed by the pick of Egypt's chariot corps—600 chariots in all—and other chariots driven by Egyptian officers. He pursued the people of Israel, for they had taken much of the wealth of Egypt with them. Pharaoh's entire cavalry—horses, chariots and charioteers—was used in the chase; and the Egyptian army overtook the people of Israel as they were camped beside the shore near Piha-hiroth, across from Baal-zephon.

As the Egyptian army approached, the people of Israel saw them far in the distance speeding after them. They were terribly frightened and cried out to the Lord to help them. And they turned against Moses, whining, "Have you brought us out here to die in the desert because there were not enough graves for us in Egypt? Why did you make us leave Egypt? Isn't this what we told you, while we were slaves, to leave us alone? We said it would be better to be slaves to the Egyptians than dead in the wilderness."

But Moses told the people, "Don't be afraid. Just stand where you are and watch, and you will see the wonderful way the Lord will rescue you today. The Egyptians you are looking at—you will never see them again. The Lord will fight for you, and you won't need to lift a finger!"

Then the Lord said to Moses, "Quit praying and get the people moving! Forward, march! Use your rod—hold it out over the water, and the sea will open up a path before you, and all the people of Israel shall walk through on dry ground!"

Then the Angel of God, who was leading the people of Israel, moved the cloud around behind them, and it stood between the people of Israel and the Egyptians. And that night, as it changed to a pillar of fire, it gave darkness to the Egyptians but light to the people of Israel! So the Egyptians couldn't find the Israeli! Meanwhile, Moses stretched his rod over the sea, and the Lord opened up a path through the sea with walls of water on each side. A strong east wind blew all that night, drying the sea bottom. So the people of Israel walked through the sea on dry ground!

Then the Egyptians followed them between the walls of water along the bottom of the sea—all of Pharaoh's horses, chariots and horsemen. But in the early morning Jehovah looked down from the cloud of fire upon the array of the Egyptians and began to harass them. Their chariot wheels began coming off, so that their chariots scraped along the dry ground. "Let's get out of here," the Egyptians yelled. "Jehovah is fighting for them and against us."

When all the Israelites were on the other side, the Lord said to Moses, "Stretch out your hand again over the sea, so that the waters will come back over the Egyptians and their chariots and horsemen." Moses did, and the sea returned to normal beneath the morning light. The Egyptians tried to flee, but the Lord drowned them in the sea. The water covered the path and the chariots and horsemen. And of all the army of Pharaoh that chased after Israel through the sea, not one remained alive.

9. The Song of Moses

Then Moses and the people of Israel sang this song to the Lord:

> I will sing to the Lord, for He has triumphed gloriously;
> He has thrown both horse and rider into the sea.
> The Lord is my strength, my song and my salvation.
> He is my God, and I will praise Him.
> He is my father's God—I will exalt Him.
>
> The Lord is a warrior—
> Yes, Jehovah is His name.
> He has overthrown Pharaoh's chariots and armies,
> Drowning them in the sea.
> The famous Egyptian captains are dead beneath the
>   waves.
> The water covers them.
> They went down into the depths like a stone.
>
> Your right hand, O Lord, is glorious in power;
> It dashes the enemy to pieces.
> In the greatness of Your majesty
> You overthrew all those who rose against You.
> You sent forth your anger, and it consumed them as fire
>   consumes straw.
> At the blast of Your breath
> The waters divided!
> They stood as solid walls to hold the seas apart.

The enemy said, "I will chase after them,
Catch up with them, destroy them.
I will cut them apart with my sword
And divide the captured booty."
But God blew with His wind, and the sea covered them.
They sank as lead in the mighty waters.
Who else is like the Lord among the gods?
Who is glorious in holiness like Him?
Who is so awesome in splendor,
A wonder-working God?

Jehovah shall reign forever and forever.
The horses of Pharaoh, his horsemen, and his chariots
Tried to follow through the sea;
But the Lord let down the walls of water on them
While the people of Israel walked through on dry land.

Also Miriam, the prophetess, the sister of Aaron, took a
timbrel and led the women in dances.

And Miriam sang this song:

Sing to the Lord, for He has triumphed gloriously.
The horse and rider have been drowned in the sea.

Then Moses led the people of Israel on from the Red Sea,
and they moved out into the wilderness of Shur and were there
three days without water. And they came to Elim where there
were 12 springs and 70 palm trees; and they camped there
beside the springs.

10. Manna from Heaven

Now they left Elim and journeyed on into the Zin wilderness, between Elim and Mount Sinai, arriving there on the fifteenth day of the second month after leaving Egypt.

There too the people spoke bitterly against Moses and
Aaron, "Oh, that we were back in Egypt," they moaned, "and
that the Lord had killed us there! For there we had plenty to
eat. But now you have brought us into this wilderness to kill
us with starvation."

Then the Lord said to Moses, "Look, I'm going to rain down food from heaven for them. Everyone can go out each day and gather as much food as he wishes. And I will test them in this, to see whether they will follow My instructions or not. Tell them to gather twice as much as usual on the sixth day of each week."

That evening vast numbers of quail arrived and covered the camp, and in the morning the desert all around the camp was wet with dew. And when the dew disappeared later in the morning it left tiny flakes of something as small as hoarfrost on the ground. When the people of Israel saw it they asked each other, "What is it?"

And Moses told them, "It is the food Jehovah has given you to eat. Jehovah has said for everyone to gather as much as is needed for his household—about three quarts for each person in his home." So the people of Israel went out and gathered it. And when they poured it into a three-quart measure, there was just enough for everyone—three quarts apiece; those who gathered a lot had nothing left over and those who gathered little had no lack! Each home had just enough. And Moses told them, "Don't leave it overnight."

But of course some of them wouldn't listen, and left it until morning. And when they looked, it was full of maggots and had a terrible odor. Moses was very angry with them. So they gathered the food morning by morning, each home according to its need; and when the sun became hot upon the ground, the food melted and disappeared. On the sixth day they gathered twice as much as usual, six quarts instead of three; then the leaders of the people came and asked Moses why this had been commanded them.

And he told them, "Because the Lord has appointed tomorrow as a day of seriousness and rest, a holy Sabbath to the Lord when we must refrain from doing our daily tasks. So cook as much as you want to today, and keep what is left overnight." And the next morning the food was wholesome and good, without maggots or odor. So the people rested on the seventh day.

And the food became known as "manna" (meaning "What is it?"); it was white like corriander seed and flat. It tasted like honey bread. So the people of Israel ate the manna 40 years until they arrived in the land of Canaan where there were crops to eat.

11. Victory over Amalek

But now the warriors of Amalek came to fight against the people of Israel at Rephidim. Moses instructed Joshua to issue a call to arms to the Israeli to fight the army of Amalek. "Tomorrow," Moses told him, "I will stand at the top of the hill with the rod of God in my hand!"

So Joshua and his men went out to fight the army of Amalek. Meanwhile, Moses, Aaron and Hur went to the top of the hill. And as long as Moses held up the rod in his hands, Israel was winning; but whenever he rested his arms at his sides, the soldiers of Amalek were winning. Moses' arms finally became too tired to hold up the rod any longer, so Aaron and Hur rolled a stone for him to sit on, and they stood on each side, holding up his hands until sunset. As a result, Joshua and his troops crushed the army of Amalek, putting them to the sword.

12. The Ten Commandments

The Israeli arrived in the Sinai peninsula three months after the night of their departure from Egypt. After breaking camp at Rephidim, they came to the base of Mount Sinai and set up camp there. Moses climbed the rugged mountain to meet with God, and from somewhere in the mountain God called to him and said, "Give these instructions to the people of Israel. Tell them God said, 'You have seen what I did to the Egyptians, and how I brought you to Myself as though on eagle's wings. Now if you will obey Me and keep your part of My contract with you, you shall be My own little flock from among all the nations of the earth; for all the earth is Mine. And you shall be a kingdom of priests to God, a holy nation.' "

On the morning of the third day there was a terrific thunder and lightning storm, and a huge cloud came down upon the mountain, and there was a long, loud blast as from a ram's horn. All the people trembled. Moses led them out from the camp to meet God, and they stood at the foot of the mountain. All Mount Sinai was covered with smoke because Jehovah descended upon it in the form of fire. The smoke billowed into the sky as from a furnace, and the whole mountain shook with a violent earthquake. As the trumpet blast grew louder and louder, Moses spoke and God thundered His reply. Then God issued this edict:

"I am Jehovah your God who liberated you from your slavery in Egypt. You may worship no other god than Me.

"You shall not make yourselves any idols: any images resembling animals, birds or fish. You must never bow to an image or worship it in any way; for I, the Lord your God, am very possessive. I will not share your affection with any other god! And when I punish people for their sins, the punishment continues upon the children, grandchildren and great-grandchildren of those who hate Me. But I lavish My love upon thousands of those who love Me and obey My commandments.

"You shall not use the name of Jehovah your God irreverently, nor use it to swear a falsehood. You will not escape punishment if you do.

"Remember to observe the Sabbath as a holy day. Six days a week are for your daily duties and your regular work, but the seventh day is a day of Sabbath rest before the Lord your God. On that day you are to do no work of any kind, nor shall your son, daughter, or slaves—whether men or women—or your cattle or your house guests. For in six days the Lord made the heaven, earth and sea, and everything in them, and rested the seventh day; so He blessed the Sabbath day and set it aside for rest.

"Honor your father and mother, that you may have a long, good life in the land the Lord your God will give you.

"You must not murder.

"You must not commit adultery.

"You must not steal.

"You must not lie.

"You must not be envious of your neighbor's house, or want to sleep with his wife, or want to own his slaves, oxen, donkeys, or anything else he has."

As the people stood in the distance, Moses entered into the deep darkness where God was. And the Lord told him: "Tell the people of Israel I have said, 'You are witnesses to the fact that I have made known My will to you from heaven.' "

13. Building Instructions for the Tabernacle

Jehovah said to Moses, "Tell the people of Israel that everyone who wants to may bring Me an offering from this list:

Gold	Goat's hair
Silver	Acacia wood
Bronze	Fine-twined linen
Blue cloth	Goats' skins
Purple cloth	Red-dyed rams' skins
Scarlet cloth	Onyx stones
Olive oil for the lamps	
Stones (to set in ephod and in breastplate)	
Spices (for anointing oil and for fragrant incense)	

"For I want the people of Israel to make Me a sacred Temple where I can live among them. Be sure that everything you make follows the pattern I am showing you here on the mountain.

"This home of Mine shall be a tent pavilion—a Tabernacle. I will give you a drawing of the construction plan and the details of each furnishing. Using acacia wood, make an Ark 3¾ feet long, 2¼ feet wide and 2¼ feet high. Overlay it inside and outside with pure gold, with a molding of gold all around it. Cast four rings of gold for it and attach them to the four lower corners, two rings on each side. Make poles from acacia wood overlaid with gold, and fit the poles into the rings at the sides of the Ark, to carry it. These carrying poles shall never be taken from the rings, but are to be left there permanently.

"When the Ark is finished, place inside it the tablets of stone I will give you, with the Ten Commandments engraved on them. And make a lid of pure gold, 3¾ feet long and 2¼ feet wide. This is the place of mercy for your sins.

"Then make images of angels, using beaten gold, and place them at the two ends of the lid of the Ark. They shall be one piece with the mercy place, one at each end. The cherubim—the angels—shall be facing each other, looking down upon the place of mercy, and shall have wings spread out above the gold lid. Install the lid upon the Ark, and place within the Ark the tablets of stone I shall give you.

"And I will meet with you there and talk with you from above the place of mercy between the cherubim; and the Ark will contain the laws of My covenant. There I will tell you My commandments for the people of Israel.

"Make the Tabernacle-tent from ten colored sheets of fine-twined linen, 42 feet long and 6 feet wide, dyed blue, purple and scarlet, with cherubim embroidered on them. The roof of the Tabernacle is made of goat's hair tarpaulins. The framework shall be made of acacia wood, each frame-piece being 15 feet high and 2¼ feet wide, standing upright, with grooves on each side to mortise into the next upright piece. Make bars of acacia wood to run across the frames, five bars on each side of the Tabernacle.

"Then make a table of acacia wood 3 feet long, 1½ feet wide and 2¼ feet high. Overlay it with pure gold. And always keep the special Bread of the Presence on the table before Me.

"Make a lampstand of pure, beaten gold. The entire lampstand and its decorations shall be one piece. It shall have three branches going out from each side of the center shaft, each branch decorated with three almond flowers.

"Inside the Tabernacle, make a veil from blue, purple and scarlet cloth, the fine-twined linen, with cherubim embroidered into the cloth. Hang the curtain from hooks. Behind this curtain place the Ark containing the stone tablets engraved with God's laws. The curtain will separate the Holy Place and the Most Holy Place.

"Place the table and the lampstand across the room from each other on the outer side of the veil. The lampstand will be on the south side of the Holy Place and the table on the north.

"Then make a smaller altar for burning incense. It is to be eighteen inches square and three feet high. Overlay the top, sides and horns of the altar with pure gold and run a gold molding around the entire altar. Place the altar just outside the veil, near the place of mercy.

"Using acacia wood, make a square altar 7½ feet wide, and 3 feet high. Make horns for the four corners of the altar, attach them firmly, and overlay everything with bronze."

And the Lord said to Moses, "Make a bronze basin with a bronze pedestal. Put it between the Tabernacle and the altar and fill it with water.

"Then make a courtyard for the Tabernacle, enclosed with curtains made of fine-twined linen. The entire court will be 150 feet long, and 75 feet wide, with curtain walls 7½ feet high, made from fine-twined linen.

"Every day you shall sacrifice a young bull as a sin offering for atonement. Each day offer two yearling lambs upon the altar, one in the morning and the other in the evening. This shall be a perpetual daily offering at the door of the Tabernacle before the Lord, where I will meet with you and speak with you. And I will meet the people of Israel there, and the Tabernacle shall be sanctified by My glory." Then, as God finished speaking with Moses on Mount Sinai, He gave him the two tablets of stone on which the Ten Commandments were written with the finger of God.

14. Seven Holy Festivals

The Lord said to Moses, "Announce to the people of Israel that they are to celebrate several annual festivals of the Lord —times when all Israel will assemble and worship Me. (These are in addition to your Sabbaths—the seventh day of every week—which are always days of solemn rest in every home, times for assembling to worship and for resting from the normal business of the week.) These are the holy festivals which are to be observed each year:

"*The Passover of the Lord:* This is to be celebrated at the end of March.

"*The Festival of Unleavened Bread:* This is to be celebrated beginning the day following the Passover. On the first day of this festival, you shall gather the people for worship, and all ordinary work shall cease. You shall do the same on the seventh day of the festival. On each of the intervening days you shall make an offering by fire to the Lord.

"*The Festival of First Fruits:* When you arrive in the land I will give you and reap your first harvest, bring the first sheaf of the harvest to the priest on the day after the Sabbath. He shall wave it before the Lord in a gesture of offering, and it will be accepted by the Lord as your gift.

"*The Festival of Pentecost:* Fifty days later you shall bring to the Lord an offering of a sample of the new grain of your later crops.

"*The Festival of Trumpets:* Mid-September is a solemn time for all the people to meet together for worship; it is a time of remembrance and is to be announced by loud blowing of trumpets. Don't do any work on the day of the celebration, but offer a sacrifice by fire to the Lord.

"*The Day of Atonement* follows nine days later: all the people are to come together before the Lord, saddened by their sin; and they shall offer sacrifices by fire to the Lord. Don't do any work that day, for it is a special day for making atonement before the Lord your God. Anyone who does not spend the day in repentance and sorrow for sin shall be excommunicated from his people.

"*The Festival of Tabernacles:* Five days later, on the last day of September, is the Festival of Shelters to be celebrated before the Lord for seven days. During those seven days, all of you who are native Israeli are to live in these shelters. The purpose of this is to remind the people of Israel, generation after generation, that I rescued you from Egypt, and caused you to live in shelters. I am Jehovah your God." So Moses announced these festivals of the Lord to the people of Israel.

Concerning the Day of Atonement, God gave to Moses these additional instructions: first Aaron shall present to the Lord a young bull as a sin offering for himself, making atonement for himself and his family. Then he shall bring two goats before the Lord at the entrance of the Tabernacle, and cast lots to determine which is the Lord's and which is to be sent away. The goat allotted to the Lord shall then be sacrificed by Aaron as a sin offering. The other goat shall be kept alive and placed before the Lord.

After Aaron has sacrificed the young bull as a sin offering, he shall take a censer full of live coals from the altar of the Lord, fill his hands with sweet incense beaten into fine powder and bring it inside the veil. There before the Lord he shall put the incense upon the coals, so that a cloud of incense will cover the mercy place above the Ark (containing the stone tablets of the Ten Commandments); thus he will not die. But he shall bring some of the blood of the young bull and sprinkle it with his finger upon the east side of the mercy place, and then seven times in front of it.

Then he must go out and sacrifice the people's sin offering goat, and bring its blood within the veil and sprinkle it upon the place of mercy and in front of it, just as he did with the blood of the young bull. Thus he shall make atonement for the Holy Place because it is defiled by the sins of the people of Israel, and for the Tabernacle, located right among them, and surrounded by their defilement. Not another soul shall be inside the Tabernacle when Aaron enters to make atonement in the Holy Place. Then he shall go out to the altar before the Lord and make atonement for it. He must smear the blood of the young bull and the goat on the horns of the altar, and sprinkle blood upon the altar seven times with his finger, thus cleansing it from the sinfulness of Israel, and making it holy.

When he has completed the rite of atonement for the Holy Place, the entire Tabernacle, and the altar, he shall bring the live goat and, laying both hands upon its head, confess over it all the sins of the people of Israel. He shall lay all their sins upon the head of the goat and send it into the desert, led by a man appointed for the task. So the goat shall carry all the sins of the people into a land where no one lives, and the man shall let it loose in the wilderness.

This is a permanent law: you must do no work on the twenty-fifth day of September, but must spend the day in self-examination and humility. This applies whether you are born in the land or are a foreigner living among the people of Israel; for this is the day commemorating the atonement, cleansing you in the Lord's eyes from all your sins.

Any Israelite who sacrifices an ox, lamb, or goat anywhere except at the Tabernacle is guilty of murder and shall be ex-communicated from his nation. I repeat: Anyone, whether an Israeli or a foreigner living among you, who eats blood in any form—I will excommunicate him from his people. For the life of the flesh is in the blood, and I have given you the blood to sprinkle upon the altar as an atonement for your souls; it is the blood that makes atonement, because it is the life. That is the reasoning behind My decree to the people of Israel, for the blood is the life.

16. Aaron's Golden Calf

When Moses didn't come back down the mountain right away, the people went to Aaron. "Look," they said, "make us a god to lead us, for this fellow Moses who brought us here from Egypt has disappeared; something must have happened to him."

"Give me your golden earrings," Aaron replied. So they all did—men and women, boys and girls. Aaron melted the gold, then molded and tooled it into the form of a calf.

The people exclaimed, "O Israel, this is the god that brought you out of Egypt!" When Aaron saw how happy the people were about it, he built an altar before the calf and announced, "Tomorrow there will be a feast to Jehovah!" So they were up early the next morning and began offering burnt offerings and peace offerings to the calf-idol; afterwards they sat down to feast and drink at a wild party, followed by sexual immorality.

Then the Lord told Moses, "Quick! Go on down, for your people that you brought from Egypt have defiled themselves, and have quickly abandoned all My laws. They have molded themselves a calf and worshiped it and sacrificed to it. They said, 'This is your god, O Israel, that brought you out of Egypt.' "

Then Moses went down the mountain, holding in his hands the Ten Commandments written on both sides of two stone tablets. (God Himself had written the commandments on the tablets.) When Joshua heard the noise below them of all the people shouting, he exclaimed to Moses, "It sounds as if they are preparing for war!"

But Moses replied, "No, it's not a cry of victory or defeat, but singing." When they came near the camp, Moses saw the calf and the dancing, and in terrible anger he threw the tablets to the ground and they lay broken at the foot of the mountain.

He took the calf and melted it in the fire, and when the metal cooled, he ground it into powder and spread it upon the water and made the people drink it.

Then he turned to Aaron. "What in the world did the people do to you," he demanded, "to make you bring such a terrible sin upon them?"

"Don't get so upset," Aaron replied. "You know these people and what a wicked bunch they are. They said to me, 'Make us a god to lead us, for something has happened to this fellow Moses who led us out of Egypt.' Well, I told them, 'Bring me your gold earrings.' So they brought them to me and I threw them into the fire, and . . . well . . . this calf came out!"

The next day Moses said to the people, "You have sinned a great sin, but I will return to the Lord on the mountain—perhaps I will be able to obtain His forgiveness for you."

So Moses returned to the Lord and said, "Oh, these people have sinned a great sin and have made themselves gods of gold. Yet now if You will only forgive their sin—and if not, then blot *me* out of the book You have written."

And the Lord replied to Moses, "Whoever has sinned

against Me will be blotted out of My book. And now go, lead the people to the place I told you about, and I assure you that My Angel shall travel on ahead of you; however, when I come to visit these people, I will punish them for their sins." And the Lord sent a great plague upon the people because they had worshiped Aaron's calf.

17. Moses and God's Glory

Moses always erected the sacred tent (the "Tent for Meeting with God," he called it) far outside the camp, and everyone who wanted to consult with Jehovah went out there. Whenever Moses went to the Tabernacle, all the people would rise and stand in their tent doors watching until he reached its entrance. As he entered, the pillar of cloud would come down and stand at the door while the Lord spoke with Moses. Then all the people worshiped from their tent doors, bowing low to the pillar of cloud. Inside the tent the Lord spoke to Moses face-to-face, as a man speaks to his friend. Afterwards Moses would return to the camp, but the young man who assisted him (Joshua, son of Nun), stayed behind in the Tabernacle.

Moses talked there with the Lord and said to Him, "You have been telling me, 'Take these people to the Promised Land,' but You haven't told me whom You will send with me. You say You are my friend, and that I have found favor before You. Please, if this is really so, guide me clearly along the way You want me to travel so that I will understand You and walk acceptably before You. For don't forget that this nation is Your people."

And the Lord replied, "I Myself will go with you and give you success." (For Moses had said, "If You aren't going with us, don't let us move a step from this place.") Then Moses asked to see God's glory.

The Lord replied, "I will make My goodness pass before you, and I will announce to you the meaning of My name Jehovah, the Lord. I show kindness and mercy to anyone I want to. But you may not see the glory of My face, for man may not see Me and live. However, stand here on this rock beside Me.

And when My glory goes by, I will put you in the cleft of the rock and cover you with My hand until I have passed. Then I will remove My hand and you shall see My back, but not My face."

The Lord told Moses, "Prepare two stone tablets like the first ones and I will write upon them the same commands that were on the tablets you broke. Be ready in the morning to come up into Mount Sinai and present yourself to Me on the top of the mountain. No one shall come with you and no one must be anywhere on the mountain. Do not let the flocks or herds feed close to the mountain."

So Moses took two tablets of stone like the first ones, and was up early and climbed Mount Sinai, as the Lord had told him to, taking the two stone tablets in his hands. Then the Lord descended in the form of a pillar of cloud and stood there with him, and passed in front of him and announced the meaning of His name. "I am Jehovah, the merciful and gracious God," He said, "slow to anger and rich in steadfast love and truth. I, Jehovah, show this steadfast love to many thousands by forgiving their sins; or else I refuse to clear the guilty, and require that a father's sins be punished in the sons and grandsons and even later generations."

Moses fell down before the Lord and worshiped. And he said, "If it is true that I have found favor in Your sight, O Lord, then please go with us to the Promised Land; yes, it is an unruly, stubborn people, but pardon our iniquity and our sins, and accept us as Your own." Moses was up on the mountain with the Lord for 40 days and 40 nights, and in all that time he neither ate nor drank. At that time God wrote out the Covenant—the Ten Commandments—on the stone tablets.

Moses didn't realize as he came back down the mountain with the tablets that his face glowed from being in the presence of God. Because of this radiance upon his face, Aaron and the people of Israel were afraid to come near him. But Moses called them over to him, and Aaron and the leaders of the congregation came and talked with him. Afterwards, all the people came to him, and he gave them the commandments the Lord had given him upon the mountain.

When Moses had finished speaking with them, he put a veil

over his face. But whenever he went into the Tabernacle to speak with the Lord, he removed the veil until he came out again; then he would pass on to the people whatever instructions God had given him, and the people would see his face aglow. Afterwards he would put the veil on again until he returned to speak with God.

18. The Fiery Cloud

At last the Tabernacle was finished, following all the Lord's instructions to Moses. On the first day of the first month in the second year, it was put together. Then Moses brought the Ark into the Tabernacle and set up the veil to screen it, just as the Lord had commanded.

That same day the cloud covered the Tabernacle and the glory of the Lord filled it. The cloud rested upon the Tabernacle during the daytime, and at night there was fire in the cloud so that all the people of Israel could see it. This continued throughout all their journeys.

It was always so—the daytime cloud changing to the appearance of fire at night. When the cloud lifted, the people of Israel moved on to wherever it stopped and camped there. In this way they journeyed at the command of the Lord and stopped where He told them to, then remained there as long as the cloud stayed. If it stayed a long time, they stayed a long time. But if it stayed only a few days, they remained only a few days; for so the Lord had instructed them. Sometimes the fire-cloud stayed only during the night and moved on the next morning. But day or night when it moved, the people broke camp and followed. If the cloud stayed above the Tabernacle two days, a month, or a year, that is how long the people of Israel stayed; but as soon as it moved, they moved. So it was that they camped or traveled at the commandment of the Lord; whatever the Lord told Moses they should do, they did.

19. The Priestly Benediction

Now the Lord said to Moses, "Tell Aaron and his sons that they are to give this special blessing to the people of Israel:

'May the Lord bless and protect you;
May the Lord's face radiate with joy because of you;
May He be gracious to you,
Show you His favor,
And give you His peace.'

"This is how Aaron and his sons shall call down My blessings upon the people of Israel; and I Myself will personally bless them."

20. Dedication of the Levites

Then the Lord said to Moses, "Now set apart the Levites from the other people of Israel. Do this by sprinkling water of purification upon them, then have them shave their entire bodies and wash their clothing and themselves. Have them bring a young bull and a grain offering of fine flour mingled with oil, along with another young bull for a sin offering. Then bring the Levites to the door of the Tabernacle as all the people watch. There the leaders of the tribes shall lay their hands upon them.

"And Aaron, with a gesture of offering, shall present them to the Lord as a gift from the entire nation of Israel. The Levites will represent all the people in serving the Lord. Next, the Levite leaders shall lay their hands upon the heads of the young bulls and offer them before the Lord; one for a sin offering and the other for a burnt offering, to make atonement for the Levites. Then the Levites are to be presented to Aaron and his sons, just as any other gift to the Lord is given to the priests! In this way you will dedicate the Levites from among the rest of the people of Israel, and the Levites shall be Mine. After you have sanctified them and presented them in this way, they shall go in and out of the Tabernacle to do their work."

"So Moses and Aaron and all the people of Israel dedicated the Levites, carefully following Jehovah's instructions to Moses. The Levites purified themselves and washed their clothes, and Aaron presented them to the Lord in a gesture of offering. He then performed the rite of atonement over them to purify them. After that they went into the Tabernacle as assistants to Aaron and his sons; everything was done just as the Lord had commanded Moses.

The Lord also instructed Moses, "The Levites are to begin serving in the Tabernacle at the age of 25, and are to retire at the age of 50. After retirement they can assist with various light duties in the Tabernacle, but will have no regular responsibilities."

21. Rules for Day-by-Day Living

The Lord also told Moses to tell the people of Israel, "You must be holy because I, the Lord your God, am holy. You must respect your mothers and fathers, and obey My Sabbath law, for I am the Lord your God.

"When you harvest your crops, don't reap the corners of your fields, and don't pick up stray grains of wheat from the ground. It is the same with your grape crop—don't strip every last piece of fruit from the vines, and don't pick up the grapes that fall to the ground. Leave them for the poor and for those traveling through, for I am Jehovah your God.

"You must not steal nor lie nor defraud. You must not swear to a falsehood, thus bringing reproach upon the name of your God, for I am Jehovah.

"Don't gossip. Don't falsely accuse your neighbor of some crime, for I am Jehovah. You shall not rob nor oppress anyone, and you shall pay your hired workers promptly. If something is due them, don't even keep it overnight.

"You must not curse the deaf nor trip up a blind man as he walks. Fear your God; I am Jehovah!

"Judges must always be just in their sentences, not noticing whether a person is poor or rich; they must always be perfectly fair. You must be impartial in judgment. Use accurate measurements—lengths, weights and volumes—and give full measure, for I am Jehovah your God, who brought you from the land of Egypt.

"Don't hate your brother. Rebuke anyone who sins; don't let him get away with it, or you will be equally guilty. Don't seek vengeance. Don't bear a grudge; but love your neighbor as yourself, for I am Jehovah.

"Do not defile yourselves by consulting mediums and wizards, for I am Jehovah your God.

"You shall give due honor and respect to the elderly, in the fear of God. I am Jehovah.

"Do not take advantage of foreigners in your land; do not wrong them. They must be treated like any other citizen; love them as yourself, for remember that you too were foreigners in the land of Egypt. I am Jehovah your God.

"You must heed all of My commandments and ordinances, carefully obeying them, for I am Jehovah."

22. Moses and Hobab

One day Moses said to his brother-in-law Hobab (son of Reuel the Midianite), "At last we are on our way to the Promised Land. Come with us and we will do you good; for the Lord has given wonderful promises to Israel!" But his brother-in-law replied, "No, I must return to my own land and kinfolk."

"Stay with us," Moses pleaded, "for you know the ways of the wilderness and will be a great help to us. If you come, you will share in all the good things the Lord does for us." They traveled for three days after leaving Mount Sinai, with the Ark at the front of the column to choose a place for them to stop.

It was daytime when they left, with the cloud moving along ahead of them as they began their march. As the Ark was carried forward, Moses cried out, "Arise, O Lord, and scatter Your enemies; let them flee before You." And when the Ark was set down he said, "Return, O Lord, to the millions of Israel."

23. The Quail

Then the Egyptians who had come with them began to long

for the good things of Egypt. This added to the discontent of the people of Israel and they wept, "Oh, for a few bites of meat! Oh, that we had some of the delicious fish we enjoyed so much in Egypt, and the wonderful cucumbers and melons, leeks, onions and garlic! But now our strength is gone, and day after day we have to face this manna!"

Then the Lord said to Moses, "Summon before Me seventy of the leaders of Israel; bring them to the Tabernacle to stand there with you. I will come down and talk with you there and I will take of the Spirit which is on you and will put it upon them also; they shall bear the burden of the people along with you, so that you will not have the task alone. And tell the people to purify themselves, for tomorrow they shall have meat to eat. Tell them, 'The Lord has heard your tearful complaints about all you left behind in Egypt, and He is going to give you meat.'"

So Moses left the Tabernacle and reported Jehovah's words to the people; and he gathered the 70 elders and placed them around the Tabernacle. And the Lord came down in the cloud and talked with Moses, and the Lord took of the Spirit that was upon Moses and put it upon the 70 elders. And when the Spirit rested upon them, they prophesied for some time. But two of the 70—Eldad and Medad—were still in the camp, and when the Spirit rested upon them, they prophesied there.

Some young men ran and told Moses what was happening, and Joshua (the son of Nun), one of Moses' personally chosen assistants, protested, "Sir, make them stop!"

But Moses replied, "Are you jealous for my sake? I only wish that all of the Lord's people were prophets, and that the Lord would put His Spirit upon them all!" Then Moses returned to the camp with the elders of Israel.

The Lord sent a wind that brought quail from the sea, and let them fall into the camp and all around it! As far as one could walk in a day in any direction, there were quail flying three or four feet above the ground. So the people caught and killed quail all that day and through the night and all the next day too! The least anyone gathered was 100 bushels! Quail were spread out all around the camp.

24. Report of the Spies

Jehovah now instructed Moses, "Send spies into the land of Canaan—the land I am giving to Israel; send one leader from each tribe." The Israeli were camped in the wilderness of Paran at the time.

Moses did as the Lord had commanded and sent 12 tribal leaders. He sent them out with these instructions: "Go northward into the hill country of the Negeb, and see what the land is like; see also what the people are like who live there, whether they are strong or weak, many or few; and whether the land is fertile or not; and what cities there are, and whether they are villages or are fortified; whether the land is rich or poor, and whether there are many trees. Don't be afraid, and bring back some samples of the crops you see." (The first of the grapes were being harvested at that time.)

So they spied out the land all the way from the wilderness of Zin to Rehob near Hamath. Going northward, they passed first through the Negeb and arrived at Hebron. There they saw the Ahimanites, Sheshites and Talmites, all families descended from Anak. (By the way, Hebron was very ancient, having been founded seven years before Tanis in Egypt.) Then they came to what is now known as the Valley of Eshcol where they cut down a single cluster of grapes so large that it took two of them to carry it on a pole between them! The Israeli named the valley Eshcol at that time (meaning "Cluster") because of the cluster of grapes they found! They also took some samples of the pomegranates and figs.

After 40 days they returned from their tour. They made their report to Moses, Aaron and all the people of Israel in the wilderness of Paran at Kadesh, and they showed the fruit they had brought with them.

This was their report: "We arrived in the land you sent us to see, and it is indeed a magnificent country—a land flowing with milk and honey. Here is some fruit we have brought as proof. But the people living there are powerful, and their cities are fortified and very large. What's more, we saw Anakim giants there! The Amalekites live in the south, while in the hill country there are the Hittites, Jebusites and Amorites; down along the coast of the Mediterranean Sea and in the Jordan River valley are the Canaanites."

But Caleb reassured the people as they stood before Moses. "Let us go up at once and possess it," he said, "for we are well able to conquer it!"

"Not against people as strong as they are!" the other spies said. "They would crush us!" So the majority report of the spies was negative: "The land is full of warriors, the people are powerfully built, and we saw some of the Anakim there, descendants of the ancient race of giants. We felt like grasshoppers before them, they were so tall!"

Then all the people began weeping aloud, and they carried on all night. Their voices rose in a great chorus of complaint against Moses and Aaron. "We wish we had died in Egypt," they wailed, "or even here in the wilderness, rather than be taken into this country ahead of us. Jehovah will kill us there, and our wives and little ones will become slaves. Let's get out of here and return to Egypt!" The idea swept the camp. "Let's elect a leader to take us back to Egypt!" they shouted.

Then Moses and Aaron fell face downward on the ground before the people of Israel; two of the spies, Joshua (the son of Nun) and Caleb (the son of Jephunneh) ripped their clothing and said to all the people, "It is a wonderful country ahead, and the Lord loves us. He will bring us safely into the land and give it to us. It is *very* fertile, a land flowing with milk and honey! Oh, do not rebel against the Lord, and do not fear the people of the land. For they are but bread for us to eat! The Lord is with us and He has removed His protection from them! Don't be afraid of them!"

But the only response of the people was to talk of stoning the two.

Then the glory of the Lord appeared, and the Lord said to Moses, "How long will these people despise Me? Will they *never* believe Me, even after all the miracles I have done among them? I will disinherit them and destroy them with a plague, and I will make you into a nation far greater and mightier than they are!"

"But what will the Egyptians think when they hear about

it?" Moses pleaded with the Lord. "They know full well the power You displayed in rescuing Your people. They have told this to the inhabitants of this land, who are well aware that You are with Israel and that You talk with her face-to-face. They see the pillar of cloud and fire standing above us, and they know that You lead and protect us day and night. Now if You kill all Your people, the nations that have heard Your fame will say, 'The Lord had to kill them because He wasn't able to take care of them in the wilderness. He wasn't strong enough to bring them into the land He swore He would give them.'

"Oh, please, show the great power of Your patience by forgiving our sins and showing us Your steadfast love. Forgive us even though You have said that You don't let sin go unpunished, and that You punish the father's fault in the children to the third and fourth generation. Oh, I plead with You, pardon the sins of this people because of Your magnificent, steadfast love, just as You have forgiven them all the time from when we left Egypt until now."

Then the Lord said, "All right, I will pardon them as you have requested. But I vow by My own name that just as it is true that all the earth shall be filled with the glory of the Lord, so it is true that not one of the men who has seen My glory and the miracles I did both in Egypt and in the wilderness—and ten times refused to trust Me and obey Me—shall even see the land I promised to this people's ancestors. But My servant Caleb is a different kind of man—he has obeyed Me fully. I will bring him into the land he entered as a spy, and his descendants shall have their full share in it. Only Caleb (son of Jephunneh) and Joshua (son of Nun) are permitted to enter it. But now, since the people of Israel are so afraid of the Amalekites and the Canaanites living in the valleys, tomorrow you must turn back into the wilderness in the direction of the Red Sea."

What sorrow there was throughout the camp when Moses reported God's words to the people! They were up early the next morning, and started towards the Promised Land. "Here we are!" they said. "We realize that we have sinned, but now we are ready to go on into the land the Lord has promised us."

But Moses said, "It's too late. Now you are disobeying the Lord's orders to return to the wilderness. Don't go ahead with your plan or you will be crushed by your enemies, for the Lord is not with you. Don't you remember? The Amalekites and the Canaanites are there! You have deserted the Lord, and now He will desert you." But they went ahead into the hill country despite the fact that neither the Ark nor Moses left the camp. Then the Amalekites and the Canaanites who lived in the hills came down and attacked them and chased them to Hormah.

25. Water in the Wilderness

The people of Israel arrived in the wilderness of Zin in April and camped at Kadesh where Miriam died and was buried. There was not enough water to drink at that place, so the people again rebelled against Moses and Aaron. A great mob formed, and they held a protest meeting. "Would that we too had died with our dear brothers the Lord killed!" they shouted at Moses. "You have deliberately brought us into this wilderness to get rid of us, along with our flocks and herds. Why did you ever make us leave Egypt and bring us here to this evil place? Where is the fertile land of wonderful crops— the figs, vines and pomegranates you told us about? Why, there isn't even water enough to drink!"

Moses and Aaron turned away and went to the entrance of the Tabernacle, where they fell face downward before the Lord; and the glory of Jehovah appeared to them. And He said to Moses, "Get Aaron's rod; then you and Aaron must summon the people. As they watch, speak to that rock over there and tell it to pour out its water! You will give them water from a rock, enough for all the people and all their cattle!"

Then Moses and Aaron summoned the people to come and gather at the rock, and he said to them, "Listen, you rebels! Must we bring you water from this rock?" Then Moses lifted the rod and struck the rock twice, and water gushed out and the people and their cattle drank.

But the Lord said to Moses and Aaron, "Because you did

not believe Me and did not sanctify Me in the eyes of the people of Israel, you shall not bring them into the land I have promised them!" This place was named Meribah (meaning "Rebel Waters"), because it was where the people of Israel fought against Jehovah and where He showed Himself to be holy before them.

26. Detour for Israel

While Moses was at Kadesh he sent messengers to the king of Edom: "We are the descendants of your brother Israel," he declared. "You know our sad history, how our ancestors went down to visit Egypt and stayed there so long and became slaves of the Egyptians. But when we cried to the Lord He heard us and sent an Angel who brought us out of Egypt. Now we are here at Kadesh, encamped on the borders of your land. Please let us pass through your country. We will be careful not to go through your planted fields, nor through your vineyards; we won't even drink water from your wells, but will stay on the main road and not leave it until we have crossed your border on the other side."

But the king of Edom said, "Stay out! If you attempt to enter my land I will meet you with an army!"

"But sir," protested the Israeli ambassadors, "we will stay on the main road and will not even drink your water unless we pay whatever you demand for it. We only want to pass through, and nothing else."

But the king was adamant. "Stay out!" he warned and, mobilizing his army, he marched to the frontier with a great force. Because Edom refused to allow Israel to pass through their country, Israel turned back and journeyed from Kadesh to Mount Hor.

27. The Death of Aaron

Then the Lord said to Moses and Aaron at the border of the land of Edom, "The time has come for Aaron to die—for he shall not enter the land I have given the people of Israel, for the two of you rebelled against My instructions concerning the water at Meribah. Now summon Aaron and his son Eleazar and take them up onto Mount Hor. There you shall remove Aaron's priestly garments from him and put them on Eleazer his son; and Aaron shall die there."

So Moses did as the Lord commanded him. The three of them went up together into Mount Hor as all the people watched. When they reached the summit, Moses removed the priestly garments from Aaron and put them on his son Eleazar; and Aaron died on the top of the mountain.

Then Moses and Eleazar returned, and when the people were informed of Aaron's death, they mourned for him for 30 days.

28. The Bronze Snake

Then the people of Israel returned to Mount Hor and from there continued southward along the road to the Red Sea in order to go around the land of Edom. The people were very discouraged; they began to murmur against God and to complain against Moses. "Why have you brought us out of Egypt to die here in the wilderness?" they whined. "There is nothing to eat here and nothing to drink, and we hate this insipid manna." So the Lord sent poisonous snakes among them to punish them, and many of them were bitten and died.

Then the people came to Moses and cried out, "We have sinned, for we have spoken against Jehovah and against you. Pray to Him to take away the snakes."

Moses prayed for the people.

Then the Lord told him, "Make a bronze replica of one of these snakes and attach it to the top of a pole; anyone who is bitten shall live if he simply looks at it!" So Moses made the replica, and whenever anyone who had been bitten looked at the bronze snake, he recovered!

29. Joshua the New Leader

One day the Lord said to Moses, "Go up into Mount Abarim and look across the river to the land I have given to the people of Israel. After you have seen it, you shall die as Aaron your brother did, for you rebelled against My instructions in the wilderness of Zin. When the people of Israel rebelled, you did not glorify Me before them by following My instructions to order water to come out of the rock." He was referring to the incident at the waters of Meribah ("Place of Strife") in Kadesh, in the wilderness of Zin.

Then Moses said to the Lord, "O Jehovah, the God of the spirits of all mankind, please appoint a new leader for the people, a man who will lead them into battle and care for them, so that the people of the Lord will not be as sheep without a shepherd."

The Lord replied, "Go and get Joshua (son of Nun) who has the Spirit in him, and take him to Eleazar the priest. As all the people watch, charge him with the responsibility of leading the people. Publicly give him your authority so that all the people of Israel will obey him. He shall be the one to consult with Eleazar the priest in order to get directions from the Lord. The Lord will speak to Eleazar through the use of the Urim, and Eleazar will pass on these instructions to Joshua and the people. In this way the Lord will continue to give them guidance."

So Moses did as Jehovah commanded and took Joshua to Eleazar the priest. As the people watched, Moses laid his hands upon him and dedicated him to his responsibilities, as the Lord had commanded.

30. Advice to Parents

Then Moses said, "The Lord your God told me to give you all these commandments which you are to obey in the land you will soon be entering, where you will live. The purpose of these laws is to cause you, your sons, and your grandsons to reverence the Lord your God by obeying all of his instructions as long as you live."

O Israel listen! Jehovah is our God, Jehovah alone. You must love Him with *all* your heart, soul and might. And you must think constantly about these commandments I am giving you today. You must teach them to your children and talk about them when you are at home or out for a walk; at bedtime and the first thing in the morning. Tie them on your finger, wear them on your forehead, and write them on the doorposts of your house!

When the Lord your God has brought you into the land He promised your ancestors Abraham, Isaac and Jacob, and when He has given you great cities full of good things—cities you didn't build, wells you didn't dig and vineyards and olive trees you didn't plant—and when you have eaten until you can hold no more, then beware lest you forget the Lord who brought you out of the land of Egypt, the land of slavery.

In the years to come your son will ask you, "What is the purpose of these laws which the Lord our God has given us?"

You must tell him, "We were Pharaoh's slaves in Egypt, and the Lord brought us out of Egypt with great power and mighty miracles—with terrible blows against Egypt and Pharaoh and all his people. We saw it all with our own eyes. He brought us out of Egypt so that He could give us this land He had promised to our ancestors. And He has commanded us to obey all of these laws and to reverence Him so that He can preserve us alive as He has until now. For it always goes well with us when we obey all the laws of the Lord our God."

For you are a holy people, dedicated to the Lord your God. He has chosen you from all the people on the face of the whole earth to be His own chosen ones. He didn't choose you and pour out His love upon you because you were a larger nation than any other, for you were the smallest of all! It was just because He loves you and because He kept His promise to your ancestors. That is why He brought you out of slavery in Egypt with such amazing power and mighty miracles. Understand, therefore, that the Lord your God is the faithful God who for a thousand generations keeps His promises and constantly loves those who love Him and who obey His commands.

Moses' instructions continued:

Do you remember how the Lord led you through the wilderness for all those 40 years, humbling you and testing you to find out how you would respond and whether or not you would really obey Him? Yes, He humbled you by letting you go hungry and then feeding you with manna, a food previously unknown to both you and your ancestors. He did it to help you realize that food isn't everything, and that real life comes by obeying every command of God. For the Lord your God is bringing you into a good land of brooks, pools, gushing springs, valleys and hills; it is a land of wheat and barley, of grape vines, fig trees, pomegranates, olives and honey; it is a land where food is plentiful and nothing is lacking; it is a land where iron is as common as stone and copper is abundant in the hills. When you have eaten your fill, bless the Lord your God for the good land He has given you.

But that is the time to be careful! Beware that in your plenty you don't forget the Lord your God and begin to disobey Him. For when you have become full and prosperous and have built fine homes to live in, and when your flocks and herds have become very large and your silver and gold have multiplied, that is the time to watch out that you don't become proud, and forget the Lord your God who brought you out of your slavery in the land of Egypt. Beware that you don't forget the God who led you through the great and terrible wilderness with the dangerous snakes and scorpions, where it was so hot and dry. He gave you water from the rock!

He fed you with manna in the wilderness (it was a kind of bread unknown before) so that you would become humble and so that your trust in Him would grow, and He could do you good. He did it so that you would never feel that it was your own power and might that made you wealthy. Always remember that it is the Lord your God who gives you power to become rich, and He does it to fulfill His promise to your ancestors. But if you forget about the Lord your God and worship other gods instead, and follow evil ways, you shall certainly perish, just as the Lord has caused other nations in the past to perish. That will be your fate, too, if you don't obey the Lord your God.

32. Blessings or Curses

Moses continued:

And now, Israel, what does the Lord your God require of you except to listen carefully to all He says to you, and to obey for your own good the commandments I am giving you today, to love Him and to worship Him with all your hearts and souls?

Earth and highest heaven belong to the Lord your God. And if you will carefully obey all of His commandments that I am going to give you today, and if you will love the Lord your God with all your hearts and souls, and will worship Him, then He will continue to send both the early and late rains that will produce wonderful crops of grain, grapes for your wine and olive oil.

I am giving you the choice today between God's blessing or God's curse! There will be blessing if you obey the commandments of the Lord your God which I am giving you today, and a curse if you refuse them and worship the gods of these other nations. So today you must begin to obey all of these commandments I have given you.

When you cross into the Promised Land, the tribes of Simeon, Levi, Judah, Issachar, Joseph and Benjamin shall stand upon Mount Gerizim to proclaim a blessing, and the tribes of Reuben, Gad, Asher, Zebulun, Dan and Naphtali shall stand upon Mount Ebal to proclaim a curse. Then the Levites standing between them shall shout to all Israel, "The curse of God be upon anyone who makes and worships an idol, even in secret, whether carved of wood or made from molten metal—for these handmade gods are hated by the Lord!" And all the people shall reply, "Amen."

"Cursed is anyone who despises his father or mother." And all the people shall reply, "Amen."

"Cursed is he who moves the boundary marker between his land and his neighbor's." And all the people shall reply, "Amen."

"Cursed is he who takes advantage of a blind man." And all the people shall reply, "Amen."

"Cursed is he who is unjust to the foreigner, the orphan and the widow." And all the people shall reply, "Amen."

"Cursed is he who commits adultery with one of his father's wives, for she belongs to his father." And all the people shall reply, "Amen."

"Cursed is he who has sexual intercourse with an animal." And all the people shall reply, "Amen."

"Cursed is he who has sexual intercourse with his sister, whether she be a full sister or a half sister." And all the people shall reply, "Amen."

"Cursed is he who has sexual intercourse with his widowed mother-in-law." And all the people shall reply, "Amen."

"Cursed is he who secretly slays another." And all the people shall reply, "Amen."

"Cursed is he who accepts a bribe to kill an innocent person." And all the people shall reply, "Amen."

"Cursed is anyone who does not obey these laws." And all the people shall reply, "Amen."

If you fully obey all of these commandments of the Lord your God, the laws I am declaring to you today, God will transform you into the greatest nation in the world. These are the blessings that will come upon you:

> Blessings in the city,
> Blessings in the field;
> Many children,
> Ample crops,
> Large flocks and herds;
> Blessings of fruit and bread;
> Blessings when you come in,
> Blessings when you go out.

If you won't listen to the Lord your God and won't obey these laws I am giving you today, then all of these curses shall come upon you:

> Curses in the city;
> Curses in the fields;
> Curses on your fruit and bread;
> The curse of barren wombs;

Curses upon your crops;
Curses upon the fertility of your cattle and flocks;
Curses when you come in;
Curses when you go out.

Obeying these commandments is not something beyond your strength and reach; for these laws are not in the far heavens, so distant that you can't hear and obey them, and with no one to bring them down to you; nor are they beyond the ocean, so far that no one can bring you their message; but they are very close at hand—in your hearts and on your lips—so that you can obey them.

Look, today I have set before you life and death, depending on whether you obey or disobey. Oh, that you would choose life; that you and your children might live!

33. Moses' Farewell Message

After Moses had said all these things to the people of Israel, he told them, "I am now 120 years old! I am no longer able to lead you, for the Lord has told me that I shall not cross the Jordan River. But the Lord Himself will lead you and will destroy the nations living there, and you shall overcome them. Joshua is your new commander, as the Lord has instructed."

Then Moses called for Joshua and said to him, as all Israel watched, "Be strong! Be courageous! For you shall lead these people into the land promised by the Lord to their ancestors; see to it that they conquer it. Don't be afraid, for the Lord will go before you and will be with you; He will not fail nor forsake you."

Then the Lord said to Moses, "The time has come when you must die. Summon Joshua and come into the Tabernacle where I can give him his instructions." So Moses and Joshua came and stood before the Lord. He appeared to them in a great cloud at the Tabernacle entrance and said to Moses, "You shall die and join your ancestors. After you are gone, these people will begin worshiping foreign gods in the Promised Land. They will forget about Me and break the contract I have made with them. Now write down the words of this song, and teach it to the people of Israel as My warning to them."

34. Moses' Farewell Song

So Moses recited this entire song to the whole assembly of Israel:

> Listen, O heavens and earth!
> Listen to what I say!
> My words shall fall upon you
> Like the gentle rain and dew,
> Like rain upon the tender grass,
> Like showers on the hillside.
>
> I will proclaim the greatness of the Lord.
> How glorious He is!
> He is the Rock. His work is perfect.
> Everything He does is just and fair.
> He is faithful, without sin.
>
> But Israel has become corrupt,
> Smeared with sin. They are no longer His,
> They are a stubborn, twisted generation.
> Is this the way you treat Jehovah?
> O foolish people,
> Is not God your Father?
> Has He not created you?
> Has He not established you and made you strong?
> Remember the days of long ago!
> (Ask your father and the aged men;
> They will tell you all about it.)
>
> When God divided up the world among the nations,
> He gave each of them a supervising angel!
> But He appointed none for Israel;
> For Israel was God's own personal possession!
> God protected them in the howling wilderness
> As though they were the apple of His eye.

He spreads His wings over them,
Even as an eagle overspreads her young.
She carries them upon her wings—
As does the Lord His people!

When the Lord alone was leading them,
And they lived without foreign gods,
God gave them fertile hilltops,
Rolling, fertile fields,
Honey from the rock,
And olive oil from stony ground!
He gave them milk and meat—
Choice Bashan rams, and goats—
And the finest of the wheat;
They drank the sparkling wine.
But Israel was soon overfed;
Yes, fat and bloated;
Then, in plenty, they forsook their God.
They shrugged away the rock of their salvation.

God saw what they were doing,
He said, "I will abandon them;
Israel is a stupid nation;
Foolish, without understanding.
Oh, that they were wise!
Oh, that they could understand!
Oh, that they would know what they are getting into!
But Israel is My special people,
Sealed as jewels with My treasury.

Vengeance is Mine,
And I decree the punishment of all her enemies:
Their doom is sealed."
The Lord will see His people righted,
And will have compassion on them when they slip.
He will watch their power ebb away,
Both slave and free.
Then God will ask,
"Where are their gods—
The rocks they claimed to be their refuge?

Where are these gods now,
To whom they sacrificed their fat and wine?
Let those gods arise,
And help them!

Don't you see that I alone am God?
I kill and make live.
I wound and heal—
No one delivers from my power."

Praise His people,
O Gentile nations,
For He will avenge His people,
Taking vengeance on His enemies,
Purifying His land
And His people.

When Moses and Joshua had recited all the words of this song to the people, Moses made these comments: "Meditate upon all the laws I have given you today and pass them on to your children. These laws are not mere words—they are your life! Through obeying them you will live long, plentiful lives in the land you are going to possess across the Jordan River."

35. Moses' Farewell Blessing

This is the blessing that Moses the man of God, gave to the people of Israel before his death:

The Lord came to us at Mount Sinai,
And dawned upon us from Mount Seir;
He shone from Mount Paran,
Surrounded by ten thousands of holy angels,
And with flaming fire at His right hand.
How He loves His people—
His holy ones are in His hands.
"They followed in Your steps, O Lord.
They have received their directions from You.
The laws I have given
Are Your precious possession."

There is none like the God of Jerusalem—
He descends from the heavens
In majestic splendor to help you.
The eternal God is your refuge,
And underneath are the everlasting arms.
He thrusts out your enemies before you;
It is He who cries, "Destroy them!"
So Israel dwells safely,
Prospering in a land of corn and wine,
While the gentle rains descend from heaven.

What blessings are yours, O Israel!
Who else has been saved by the Lord?
He is your shield and your helper!
He is your excellent sword!
Your enemies shall bow low before you,
And you shall trample on their backs!

36. Moses' Death

That same day, the Lord said to Moses, "Go to Mount
Nebo in the Abarim mountains, in the land of Moab
across from Jericho. Climb to its heights and look out
across the land of Canaan, the land I am giving to the
people of Israel. After you see the land you must die and
join your ancestors, just as Aaron your brother died in
Mount Hor and joined them. For you dishonored Me
among the people of Israel at the springs of Meribath-
Kadesh, in the wilderness of Zin. You will see spread out
before you the land I am giving the people of Israel, but
you will not enter it."

Then Moses climbed from the plains of Moab to Pis-
gah Peak in Mount Nebo, across from Jericho. And the
Lord pointed out to him the Promised Land, as they
gazed out across Gilead as far as Dan.

"There is Naphtali; and there is Ephraim and Manasseh; and across there, Judah extending to the Mediterranean Sea; there is the Negeb; and the Jordan Valley; and

Jericho the city of palm trees; and Zoar," the Lord told him. "It is the Promised Land," the Lord told Moses. "I promised Abraham, Isaac and Jacob that I would give it to their descendants. Now you have seen it but you will not enter it."

So Moses, the disciple of the Lord, died in the land of Moab as the Lord had said. The Lord buried him in a valley near Beth-peor in Moab, but no one knows the exact place. Moses was 120 years old when he died, yet his eyesight was perfect and he was as strong as a young man.

The people of Israel mourned for him for 30 days on the plains of Moab.

Joshua (son of Nun) was full of the spirit of wisdom, for Moses had laid his hands upon him. So the people of Israel obeyed him and followed the commandments that the Lord had given to Moses.

There has never been another prophet like Moses, for the Lord talked to him face-to-face. At God's command he performed amazing miracles which have never been equaled. He did great and terrifying wonders before Pharaoh and his entire court in Egypt and before the people of Israel in the wilderness.

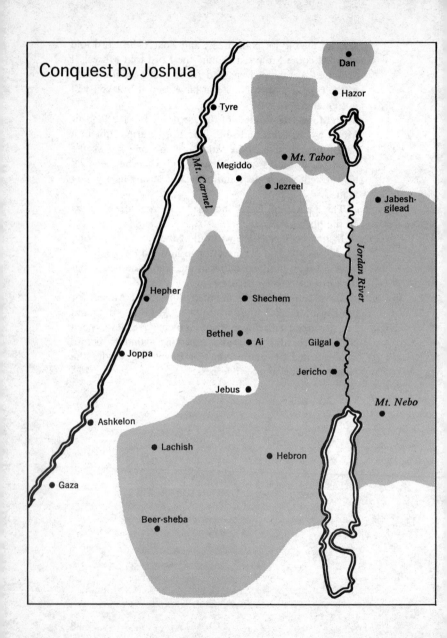

Conquest by Joshua

Dan
Hazor
Tyre
Mt. Tabor
Mt. Carmel
Megiddo
Jezreel
Jabesh-gilead
Hepher
Shechem
Jordan River
Bethel
Ai
Gilgal
Joppa
Jericho
Jebus
Mt. Nebo
Ashkelon
Lachish
Hebron
Gaza
Beer-sheba

PART 3 Palestine Under New Management

JOSHUA

The book of Joshua records the success of Israel in conquering the land of Canaan under the leadership of Moses' courageous successor. It covers a period of some 30 to 40 years.

1. God's Charge to Joshua

AFTER the death of Moses, the Lord's disciple, God spoke to Moses' assistant whose name was Joshua (the son of Nun) and said to him, "Now that My disciple is dead, you are the new leader of Israel. Lead My people across the Jordan River into the Promised Land. You need only to be strong and courageous and to obey to the letter every law Moses gave you, for if you are careful to obey every one of them you will be successful in everything you do.

"Constantly remind the people about these laws, and you yourself must think about them every day and every night so that you will be sure to obey all of them. For only then will you succeed. Yes, be bold and strong! Banish fear and doubt! For remember, the Lord your God is with you wherever you go."

2. Rahab and the Spies

Then Joshua sent two spies from the Israeli camp at Acacia to cross the river and check out the situation on the other side, especially at Jericho. They arrived at an inn operated by a woman named Rahab who was a prostitute. They were planning to spend the night there, but someone informed the king of Jericho that two Israelis who were suspected of being spies had arrived in the city that evening. He dispatched a police squadron to Rahab's home, demanding that she surrender them. "They are spies," the police explained. "They have been sent by the Israeli leaders to discover the best way to attack us."

But she had hidden them, so she told the officer in charge, "The men were here earlier, but I didn't know they were spies. They left the city at dusk as the city gates were about to close, and I don't know where they went. If you hurry you can probably catch up with them!"

But actually she had taken them up to the roof and hidden them beneath piles of flax that were drying there. So the constable and his men went all the way to the Jordan River looking for them; meanwhile, the city gates were kept shut. Rahab went up to talk to the men before they retired for the night. "I know perfectly well that your God is going to give my country to you," she told them. "We are all afraid of you; everyone is terrified if the word *Israel* is even mentioned. Now I beg for this one thing: Swear to me by the sacred name of your God that when Jericho is conquered you will let me live, along with my father and mother, my brothers and sisters and all their families. This is only fair after the way I have helped you."

The men agreed. "If you won't betray us, we'll see to it that you and your family aren't harmed," they promised. "We'll defend you with our lives." Then, since her house was on top of the city wall, she let them down by a rope from a window.

"I accept your terms," she replied. And she left the scarlet rope hanging from the window.

The spies went up into the mountains and stayed there three days, until the men who were chasing them had returned to the city after searching everywhere along the road without success. Then the two spies came down from the mountain and crossed the river and reported to Joshua all that had happened to them. "The Lord will certainly give us the entire land," they said, "for all the people over there are scared to death of us."

3. Crossing the Jordan

Early the next morning Joshua and all the people of Israel left Acacia and arrived that evening at the banks of the Jordan River, where they camped for a few days before crossing.

"Today," the Lord told Joshua, "I will give you great honor, so that all Israel will know that I am with you just as I was with Moses. Instruct the priests who are carrying the Ark to stop at the edge of the river."

Now it was the harvest season and the Jordan was overflowing all its banks; but as the people set out to cross the river and as the feet of the priests who were carrying the Ark touched the water at the river's edge, suddenly, far up the river at the city of Adam near Zarethan, the water began piling up as though against a dam! And the water below that point flowed on to the Salt Sea until the riverbed was empty. Then all the people crossed at a spot where the river was close to the city of Jericho, and the priests who were carrying the Ark stood on dry ground in the middle of the Jordan and waited as all the people passed by.

When all the people were safely across, the Lord said to Joshua, "Tell the 12 men chosen for a special task—one from each tribe—each to take a stone from where the priests are standing in the middle of the Jordan, and to carry them out and pile them up as a monument at the place where you camp tonight."

So the men did as Joshua told them. They took 12 stones from the middle of the Jordan River—one for each tribe, just as the Lord had commanded Joshua. They carried them to the place where they were camped for the night and constructed a monument there. Then Joshua explained the purpose of the stones. "In the future," he said, "when your children ask you why these stones are here and what they mean, you are to tell them that these stones are a reminder of this amazing miracle—that the nation of Israel crossed the Jordan River on dry ground! Tell them how the Lord our God dried up the river right before our eyes, and then kept it dry until we were all across! It is the same thing the Lord did 40 years ago at the Red Sea! He did this so that all the nations of the earth will realize that Jehovah is the mighty God, and so that all of you will worship Him forever."

4. The Fall of Jericho

The gates of Jericho were kept tightly shut because the people were afraid of the Israelis; no one was allowed to go in or out. But the Lord said to Joshua, "Jericho and its king and all its mighty warriors are already defeated, for I have given them to you!"

So Joshua summoned the priests and gave them their instructions: the armed men would lead the procession followed by seven priests blowing continually on their trumpets. Behind them would come the priests carrying the Ark, followed by a rearguard. "Let there be complete silence except for the trumpets," Joshua commanded. "Not a single word from any of you until I tell you to shout; then *shout!*"

The Ark was carried around the city once that day, after which everyone returned to the camp again and spent the night there. At dawn the next morning they went around again, and returned again to the camp. They followed this pattern for six days.

At dawn of the seventh day they started out again, but this time they went around the city not once, but seven times. The seventh time, as the priests blew a long, loud trumpet blast, Joshua yelled to the people, *"Shout!* The Lord has given us the city!"

When the people heard the trumpets blast, they shouted as loud as they could. And suddenly the walls of Jericho crumbled and fell before them, and the people of Israel poured into the city from every side and captured it! They destroyed everything in it—men and women, young and old; oxen, sheep, donkeys—everything.

Then Joshua said to the two spies, "Keep your promise. Go and rescue the prostitute and everyone with her." The young men found her and rescued her, along with her father, mother, brothers and other relatives who were with her. Arrangements were made for them to live outside the camp of Israel. Then the Israelis burned the city and everything in it except that the silver and gold and the bronze and iron utensils were kept for the Lord's treasury.

So the Lord was with Joshua, and his name became famous everywhere.

5. The Capture of Ai

Then the Lord said to Joshua, "Don't be afraid or discouraged; take the entire army and go to Ai, for it is now yours to conquer. I have given the king of Ai and all of his people to you. You shall do to them as you did to Jericho and her king; but this time you may keep the loot and the cattle for yourselves. Set an ambush behind the city."

Before the main army left for Ai, Joshua sent thirty thousand of his bravest troops to hide in ambush close behind the city, alert for action. Early the next morning Joshua roused his men and started toward Ai, accompanied by the elders of Israel, and stopped at the edge of a valley north of the city. That night Joshua sent another five thousand men to join the troops ambushed on the west side of the city. He himself spent the night in the valley.

The king of Ai, seeing the Israeli across the valley, went out early the next morning and attacked at the Plain of Arabah. But of course he didn't realize that there was an ambush behind the city. Joshua and the Israeli army fled across the wilderness as though badly beaten, and all the soldiers in the city were called out to chase after them; so the city was left defenseless. There was not a soldier left in Ai or Bethel and the city gates were left wide open.

Then the Lord said to Joshua, "Point your spear toward Ai, for I will give you the city." Joshua did. And when the men in ambush saw his signal, they jumped up and poured into the city and set it on fire. When the men of Ai looked behind them smoke from the city was filling the sky and they had nowhere to go. When Joshua and the troops who were with him saw the smoke, they knew that their men who had been in ambush were inside the city. So they turned upon their pursuers and began killing them. Then the Israelis who were inside the city came out and began destroying the enemy from the rear. So the men of Ai were caught in a trap and all of them died; not one man survived or escaped.

6. The Law Recorded and Read

Joshua built an altar to the Lord God of Israel at Mount Ebal, as Moses had commanded in the book of his laws. "Make Me an altar of boulders that have neither been broken nor carved," the Lord had said concerning Mount Ebal. Then the priests offered burnt sacrifices and peace offerings to the Lord on the altar. And as the people of Israel watched, Joshua carved upon the stones of the altar each of the Ten Commandments.

Then all the people of Israel—including the elders, officers, judges, and the foreigners living among them—divided into two groups, half of them standing at the foot of Mount Gerizim and half at the foot of Mount Ebal. Between them stood the priests with the Ark, ready to pronounce their blessing. (This was all done in accordance with the instructions given long before by Moses.) Joshua then read to them all of the statements of blessings and curses that Moses had written in the book of God's laws. Every commandment Moses had ever given was read before the entire assembly, including the women and children and the foreigners who lived among the Israelis.

7. Strategy of the Gibeonites

When the people of Gibeon heard what had happened to Jericho and Ai, they resorted to trickery to save themselves. They sent ambassadors to Joshua wearing worn-out clothing, as though from a long journey, with patched shoes, weather-worn saddlebags on their donkeys, old patched wineskins and dry, moldy bread. When they arrived at the camp of Israel at Gilgal, they told Joshua and the men of Israel, "We have come from a distant land to ask for a peace treaty with you."

Joshua and the other leaders believed them. They did not bother to ask the Lord, but went ahead and signed a peace treaty. And the leaders of Israel ratified the agreement with a binding oath.

Three days later the facts came out—these men were close neighbors. The Israeli army set out at once to investigate and reached their cities in three days. The names of the cities were Gibeon, Chephirah, Be-eroth and Kiriath-jearim. But the cities were not harmed because of the vow which the leaders of Israel had made before the Lord God. The people of Israel were angry with their leaders because of the peace treaty, but the leaders replied, "We have sworn before the Lord God of Israel that we will not touch them, and we won't. We must let them live, for if we break our oath the wrath of Jehovah will be upon us." So they became servants of the Israelis, chopping their wood and carrying their water.

8. When the Sun Stood Still

When Adoni-zedek, the king of Jerusalem, heard how Joshua had captured and destroyed Ai and had killed its king the same as he had done at Jericho, and how the people of Gibeon had made peace with Israel and were now their allies, he was very frightened. For Gibeon was a great city, as great as the royal cities and much larger than Ai, and its men were known as hard fighters. So King Adoni-zedek of Jerusalem sent messengers to several other kings: King Hoham of Hebron, King Piram of Jarmuth, King Japhia of Lachish and King Debir of Eglon.

"Come and help me destroy Gibeon," he urged them, "for they have made peace with Joshua and the people of Israel." So these five Amorite kings combined their armies for a united attack on Gibeon.

The men of Gibeon hurriedly sent messengers to Joshua at Gilgal. "Come and help your servants!" they demanded. "Come quickly and save us! For all the kings of the Amorites who live in the hills are here with their armies." So Joshua and the Israeli army left Gilgal and went to rescue Gibeon.

"Don't be afraid of them," the Lord said to Joshua, "for they are already defeated! I have given them to you to destroy. Not a single one of them will be able to stand up to you."

Joshua traveled all night from Gilgal and took the enemy armies by surprise. Then the Lord threw them into a panic so that the army of Israel slaughtered great numbers of them at Gibeon and chased the others all the way to Beth-horon and Azekah and Makkedah, killing them along the way. And as the enemy was racing down the hill to Beth-horon, the Lord destroyed them with a great hailstorm that continued all the way to Azekah; in fact, more men died from the hail than by the swords of the Israelis.

As the men of Israel were pursuing and harassing the foe, Joshua prayed aloud, "Let the sun stand still over Gibeon, and let the moon stand in its place over the valley of Aijalon!" And the sun and the moon didn't move until the Israeli army had finished the destruction of its enemies! This is described in greater detail in *The Book of Jashar*. So the sun stopped in the heavens and stayed there for almost 24 hours! There had never been such a day before, and there has never been another since when the Lord stopped the sun and moon—all because of the prayer of one man.

9. Hebron Assigned to Caleb

A delegation from the tribe of Judah led by Caleb came to Joshua in Gilgal. "Remember what the Lord said to Moses about you and me when we were at Kadesh-barnea?" Caleb asked Joshua. "I was 40 years old at the time, and Moses had sent us from Kadesh-barnea to spy out the land of Canaan. I reported what I felt was the truth, but our brothers who went with us frightened the people and discouraged them from entering the Promised Land. But since I had followed the Lord my God, Moses told me, 'The section of Canaan you were just in shall belong to you and your descendants forever.'

"Now, as you see, from that time until now the Lord has kept me alive and well for all these 45 years since crisscrossing the wilderness, and today I am 85 years old. I am as strong now as I was when Moses sent us on that journey, and I can still travel and fight as well as I could then! So I'm asking that you give me the hill country which the Lord promised me. You will remember that as spies we found the Anakim living there in great, walled cities, but if the Lord is with me I shall drive them out of the land."

So Joshua blessed him and gave him Hebron as a permanent inheritance because he had followed the Lord God of Israel.

10. Joshua's Farewell Address

Long after this when the Lord had given success to the people of Israel against their enemies and when Joshua was very old, he called for the leaders of Israel, the elders, judges and officers, and said to them, "I am an old man now, and you have seen all that the Lord your God has done for you during my lifetime. He has fought for you against your enemies and has given you their land. Soon I will be going the way of all the earth—I am going to die.

"You know very well that God's promises to you have all come true. But as certainly as the Lord has given you the good things He promised, just as certainly He will bring evil upon you if you disobey Him. For if you worship other gods He will completely wipe you out from this good land which the Lord has given you. His anger will rise hot against you, and you will quickly perish. So revere Jehovah and serve Him in sincerity and truth. Put away forever the idols which your ancestors worshiped when they lived beyond the Euphrates River and in Egypt. Worship the Lord alone. But if you are unwilling to obey the Lord, then decide today whom you will obey. Will it be the gods of your ancestors beyond the Euphrates or the gods of the Amorites here in this land? But as for me and my family, we will serve the Lord."

And the people replied, "We would never forsake the Lord

and worship other gods! For the Lord our God is the one who rescued our fathers from their slavery in the land of Egypt. He is the God who did mighty miracles before the eyes of Israel as we traveled through the wilderness and preserved us from our enemies when we passed through their land."

So Joshua made a covenant with them that day at Shechem, committing them to a permanent and binding contract between themselves and God. Joshua recorded the people's reply in the book of the laws of God, and took a huge stone as a reminder and rolled it beneath the oak tree that was beside the Tabernacle. He said to all the people, "This stone has heard everything the Lord said, so it will be a witness to testify against you if you go back on your word."

Then Joshua sent the people away to their own sections of the country. Soon after this he died at the age of 110. He was buried on his own estate of Timnath-serah in the hill country of Ephraim on the north side of the mountains of Gaash.

The bones of Joseph which the people of Israel had brought with them when they left Egypt were buried in Shechem in the parcel of ground which Jacob had bought for $200 from the sons of Hamor.

THE JUDGES

The events recorded in Judges embrace a period of over 300 years. The book moves in cycles: apostasy, followed by oppression, leading to repentance, and after that, deliverance—over and over again! This period may be called the "dark age of the nation" when "there was no king in Israel . . . and every man did whatever he thought was right."

1. Every Man a King

The people had remained true to the Lord throughout Joshua's lifetime and as long afterwards as the old men of his generation were still living—those who had seen the mighty miracles the Lord had done for Israel. But finally all that generation died; and the next generation did not worship Jehovah as their God, and did not care about the mighty miracles He had done for Israel. They did many things which the Lord had expressly forbidden, including the worshiping of heathen gods. They abandoned Jehovah, the God loved and worshiped by their ancestors, the God who had brought them out of Egypt. Instead, they were worshiping and bowing low before the idols of the neighboring nations. So the anger of the Lord flamed out against all Israel. He left them to the mercy of their enemies, for they had departed from Jehovah and were worshiping Baal and the Ashtaroth idols.

So now when the Israelis went out to battle against their enemies, the Lord blocked their path. He had warned them about this, and in fact had vowed that He would do it. But when the people were in this terrible plight, the Lord raised up judges to save them from their enemies. Yet even then Israel would not listen to the judges, but broke faith with Jehovah by worshiping other gods instead. How quickly they turned away from the true faith of their ancestors, for they refused to obey God's commands.

There was no king in Israel in those days, and every man did whatever he thought was right.

2. Deliverance from the Moabites

Not long after the death of Joshua, the people of Israel turned again to their sinful ways, so God helped King Eglon of Moab to conquer part of Israel at that time. Allied with him were the armies of the Ammonites and the Amalekites. These forces defeated the Israelis and took possession of Jericho, often called "The City of Palm Trees." For the next 18 years the people of Israel were required to pay crushing taxes to King Eglon.

But when they cried to the Lord, He sent them a saviour, Ehud (son of Gera, a Benjaminite) who was left-handed. Ehud was the man chosen to carry Israel's annual tax money to the Moabite capital. Before he went on this journey he made himself a double-edged dagger eighteen inches long and hid it in his clothing, strapped against his right thigh.

After delivering the money to King Eglon (who, by the way, was very fat!) he started home again. But outside the city, at the quarries of Gilgal, he sent his companions on and returned alone to the king. "I have a secret message for you," he told him. The king immediately dismissed all those who were with him so that he could have a private interview.

Ehud walked over to him as he was sitting in a cool upstairs room and said to him, "It is a message from God!" King Eglon stood up at once to receive it, whereupon Ehud reached beneath his robe with his strong left hand, pulled out the double-bladed dagger strapped against his right thigh and plunged it deep into the king's belly. The hilt of the dagger disappeared beneath the flesh, and the fat closed over it as the entrails oozed out. Leaving the dagger there, Ehud locked the doors behind him and escaped across an upstairs porch.

When the king's servants returned and saw that the doors were locked they waited, thinking that perhaps he was using the bathroom. But when, after a long time, he still didn't come out, they became concerned and got a key. And when they opened the door, they found their master dead on the floor. Meanwhile Ehud had escaped past the quarries to Seirah.

When he arrived in the hill country of Ephraim, he blew a trumpet as a call to arms and mustered an army under his own command. "Follow me," he told them, "for the Lord has put your enemies the Moabites at your mercy!" The army then proceeded to seize the fords of the Jordan River near Moab, preventing anyone from crossing. Then they attacked the Moabites and killed about ten thousand of the strongest and most skillful of their fighting men, letting not one escape. So Moab was conquered by Israel that day, and the land was at peace for the next 80 years.

3. The Defeat of Sisera

After Ehud's death the people of Israel again sinned against the Lord, so the Lord let them be conquered by King Jabin of Hazor in Canaan. The commander-in-chief of his army was Sisera who lived in Harosheth-hagoiim. He had 900 iron chariots and made life unbearable for the Israelis for 20 years. But finally they begged the Lord for help.

Israel's leader at that time, the one who was responsible for bringing the people back to God, was Deborah, a prophetess, the wife of Lappidoth. She held court at a place now called "Deborah's Palm Tree," between Ramah and Bethel, in the hill country of Ephraim; and the Israelites came to her to decide their disputes.

One day she summoned Barak (son of Abinoam), who lived in Kedesh, in the land of Naphtali, and said to him, "The Lord God of Israel has commanded you to mobilize ten thousand men from the tribes of Naphtali and Zebulun. Lead them to Mount Tabor to fight King Jabin's mighty army with all his chariots under General Sisera's command. The Lord says, 'I will draw them to the Kishon River and you will defeat them there.' "

"I'll go, but only if you go with me!" Barak told her.

"All right," she replied, "I'll go with you; but I'm warning you now that the honor of conquering Sisera will go to a woman instead of to you!" So she went with him to Kedesh. When Barak summoned the men of Zebulun and Naphtali to mobilize at Kedesh, ten thousand men volunteered. And Deborah marched with them.

When General Sisera was told that Barak and his army were camped at Mount Tabor, he mobilized his entire army including the 900 iron chariots and marched from Harosheth-hagoiim to the Kishon River. Then Deborah said to Barak, "Now is the time for action! The Lord leads on! He has already delivered Sisera into your hand!"

So Barak led his ten thousand men down the slopes of Mount Tabor into battle. Then the Lord threw the enemy into a panic, both the soldiers and the charioteers, and Sisera leaped from his chariot and escaped on foot. Barak and his men chased the enemy and the chariots as far as Harosheth-hagoiim until all of Sisera's army was destroyed; not one man was left alive.

Meanwhile Sisera had escaped to the tent of Jael the wife of Heber the Kenite, for there was a mutual-assistance agreement between King Jabin of Hazor and the clan of Heber. Jael went out to meet Sisera and said to him, "Come into my tent, sir. You will be safe here in our protection. Don't be afraid." So he went into her tent and she covered him with a blanket.

"Please give me some water," he said, "for I am very thirsty." So she gave him some milk and covered him again.

"Stand in the door of the tent," he told her, "and if anyone comes by looking for me, tell them that no one is here." Sisera was soon fast asleep from weariness. Then Jael took a sharp tent peg and a hammer and, quietly creeping up to him as he slept, she drove the peg through his temples and into the ground, and so he died.

When Barak came by looking for Sisera, Jael went out to meet him and said, "Come, and I will show you the man you are looking for." So he followed her into the tent and found Sisera lying there dead, with the tent peg through his temples. So that day the Lord used Israel to subdue King Jabin of Canaan.

4. Deborah's Song

Then Deborah and Barak sang this song about the wonderful victory:

> Praise the Lord!
> Israel's leaders bravely led;
> The people gladly followed!
> Yes, bless the Lord!
> Listen, O you kings and princes,
> For I shall sing about the Lord,
> The God of Israel.
>
> In the days of Shamgar and of Jael,
> The main roads were deserted.
> Travelers used the narrow, crooked side paths.
> Israel's population dwindled,
> Until Deborah became a mother to Israel.
>
> When Israel chose new gods,
> Everything collapsed.
> Our masters would not let us have
> A shield or spear.
> Among forty thousand men of Israel,
> Not a weapon could be found!
> How I rejoice
> In the leaders of Israel
> Who offered themselves so willingly!
> Praise the Lord!
>
> The very stars of heaven
> Fought Sisera.
> The rushing Kishon River
> Swept them away.

March on, my soul, with strength!
Hear the stamping
Of the horsehoofs of the enemy!
See the prancing of his steeds!
But the angel of Jehovah
Put a curse on Meroz.
"Curse them bitterly," he said,
"Because they did not come to help the Lord
Against His enemies."

The mother of Sisera watched through the window
For his return.
"Why is his chariot so long in coming?
Why don't we hear the sound of the wheels?"
But her ladies-in-waiting—and she herself—replied,
"There is much loot to be divided,
And it takes time.
Each man receives a girl or two;
And Sisera will get gorgeous robes,
And he will bring home
Many gifts for me."

O Lord, may all Your enemies
Perish as Sisera did,
But may those who love the Lord
Shine as the sun!

5. Gideon's Victory

There was peace in the land for 40 years. Then the people of Israel began once again to worship other gods, and once again the Lord let their enemies harass them. This time for seven years it was by the people of Midian. The Midianites were so cruel that the Israelis took to the mountains, living in caves and dens.

But one day the Angel of the Lord came and sat beneath the oak tree at Ophrah, on the farm of Joash the Abiezrite. Joash's son Gideon had been threshing wheat by hand in the bottom of a grape press—a pit where grapes were pressed to make wine—for he was hiding from the Midianites. The Angel of the Lord appeared to him and said, "Mighty soldier, the Lord is with you!"

"Stranger," Gideon replied, "if the Lord is with us, why has all this happened to us? And where are all the miracles our ancestors have told us about—such as when God brought them out of Egypt? Now the Lord has thrown us away and has let the Midianites completely ruin us."

Then the Lord turned to him and said, "I will make you strong! Go and save Israel from the Midianites! I am sending you!"

But Gideon replied, "Sir, how can *I* save Israel? My family is the poorest in the whole tribe of Manasseh, and I am the least thought of in the entire family!"

Whereupon the Lord said to him, "But I, Jehovah, will be with you! And you shall quickly destroy the Midianite hordes!"

Gideon said to God, "If You are really going to use me to save Israel as You promised, prove it to me in this way: I'll put some wool on the threshing floor tonight, and if, in the morning, the fleece is wet and the ground is dry, I will know You are going to help me!" And it happened just that way! When he got up the next morning he pressed the fleece together and wrung out a whole bowlful of water!

Then Gideon said to the Lord, "Please don't be angry with me, but let me make one more test: this time let the fleece remain dry while the ground around it is wet!" So the Lord did as he asked; that night the fleece stayed dry, but the ground was covered with dew!

Gideon gathered an army of thirty thousand men. He and his army got an early start and went as far as the spring of Harod. The armies of Midian were camped north of them, down in the valley beside the hill of Moreh. The Lord then said to Gideon, "There are too many of you! I can't let all of you fight the Midianites, for then the people of Israel will boast to Me that they saved themselves by their own strength! Send home any of your men who are timid and frightened."

So twenty-two thousand of them left, and only ten thousand remained who were willing to fight. But the Lord told Gideon,

"There are still too many! Bring them down to the spring and I'll show you which ones shall go with you and which ones shall not." So Gideon assembled them at the water. There the Lord told him, "Divide them into two groups decided by the way they drink. In group one will be all the men who cup the water in their hands to get it to their mouths and lap it like dogs. In group two will be those who kneel, with their mouths in the stream." Only 300 of the men drank from their hands; all the others drank with their mouths to the stream.

"I'll conquer the Midianites with these 300!" the Lord told Gideon. "Send all the others home!" So after Gideon had collected all the clay jars and trumpets they had among them, he sent them home, leaving only 300 men with him. He divided the 300 men into three groups and gave each man a trumpet and a clay jar with a torch in it.

Then he explained his plan. "When we arrive at the outer guardposts of the camp," he told them, "do just as I do. As soon as I and the men in my group blow our trumpets, you blow yours on all sides of the camp and shout, 'We fight for God and for Gideon!' "

It was just after midnight and the change of guards when Gideon and the hundred men with him crept to the outer edge of the camp of Midian. Suddenly they blew their trumpets and broke their clay jars so that their torches blazed into the night. Then the other two hundred of his men did the same, blowing the trumpets in their right hands, and holding the flaming torches in their left hands, all yelling, "For the Lord and for Gideon!"

Then they just stood and watched as the whole vast enemy army began rushing around in a panic, shouting and running away. For in the confusion the Lord caused the enemy troops to begin fighting and killing each other from one end of the camp to the other, and they fled into the night to places as far away as Beth-shittah near Zererah, and to the border of Abel-meholah near Tabbath.

Then Gideon sent for the troops of Naphtali, Asher and Manasseh and told them to come and chase and destroy the fleeing army of Midian. Gideon also sent messengers throughout the hill country of Ephraim summoning troops who seized the fords of the Jordan River at Beth-barah, thus preventing the Midianites from escaping by going across.

This is the true account of how Midian was subdued by Israel. Midian never recovered and the land was at peace for forty years—all during Gideon's lifetime.

Now the men of Israel said to Gideon, "Be our king! You and your sons and all your descendants shall be our rulers, for you have saved us from Midian."

But Gideon replied, "I will not be your king, nor shall my son; the Lord is your king!"

Gideon finally died, an old, old man, and was buried in the sepulcher of his father Joash in Ophrah, in the land of the Abiezrites. But as soon as Gideon was dead, the Israeli began to worship the idols Baal and Baal-berith. They no longer considered the Lord as their God, though He had rescued them from all their enemies on every side. Nor did they show any kindness to the family of Gideon despite all he had done for them.

6. Jephthah's Foolish Vow

Now Jephthah was a great warrior from the land of Gilead, but his mother was a prostitute. His father (whose name was Gilead) had several other sons by his legitimate wife, and when these half-brothers grew up, they chased Jephthah out of the country. "You son of a whore!" they said. You'll not get any of our father's estate." So Jephthah fled from his father's home and lived in the land of Tob. Soon he had quite a band of malcontents as his followers, living off the land as bandits.

It was about this time that the Ammonites began their war against Israel. The leaders of Gilead sent for Jephthah, begging him to come and lead their army against the Ammonites. But Jephthah said to them, "Why do you come to me when you hate me and have driven me out of my father's house? Why come now when you're in trouble?"

"Because we need you," they replied. "If you will be our commander-in-chief against the Ammonites, we will make you the king of Gilead."

"Sure!" Jephthah exclaimed. "Do you expect me to believe that?"

"We swear it," they replied. "We promise with a solemn oath."

So Jephthah accepted the commission and was made commander-in-chief and king. The contract was ratified before the Lord in Mizpah at a general assembly of all the people. He attempted to avoid war through diplomacy but failed. Thereafter the Spirit of the Lord came upon Jephthah and he led his army across the land of Gilead and Manasseh, past Mizpah in Gilead, and attacked the army of Ammon.

Meanwhile Jephthah had vowed to the Lord that if God would help Israel conquer the Ammonites, then when he returned home in peace, the first person coming out of his house to meet him would be sacrificed as a burnt offering to the Lord!

So Jephthah led his army against the Ammonites, and the Lord gave him the victory. He destroyed the Ammonites with a terrible slaughter all the way from Aroer to Minnith, including twenty cities, and as far away as Vineyard Meadow. Thus the Ammonites were subdued by the people of Israel.

When Jephthah returned home his daughter—his only child —ran out to meet him, playing on a tambourine and dancing for joy. When he saw her he tore his clothes in anguish. "Alas, my daughter!" he cried out. "You have brought me to the dust. For I have made a vow to the Lord and I cannot take it back."

And she said, "Father, you must do whatever you promised the Lord, for He has given you a great victory over your enemies the Ammonites. But first let me go up into the hills and roam with my girl friends for two months, weeping because I'll never marry."

"Yes," he said. "Go." And so she did, bewailing her fate with her friends for two months. Then she returned to her father, who did as he had vowed. So she was never married. And after that it became a custom in Israel that the young girls went away for four days each year to lament the fate of Jephthah's daughter.

7. The Birth of Samson

Once again Israel sinned by worshiping other gods, so the Lord let them be conquered by the Philistines who kept them in subjection for forty years. Then one day the angel of the Lord appeared to the wife of Manoah, of the tribe of Dan, who lived in the city of Zorah. She had no children, but the angel said to her, "Even though you have been barren so long, you will soon conceive and have a son! Don't drink any wine or beer, and don't eat any food that isn't kosher. Your son's hair must never be cut, for he shall be a Nazirite, a special servant of God from the time of his birth; and he will begin to rescue Israel from the Philistines."

The woman ran and told her husband, "A man from God appeared to me and I think He must be the angel of the Lord, for He was almost too glorious to look at. I didn't ask where He was from, and He didn't tell me His name, but He told me, 'You are going to have a baby boy!' And He told me not to drink any wine or beer, and not to eat food that isn't kosher, for the baby is going to be a Nazirite—he will be dedicated to God from the moment of his birth until the day of his death!"

Then Manoah prayed, "O Lord, please let the man from God come back to us again and give us more instructions about the child You are going to give us." The Lord answered his prayer, and the angel of God appeared once again. Then Manoah took a young goat and a grain offering and offered it as a sacrifice to the Lord; and the angel did a strange and wonderful thing, for as the flames from the altar were leaping up toward the sky and as Manoah and his wife watched, the angel ascended in the fire! Manoah and his wife fell face downward to the ground, and that was the last they ever saw of him. It was then that Manoah finally realized that it had been the angel of the Lord.

"We will die," Manoah cried out to his wife, "for we have seen God!"

But his wife said, "If the Lord were going to kill us He wouldn't have accepted our burnt offerings and wouldn't have appeared to us and told us this wonderful thing and done these miracles."

When her son was born they named him Samson, and the Lord blessed him as he grew up. And the Spirit of the Lord began to excite him whenever he visited the parade grounds of the army of the tribe of Dan located between the cities of Zorah and Eshtaol.

8. Samson's Riddle

One day when Samson was in Timnah, he noticed a certain Philistine girl, and when he got home he told his father and mother that he wanted to marry her. They objected strenuously.

"Why don't you marry a Jewish girl?" they asked. "Why must you go and get a wife from these heathen Philistines? Isn't there one girl among all the people of Israel you could marry?"

But Samson told his father, "She is the one I want. Get her for me." His father and mother didn't realize that the Lord was behind the request, for God was setting a trap for the Philistines who at that time were the rulers of Israel.

As Samson and his parents were going to Timnah, a young lion attacked Samson in the vineyards on the outskirts of the town. At that moment the Spirit of the Lord came mightily upon him and, since he had no weapon, he ripped the lion's jaws apart and did it as easily as though it were a young goat! But he didn't tell his father or mother about it.

Upon arriving at Timnah he talked with the girl and found her to be just what he wanted, so the arrangements were made.

When he returned for the wedding, he turned off the path to look at the carcass of the lion. And he found a swarm of bees in it, and some honey! He took some of the honey with him, eating as he went, and gave some of it to his father and mother. But he didn't tell them where he had gotten it.

As his father was making final arrangements for the marriage, Samson threw a party for thirty young men of the village, as was the custom of the day. When Samson asked if they would like to hear a riddle, they replied that they would. "If you solve my riddle during these seven days of the celebration," he said, "I'll give you 30 plain robes and 30 fancy robes. But if you can't solve it, then you must give the robes to me!"

"All right," they agreed, "let's hear it."

This was his riddle: "Food came out of the eater, and sweetness from the strong!" Three days later they were still trying to figure it out.

On the fourth day they said to his new wife, "Get the answer from your husband, or we'll burn down your father's house with you in it. Were we invited to this party just to make us poor?"

So Samson's wife broke down in tears before him and said, "You don't love me at all; you hate me, for you have told a riddle to my people and haven't told me the answer!"

"I haven't even told it to my father or mother; why should I tell you?" he replied.

So she cried whenever she was with him and kept it up for the remainder of the celebration. At last, on the seventh day he told her the answer and she, of course, gave the answer to the young men. So before sunset of the seventh day they gave him their reply. "What is sweeter than honey?" they asked, "and what is stronger than a lion?"

"If you hadn't plowed with my heifer, you wouldn't have found the answer to my riddle!" he retorted.

Then the Spirit of the Lord came upon him and he went to the city of Ashkelon, killed 30 men, took their clothing, and gave it to the young men who had told him the answer to his riddle. But he was furious about it and abandoned his wife and went back home to live with his father and mother. So his wife was married instead to the fellow who had been best man at Samson's wedding.

9. Samson's Vengeance

Later on during the wheat harvest, Samson took a young goat as a present to his wife, intending to sleep with her; but her father wouldn't let him in. "I really thought you hated her," he explained, "so I married her to your best man. But look, her sister is prettier than she is. Marry her instead."

Samson was furious. "You can't blame me for whatever happens now," he shouted. He went out and caught 300 foxes and tied their tails together in pairs, with a torch between each pair. Then he lit the torches and let the foxes run through the field of the Philistines, burning the grain to the ground along with all the sheaves and shocks of grain and destroying the olive trees.

"Who did this?" the Philistines demanded. "Samson," was the reply, "because his wife's father gave her to another man." So the Philistines came and got the girl and her father and burned them alive.

"Now my vengeance will strike again!" Samson vowed. So he attacked them with great fury and killed many of them. Then he went to live in a cave in the rock of Etam. The Philistines in turn sent a huge posse into Judah and raided Lehi.

"Why have you come here?" the men of Judah asked.

And the Philistines replied, "To capture Samson and do to him as he has done to us."

So three thousand men of Judah went down to get Samson at the cave in the rock of Etam. "What are you doing to us?" they demanded of him. "Don't you realize that the Philistines are our rulers?"

But Samson replied, "I only paid them back for what they did to me."

"We have come to capture you and take you to the Philistines," the men of Judah told him.

"All right," Samson said, "but promise me that you won't kill me yourselves."

"No," they replied, "we won't do that." So they tied him with two new ropes and led him away.

As Samson and his captors arrived at Lehi, the Philistines shouted with glee; but then the strength of the Lord came upon Samson, and the ropes with which he was tied snapped like thread and fell from his wrists! He picked up a donkey's jawbone that was lying on the ground and killed a thousand Philistines with it. Tossing away the jawbone, he remarked,

"Heaps upon heaps,
All with a donkey's jaw!
I've killed a thousand men,
All with a donkey's jaw!"
The place has been called "Jawbone Hill" ever since.

Samson was Israel's judge for the next 20 years, but the Philistines still controlled the land.

10. Samson and Delilah

Later on he fell in love with a girl named Delilah over in the valley of Sorek. The five heads of the Philistine nation went personally to her and demanded that she find out from Samson what made him so strong, so that they would know how to overpower and subdue him and put him in chains. "Each of us will give you a thousand dollars for this job," they promised.

So Delilah begged Samson to tell her his secret. *"Please* tell me, Samson, why you are so strong," she pleaded. "I don't think anyone could ever capture you!"

"Well," Samson replied, "if I were tied with seven raw-leather bowstrings, I would become as weak as anyone else."

So they brought her the seven bowstrings and while he slept she tied him with them. Some men were hiding in the next room, so as soon as she had tied him up she exclaimed, "Samson! the Philistines are here!" Then he snapped the bowstrings like cotton thread, and so his secret was not discovered.

Afterwards Delilah said to him, "You are making fun of me! You told me a lie! *Please* tell me how you can be captured!"

"Well," he said, "if I am tied with brand new ropes which have never been used, I will be as weak as other men." So that time, as he slept, Delilah took new ropes and tied him with them. The men were hiding in the next room, as before.

Again Delilah exclaimed, "Samson! The Philistines have come to capture you!" But he broke the ropes from his arms like spiderwebs!

"You have mocked me again, and told me more lies!" Delilah complained. "Now tell me how you can *really* be captured."

"Well," he said, "if you weave my hair into your loom . . .!"

So while he slept, she did just that and then screamed, "The Philistines have come, Samson!" And he woke up and yanked his hair away, breaking the loom.

"How can you say you love me when you don't confide in me?" she whined. "You've made fun of me three times now, and you still haven't told me what makes you so strong!" She nagged at him every day until he couldn't stand it any longer and finally told her his secret.

"My hair has never been cut," he confessed, "for I've been a Nazirite to God since before my birth. If my hair were cut, my strength would leave me and I would become as weak as anyone else." Delilah realized that he had finally told her the truth, so she sent for the five Philistine leaders.

"Come just this once more," she said, "for this time he has told me everything." So they brought the money with them. She lulled him to sleep with his head in her lap, and they brought in a barber and cut off his hair. Then she screamed, "The Philistines are here to capture you, Samson!"

He woke up and thought, "I will do as before; I'll just shake myself free." But he didn't realize that the Lord had left him. So the Philistines captured him and gouged out his eyes and took him to Gaza where he was bound with bronze chains and made to grind grain in the prison. But before long his hair began to grow again.

The Philistine leaders declared a great festival to celebrate the capture of Samson. The people made sacrifices to their god Dagon and excitedly praised him. "Our god has delivered our enemy Samson to us!" they thrilled as they saw him there in chains. "The scourge of our nation who killed so many of us is now in our power!" Half-drunk by now, the people demanded, "Bring out Samson so we can have some fun with him!" So he was brought from the prison and made to stand at the center of the temple, between the two pillars supporting the roof.

Samson said to the boy who was leading him by the hand, "Place my hands against the two pillars. I want to rest against them." By then the temple was completely filled with people. The five Philistine leaders were there as well as three thousand people in the balconies who were watching Samson and making fun of him. Then Samson prayed to the Lord and said, "O Lord Jehovah, remember me again—please strengthen me one more time, so that I may pay back the Philistines for the loss of at least one of my eyes."

Then Samson pushed against the pillars with all his might. "Let me die with the Philistines," he prayed. And the temple crashed down upon the Philistine leaders and all the people. So those he killed at the moment of his death were more than those he had killed during his entire lifetime.

Later his brothers and other relatives came down to get his body, and they brought him back home and buried him between Zorah and Eshtaol, where his father, Manoah, was buried. He had judged Israel for 20 years.

RUTH

In sharp and welcome contrast with the events of cruelty, bloodshed and lawlessness described in Judges, the story of Ruth (belonging to the same time) is a heart-warming idyll of love, marriage, family loyalty and faith in God. It is like a lovely lily growing out of the muck of a swamp.

1. Ruth and Naomi

Long ago when judges ruled in Israel, a man named Elimelech from Bethlehem left the country because of a famine and moved to the land of Moab. With him were his wife Naomi and his two sons, Mahlon and Chilion. During the time of their residence there, Elimelech died and Naomi was left with her two sons. These young men, Mahlon and Chilion, married girls of Moab, Orpah and Ruth. But later, both men died, so that Naomi was left alone without her husband or sons.

She decided to return to Israel with her daughters-in-law, for she had heard that the Lord had blessed His people by giving them good crops again. But after they had begun their homeward journey, she changed her mind and said to her two daughters-in-law, "Why don't you return to your parents' homes instead of coming with me? And may the Lord reward you for your faithfulness to your husbands and to me. And may He bless you with another happy marriage." Then she kissed them and they all broke down and cried.

"No," they said. "We want to go with you to your people."

But Naomi replied, "It is better for you to return to your own people. Do I have younger sons who could grow up to be your husbands?" And again they cried together, and Orpah kissed her mother-in-law good-bye and returned to her childhood home; but Ruth insisted on staying with Naomi. "See," Naomi said to her, "your sister-in-law has gone back to her people and to her gods; you should do the same."

But Ruth replied, "Don't make me leave you, for I want to go wherever you go and to live wherever you live; your people shall be my people and your God shall be my God; I want to die where you die and be buried there. May the Lord do terrible things to me if I allow anything but death to separate us."

And when Naomi saw that Ruth had made up her mind and could not be persuaded otherwise, she stopped urging her. So they both came to Bethlehem and the entire village was stirred by their arrival. "Is it really Naomi?" the women asked.

But she told them, "Don't call me Naomi. Call me Mara" (Naomi means "pleasant," Mara means "bitter"), "for Almighty God has dealt me bitter blows."

2. Ruth and Boaz

Now Naomi had an in-law there in Bethlehem who was a very wealthy man. His name was Boaz. One day Ruth said to Naomi, "Perhaps I can go out into the fields of some kind man to glean the free grain behind his reapers."

And Naomi said, "All right, dear daughter. Go ahead." So she did. And as it happened the field where she found herself belonged to Boaz, this relative of Naomi's husband. Boaz arrived from the city while she was there.

After exchanging greetings with the reapers he said to his foreman, "Say, who's that girl over there?"

And the foreman replied, "It's that girl from the land of Moab who came back with Naomi."

Boaz went over and talked to her, "Listen, my child," he said to her. "Stay right here with us to glean; don't think of going to any other fields. Stay right behind my women workers; I have warned the young men not to bother you; when you are thirsty, go and help yourself to the water."

She thanked him warmly. "How can you be so kind to me?" she asked. "You must know I am only a foreigner."

"Yes, I know," Boaz replied, "and I also know about all the love and kindness you have shown your mother-in-law since the death of your husband, and how you left your father and mother in your own land and have come here to live among strangers. May the Lord God of Israel, under whose wings you have come to take refuge, bless you for it." At lunch time Boaz called to her, "Come and eat with us." So she sat with his reapers and he gave her food, more than she could eat.

She worked there all day and in the evening when she had beaten out the barley she had gleaned, it came to a whole bushel! She carried it back into the city and gave it to her mother-in-law, with what was left of her lunch.

"So much!" Naomi exclaimed. "Where in the world did you glean today? Praise the Lord for whoever was so kind to you." So Ruth told her mother-in-law all about it and mentioned that the owner of the field was Boaz. "Praise the Lord for a man like that! God has continued His kindness to us as well as to your dead husband!" Naomi cried excitedly, "Why, that man is one of our closest relatives!"

3. Ruth's Betrothal

One day Naomi said to Ruth, "My dear, isn't it time that I try to find a husband for you and get you happily married again? The man I'm thinking of is Boaz! He has been so kind to us and he is a close relative. I happen to know that he will be winnowing barley tonight out on the threshing floor. Now do what I tell you—bathe and put on some perfume and some nice clothes and go on down to the threshing floor, but don't let him see you until he has finished his supper. Notice where he lies down to sleep; then go and lift the cover off his feet and lie down there, and he will tell you what to do concerning marriage."

And Ruth replied, "All right. I'll do whatever you say." So she went down to the threshing floor that night and followed her mother-in-law's instructions. After Boaz had finished a good meal, he lay down very contentedly beside a heap of grain and went to sleep. Then Ruth came quietly and lifted the covering off his feet and lay there. Suddenly around midnight he wakened and sat up, startled. There was a woman lying at his feet!

"Who are you?" he demanded.

"It's I, sir—Ruth," she replied. "Make me your wife according to God's law, for you are my close relative."

"Thank God for a girl like you!" he exclaimed. "But there is one problem. It's true that I am a close relative, but there is someone else who is more closely related to you than I am. Stay here tonight and in the morning I'll talk to him. And if he will marry you, fine, let him do his duty; but if he won't, then I will, I swear by Jehovah. Lie down until the morning."

So she lay at his feet until the morning and was up early before daybreak, for he had said to her, "Don't let it be known that a woman was here at the threshing floor. Bring your shawl," he told her. She opened it up and he poured in a bushel and a half of barley as a present for her mother-in-law.

"Well, what happened, dear?" Naomi asked her when she arrived home. She told Naomi everything and gave her the barley from Boaz and mentioned his remark that she mustn't go home without a present. Then Naomi said to her, "Just be patient until we hear what happens, for Boaz won't rest until he has followed through on this. He'll settle it today."

4. Ruth's Marriage

So Boaz went down to the market place and found the relative he had mentioned. "Say, come over here," he called to him. "I want to talk to you a minute." So they sat down together. Then Boaz called for ten of the chief men of the village and asked them to sit as witnesses. He said to his relative, "You know Naomi, who came back to us from Moab. She is selling our brother Elimelech's property. Your purchase of the land from Naomi requires your marriage to Ruth so that she can have children to carry on her husband's name and to inherit the land."

"Then I can't do it," the man replied. "For her son would become an heir to my property too; you buy it."

Then Boaz said to the witnesses and to the crowd standing around, "You have seen that today I have bought all the property of Elimelech, Chilion and Mahlon from Naomi, and that with it I have purchased Ruth the Moabitess, the widow of Mahlon, to be my wife so that she can have a son to carry on the family name of her dead husband."

And all the people standing there and the witnesses replied, "We are witnesses. May the Lord make this woman who has now come into your home as fertile as Rachel and Leah from whom all the nation of Israel descended! May you be a great and successful man in Bethlehem, and may the descendants the Lord will give you from this young woman be numerous and honorable."

So Boaz married Ruth, and when he slept with her the Lord gave her a son. And the women of the city said to Naomi, "Bless the Lord who has given you this little grandson; may he be famous in Israel. May he restore your youth and take care of you in your old age; for he is the son of your daughter-in-law who loves you so much and who has been kinder to you than seven sons!"

Naomi took care of the baby, and the neighbor women said, "Now at last Naomi has a son again!" And they named him Obed. He was the father of Jesse and grandfather of King David.

SAMUEL

The books of 1 and 2 Samuel record the history of Israel from the end of the period covered by Judges to the close of the reign of David. The stories revolve around three main characters: Samuel, Saul and David.

1. The Birth of Samuel

This is the story of Elkanah, a man of the tribe of Ephraim who lived in Ramathaim-zophim in the hills of Ephraim. He had two wives, Hannah and Peninnah. Peninnah had some children but Hannah didn't. Each year Elkanah and his families journeyed to the Tabernacle at Shiloh to worship the Lord of the heavens and to sacrifice to Him. The priests on duty at that time were the two sons of Eli, Hophni and Phinehas.

One evening after supper, when they were at Shiloh, Hannah went over to the Tabernacle. Eli the priest was sitting at his customary place beside the entrance. She was in deep anguish and was crying bitterly as she prayed to the Lord. And she made this vow: "O Lord of heaven, if You will look down upon my sorrow and answer my prayer and give me a son, then I will give him back to You, and he'll be Yours for his entire lifetime, and his hair shall never be cut."

Eli noticed her mouth moving as she was praying silently. He said, "May the Lord grant you your petition, whatever it is."

The entire family was up early the next morning and went to the Tabernacle to worship the Lord once more. Then they returned home to Ramah, and when Elkanah slept with Hannah, the Lord remembered her petition; in the process of time a baby boy was born to her. She named him Samuel (meaning "asked of God") because, as she said, "I asked the Lord for him."

The next year Elkanah and Peninnah and her children went on the annual trip to the Tabernacle without Hannah, for she told her husband, "Wait until the baby is weaned, and then I will take him to the Tabernacle and leave him there."

"Well, whatever you think best," Elkanah agreed. "May the Lord's will be done." So she stayed home until the baby was weaned. Then though he was still so small, they took him to the Tabernacle in Shiloh, along with a three-year-old bull for the sacrifice and a bushel of flour and some wine.

After the sacrifice they took the child to Eli. "Sir, do you remember me?" Hannah asked him. "I am the woman who stood here that time praying to the Lord! I asked Him to give me this child, and He has given me my request; and now I am giving him to the Lord for as long as he lives." So she left him there at the Tabernacle for the Lord to use.

This was Hannah's prayer:
How I rejoice in the Lord!
How He has blessed me!
Now I have an answer for my enemies,
For the Lord has solved my problem.
How I rejoice!
No one is as holy as the Lord!
There is no other God,
Nor any Rock like our God.
Those who were mighty are mighty no more!
Those who were well are now starving;
Those who were starving are fed.
The barren woman now has seven children;
She with many children has no more!
He lifts the poor from the dust—
Yes, from a pile of ashes—
And treats them as princes
Sitting in the seats of honor.

For the earth is the Lord's
and He has set the world in order.
No one shall succeed by strength alone.
Those who fight against the Lord shall be broken;
He thunders against them from heaven.
He judges throughout the earth.

They returned home to Ramah without Samuel; and the child became the Lord's helper, for he assisted Eli the priest, and wore a little linen robe just like the priest's. Each year his mother made a little coat for him and brought it to him when she came with her husband for the sacrifice. Before they returned home Eli would bless Elkanah and Hannah and ask God to give them other children to take the place of this one they had given to the Lord. And the Lord gave Hannah three sons and two daughters. Meanwhile Samuel grew up in the service of the Lord.

Little Samuel was growing in two ways—he was getting taller and he was becoming everyone's favorite (and he was a favorite of the Lord's too!).

2. Samuel's Call

However, the sons of Eli were evil men who didn't love the Lord. Eli was now very old, but he was aware of what was going on around him. He knew, for instance, that his sons were seducing the young women who assisted at the entrance to the Tabernacle. "I have been hearing terrible reports from the Lord's people about what you are doing," Eli told his sons. "It is an awful thing to make the Lord's people sin. Ordinary sin receives heavy punishment, but how much more this sin of yours which has been committed against the Lord?" But they wouldn't listen to their father.

Meanwhile little Samuel was helping the Lord by assisting Eli. Messages from the Lord were very rare in those days, but one night after Eli had gone to bed (he was almost blind with age by now) and Samuel was sleeping in the Temple near the Ark, the Lord called out, "Samuel! Samuel!"

"Yes?" Samuel replied. "What is it?" He jumped up and ran to Eli. "Here I am. What do you want?" he asked.

"I didn't call you," Eli said. "Go on back to bed." So he did.

Then the Lord called again, "Samuel!" And again Samuel jumped up and ran to Eli.

"Yes?" he asked. "What do you need?"

"No, I didn't call you, my son," Eli said. "Go on back to bed."

So now the Lord called the third time, and once more Samuel jumped and ran to Eli. "Yes?" he asked, "what do you need?"

Then Eli realized it was the Lord who had spoken to the child. So he said to Samuel, "Go and lie down again, and if He calls again, say, 'Yes, Lord, I'm listening.'" So Samuel went back to bed.

And the Lord came and called as before, "Samuel! Samuel!"

And Samuel replied, "Yes, I'm listening."

Then the Lord said to Samuel, "I am going to do a shocking thing in Israel. I am going to do all of the dreadful things I warned Eli about. I have continually threatened him and his entire family with punishment because his sons are blaspheming God, and he doesn't stop them. So I have vowed that the sins of Eli and of his sons shall never be forgiven by sacrifices and offerings."

Samuel stayed in bed until morning, then opened the doors of the Temple as usual, for he was afraid to tell Eli what the Lord had said to him. But Eli called him. "My son," he said, "what did the Lord say to you? Tell me everything. And may God punish you if you hide anything from me!" So Samuel told him what the Lord had said. "It is the Lord's will," Eli replied; "let Him do what He thinks best."

As Samuel grew, the Lord was with him and people listened carefully to his advice. And all Israel from Dan to Beer-sheba knew that Samuel was going to be a prophet of the Lord. Then the Lord began to give messages to him there at the Tabernacle in Shiloh, and he passed them on to the people of Israel.

3. The Ark of the Covenant Captured

At that time Israel was at war with the Philistines. The Israeli army was camped near Ebenezer, the Philistines at Aphek. And the Philistines defeated Israel, killing four thousand of them. After the battle was over, the army of Israel returned to their camp and their leaders discussed why the Lord had let them be defeated. "Let's bring the Ark here from Shiloh," they said. "If we carry it into battle with us the Lord will be among us and He will surely save us from our enemies." So they sent for the Ark of the Lord of heaven who is enthroned above the angels. Hophni and Phinehas, the sons of Eli, accompanied it into the battle.

When the Israelis saw the Ark coming, their shout of joy was so loud that it almost made the ground shake!

"What's going on?" the Philistines asked. "What's all the shouting about over in the camp of the Hebrews?" When they were told it was because the Ark of the Lord had arrived, they panicked. "God has come into their camp!" they cried out. "Woe upon us, for we have never had to face anything like this before! Who can save us from these mighty gods of Israel? They are the same gods who destroyed the Egyptians with plagues when Israel was in the wilderness. Fight as you never have before, O Philistines, or we will become their slaves just as they have been ours."

So the Philistines fought desperately and Israel was defeated again. Thirty thousand men of Israel died that day and the remainder fled to their tents. And the Ark of God was captured and Hophni and Phinehas were killed.

A man from the tribe of Benjamin ran from the battle and arrived at Shiloh the same day with his clothes torn and dirt on his head. Eli was waiting beside the road to hear the news of the battle, for his heart trembled for the safety of the Ark of God. As the messenger from the battlefront arrived and told what had happened, a great cry arose throughout the city. "What is all the noise about?" Eli asked. And the messenger rushed over to Eli and told him what had happened. Eli was 98 years old and was blind.

139

"I have just come from the battle—I was there today," he told Eli, "and Israel has been defeated and thousands of the Israeli troops are dead on the battlefield. Hophni and Phinehas were killed too, and the Ark has been captured."

As the messenger mentioned what had happened to the Ark, Eli fell backward from his seat beside the gate and his neck was broken by the fall and he died (for he was old and fat). He had judged Israel for 40 years.

When Eli's daughter-in-law, Phinehas' wife who was pregnant, heard that the Ark had been captured and that her husband and father-in-law were dead, her labor pains suddenly began. Just before she died, the women who were attending her told her that everything was all right and that the baby was a boy. But she did not reply or respond in any way. Then she murmured, "Name the child Ichabod, for Israel's glory is gone." (Ichabod means "there is no glory.") She named him this because the Ark of God had been captured and because her husband and her father-in-law were dead.

4. The Ark Returned

The Philistines took the captured Ark of God from the battleground at Ebenezer to the temple of their idol Dagon in the city of Ashdod. But when the local citizens went to see it the next morning, Dagon had fallen with his face to the ground before the Ark of Jehovah! They set him up again, but the next morning the same thing had happened—the idol had fallen face down before the Ark of the Lord again. This time his head and hands had been cut off and were lying in the doorway; only the trunk of his body was left intact.

The Lord also began to destroy the people of Ashdod and the nearby villages with a plague of boils. When the people realized what was happening, they exclaimed, "We can't keep the Ark of the God of Israel here any longer. We will all perish along with our god Dagon."

The Ark remained in the Philistine country for seven months in all. Then the Philistines called for their priests and diviners and asked them, "What shall we do about the Ark of

God? What sort of gift shall we send with it when we return it to its own land?"

"Yes, send it back with a gift," they were told.

"What guilt offering shall we send?" they asked.

And they were told, "Send five gold models of the tumor caused by the plague and five gold models of the rats that have ravaged the whole land—the capital cities and villages alike. If you send these gifts and then praise the God of Israel, perhaps He will stop persecuting you and your god."

These instructions were carried out. Two fresh cows were hitched to the cart and their calves were shut up in the barn. Then the Ark of the Lord and the chest containing the gold rats and tumors were placed upon the cart. And the cows went straight along the road toward Beth-shemesh, lowing as they went; and the Philistine mayors followed them as far as the border of Beth-shemesh.

The people of Beth-shemesh were reaping wheat in the valley, and when they saw the Ark they went wild with joy! The cart came into the field of a man named Joshua and stopped beside a large rock. So the people broke up the wood of the cart for a fire and killed the cows and sacrificed them to the Lord as a burnt offering. Several men of the tribe of Levi lifted the Ark and the chest containing the golden rats and tumors from the cart and laid them on the rock. And many burnt offerings and sacrifices were offered to the Lord that day by the men of Beth-shemesh. After the five Philistine mayors had watched for awhile, they returned to Ekron that same day.

5. Revival at Mizpah

Later the men of Kiriath-jearim came and took the Ark to the hillside home of Abinadab and installed his son Eleazar to be in charge of it. The Ark remained there for 20 years and during that time all Israel was in sorrow because the Lord had seemingly abandoned them.

At that time Samuel said to them, "If you are really serious about wanting to return to the Lord, get rid of your foreign gods and your Ashtaroth idols. Determine to obey only the

Lord; then He will rescue you from the Philistines." So they destroyed their idols of Baal and Ashtaroth and worshiped only the Lord. Then Samuel told them, "Come to Mizpah, all of you, and I will pray to the Lord for you." So they gathered there and in a great ceremony drew water from the well and poured it out before the Lord. They also went without food all day as a sign of sorrow for their sins. So it was at Mizpah that Samuel became Israel's judge. Samuel then took a stone and placed it between Mizpah and Jeshanah and named it Ebenezer (meaning "the Stone of Help"), for he said, "The Lord has certainly helped us!"

So the Philistines were subdued and didn't invade Israel again at that time because the Lord was against them throughout the remainder of Samuel's lifetime. The Israeli cities between Ekron and Gath, which had been conquered by the Philistines, were now returned to Israel, for the Israeli army rescued them from their Philistine captors. And there was peace between Israel and the Amorites in those days. Samuel continued as Israel's judge for the remainder of his life. He rode circuit annually, setting up his court first at Bethel, then Gilgal and then Mizpah, and cases of dispute were brought to him in each of those three cities from all the surrounding territory. Then he would come back to Ramah, for his home was there, and he would hear cases there too. And he built an altar to the Lord at Ramah.

6. Demand for a King

In his old age, Samuel retired and appointed his sons as judges in his place. Joel and Abijah, his oldest sons, held court in Beer-sheba; but they were not like their father, for they were greedy for money. They accepted bribes and were very corrupt in the administration of justice.

Finally the leaders of Israel met in Ramah to discuss the matter with Samuel. They told him that since his retirement things hadn't been the same, for his sons were not good men. "Give us a king like all the other nations have," they pleaded. Samuel was terribly upset and went to the Lord for advice.

"Do as they say," the Lord replied, "for I am the one they are rejecting, not you—they don't want Me to be their king any longer. Ever since I brought them from Egypt they have continually forsaken Me and followed other gods. And now they are giving you the same treatment. Do as they ask, but warn them about what it will be like to have a king!"

So Samuel told the people what the Lord had said: "If you insist on having a king, he will conscript your sons and make them run before his chariots."

But the people refused to listen to Samuel's warning. "Even so we still want a king," they said, "for we want to be like the nations around us. He will govern us and lead us to battle."

Samuel told the Lord what the people had said, and the Lord replied, "Then do as they say and give them a king." So Samuel agreed and sent the men home again.

7. The Anointing of Saul

Kish was a rich, influential man from the tribe of Benjamin. He was the son of Abiel, grandson of Zeror, great-grandson of Becorath and great-great-grandson of Aphiah. His son Saul was the most handsome man in Israel. And he was head and shoulders taller than anyone else in the land!

One day Kish's donkeys strayed away, so he sent Saul and a servant to look for them. They traveled all through the hill country of Ephraim, the land of Shalishah, the Shaalim area, and the entire land of Benjamin, but couldn't find them anywhere. Finally, after searching in the land of Zuph, Saul said to the servant, "Let's go home; by now my father will be more worried about us than about the donkeys!"

But the servant said, "I've just thought of something! There is a prophet who lives here in this city; he is held in high honor by all the people because everything he says comes true; let's go and find him and perhaps he can tell us where the donkeys are." So they went into the city, and as they were entering the gates they saw Samuel coming out towards them to go up the hill.

The Lord had told Samuel the previous day, "About this

time tomorrow I will send you a man from the land of Benjamin. You are to anoint him as the leader of My people. He will save them from the Philistines, for I have looked down on them in mercy and have heard their cry."

When Samuel saw Saul the Lord said, "That's the man I told you about! He will rule My people."

Just then Saul approached Samuel and asked, "Can you please tell me where the seer's house is?"

"I am the seer!" Samuel replied. Then Samuel took a flask of olive oil and poured it over Saul's head and kissed him on the cheek and said, "I am doing this because the Lord has appointed you to be the king of His people, Israel!"

Samuel now called a convocation of all Israel at Mizpah, and gave them this message from the Lord God: "I brought you from Egypt and rescued you from the Egyptians and from all of the nations that were torturing you. But although I have done so much for you, you have rejected Me and have said you want a king instead! All right then, present yourselves before the Lord by tribes and clans."

So Samuel called the tribal leaders together before the Lord and the tribe of Benjamin was chosen by sacred lot. Then he brought each family of the tribe of Benjamin before the Lord and the family of the Matrites was chosen. And finally, the sacred lot selected Saul the son of Kish. But when they looked for him he had disappeared!

So they asked the Lord, "Where is he? Is he here among us?"

And the Lord replied, "He is hiding in the baggage."

Thus they found him and brought him out, and he stood head and shoulders above anyone else. Then Samuel said to all the people, "This is the man the Lord has chosen as your king. There isn't his equal in all of Israel!"

And all the people shouted, "Long live the king!"

(Saul soon had an opportunity to prove himself. He won a signal military victory at Jabesh.) Then Samuel said to the people, "Come, let us all go to Gilgal and reconfirm Saul as our king." So they went to Gilgal and in a solemn ceremony before the Lord they crowned him king. Then they offered peace offerings to the Lord, and Saul and all Israel were very happy.

8. Jonathan's Rescue

Saul had reigned for one year, and in the second year of his reign, he selected three thousand special troops and took two thousand of them with him to Michmash and Mount Bethel while the other thousand remained with Jonathan, Saul's son, in Gibe-ah in the land of Benjamin. The rest of the army was sent home.

A day or so later, Prince Jonathan said to his young bodyguard, "Come on, let's cross the valley to the garrison of the Philistines." There were no blacksmiths in Israel in those days. So there was not a single sword or spear in the entire "army" except for Saul's and Jonathan's.

When the Philistines saw them coming they shouted, "Look! The Israelis are crawling out of their holes!" Then they shouted to Jonathan, "Come on up here and we'll show you how to fight!"

"Come on, climb right behind me," Jonathan exclaimed to his bodyguard, "for the Lord will help us defeat them!" So they clambered up on their hands and knees, and the Philistines fell back as Jonathan and the lad killed them right and left, about 20 men in all, and their bodies were scattered over about half an acre of land. Suddenly panic broke out throughout the entire Philistine army and even among the raiders. And just then there was a great earthquake, increasing the terror. Saul's lookouts in Gibe-ah saw a strange sight— the vast army of the Philistines began to melt away in all directions.

Then Saul and his 600 men rushed out to the battle and found the Philistines killing each other, and there was terrible confusion everywhere. Finally even the men hiding in the hills joined the chase when they saw that the Philistines were running away. So the Lord saved Israel that day, and the battle continued out beyond Beth-aven.

Saul had declared, "A curse upon anyone who eats anything before evening—before I have full revenge on my enemies." So no one ate anything all day, even though they found honeycomb on the ground in the forest, for they all feared Saul's curse. Jonathan, however, had not heard his father's command; so he dipped a stick into a honeycomb, and when he had eaten the honey he felt much better. Then someone told him that his father had laid a curse upon anyone who ate food that day, and everyone was weary and faint as a result.

"That's ridiculous!" Johathan exclaimed, "A command like that only hurts us. See how much better I feel now that I have eaten this little bit of honey. If the people had been allowed to eat freely from the food they found among our enemies, think how many more we could have slaughtered!"

Afterwards Saul said, "Let's chase the Philistines all night and destroy every last one of them."

"Fine!" his men replied. "Do as you think best."

But the priest said, "Let's ask God first."

So Saul asked God, "Shall we go after the Philistines? Will You help us defeat them?" But the Lord made no reply all night.

Then Saul said to the leaders, "Something's wrong! We must find out what sin was committed today. I vow by the name of the God who saved Israel that though the sinner be my own son Jonathan, he shall surely die!" But no one would tell him what the trouble was.

Then Saul proposed, "Jonathan and I will stand over here and all of you stand over there." And the people agreed. Then Saul said, "O Lord God of Israel, why haven't You answered my question? What is wrong? Are Jonathan and I guilty or is the sin among the others? O Lord God, show us who is guilty." And Jonathan and Saul were chosen by sacred lot as the guilty ones and the people were declared innocent. Then Saul said, "Now draw lots between me and Jonathan." And Jonathan was chosen as the guilty one.

"Tell me what you've done," Saul demanded of Jonathan.

"I tasted a little honey," Jonathan admitted. "It was only a little bit on the end of a stick; but now I must die."

"Yes, Jonathan," Saul said, "you must die; may God strike me dead if you are not executed for this."

But the troops retorted, "Jonathan who saved Israel today shall die? Far from it! We vow by the the life of God that not one hair on his head will be touched, for he has been used of

God to do a mighty miracle today." So the people rescued Jonathan. Then Saul called back the army, and the Philistines returned home.

9. Saul Rejected

At this same time, the Philistines recruited a mighty army of three thousand chariots, six thousand horsemen, and so many soldiers that they were as thick as sand along the seashore; and they camped at Michmash east of Beth-aven. When the men of Israel saw the vast mass of enemy troops, they lost their nerve entirely and tried to hide in caves, thickets, coverts, among the rocks and even in tombs and cisterns. Some of them crossed the Jordan River and escaped to the land of Gad and Gilead. Meanwhile, Saul stayed at Gilgal and those who were with him trembled with fear at what awaited them.

Samuel had told Saul earlier to wait seven days for his arrival, but when he still didn't come, and Saul's troops were rapidly slipping away, he decided to sacrifice the burnt offering and the peace offerings himself. But just as he was finishing, Samuel arrived. Saul went out to meet him and to receive his blessing.

But Samuel said, "What is this you have done?"

"Well," Saul replied, "when I saw that my men were scattering from me, and that you hadn't arrived by the time you said you would, and that the Philistines were at Michmash ready for battle I said, 'The Philistines are ready to march against us and I haven't even asked for the Lord's help!' So I reluctantly offered the burnt offering without waiting for you to arrive."

"You fool!" Samuel exclaimed. "You have disobeyed the commandment of the Lord your God. He was planning to make you and your descendants kings of Israel forever, but now your dynasty must end; for the Lord wants a man who will obey Him. And He has discovered the man He wants and has already appointed him as king over His people; for you have not obeyed the Lord's commandment."

Later, since he was securely in the saddle as king of

Israel, Saul sent the Israeli army out in every direction against Moab, Ammon, Edom, the kings of Zobah and the Philistines. And wherever he turned, he was successful.

One day God said, "Now go and completely destroy the Amalek nation." Saul won a great victory but he and his men kept Agag the king and the best of the sheep and oxen and the fattest of the lambs.

Samuel finally found him. "What was all the bleating of sheep and lowing of oxen I heard?"

"It's true that the army spared the best of the sheep and oxen," Saul admitted, "but they are going to sacrifice them to the Lord your God."

Samuel replied, "Has the Lord as much pleasure in your burnt offerings and sacrifices as in your obedience? Obedience is far better than sacrifice. He is much more interested in your listening to Him than in your offering the fat of rams to Him. For rebellion is as bad as the sin of witchcraft, and stubbornness is as bad as worshiping idols. And now because you have rejected the word of Jehovah, He has rejected you from being king."

"I have sinned," Saul finally admitted. "Yes, I have disobeyed your instructions and the command of the Lord, for I was afraid of the people and did what they demanded. Oh, please pardon my sin now and go with me to worship the Lord."

But Samuel replied, "It's no use! Since you have rejected the commandment of the Lord, He has rejected you from being the king of Israel."

Then Samuel went home to Ramah, and Saul returned to Gibe-ah. Samuel never saw Saul again, but he mourned constantly for him; and the Lord was sorry that He had ever made Saul king of Israel.

10. The Anointing of David

Finally the Lord said to Samuel, "You have mourned long enough for Saul, for I have rejected him as king of Israel. Now take a vial of olive oil and go to Bethlehem and find a man named Jesse, for I have selected one of his sons to be the new king."

Samuel did as the Lord had told him to. When he arrived at Bethlehem the elders of the city came trembling to meet him. "What is wrong?" they asked. "Why have you come?"

But he replied, "All is well. I have come to sacrifice to the Lord. Purify yourselves and come with me to the sacrifice." And he performed the purification rite on Jesse and his sons, and invited them too. When they arrived, Samuel took one look at Eliab and thought, "Surely this is the man the Lord has chosen!"

But the Lord said to Samuel, "Don't judge by a man's face or height, for this is not the one. I don't make decisions the way you do! Men judge by outward appearance, but I look at a man's thoughts and intentions."

Then Jesse told his son Abinadab to step forward and walk in front of Samuel. But the Lord said, "This is not the right man either." Next Jesse summoned Shammah, but the Lord said, "No, this is not the one." In the same way all seven of his sons presented themselves to Samuel and were rejected.

The Lord has not chosen any of them," Samuel told Jesse; "are these all there are?"

"Well, there is the youngest," Jesse replied. "But he's out in the fields watching the sheep."

"Send for him at once," Samuel said, "for we will not sit down to eat until he arrives."

So Jesse sent for him. He was a fine looking boy, ruddy-faced, and with pleasant eyes. And the Lord said, "This is the one; anoint him." So as David stood there among his brothers, Samuel took the olive oil he had brought and poured it upon David's head; and the Spirit of Jehovah came upon him and gave him great power from that day onward. Then Samuel returned to Ramah.

11. David, Musician to the King

The Spirit of the Lord had left Saul and, instead, the Lord had sent a tormenting spirit that filled him with depression and fear. Some of Saul's aides suggested a cure. "We'll find a good harpist to play for you whenever the tormenting spirit is bothering you," they said. "The harp music will quiet you and you'll soon be well again."

"All right," Saul said. "Find me a harpist."

One of them said he knew a young fellow in Bethlehem, the son of a man named Jesse, who was not only a talented harp player but was handsome, brave and strong, and had good, solid judgement. "What's more," he added, "the Lord is with him."

So Saul sent messengers to Jesse, asking that he send his son David the shepherd. Jesse responded by sending not only David but a young goat and a donkey carrying a load of food and wine. From the instant he saw David, Saul admired and loved him, and David became his bodyguard.

Then Saul wrote to Jesse, "Please let David join my staff, for I am very fond of him." And whenever the tormenting spirit from God troubled Saul, David would play the harp and Saul would feel better and the evil spirit would go away.

12. David and Goliath

The Philistines now mustered their army for battle and camped between Socoh and Judah and Azekah in Ephes-dammim. Saul countered with a buildup of forces at Elah Valley. So the Philistines and Israelis faced each other on opposite hills with the valley between them.

Then Goliath, a Philistine champion from Gath, came out of the Philistine ranks to face the forces of Israel. He was a giant of a man, measuring over nine feet tall! He wore a bronze helmet, a 200-pound coat of mail, bronze leggings, and carried a bronze javelin several inches thick tipped with a 20-pound iron spearhead. His armor bearer walked ahead of him with a huge shield. He stood and shouted across to the Israelis, "Do you need a whole army to settle this? I will represent the Philistines and you choose someone to represent you, and we will settle this in single combat! If your man is able to kill me, then we will be your slaves. But if I kill him, then you must be our slaves! I defy the armies of Israel! Send me a man who will fight with me!"

When Saul and the Israeli army heard this, they were dismayed and frightened.

David (the son of aging Jesse, a member of the tribe of Ephraim who lived in Bethlehem-Judah) had seven older brothers. The three oldest—Eliab, Abinadab and Shammah—had already volunteered for Saul's army to fight the Philistines. One day Jesse said to David, "Take this bushel of roasted grain and these ten loaves of bread to your brothers. Give this cheese to their captain and see how the boys are getting along; and bring us back a letter from them!"

So David left the sheep with another shepherd and took off early the next morning with the gifts. He arrived at the outskirts of the camp just as the Israeli army was leaving for the battlefield with shouts and battle cries.

David left his luggage with a baggage officer and hurried out to the ranks to find his brothers. As he was talking with them, he saw Goliath the giant step out from the Philistine troops and shout his challenge to the army of Israel. As soon as they saw him the Israeli army began to run away in fright.

"Have you seen the giant?" the soldiers were asking. "He has insulted the entire army of Israel. And have you heard about the huge reward the king has offered to anyone who kills him? And the king will give him one of his daughters for a wife, and his family will be exempted from paying taxes!"

David talked to some others standing there to verify the report. "What will a man get for killing this Philistine and ending his insults to Israel?" he asked them. "Who is this heathen Philistine, anyway, that he is allowed to defy the armies of the living God?"

When it was finally realized what David meant, someone told King Saul, and the king sent for him.

"Don't worry about a thing," David told him, "I'll take care of this Philistine!"

"Don't be ridiculous!" Saul replied. "How can a kid like you fight with a man like him? You are only a boy and he has been in the army *since* he was a boy!" But David persisted.

Saul finally consented, "All right, go ahead," he said, "and may the Lord be with you!"

Then Saul gave David his own armor, a bronze helmet and a coat of mail. David put it on, strapped the sword over it, and took a step or two to see what it was like, for he had never worn such things before. "I can hardly move!" he exclaimed, and took them off again.

Then he picked up five smooth stones from a stream and put them in his shepherd's bag and, armed only with his shepherd's staff and sling, started across to Goliath. Goliath walked out towards David with his shield bearer ahead of him, sneering in contempt at this nice little red-cheeked boy! "Am I a dog," he roared at David, "that you come at me with a stick?" And he cursed David by the names of his gods. "Come over here and I'll give your flesh to the birds and wild animals," Goliath yelled.

David shouted in reply, "You come to me with a sword and a spear, but I come to you in the name of the Lord of the armies of heaven and of Israel—the very God whom you have defied."

As Goliath approached, David ran out to meet him and reaching into his shepherd's bag took out a stone, hurled it from his sling, and hit the Philistine in the forehead. The stone sank in, and the man fell on his face to the ground. So David conquered the Philistine giant with a sling and a stone. Since he had no sword, he ran over and pulled Goliath's from its sheath and killed him with it, and then cut off his head. When the Philistines saw that their champion was dead, they turned and ran.

Then the Israelis gave a great shout of triumph and rushed after the Philistines, chasing them as far as Gath and the gates of Ekron. The bodies of the dead and wounded Philistines were strewn all along the road to Shaaraim. Then the Israeli army returned and plundered the deserted Philistine camp.

13. Saul's Jealousy

Something happened when the victorious Israeli army was

returning home after David had killed Goliath. Women came out from all the towns along the way to celebrate and to cheer for King Saul, and were singing and dancing for joy with tambourines and cymbals. However this was their song: "Saul has slain his thousands and David his ten thousands!"

Of course Saul was very angry. "What's this?" he said to himself. "They credit David with ten thousands and me with only thousands. Next they'll be making him their king!"

So from that time on King Saul kept a jealous watch on David. The very next day, in fact, a tormenting spirit from God overwhelmed Saul, and he began to rave like a madman. David began to soothe him by playing the harp, as he did whenever this happened. But Saul who was fiddling with his spear suddenly hurled it at David, intending to pin him to the wall. But David jumped aside and escaped. This happened another time, too, for Saul was afraid of him and jealous because the Lord had left him and was now with David.

One day Saul said to David, "I am ready to give you my oldest daughter Merab as your wife. But first you must prove yourself to be a real soldier by fighting the Lord's battles." For Saul thought to himself, "I'll send him out against the Philistines and let them kill him rather than doing it myself."

"Who am I that I should be the king's son-in-law?" David exclaimed. "My father's family is nothing!" But when the time arrived for the wedding, Saul married her to Adriel, a man from Meholath, instead.

In the meantime Saul's daughter Michal had fallen in love with David, and Saul was delighted when he heard about it. "Here's another opportunity to see him killed by the Philistines!" Saul said to himself. But to David he said, "You can be my son-in-law after all, for I will give you my youngest daughter." So Saul gave Michal to him.

When the king realized how much the Lord was with David and how immensely popular he was with all the people, he became even more afraid of him, and grew to hate him more with every passing day.

War broke out shortly after that and David led his troops against the Philistines and slaughtered many of them, and put to flight their entire army. But one day as Saul was sitting at home listening to David playing the harp, suddenly the tormenting spirit from the Lord attacked him. He had his spear in his hand and hurled it at David in an attempt to kill him. But David dodged out of the way and fled into the night, leaving the spear imbedded in the timber of the wall.

Saul sent troops to watch David's house and kill him when he came out in the morning. "If you don't get away tonight," Michal warned him, "you'll be dead by morning." And she helped him get down to the ground through a window.

14. Jonathan's Friendship for David

David fled from Naioth in Ramah and found Jonathan.

"What have I done?" David exclaimed. "Why is your father so determined to kill me?"

"That's not true!" Jonathan protested. "I'm sure he's not planning any such thing, for he always tells me everything he's going to do, even little things, and I know he wouldn't hide something like this from me. It just isn't so."

Later Jonathan told David, "I promise by the Lord God of Israel that about this time tomorrow, or the next day at the latest, I will talk to my father about you and let you know at once how he feels about you. If he is angry and wants you killed, then may the Lord kill me if I don't tell you, so you can escape and live. May the Lord be with you as He used to be with my father. And remember, you must demonstrate the love and kindness of the Lord not only to me during my own lifetime, but also to my children after the Lord has destroyed all of your enemies."

So Jonathan made a covenant with the family of David, and David swore to it with a terrible curse against himself and his descendants should he be unfaithful to his promise. But Jonathan made David swear to it again, this time by his love for him, for he loved him as much as he loved himself. Jonathan said to David, "Cheer up, for we have entrusted each other and each other's children into God's hands for ever." So they parted, David going away and Jonathan returning to the city.

15. Saul's Life Spared

David left and escaped to the cave of Adullam where his brothers and other relatives soon joined him. Then others began coming—those who were in any kind of trouble, such as being in debt or merely discontented—until David was the leader of about four hundred men. In time, David and his men, about six hundred of them now, left Keilah and began roaming the countryside. Word soon reached Saul that David had escaped, so he didn't go there after all.

David now lived in the wilderness caves in the hill country of Ziph. One day near Horesh he received the news that Saul was on the way to Ziph to search for him and kill him. Saul hunted him day after day, but the Lord didn't let him find him. Prince Jonathan now went to find David; he met him at Horesh and encouraged him in his faith in God. "Don't be afraid," Jonathan reassured him. "My father will never find you! You are going to be the king of Israel and I will be next to you, as my father is well aware."

So the two of them renewed their pact of friendship; and David stayed at Horesh while Jonathan returned home.

Now the men from Ziph came back to Saul at Gibeah to tell him that David had returned to the wilderness and was hiding on Hachilah Hill. So Saul took his elite corps of three thousand troops and went to hunt him down. He camped along the road at the edge of the wilderness where David was hiding, but David knew of Saul's arrival and sent out spies to watch his movements.

David slipped over to Saul's camp one night to look around. King Saul and General Abner were sleeping inside a ring formed by the slumbering soldiers. "Any volunteers to go down there with me?" David asked Ahimelech (the Hittite) and Abishai (Joab's brother and the son of Zeruiah).

"I'll go with you," Abishai replied. So David and Abishai went to Saul's camp and found him asleep with his spear in the ground beside his head.

"God has put your enemy within your power this time for sure," Abishai whispered to David. "Let me go and put that spear through him. I'll pin him to the earth with it—I'll not need to strike a second time!"

"No," David said. "Don't kill him, for who can remain innocent after attacking the Lord's chosen king?" But David took the spear and a jug of water, and they got away without anyone seeing them or even waking up, because the Lord had put them sound asleep. They climbed the mountain slope opposite the camp until they were at a safe distance. Then David shouted down to Abner and Saul, "Wake up, Abner!"

"Who is it?" Abner demanded.

"Well, Abner, you're a great fellow, aren't you?" David taunted. "Where in all Israel is there anyone as wonderful? So why haven't you guarded your master the king when someone came to kill him? This isn't good at all! I swear by the Lord that you ought to die for your carelessness. Where is the king's spear and the jug of water that was beside his head? Look and see!"

Saul recognized David's voice and said, "Is that you, my son David?" Then Saul confessed, "I have done wrong. Come back home, my son, and I'll no longer try to harm you; for you saved my life today. I have been a fool and very, very wrong."

"Here is your spear, sir," David replied. "Let one of your young men come over and get it. The Lord gives His own reward for doing good and for being loyal, and I refused to kill you even when the Lord placed you in my power. Now may the Lord save my life, even as I have saved yours today. May He rescue me from all my troubles."

And Saul said to David, "Blessings on you, my son David. You shall do heroic deeds and be a great conqueror." Then David went away and Saul returned home.

16. David and Abigail

Shortly afterwards Samuel died and all Israel gathered for his funeral and buried him in his family plot at Ramah. Meanwhile David went down to the wilderness of Paran. A wealthy man from Maon owned a sheep ranch there near the village of Carmel. He had three thousand sheep and a thousand goats and was at his ranch at this time for the sheep shearing. His name was Nabal and his wife, a beautiful and very intelligent woman, was named Abigail. But the man who was a descendant of Caleb was uncouth, churlish, stubborn and ill-mannered.

When David heard that Nabal was shearing his sheep, he sent ten of his young men to Carmel to give him this message: "May God prosper you and your family and multiply everything you own. I am told that you are shearing your sheep and goats. While your shepherds have lived among us, we have never harmed them, nor stolen anything from them the whole time they have been in Carmel. Ask your young men and they will tell you whether or not this is true. Now I have sent my men to ask for a little contribution from you, for we have come at a happy time of holiday. Please give us a present of whatever is at hand."

The young men gave David's message to Nabal and waited for his reply. "Who is this fellow David?" he asked. "Who does this son of Jesse think he is? There are lots of servants these days who run away from their masters. Should I take my bread and my water and my meat that I've slaughtered for my shearers and give it to a gang who suddenly appear from nowhere?"

So David's messengers returned and told him what Nabal had said. "Get your swords!" was David's reply as he strapped on his own. Four hundred of them started off with David and 200 remained behind to guard their gear.

Meanwhile one of Nabal's men went and told Abigail, "David sent men from the wilderness to talk to our master, but he insulted them and railed at them."

Then Abigail hurriedly took 200 loaves of bread, two barrels of wine, five dressed sheep, two bushels of roasted grain, 100 raisin cakes and 200 fig cakes, and packed them onto donkeys. "Go on ahead," she said to her young men, "and I will follow." But she didn't tell her husband what she was doing.

As she was riding down the trail on her donkey, she met David coming towards her. When Abigail saw David, she quickly dismounted and bowed low before him. "I accept all blame in this matter, my lord," she said. "Please listen to what I want to say. Forgive me for my boldness in coming out here.

The Lord will surely reward you with eternal royalty for your descendants, for you are fighting His battles; and you will never do wrong throughout your entire life. Even when you are chased by those who seek your life, you are safe in the care of the Lord your God, just as though you were safe inside his purse! But the lives of your enemies shall disappear like stones from a sling! When the Lord has done all the good things He promised you and has made you king of Israel, you won't want the conscience of a murderer who took the law into his own hands! And when the Lord has done these great things for you, please remember me!"

David replied to Abigail, "Bless the Lord God of Israel who has sent you to meet me today! Thank God for your good sense! Bless you for keeping me from murdering the man and carrying out vengeance with my own hands. For I swear by the Lord, the God of Israel who has kept me from hurting you, that if you had not come out to meet me, not one of Nabal's men would be alive tomorrow morning." Then David accepted her gifts and told her to return home without fear, for he would not kill her husband.

When she arrived home she found that Nabal had thrown a big party. He was roaring drunk, so she didn't tell him anything about her meeting with David until the next morning. By that time he was sober, and when his wife told him what had happened, he had a stroke and lay paralyzed for about ten days, then died.

When David heard that Nabal was dead, he wasted no time in sending messengers to Abigail to ask her to become his wife. When the messengers arrived at Carmel and told her why they had come, she readily agreed to his request. Quickly getting ready, she took along five of her serving girls as attendants, mounted her donkey and followed the men back to David. So she became his wife.

17. Saul and the Witch of Endor

About that time the Philistines mustered their armies for another war with Israel. The Philistines set up their camp at

Shunem, and Saul and the armies of Israel were at Gilboa. When Saul saw the vast army of the Philistines, he was frantic with fear and asked the Lord what he should do. But the Lord refused to answer him either by dreams or by Urim, or by the prophets. Saul then instructed his aides to try to find a medium so that he could ask her what to do. They found one at Endor. Saul disguised himself by wearing ordinary clothing instead of his royal robes. He went to the woman's home at night, accompanied by two of his men. "I've got to talk to a dead man," he pleaded. "Will you bring his spirit up?"

"Are you trying to get me killed?" the woman demanded. "You know that Saul has had all of the mediums and fortune-tellers executed. You are spying on me." But Saul took a solemn oath that he wouldn't betray her. Finally the woman said, "Well, whom do you want me to bring up?"

"Bring me Samuel," Saul replied.

When the woman saw Samuel, she screamed, "You've deceived me! You are Saul!"

"Don't be frightened!" the king told her. "What do you see?"

"I see a specter coming up out of the earth," she said.

"What does he look like?"

"He is an old man wrapped in a robe." Saul realized that it was Samuel and bowed low before him.

"Why have you disturbed me by bringing me back?" Samuel asked Saul.

"Because I am in deep trouble," he replied. "The Philistines are at war with us, and God has left me and won't reply by prophets or dreams; so I have called for you to ask you what to do."

But Samuel replied, "Why ask me if the Lord has left you and has become your enemy? He has done just as He said He would and has taken the kingdom from you and given it to your rival, David. What's more, the entire Israeli army will be routed and destroyed by the Philistines tomorrow, and you and your sons will be here with me."

Saul now fell full length upon the ground, paralyzed with fright because of Samuel's words. He was also faint with hunger for he had eaten nothing all day. The woman had been fattening a calf, so she hurried out and killed it and kneaded dough and baked unleavened bread. She brought the meal to the king and his men, and they ate it. Then they went out into the night.

18. Saul's Death

Meanwhile the Philistines had begun the battle against Israel, and the Israelis fled from them and were slaughtered wholesale on Mount Gilboa. The Philistines closed in on Saul and killed his sons Jonathan, Abinidab and Malchishua.

Then the archers overtook Saul and wounded him badly. He groaned to his armor bearer, "Kill me with your sword before these heathen Philistines capture me and torture me." But his armor bearer was afraid to, so Saul took his own sword and fell upon the point of the blade, and it pierced him through. When his armor bearer saw that he was dead, he also fell upon his sword and died with him. So Saul, his armor bearer, his three sons and his troops died together that same day.

When the Israelis on the other side of the valley and beyond the Jordan heard that their comrades had fled and that Saul and his sons were dead, they abandoned their cities; and the Philistines lived in them.

The next day when the Philistines went out to strip the dead, they found the bodies of Saul and his three sons on Mount Gilboa. They cut off Saul's head and stripped off his armor and sent the wonderful news of Saul's death to their idols and to the people throughout their land. His armor was placed in the temple of Ashtaroth, and his body was fastened to the wall of Bethshan.

But when the people of Jabesh-gilead heard what the Philistines had done, warriors from that town traveled all night to Bethshan and took down the bodies of Saul and his sons from the wall and brought them to Jabesh where they cremated them. Then they buried their remains beneath the oak tree at Jabesh and fasted for seven days.

19. David's Lament for Saul and Jonathan

When David and his men heard this news, they tore their clothes in sorrow. They mourned and wept and fasted all day for Saul and his son Jonathan, and for the Lord's people, and for the men of Israel who had died that day.

Then David composed a dirge for Saul and Jonathan and afterward commanded that it be sung throughout Israel. It is quoted here from the book, *Heroic Ballads*.

O Israel, your pride and joy lies dead upon the hills;
Mighty heroes have fallen.
Don't tell the Philistines, lest they rejoice.
Hide it from the cities of Gath and Ashkelon,
Lest the heathen nations laugh in triumph.

O Mount Gilboa,
Let there be no dew nor rain upon you,
Let no crops of grain grow on your slopes.
For there the mighty Saul has died;
He is God's appointed king no more.
Both Saul and Jonathan slew their strongest foes,
And did not return from battle empty-handed.

How much they were loved, how wonderful they were—
Both Saul and Jonathan!
They were together in life and in death.
They were swifter than eagles, stronger than lions.
But now, O women of Israel, weep for Saul;
He enriched you
With fine clothing and golden ornaments.
These mighty heroes have fallen in the midst of the battle.
Jonathan is slain upon the hills.

How I weep for you, my brother Jonathan;
How much I loved you!
And your love for me was deeper
Than the love of women!
The mighty ones have fallen,
Stripped of their weapons, and dead.

20. David and Ish-bosheth

David then asked the Lord, "Shall I move back to Judah?"
And the Lord replied, "Yes."

"Which city shall I go to?"

And the Lord replied, "Hebron." So David and his wives—
Ahino-am from Jezreel and Abigail the widow of Nabal from
Carmel—and his men and their families all moved to Hebron.
Then the leaders of Judah came to David and crowned him
king of the Judean confederacy.

When David heard that the men of Jabesh-gilead had
buried Saul, he sent them this message: "May the Lord bless
you for being so loyal to your king and giving him a decent
burial. May the Lord be loyal to you in return, and reward
you with many demonstrations of His love! And I too will be
kind to you because of what you have done. And now I ask
you to be my strong and loyal subjects now that Saul is dead.
Be like the tribe of Judah who have appointed me as their new
king."

But Abner, Saul's commander-in-chief, had gone to Mahanaim to crown Saul's son Ish-bosheth as king. His territory
included Gilead, Ashuri, Jezreel, Ephraim, the tribe of Benjamin and all the rest of Israel. Ish-bosheth was 40 years old
at the time. He reigned in Mahanaim for two years; meanwhile, David was reigning in Hebron as king of the Judean
confederacy for seven and one-half years.

One day Rechab and Baanah arrived at King Ish-bosheth's
home at noon as he was taking a nap. They walked into the
kitchen as though to get a sack of wheat, but then sneaked into
his bedroom, murdered him and cut off his head.

Taking his head with them, they fled across the desert that
night and escaped. They presented the head to David at Hebron. But David replied, "I swear by the Lord who saved me
from my enemies, that when someone told me, 'Saul is dead,'
thinking he was bringing me good news, I killed him. And
how much more shall I do to wicked men who kill a good man
in his own house and on his bed! Shall I not demand your
lives?" So David ordered his young men to kill them, and they
did.

21. Conquest of Jerusalem

There was a long war between the followers of Saul and of David. David's position now became stronger and stronger, while Saul's dynasty became weaker and weaker. Then representatives of all the tribes of Israel came to David at Hebron and gave him their pledge of loyalty. "We are your blood brothers," they said, "and even when Saul was our king you were our real leader. The Lord has said that you should be the shepherd and leader of His people."

So David made a contract before the Lord with the leaders of Israel there at Hebron, and they crowned him king of Israel. He had already been the king of Judah for seven years, since the age of 30. He then ruled 33 years in Jerusalem as king of both Israel and Judah; so he reigned for 40 years altogether.

David now led his troops to Jerusalem to fight against the Jebusites who lived there. "You'll never come in here," they told him. "Even the blind and lame could keep you out!" For they thought they were safe. But David and his troops defeated them and captured the stronghold of Zion now called the City of David.

When the insulting message from the defenders of the city reached David, he told his troops, "Go up through the water tunnel into the city and destroy those 'lame' and 'blind' Jebusites. How I hate them." (That is the origin of the saying, "Even the blind and the lame could conquer you!")

David made the stronghold of Zion (City of David) his headquarters. Then beginning at the old Millo section of the city, he built northward toward the present city center. So David became greater and greater, for the Lord God of heaven was with him.

22. Two Victories for David

When the Philistines heard that David had been crowned king of Israel, they tried to capture him; but David was told that they were coming and went into the stronghold. The Philistines arrived and spread out across the Valley of Rephaim.

Then David asked the Lord, "Shall I go out and fight against them? Will You defeat them for me?"

And the Lord replied, "Yes, go ahead, for I will give them to you."

So David went out and fought with them at Baal-perazim, and defeated them. "The Lord did it!" he exclaimed. "He burst through my enemies like a raging flood." So he named the place "Bursting." At that time David and his troops confiscated many idols which had been abandoned by the Philistines.

But the Philistines returned and again spread out across the Valley of Rephaim. When David asked the Lord what to do, He replied, "Don't make a frontal attack. Go behind them and come out by the balsam trees. When you hear a sound like marching feet in the tops of the balsam trees, attack! for it will signify that the Lord has prepared the way for you and will destroy them." So David did as the Lord had instructed him and destroyed the Philistines all the way from Geba to Gezer.

23. David's Mighty Men

David became more and more famous and powerful, for the Lord of the heavens was with him.

These are the names of some of the bravest of David's warriors (who also encouraged the leaders of Israel to make David their king, as the Lord had said would happen):

Jashobeam (the son of a man from Hachmon) was the leader of the Top Three—the three greatest heroes among David's men. He once killed 300 men with his spear.

The second of the Top Three was Eleazar, the son of Dodo, a member of the subclan of Ahoh. He was with David in the battle against the Philistines at Pas-dammim. The Israeli army was in a barley field and had begun to run away, but he held his ground in the middle of the field, and recovered it and slaughtered the Philistines; and the Lord saved them with a great victory.

Abishai, Joab's brother, was commander of the Thirty. He had gained his place among the Thirty by killing 300 men at one time with his spear. He was the chief and the most famous of the Thirty, but he was not as great as the Three.

Benaiah, whose father was a mighty warrior from Kabzeel, killed the two famous giants from Moab. He also killed a lion in a slippery pit when there was snow on the ground. Once he killed an Egyptian who was seven and one-half feet tall whose spear was as thick as a weaver's beam. But Benaiah went up to him with only a club in his hand and pulled the spear away from him and used it to kill him. He was nearly as great as the Three and very famous among the Thirty. David made him captain of his bodyguard.

Another time three of the Thirty went to David while he was hiding in the cave of Adullam. The Philistines were camped in the Valley of Rephaim, and David was in the stronghold at the time; an outpost of the Philistines had occupied Bethlehem. David wanted a drink from the Bethlehem well beside the gate, and when he mentioned this to his men, these three broke through to the Philistine camp, drew some water from the well, and brought it back to David. But he refused to drink it! Instead, he poured it out as an offering to the Lord and said, "God forbid that I should drink it! It is the very blood of these men who risked their lives to get it."

24. Return of the Ark

Then David mobilized thirty thousand special troops and led them to Baal-judah to bring home the Ark of the Lord of heaven enthroned above the cherubim. After the men who were carrying it had gone six paces, they stopped and waited so that he could sacrifice an ox and a fat lamb. And David danced before the Lord with all his might, and was wearing priests' clothing. So Israel brought home the Ark of the Lord with much shouting and blowing of trumpets.

The Ark was placed inside the tent which David had prepared for it; and he sacrificed burnt offerings and peace offerings to the Lord. Then he blessed the people in the name of the Lord of heaven, and gave a present to everyone—men and women alike—of a loaf of bread, some wine and a cake of raisins.

When the Lord finally sent peace upon the land, and Israel was no longer at war with the surrounding nations, David said to Nathan the prophet, "Look! Here I am living in this beautiful cedar palace while the Ark of God is out in a tent!"

"Go ahead with what you have in mind," Nathan replied, "for the Lord is with you."

But that night the Lord said to Nathan, "Tell My servant David not to do it! Give this message to David from the Lord of heaven: 'For when you die, I will put one of your sons upon your throne and I will make his kingdom strong. He is the one who shall build Me a Temple. And I will continue his kingdom into eternity. I will be his father and he shall be My son. If he sins, I will use other nations to punish him, but My love and kindness shall not leave him as I took it from Saul, your predecessor. Your family shall rule My kingdom forever!' "

So Nathan went back to David and told him everything the Lord had said.

Then David went into the Tabernacle and sat before the Lord and prayed, "O Lord God, why have You showered Your blessings on such an insignificant person as I am? And now, in addition to everything else, You speak of giving me an eternal dynasty! Such generosity is far beyond any human standard! Oh, Lord God! What can I say? For You know what I am like! You are doing all these things just because You promised to and because You want to!

"How great You are, Lord God! For You are indeed God, and Your words are truth; and You have promised me these good things—so do as You have promised! Bless me and my family forever! May our dynasty continue on and on before You; for You, Lord God, have promised it. And may You be eternally honored when You have established Israel as Your people and have established my dynasty before You."

25. David and Mephibosheth

There was a little lame grandson of King Saul's named Mephibosheth who was the son of Prince Jonathan. He was five years old at the time Saul and Jonathan were killed at the battle of Jezreel. When the news of the outcome of the battle reached the capital, the child's nurse grabbed him and fled, but she fell and dropped him as she was running, and he became lame.

One day, years later, David began wondering if any of Saul's family was still living, for he wanted to be kind to them as he had promised Prince Jonathan. He heard about a man named Ziba who had been one of Saul's servants and summoned him.

"Are you Ziba?" the king asked.

"Yes, sir, I am," he replied.

The king then asked him, "Is anyone left from Saul's family? If so, I want to fulfill a sacred vow by being kind to him."

"Yes," Ziba replied, "Jonathan's lame son is still alive."

"Where is he?" the king asked.

"In Lo-debar," Ziba told him. "At the home of Machir."

So King David sent for Mephibosheth, Jonathan's son and Saul's grandson. Mephibosheth arrived in great fear and greeted the king in deep humility, bowing low before him. But David said, "Don't be afraid! I've asked you to come so that I can be kind to you because of my vow to your father Jonathan. I will restore to you all the land of your grandfather Saul, and you shall live here at the palace!"

Mephibosheth fell to the ground before the king. "Should the king show kindness to a dead dog like me?" he exclaimed.

Then the king summoned Saul's servant Ziba. "I have given your master's grandson everything that belonged to Saul and his family," he said. "You and your sons and servants are to farm the land for him, to produce food for his family; but he will live here with me."

Ziba, who had 15 sons and 20 servants, replied, "Sir, I will do all that you have commanded." And from that time on Mephibosheth ate regularly with King David, as though he were one of his own sons.

26. David and Bathsheba

In the spring of the following year, at the time when wars begin, David sent Joab and the Israeli army to destroy the Ammonites. They began by laying siege to the city of Rabbah. But David stayed in Jerusalem.

One evening he got up and went for a stroll on the roof of the palace. As he looked out over the city he noticed a woman of unusual beauty taking her evening bath. He sent to find out who she was and was told that she was Bath-sheba, the daughter of Eliam and the wife of Uriah. Then David sent for her and when she came he slept with her. Then she returned home. When she found that he had gotten her pregnant she sent a message to inform him.

So David dispatched a memo to Joab: "Send me Uriah the Hittite." When he arrived, David asked him how Joab and the army were getting along and how the war was prospering. Then he told him to go home and relax and he sent a present to him at his home. But Uriah didn't go there. He stayed that night at the gateway of the palace with the other servants of the king.

When David heard what Uriah had done, he summoned him and asked him, "What's the matter with you? Why didn't you go home to your wife last night after being away for so long?"

Uriah replied, "The Ark and the armies and the general and his officers are camping out in open fields, and should I go home to wine and dine and sleep with my wife? I swear that I will never be guilty of acting like that."

"Well, stay here tonight," David told him, "and tomorrow you may return to the army." So Uriah stayed around the palace. David invited him to dinner and got him drunk; but even so he didn't go home that night, but again he slept at the entry to the palace.

Finally the next morning David wrote a letter to Joab and gave it to Uriah to deliver. The letter instructed Joab to put Uriah at the front of the hottest part of the battle—and then pull back and leave him there to die! So Joab assigned Uriah to a spot close to the besieged city where he knew that the enemies' best men were fighting; and Uriah was killed along with several other Israeli soldiers.

When Joab sent a report to David of how the battle was going, he told his messenger, "If the king is angry and asks, 'Why did the troops go so close to the city? Didn't they know there would be shooting from the walls? Wasn't Abimelech killed at Thebez by a woman who threw down a millstone on him?'—then tell him, 'Uriah was killed too.' "

So the messenger arrived at Jerusalem and gave the report to David. "The enemy came out against us," he said, "and as we chased them back to the city gates, the men on the wall attacked us. Some of our men were killed, and Uriah the Hittite is dead too."

"Well, tell Joab not to be discouraged," David said. "The sword kills one as well as another! Fight harder next time and conquer the city; tell him he is doing well."

When Bath-sheba heard that her husband was dead, she mourned for him; then when the period of mourning was over, David sent for her and brought her to the palace and she became one of his wives; and she gave birth to his son. But the Lord was very displeased with what David had done.

27. Nathan and David

The Lord sent the prophet Nathan to tell David this story: "There were two men in a certain city, one very rich, owning many flocks of sheep and herds of goats, and the other very poor, owning nothing but a little lamb he had managed to buy. It was his children's pet and he fed it from his own plate and let it drink from his own cup; he cuddled it in his arms like a baby daughter. Recently a guest arrived at the home of the rich man. But instead of killing a lamb from his own flocks for food for the traveler, he took the poor man's lamb and roasted it and served it."

David was furious. "I swear by the living God," he vowed, "any man who would do a thing like that should be put to death! He shall repay four lambs to the poor man for the one he stole, and for having no pity."

Then Nathan said to David, *"You* are that rich man! The Lord God of Israel says, 'I made you king of Israel and saved you from the power of Saul. I gave you his palace and his wives and the kingdoms of Israel and Judah; and if that had not been enough, I would have given you much, much more. Why, then, have you despised the laws of God and done this horrible deed? For you have murdered Uriah and stolen his wife. Therefore murder shall be a constant threat in your family from this time on, because you have insulted Me by taking Uriah's wife."

"I have sinned against the Lord," David confessed to Nathan.

Then Nathan replied, "Yes, but the Lord has forgiven you, and you won't die for this sin. But you have given great opportunity to the enemies of the Lord to despise and blaspheme Him, so your child shall die." Then Nathan returned to his home.

And the Lord made Bath-sheba's baby deathly sick. David begged Him to spare the child and went without food and lay all night before the Lord on the bare earth. The leaders of the nation pleaded with him to get up and eat with them, but he refused. Then on the seventh day the baby died. David's aides were afraid to tell him. "He was so broken up about the baby being sick," they said, "what will he do to himself when we tell him the child is dead?"

But when David saw them whispering, he realized what had happened. "Is the baby dead?" he asked.

"Yes," they replied, "he is."

Then David got up off the ground, washed himself, brushed his hair, changed his clothes and went into the Tabernacle and worshiped the Lord. Then he returned to the palace and ate. His aides were amazed. "We don't understand you," they told him. "While the baby was still living, you wept and refused to eat; but now that the baby is dead, you have stopped your mourning and are eating again."

David replied, "I fasted and wept while the child was alive, for I said, 'Perhaps the Lord will be gracious to me and let the child live.' But why should I fast when he is dead? Can I bring him back? I shall go to him, but he shall not return to me."

28. Amnon and Tamar

Prince Absalom, David's son, had a beautiful sister named Tamar. And Prince Amnon (her half-brother) fell desperately in love with her. Amnon became so tormented by his love for her that he became ill. He had no way of talking to her, for the girls and young men were kept strictly apart. But when the king came to see him, Amnon asked him for this favor: that his sister Tamar be permitted to come and cook a little something for him to eat.

David agreed and sent word to Tamar to go to Amnon's quarters and prepare some food for him. So she went into his bedroom so that he could watch her mix some dough, then she baked some special bread for him. But as she was standing there before him, he grabbed her and demanded, "Come to bed with me, my darling."

"Oh, Amnon," she cried. "Don't be foolish! Don't do this to me! You know what a serious crime it is in Israel. Where could I go in my shame? And you would be called one of the greatest fools in Israel. Please, just speak to the king about it, for he will let you marry me."

But he wouldn't listen to her; and since he was stronger than she, he forced her. Then suddenly his love turned to hate, and now he hated her more than he had loved her. "Get out of here!" he snarled at her.

"No, no!" she cried. "To reject me now is a greater crime than the other you did to me."

But he wouldn't listen to her. He shouted for his valet and demanded, "Throw this woman out and lock the door behind her." So he put her out.

She was wearing a long robe with sleeves as was the custom in those days for virgin daughters of the king. Now she tore the robe and put ashes on her head and with her head in her hands went away crying.

29. Absalom the Murderer

When King David heard what had happened he was very

171

angry, but Absalom said nothing one way or the other about this to Amnon. However, he hated him with a deep hatred because of what he had done to his sister. Then two years later when Absalom's sheep were being sheared at Baal-hazor in Ephraim, Absalom invited his father and all his brothers to come to a feast to celebrate the occasion. Absalom kept on urging the matter until finally the king agreed and let all of his sons attend, including Amnon.

Absalom told his men, "Wait until Amnon gets drunk, then at my signal kill him! Don't be afraid. I'm the one who gives the orders around here, and this a command. Take courage and do it!" Thus they murdered Amnon. At once the other sons of the king jumped on their mules and fled.

Absalom also fled to King Talmai of Geshur (the son of Ammihud) and stayed there three years. Meanwhile David now reconciled to Amnon's death, longed day after day for fellowship with his son Absalom.

30. Absalom Returns to Jerusalem

When General Joab realized how much the king was longing to see Absalom, he sent for a woman of Tekoa who had a reputation for great wisdom and told her to ask for an appointment with the king. He told her what to say to him. "Pretend you are in mourning," Joab instructed her. "Wear mourning clothes and dishevel your hair as though you have been in deep sorrow for a long time."

When the woman approached the king, she fell face downward on the floor in front of him and cried out, "O king! Help me!"

"What's the trouble?" he asked.

"I am a widow," she replied, "and my two sons had a fight out in the field, and since no one was there to part them, one of them was killed. Now the rest of the family is demanding that I surrender my other son to them to be executed for murdering his brother. But if I do that, I will have no one left and my husband's name will be destroyed from the face of the earth. Please swear to me by God that you won't let anyone harm my son. I want no more bloodshed."

"I vow by God," he replied, "that not a hair of your son's head shall be disturbed!"

"Please let me ask one more thing of you!" she said.

"Go ahead," he replied. "Speak!"

"Why don't you do as much for all the people of God as you have promised to do for me?" she asked. "You have convicted yourself in making this decision, because you have refused to bring home your own banished son. All of us must die eventually; our lives are like water that is poured out on the ground—it can't be gathered up again. But God will bless you with a longer life if you will find a way to bring your son back from his exile."

"I want to know one thing," the king replied.

"Yes, my lord?" she asked.

"Did Joab send you here?"

And the woman replied, "How can I deny it? Yes, Joab sent me and told me what to say."

So the king sent for Joab and told him, "All right, go and bring back Absalom."

Joab fell to the ground before the king and blessed him and said, "At last I know that you like me! For you have granted me this request!" Then Joab went to Geshur and brought Absalom back to Jerusalem.

31. Absalom's Rebellion

Now no one in Israel was such a handsome specimen of manhood as Absalom, and no one else received such praise. He cut his hair only once a year—and then only because it weighed three pounds and was too much of a load to carry around!

Absalom bought a magnificent chariot and chariot horses and hired 50 footmen to run ahead of him. He got up early every morning and went out to the gate of the city; and when anyone came to bring a case to the king for trial, Absalom called him over and expressed interest in his problem. He would say, "I can see that you are right in this matter; it's unfortunate that the king doesn't have anyone to assist him in hearing these cases. I surely wish I were the judge, then anyone with a lawsuit could come to me and I would give him justice!"

And when anyone came to bow to him, Absalom wouldn't let him, but shook his hand instead. In this way Absalom stole the hearts of all the people of Israel.

After four years, Absalom said to the king, "Let me go to Hebron to sacrifice to the Lord in fulfillment of a vow I made to Him while I was at Geshur—that if He would bring me back to Jerusalem, I would sacrifice to Him."

"All right," the king told him, "Go and fulfill your vow." So Absalom went to Hebron. But while he was there, he sent spies to every part of Israel to incite rebellion against the king. "As soon as you hear the trumpets," his message read, "you will know that Absalom has been crowned in Hebron."

A messenger soon arrived in Jerusalem to tell King David, "All Israel has joined Absalom in a conspiracy against you!"

"Then we must flee at once or it will be too late!" was David's instant response to his men. "If we get out of the city before he arrives, both we and the city of Jerusalem will be saved."

"We are with you," his aides replied. "Do as you think best." So the king and his household set out at once. There was deep sadness throughout the city as the king and his retinue passed by, crossed Kidron Brook and went out into the country. David walked up the road that led to the Mount of Olives, weeping as he went. His head was covered and his feet were bare as a sign of mourning. And the people who were with him covered their heads and wept as they climbed the mountain.

32. Absalom Defeated and Slain

When David arrived at Mahanaim, he was warmly greeted by Shobi (son of Nahash of Rabbah, an Ammonite) and Machir (son of Ammiel of Lodebar) and Barzillai (a Gileadite of Rogelim). They brought him and those who were with him mats to sleep on, cooking pots, serving bowls, wheat and barley flour, parched grain, beans, lentils, honey, butter and cheese. For they said, "You must be very tired and hungry and thirsty after your long march through the wilderness."

Meanwhile, Absalom had mobilized the entire army of Israel and was leading the men across the Jordan River. David now appointed regimental colonels and company commanders over his troops. And the king commanded Joab, Abishai and Ittai, "For my sake deal gently with young Absalom." And all the troops heard the king give them this charge.

The battle began in the forest of Ephraim, and the Israeli troops were beaten back by David's men. There was a great slaughter and twenty thousand men laid down their lives that day. The battle raged all across the countryside. More men disappeared in the forest than were killed!

During the battle Absalom came upon some of David's men. As Absalom fled on his mule, it ran beneath the thick boughs of a great oak tree, and his hair caught in the branches. The mule went on, leaving Absalom dangling in the air. One of David's men saw him and told Joab. "What? You saw him there and didn't kill him?" Joab demanded. "I would have rewarded you handsomely and made you a commissioned officer."

"For a million dollars I wouldn't do it," the man replied. "We all heard the king say to you and Abishai and Ittai, 'For my sake please don't harm young Absalom.' And if I had betrayed the king by killing his son (and the king would certainly find out who did it), you yourself would be the first to accuse me."

"Enough of this nonsense," Joab said. Then he took three daggers and plunged them into the heart of Absalom as he dangled alive from the oak. Ten of Joab's young armor bearers then surrounded Absalom and finished him off. Then Joab blew the trumpet, and his men returned from chasing the army of Israel. They threw Absalom's body into a deep pit in the forest and piled a great heap of stones over it. And the army of Israel fled to their homes.

33. Heartbreak for David

Zadok's son Ahima-az said to Joab, "Let me run to King David with the good news that the Lord has saved him from his enemy Absalom."

"No," Joab told him, "it wouldn't be good news to the king that his son is dead. You can be my messenger some other time." Then Joab said to a man from Cush, "Go tell the king what you have seen." The man bowed and ran off.

But Ahima-az pleaded with Joab, "Please let me go too."

And Joab finally said, "All right, go ahead." Then Ahima-az took a short cut across the plain and got there ahead of the man from Cush.

David was sitting at the gate of the city. When the watchman climbed the stairs to his post at the top of the wall, he saw a lone man running towards them. He shouted the news down to David, and the king replied, "If he is alone, he has news."

As the messenger came closer, the watchman saw another man running towards them. He shouted down, "Here comes another one."

And the king replied, "He will have more news."

"The first man looks like Ahima-az the son of Zadok," the watchman said.

"He is a good man and comes with good news," the king replied.

Then Ahima-az cried out to the king, "All is well!" He bowed low with his face to the ground and said, "Blessed be the Lord your God who has destroyed the rebels who dared to stand against you."

"What of young Absalom?" the king demanded. "Is he all right?"

"When Joab told me to come, there was a lot of shouting; but I didn't know what was happening," Ahima-az answered.

"Wait here," the king told him. So Ahima-az stepped aside.

Then the man from Cush arrived and said, "I have good news for my lord the king. Today Jehovah has rescued you from all those who rebelled against you."

"What about young Absalom? Is he all right?" the king demanded.

And the man replied, "May all of your enemies be as that young man is!"

Then the king broke into tears and went up to his room over the gate, crying as he went. "O my son Absalom, my son, my son Absalom. If only I could have died for you! O Absalom, my son, my son."

(Absalom had built a monument to himself in the King's Valley, for he said, "I have no sons to carry on my name." He called it "Absalom's Monument," as it is still known today.)

34. Back to Jerusalem

Meanwhile there was much discussion and argument going on all across the nation: "Why aren't we talking about bringing the king back?" was the great topic everywhere. "For he saved us from our enemies the Philistines; and Absalom whom we made our king instead chased him out of the country, but now Absalom is dead. Let's ask David to return and be our king again."

So the king started back to Jerusalem. And when he arrived at the Jordan River, it seemed as if everyone in Judah had come to Gilgal to meet him and escort him across the river! Barzillai, who had fed the king and his army during their exile in Mahanaim, arrived from Rogelim to conduct the king across the river. He was very old now, about eighty, and very wealthy.

"Come across with me and live in Jerusalem," the king said to Barzillai. "I will take care of you there."

"No," he replied, "I am far too old for that. I am 80 years old today, and life has lost its excitement. Food and wine are no longer tasty and entertainment is not much fun; I would only be a burden to my lord the king. Just to go across the river with you is all the honor I need! Then let me return again to die in my own city where my father and mother are buried. But here is Chimham. Let him go with you and receive whatever good things you want to give him."

"Good," the king agreed. "Chimham shall go with me, and I will do for him whatever I would have done for you."

So all the people crossed the Jordan with the king; and after David had kissed and blessed Barzillai, he returned home. The king then went on to Gilgal, taking Chimham with him. And most of Judah and half of Israel were there to greet him. But the men of Judah stayed with their king, accompanying him from the Jordan to Jerusalem until he arrived at his palace.

35. David, Gad and Ornan

After this, Satan brought disaster upon Israel, for he made David decide to take a census. "Take a complete census throughout the land and bring me the totals," David told Joab and the other leaders.

But Joab objected. "If the Lord were to multiply His people a hundred times, would they not all be yours? So why are you asking us to do this? Why must you cause Israel to sin?" And God, too, was displeased with the census and punished Israel for it. He sent a plague upon Israel and seventy thousand men died as a result.

And David said to God, "I am the one who sinned by ordering the census. But what have these sheep done? O Lord my God, destroy me and my family, but do not destroy Your people."

Then the Lord said to Gad, David's personal prophet, "Go and tell David to build an altar to the Lord at the threshing floor of Ornan the Jebusite."

So David went to see Ornan who was threshing wheat at the time. He saw the king approaching, so he left the threshing floor and bowed to the ground before King David.

David said to Ornan, "Let me buy this threshing floor from you at its full price; then I will build an altar to the Lord and the plague will stop."

"Take it, my lord, and use it as you wish," Ornan said to David. "Take the oxen, too, for burnt offerings: use the threshing instruments for wood for the fire and use the wheat for the grain offering. I give it all to you."

"No," the king replied, "I will buy it for the full price; I cannot take what is yours and give it to the Lord. I will not offer a burnt offering that has cost me nothing!"

So David paid Ornan forty-three hundred dollars in gold. He built an altar there to the Lord and offered burnt offerings and peace offerings. And the Lord answered his prayer and the plague was stopped.

Then David said, "Right here at Ornan's threshing floor is the place where I'll build the Temple of the Lord and construct the altar for Israel's burnt offering!"

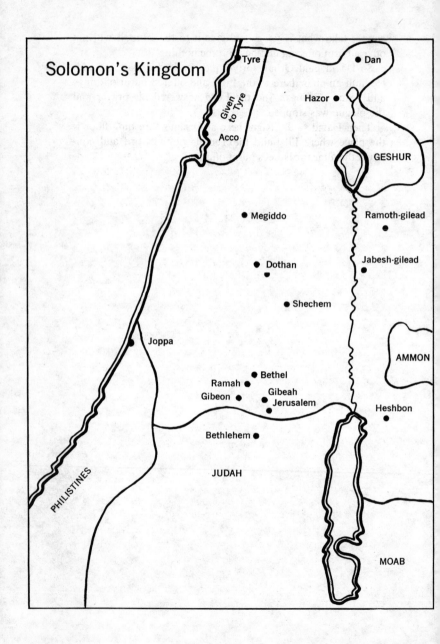

Solomon's Kingdom

PART 4 From Affluence to Pollution

BOOK OF THE KINGS

The events in this part cover a period of around 375 years: Solomon crowned in 971 B.C.; fall of Samaria, 722 B.C.; deliverance of Jerusalem under King Hezekiah in 701 B.C.; and the fall of Jerusalem in Jeremiah's time, 586 B.C.

1. The New King

DAVID'S son Adonijah (his mother was Haggith) decided to crown himself king in place of his aged father. So he hired chariots and drivers and recruited 50 men to run down the streets before him as royal footmen. Now his father, King David, had never disciplined him at any time—not so much as by a single scolding! He was Absalom's younger brother, and a very handsome man. He took General Joab and Abiathar the priest into his confidence, and they agreed to help him become king.

Then Nathan the prophet went to Bath-sheba, Solomon's mother, and asked her, "Do you realize that Haggith's son, Adonijah, is now the king and that our lord David doesn't even know about it? If you want to save your own life and the life of your son Solomon, do exactly as I say!"

So Bath-sheba went into the king's bedroom. He was an old, old man now, and Abishag was caring for him. Bath-sheba bowed low before him.

"What do you want?" he asked her.

She replied, "My lord, you vowed to me by the Lord your God that my son Solomon would be the next king and would sit upon your throne. But instead, Adonijah is the new king, and you don't even know about it. He has celebrated his coronation by sacrificing oxen, fat goats and many sheep. He has invited all your sons and Abiathar the priest and General Joab. But he didn't invite Solomon. And now, my lord the king, all Israel is waiting for your decision as to whether Adonijah is the one you have chosen to succeed you."

"Call Zadok the priest," the king ordered, "and Nathan the prophet, and Benaiah." When they arrived, he said to them, "Take Solomon and my officers to Gihon. Solomon is to ride on my personal mule, and Zadok the priest and Nathan the prophet are to anoint him there as king of Israel. Then blow the trumpets and shout, 'Long live King Solomon!' When you bring him back here, place him upon my throne as the new king; for I have appointed him king of Israel and Judah."

"Amen! Praise God!" replied Benaiah, and added, "May the Lord be with Solomon as He has been with you, and may God make Solomon's reign even greater than yours!"

So Zadok the priest, Nathan the prophet, Benaiah and David's bodyguard took Solomon to Gihon, riding on King David's own mule. At Gihon Zadok took a flask of sacred oil from the Tabernacle and poured it over Solomon; and the trumpets were blown and all the people shouted, "Long live King Solomon!" Then they all returned with him to Jerusalem, making a joyous and noisy celebration all along the way.

Adonijah and his guests heard the commotion and shouting just as they were finishing their banquet. Then Adonijah and his guests jumped up from the banquet table and fled in panic, for they were fearful for their lives. Adonijah rushed into the Tabernacle and caught hold of the horns of the sacred altar. When word reached Solomon that Adonijah was claiming sanctuary in the Tabernacle and pleading for clemency, King Solomon summoned him, and they brought him down from the altar. He came to bow low before the king, and then Solomon curtly dismissed him. "Go on home," he said.

2. David's Charge to Solomon

David now summoned all of his officials to Jerusalem—the political leaders, the commanders of the twelve army divisions, the other army officers, those in charge of his property and livestock and all the other men of authority in his kingdom. He rose and stood before them and addressed them as follows: "My brothers and my people! It was my desire to build a Temple in which the Ark of the Covenant of the Lord could rest—a place for our God to live in. I have now collected everything that is necessary for the building, but God has told me, 'You are not to build My Temple, for you are a warrior and have shed much blood.' "

Then David turned to Solomon and said: "Here before the leaders of Israel, the people of God, and in the sight of our God, I am instructing you to search out every commandment of the Lord so that you may continue to rule this good land and leave it to your children to rule forever. Solomon my son, get to know the God of your fathers. Worship and serve Him with a clean heart and a willing mind, for the Lord sees every heart and understands and knows every thought. If you seek Him, you will find Him; but if you forsake Him, He will permanently throw you aside. So be very careful, for the Lord has chosen you to build His holy Temple. Be strong and do as He commands."

3. Plans for Building the Temple

Then King David turned to the entire assembly and said: "My son Solomon whom God has chosen to be the next king of Israel is still young and inexperienced, and the work ahead of him is enormous; for the Temple he will build is not just another building—it is for the Lord God Himself! Using every resource at my command, I have gathered as much as I could for building it: enough gold, silver, bronze, iron, wood and great quantities of onyx, other precious stones, costly jewels and marble. And now because of my devotion to the Temple

183

of God, I am giving all of my own private treasures to aid in the construction. This is in addition to the building materials I have already collected. These personal contributions consist of $85 million worth of gold from Ophir and $20 million worth of purest silver to be used for overlaying the walls of the buildings. This will be used for the articles made of gold and silver and for the artistic decorations. Now then, who will follow my example? Who will give himself and all that he has to the Lord?"

Then the clan leaders, the heads of the tribes, the army officers and the administrative officers of the king pledged $145 million in gold; $50 thousand in foreign currency, $30 million in silver; 800 tons of bronze; and 4,600 tons of iron. They also contributed great amounts of jewelry which were deposited at the Temple treasury with Jehiel (a descendant of Gershom). Everyone was excited and happy for this opportunity of service, and King David was moved with deep joy.

While still in the presence of the whole assembly, David expressed his praises to the Lord: "O Lord God of our father Israel, praise Your name for ever and ever! Yours is the mighty power and glory and victory and majesty. Everything in the heavens and earth is Yours, O Lord, and this is Your kingdom. We adore You as being in control of everything. Riches and honor come from You alone, and You are the ruler of all mankind; Your hand controls power and might, and it is at Your discretion that men are made great and given strength.

"O our God, we thank You and praise Your glorious name, but who am I and who are my people that we should be permitted to give anything to You? Everything we have has come from You, and we only give You what is Yours already! For we are here for but a moment, strangers in the land as our fathers were before us; our days on earth are like a shadow, gone so soon, without a trace.

"O Lord our God, all of this material that we have gathered to build a Temple for Your holy name comes from You! It all belongs to You! I know, my God, that You test men to see if they are good; for You enjoy good men. I have done all this with good motives, and I have watched Your people offer their gifts willingly and joyously.

"O Lord God of our fathers: Abraham, Isaac and Israel! Make Your people always want to obey You, and see to it that their love for You never changes. Give my son Solomon a good heart toward God, so that he will want to obey You in the smallest detail and will look forward eagerly to finishing the building of Your Temple, for which I have made all of these preparations."

Then David said to all the people, "Give praise to the Lord your God!" And they did, bowing low before the Lord and the king.

David was king of the land of Israel for 40 years; seven of them during his reign in Hebron and 33 in Jerusalem. He died at an old age, wealthy and honored, and his son Solomon reigned in his place.

4. Solomon's Choice

In those days the people of Israel sacrificed their offerings on altars in the hills, for the Temple of the Lord hadn't yet been built. King Solomon loved the Lord and followed all of his father David's instructions except that he continued to sacrifice in the hills and to offer incense there. The most famous of the hilltop altars was at Gibeon and now the king went there and sacrificed one thousand burnt offerings! The Lord appeared to him in a dream that night and told him to ask for anything he wanted, and it would be given to him!

Solomon replied, "You were wonderfully kind to my father David because he was honest and true and faithful to You and obeyed Your commands. And You have continued Your kindness to him by giving him a son to succeed him. O Lord my God, now You have made me the king instead of my father David, but I am as a little child who doesn't know his way around. And here I am among Your own chosen people, a nation so great that there are almost too many people to count! Give me an understanding mind so that I can govern Your people well and know the difference between what is right and what is wrong. For who by himself is able to carry such a heavy responsibility?"

The Lord was pleased with his reply and was glad that Solomon had asked for wisdom. So He replied, "Because you have asked for wisdom in governing My people and haven't asked for a long life or riches for yourself, or the defeat of your enemies—yes, I'll give you what you asked for! I will give you a wiser mind than anyone else has ever had or ever will have! And I will also give you what you didn't ask for—riches and honor! And no one in all the world will be as rich and famous as you for the rest of your life! And I will give you a long life if you follow Me and obey My laws as your father David did."

Then Solomon woke up and realized it had been a dream. He returned to Jerusalem and went into the Tabernacle. And as he stood before the Ark of the Covenant of the Lord, he sacrificed burnt offerings and peace offerings. Then he invited all of his officials to a great banquet.

5. Solomon's Wise Judgment

Soon afterwards two young prostitutes came to the king to have an argument settled. "Sir," one of them began, "we live in the same house, just the two of us, and recently I had a baby. When it was three days old, this woman's baby was born too. But her baby died during the night when she rolled over on it in her sleep and smothered it. Then she got up in the night and took my son from beside me while I was asleep, laid her dead child in my arms and took mine to sleep beside her. And in the morning when I tried to feed my baby it was dead! But when it became light outside I saw that it wasn't my son at all."

Then the other woman interrupted, "It certainly was her son, and the living child is mine."

"No," the first woman said, "the dead one is yours and the living one is mine." And so they argued back and forth before the king.

Then the king said, "Let's get the facts straight: both of you claim the living child, and each says that the dead child belongs to the other. All right, bring me a sword." So a sword was brought to the king.

Then he said, "Divide the living child in two and give half to each of these women!"

Then the woman who really was the mother of the child, and who loved him very much, cried out, "Oh, no, sir! Give her the child—don't kill him!"

But the other woman said, "All right, it will be neither yours nor mine; divide it between us!"

Then the king said, "Give the baby to the woman who wants him to live, for she is the mother!" Word of the king's decision spread quickly throughout the entire nation, and all the people were awed as they realized the great wisdom God had given him.

6. Solomon's Fame and Greatness

Israel and Judah were a wealthy, populous, contented nation at this time. King Solomon ruled the whole area from the Euphrates River to the land of the Philistines and down to the borders of Egypt. The conquered peoples of those lands sent taxes to Solomon and continued to serve him throughout his lifetime. The daily food requirements for the palace were 195 bushels of fine flour, 390 bushels of meal, 10 oxen from the fattening pens, 20 pasture-fed cattle, 100 sheep and, from time to time, deer, gazelles, roebucks and plump fowl. His dominion extended over all the kingdoms west of the Euphrates River from Tiphsah to Gaza. And there was peace throughout the land.

Throughout the lifetime of Solomon all of Judah and Israel lived in peace and safety; and each family had its own home and garden. Solomon owned forty thousand chariot horses and employed twelve thousand charioteers. Each month the tax officials provided food for King Solomon and his court; also the barley and straw for the royal horses in the stables.

God gave Solomon great wisdom and understanding, and a mind with broad interests. In fact his wisdom excelled that of any of the wise men of the East, including those in Egypt. He was wiser than Ethan the Ezrahite and Heman, Calcol and Darda, the sons of Mahol; and he was famous among all the surrounding nations. He was the author of three thousand proverbs and wrote one thousand and five songs. Also, he was a great naturalist, with interest in animals, birds, snakes, fish and trees—from the great cedars of Lebanon down to the tiny hyssop which grew in cracks in the wall. And kings from many lands sent their ambassadors to him for his advice.

7. The Building of Solomon's Temple

It was in the spring of the fourth year of Solomon's reign that he began the actual construction of the Temple. This was 480 years after the people of Israel left their slavery in Egypt.

The Temple was 90 feet long, 30 feet wide and 45 feet high. All along the front of the Temple was a porch 30 feet long and 15 feet deep. The stones used in the construction of the Temple were prefinished at the quarry. So the entire structure was built without the sound of hammer, axe or any other tool at the building site.

The entire inside, from floor to ceiling, was paneled with cedar and the floors were made of cypress boards. The 30-foot inner room at the far end of the Temple—the Most Holy Place—was also paneled from the floor to the ceiling with cedar boards. The remainder of the Temple, other than the Most Holy Place, was 60 feet long. Throughout the Temple the cedar paneling laid over the stone walls was carved with designs of rosebuds and open flowers.

The inner room was where the Ark of the Covenant of the Lord was placed. This inner sanctuary was 30 feet long, 30 feet wide and 30 feet high. Its walls and ceiling were overlaid with pure gold, and Solomon made a cedarwood altar for this room. Then he overlaid the interior of the remainder of the Temple, including the cedar altar, with pure gold; and he made gold chains to protect the entrance to the Most Holy Place.

The Lord sent this message to Solomon concerning the

Temple he was building: "If you do as I tell you to and follow all of My commandments and instructions, I will do what I told your father David I would do. *I will live among the people of Israel and never forsake them.*"

The foundation of the Temple was laid in the month of May in the fourth year of Solomon's reign, and the entire building was completed in every detail in November of the eleventh year of his reign. So it took seven years to build. When the Temple was finally finished, Solomon took into the treasury of the Temple the silver, the gold and all the vessels dedicated for that purpose by his father David.

8. Dedication of the Temple

To observe the transferring of the Ark of the Covenant of the Lord from the Tabernacle in Zion (the City of David) to the Temple, Solomon called a convocation at Jerusalem of all the leaders of Israel—the heads of the tribes and clans. Then the priests took the Ark into the inner sanctuary of the Temple —the Most Holy Place—and placed it under the wings of the angels. The angels had been constructed in such a manner that their wings spread out over the spot where the Ark would be placed; so now their wings overshadowed the Ark and its carrying poles. There was nothing in the Ark at that time except the two stone tablets which Moses had placed there at Mount Horeb at the time the Lord made His covenant with the people of Israel after they left Egypt.

Now King Solomon prayed this invocation:

"The Lord has said that He would live in the thick darkness;
But, O Lord, I have built You a lovely home on earth, a place for You to live forever."

As all the people watched, Solomon stood before the altar of the Lord with his hands spread out towards heaven and said, "O Lord God of Israel, there is no God like You in heaven or earth, for You are loving and kind and You keep Your promises to Your people if they do their best to do Your will. But is it possible that God would really live on earth? Why, even the skies and the highest heavens cannot contain You, much less this Temple I have built! And yet, O Lord my God, You have heard and answered my request. Please watch over this Temple night and day—this place You have promised to live in—and as I face toward the Temple and pray, whether by night or by day, please listen to me and answer my requests. Listen to every plea of the people of Israel whenever they face this place to pray; yes, hear in heaven where You live and when You hear, forgive.

"If they sin against You (and who has never sinned?) and You become angry with them, and You let their enemies defeat them and take them away as captives to some foreign nation near or far—and if in that land of exile they turn to You again, and face toward this land You gave their fathers, and this city and Your Temple I have built, and plead with You with all their hearts to forgive them, then hear from heaven where You live and help them and forgive Your people who have sinned against You. Yes, O my God, be wide awake and attentive to all the prayers made to You in this place.

"And now, O Lord God, arise and enter this resting place of Yours where the Ark of Your strength has been placed. Let Your priests, O Lord God, be clothed with salvation, and let Your saints rejoice in Your kind deeds. O Lord God, do not ignore me—do not turn Your face away from me, Your anointed one. Oh, remember Your love for David and Your kindness to him."

As Solomon finished praying, fire flashed down from heaven and burned up the sacrifices! And the glory of the Lord filled the Temple so that the priests couldn't enter! All the people had been watching and now they fell flat on the pavement and worshiped and thanked the Lord. "How good He is!" they exclaimed. "He is always so loving and kind."

When Solomon had finished building the Temple and the palace and all the other buildings he had always wanted, the Lord appeared to him the second time (the first time had been at Gibeon) and said to him, "I have heard your prayer. I have hallowed this Temple which you have built and have put My name here forever. I will constantly watch over it and rejoice in it."

9. The Queen of Sheba's Visit

When the queen of Sheba heard how wonderfully the Lord had blessed Solomon with wisdom, she decided to test him with some hard questions. She arrived in Jerusalem with a long train of camels carrying spices, gold and jewels; and she told him all her problems. Solomon answered all her questions; nothing was too difficult for him, for the Lord gave him the right answers every time. She soon realized that everything she had ever heard about his great wisdom was true. She also saw the beautiful palace he had built, and when she saw the wonderful foods on his table, the great number of servants and aides who stood around in splendid uniforms, his cupbearers, and the many offerings he sacrificed by fire to the Lord—well, there was no more spirit in her!

She exclaimed to him, "Everything I heard in my own country about your wisdom and about the wonderful things going on here is all true. I didn't believe it until I came, but now I have seen it for myself! And really! The half had not been told me! Your wisdom and prosperity are far greater than anything I've ever heard of! Your people are happy and your palace aides are content—but how could it be otherwise, for they stand here day after day listening to your wisdom! Blessed be the Lord your God who chose you and set you on the throne of Israel. How the Lord must love Israel—for He gave you to them as their king! And you give your people a just, good government!"

Then she gave the king a gift of $3.5 million in gold, along with a huge quantity of spices and precious gems. It was, in fact, the largest single gift of spices King Solomon had ever received. In exchange for the gifts from the queen of Sheba, King Solomon gave her everything she asked him for, besides the presents he had already planned. Then she and her servants returned to their own land.

10. Solomon's Wealth

Each year Solomon received gold worth about $20 million, besides sales taxes and profits from trade with the kings of Arabia and the other surrounding territories. Solomon had some of the gold beaten into two hundred pieces of armor (gold worth $6,000 went into each piece) and 300 shields ($1,800 worth of gold in each). And he kept them in his palace in the Hall of the Forest of Lebanon.

He also made a huge ivory throne and overlaid it with pure gold. It had six steps and a rounded back with arm rests; and a lion standing on each side—there were two lions on each step—twelve in all. There was no other throne in all the world so splendid as that one.

All of King Solomon's cups were of solid gold. In the Hall of the Forest of Lebanon his entire dining service was made of solid gold. (Silver wasn't used because it wasn't considered to be of much value and cedar was of no greater value than sycamore!)

King Solomon's merchant fleet was in partnership with King Hiram's, and once every three years a great load of gold, silver, ivory, apes and peacocks arrived at the Israeli ports.

So King Solomon was richer and wiser than all the kings of the earth. Great men from many lands came to interview him and listen to his God-given wisdom. They brought him annual tribute of silver and gold dishes, beautiful cloth, myrrh, spices, horses and mules. Solomon built up a great stable of horses with a vast number of chariots and cavalry—fourteen hundred chariots in all, and twelve thousand cavalrymen who lived in the chariot cities and with the king at Jerusalem.

11. Solomon's Apostasy

King Solomon married many other girls besides the Egyptian princess. Many of them came from nations where idols were worshiped—Moab, Ammon, Edom, Sidon and from the Hittites—even though the Lord had clearly instructed His people not to marry into those nations because the women they married would get them started worshiping their gods. Yet Solomon did it anyway. He had 700 wives and 300 concubines; and sure enough, they turned his heart away from the Lord, especially in his old age. They encouraged him to worship their gods instead of trusting completely in the Lord as his father David had done.

Solomon worshiped Ashtoreth, the goddess of the Sidonians, and Milcom, the horrible god of the Ammonites. Thus Solomon did what was clearly wrong and refused to follow the Lord as his father David did. He even built a temple on the Mount of Olives across the valley from Jerusalem for Chemosh, the depraved god of Moab, and another for Molech, the unutterably vile god of the Ammonites. Solomon built temples for these foreign wives to use for burning incense and sacrificing to their gods.

Jehovah was very angry with Solomon about this, for now Solomon was no longer interested in the Lord God of Israel who had appeared to him twice to warn him specifically against worshiping other gods. But he hadn't listened, so now the Lord said to him, "Since you have not kept our agreement and have not obeyed My laws, I will tear the kingdom away from you and your family and give it to someone else. However, for the sake of your father David, I won't do this while you are still alive. I will take the kingdom away from your son. And even so I will let him be king of one tribe for David's sake and for the sake of Jerusalem, My chosen city."

Solomon was rebuilding Fort Millo, repairing the walls of this city his father had built. Jeroboam was very able, and when Solomon saw how industrious he was, he put him in charge of his labor battalions from the tribe of Joseph. One day as Jeroboam was leaving Jerusalem, the prophet Ahijah from Shiloh called him aside to talk to him. He tore his new robe into twelve parts and said to Jeroboam, "Take these ten pieces, for the Lord God of Israel says, 'I will tear the kingdom from the hand of Solomon and give ten of the tribes to you! For Solomon has not followed My paths and has not done what I consider right.' "

193

Solomon ruled in Jerusalem for 40 years, and then died and was buried in the city of his father David; and his son Rehoboam reigned in his place.

12. Rebellion Under Rehoboam

Rehoboam's inauguration was at Shechem, and all Israel came for the coronation ceremony. Jeroboam, who was still in Egypt where he had fled from King Solomon, heard about the plans from his friends. They urged him to attend, so he joined the rest of Israel at Shechem and was the ringleader in getting the people to make certain demands upon Rehoboam.

"Your father was a hard master," they told Rehoboam. "We don't want you as our king unless you promise to treat us better than he did."

"Give me three days to think this over," Rehoboam replied. "Come back then for my answer." So the people left. Rehoboam talked it over with the old men who had counseled his father Solomon. "What do you think I should do?" he asked them.

They replied, "If you give them a pleasant reply and agree to be good to them and serve them well, you can be their king forever."

But Rehoboam refused the old men's counsel and called in the young men with whom he had grown up. "What do you think I should do?" he asked them.

The young men replied, "Tell them, 'If you think my father was hard on you, well, I'll be harder! Yes, my father was harsh, but I'll be even harsher! My father used whips on you, but I'll use scorpions!' "

When Jeroboam and the people returned three days later, the new king answered them roughly. He ignored the old men's advice and followed that of the young men. So the king refused the people's demands. But the Lord's hand was in it—He caused the new king to do this in order to fulfill His promise to Jeroboam, made through Ahijah the prophet from Shiloh.

When the people realized that the king meant what he said and was refusing to listen to them, they began shouting, "Down with David and all his relatives! Let's go home! Let Rehoboam be king of his own family!" And they all deserted him except for the tribe of Judah, who remained loyal and accepted Rehoboam as their king.

King Rehoboam sent Adoram, who was in charge of the draft, to conscript men from the other tribes, but a great mob stoned him to death. However, King Rehoboam escaped by chariot and fled to Jerusalem. And Israel has been in rebellion against the dynasty of David to this day. When the people of Israel learned of Jeroboam's return from Egypt, he was asked to come before an open meeting of all the people where he was made king of Israel. Only the tribe of Judah continued under the kingship of the family of David.

Jeroboam now built the city of Shechem in the hill country of Ephraim, and it became his capital. Later he built Penuel. Jeroboam thought, "Unless I'm careful the people will want a descendant of David as their king. When they go to Jerusalem to offer sacrifices at the Temple, they will become friendly with King Rehoboam; then they will kill me and ask him to be their king instead."

So on the advice of his counselors, the king had two gold calf-idols made and told the people, "It's too much trouble to go to Jerusalem to worship; from now on these will be your gods—they rescued you from your captivity in Egypt!" One of these calf-idols was placed in Bethel and the other in Dan. This was of course a great sin, for the people worshiped them.

He also made shrines on the hills and ordained priests from the rank and file of the people—even those who were not from the priest-tribe of Levi. Jeroboam also announced that the annual Tabernacle Festival would be held at Bethel on the first of November (a date he decided upon himself), similar to the annual festival at Jerusalem. He himself offered sacrifices upon the altar to the calves at Bethel and burned incense to them. And it was there at Bethel that he ordained priests for the shrines on the hills.

13. Rehoboam's Reign over Judah

Meanwhile, Rehoboam, the son of Solomon and Naamah, an Ammonite woman, was king in Judah. He was 41 years old when he began to reign, and he was on the throne 17 years in Jerusalem, the city which among all the cities of Israel the Lord had chosen to live in. During his reign the people of Judah, like those in Israel, did wrong and angered the Lord with their sin, for it was even worse than that of their ancestors.

In the fifth year of Rehoboam's reign, King Shishak of Egypt attacked and conquered Jerusalem. He ransacked the Temple and the palace and stole everything, including all the gold shields Solomon had made. Afterwards Rehoboam made bronze shields as substitutes, and the palace guards used these instead. Whenever the king went to the Temple, the guards paraded before him and then took the shields back to the guard chamber.

There was constant war between Rehoboam and Jeroboam. When Rehoboam died, he was buried among his ancestors in Jerusalem, and his son Abijam took the throne.

Abijam reigned only three years and then Asa became king of Judah, in Jerusalem, in the twentieth year of the reign of Jeroboam over Israel and reigned 41 years. He pleased the Lord like his ancestor King David. He executed the male prostitutes and removed all the idols his father had made. He deposed his grandmother Maacah as queen mother because she had made an idol—which he cut down and burned at Kidron Brook. And when he died he was buried in the royal cemetery in Jerusalem. Then his son Jehoshaphat became the new king of Judah.

14. First Clash Between Ahab and Elijah

King Asa of Judah had been on the throne 38 years when Ahab became the king of Israel. Ahab reigned for 22 years. But he was even more wicked than his father Omri; he was worse than any other king of Israel! And as though that were not enough, he married Jezebel the daughter of King Ethbaal of the Sidonians, and then began worshiping Baal. First he built a temple and an altar for Baal in Samaria, then he made other idols and did more to anger the Lord God of Israel than any of the other kings of Israel before him.

Then Elijah the prophet from Tishbe in Gilead told King Ahab, "As surely as the Lord God of Israel lives—the God whom I worship and serve—there won't be any dew or rain for several years until I say the word!"

Then the Lord said to Elijah, "Go to the east and hide by Cherith Brook at a place east of where it enters the Jordan River. Drink from the brook and eat what the ravens bring you, for I have commanded them to feed you."

So he did as the Lord had told him to and camped beside the brook. The ravens brought him bread and meat each morning and evening, and he drank from the brook. But after awhile the brook dried up because there was no rainfall anywhere in the land.

15. The Contest on Mount Carmel

It was three years later that the Lord said to Elijah, "Go and tell King Ahab that I will soon send rain again!" So Elijah went to tell him. Meanwhile the famine had become very severe in Samaria.

"So it's you, is it?—the man who brought this disaster upon Israel!" Ahab exclaimed when he saw him.

"You're talking about yourself," Elijah answered. "For you and your family have refused to obey the Lord and have worshiped Baal instead. Now bring all the people of Israel to Mount Carmel with all 450 prophets of Baal and the 400 prophets of Asherah who are supported by Jezebel." So Ahab summoned all the people and the prophets to Mount Carmel.

Then Elijah talked to them, "How long are you going to waver between two opinions?" he asked the people. "If the Lord is God, *follow* him! But if Baal is God, then follow *him!*" Then Elijah spoke again. "I am the only prophet of the Lord who is left," he told them, "but Baal has 450 prophets. Now bring two young bulls. The prophets of Baal may choose whichever one they wish and cut it into pieces and lay it on the wood of their altar, but without putting any fire under the wood. I will prepare the other young bull and lay it on the wood on the Lord's altar with no fire under it. Then pray to your god, and I will pray to the Lord; and the god who answers by sending fire to light the wood is the true God!" And all the people agreed to this test.

Then Elijah turned to the prophets of Baal. "You first," he said, "for there are many of you. Choose one of the bulls and prepare it and call to your god; but don't put any fire under the wood."

So they prepared one of the young bulls and placed it on the altar; and they called to Baal all morning, shouting, "O Baal, hear us!" But there was no reply of any kind. Then they began to dance around the altar.

About noontime, Elijah began mocking them. "You'll have to shout louder than that," he scoffed, "to catch the attention of your god! Perhaps he is talking to someone, or is out sitting on the toilet, or maybe he is away on a trip, or is asleep and needs to be awakened!"

So they shouted louder and, as was their custom, cut themselves with knives and swords until the blood gushed out. They raved all afternoon until the time of the evening sacrifice, but there was no reply, no voice, no answer.

Then Elijah called to the people, "Come over here." And they all crowded around him as he repaired the altar of the Lord which had been torn down. He took twelve stones, one to represent each of the tribes of Israel, and used the stones to rebuild the Lord's altar. Then he dug a trench about three feet wide around the altar. He piled wood upon the altar and cut the young bull into pieces and laid the pieces on the wood.

"Fill four barrels with water," he said, "and pour the water over the carcass and the wood." After they had done this he said, "Do it again." And they did.

"Now, do it once more!" And they did. And the water ran off the altar and filled the trench.

At the customary time for offering the evening sacrifice, Elijah walked up to the altar and prayed, "O Lord God of Abraham, Isaac and Israel, prove today that You are the God of Israel and that I am Your servant; prove that I have done all this at Your command. O Lord, answer me! Answer me so these people will know that You are God and that You have brought them back to Yourself."

Then, suddenly, fire flashed down from heaven and burned up the young bull, the wood, the stones, the dust and even evaporated all the water in the ditch! And when the people saw it, they fell to their faces upon the ground shouting, "Jehovah is God! Jehovah is God!"

Elijah told them to grab the prophets of Baal. "Don't let a single one escape," he commanded. So they seized them all, and Elijah took them to Kishon Brook and killed them there.

Then Elijah said to Ahab, "Go and enjoy a good meal! For I hear a mighty rainstorm coming!" So Ahab prepared a feast.

But Elijah climbed to the top of Mount Carmel and got down on his knees, with his face between his knees, and said to his servant, "Go and look out toward the sea."

He did, but returned to Elijah and told him, "I didn't see anything."

Then Elijah told him, "Go again, and again, and again, seven times!"

Finally, the seventh time, his servant told him, "I saw a little cloud about the size of a man's hand rising from the sea."

Then Elijah shouted, "Hurry to Ahab and tell him to get into his chariot and get down the mountain, or he'll be stopped by the rain!"

And sure enough, the sky was soon black with clouds, and a heavy wind brought a terrific rainstorm. Ahab left hastily for Jezreel, and the Lord gave special strength to Elijah so that he was able to run ahead of Ahab's chariot to the entrance of the city!

16. Elijah's Despondency

When Ahab told Queen Jezebel what Elijah had done, and that he had slaughtered the prophets of Baal, she sent this message to Elijah: "You killed my prophets, and now I swear by the gods that I am going to kill you by this time tomorrow night."

So Elijah fled for his life; he went to Beersheba, a city of Judah, and left his servant there. Then he went on alone into the wilderness, traveling all day, and sat down under a broom bush and prayed that he might die. "I've had enough," he told the Lord, "Take away my life. I've got to die sometime, and it might as well be now." Then he lay down and slept beneath the broom bush.

But as he was sleeping, an angel touched him and told him to get up and eat! He looked around and saw some bread baking on hot stones, and a jar of water! So he ate and drank and lay down again.

The angel of the Lord came again and touched him and said, "Get up and eat some more, for there is a long journey ahead of you."

So he got up and ate and drank, and the food gave him enough strength to travel 40 days and 40 nights to Mount Horeb, the mountain of God, where he lived in a cave. But the Lord said to him, "What are you doing here, Elijah?"

He replied, "I have worked very hard for the Lord God of the heavens; but the people of Israel have broken their covenant with You and torn down Your altars and killed Your prophets, and only I am left. Now they are trying to kill me too."

"Go out and stand before Me on the mountain," the Lord told him. And as Elijah stood there the Lord passed by, and a mighty windstorm hit the mountain; it was such a terrible blast that the rocks were torn loose, but the Lord was not in the wind. After the wind there was an earthquake, but the Lord was not in the earthquake. And after the earthquake there was a fire, but the Lord was not in the fire.

And after the fire there was the sound of a gentle whisper. When Elijah heard it, he wrapped his face in his scarf and went out and stood at the entrance of the cave. And a voice said, "Why are you here, Elijah?"

He replied again, "I have been working very hard for the Lord God of the armies of heaven, but the people have broken their covenant and have torn down Your altars; they have killed every one of Your prophets except me; and now they are trying to kill me too."

Then the Lord told him, "Go back by the desert road to Damascus, and when you arrive, anoint Hazael to be king of Syria. Then anoint Jehu (son of Nimshi) to be king of Israel, and anoint Elisha (the son of Shaphat of Abel-meholah) to replace you as My prophet. And incidentally, there are seven thousand men in Israel who have never bowed to Baal nor kissed him!"

So Elijah went and found Elisha who was plowing a field with eleven other teams ahead of him; he was at the end of the line with the last team. Elijah went over to him and threw his coat across his shoulders and walked away again. Elisha left the oxen standing there and ran after Elijah and said to him, "First let me go and say good-bye to my father and mother, and then I'll go with you!"

Elijah replied, "Go on back! Why all the excitement?"

Elisha then returned to his oxen, killed them, and used wood from the plow to build a fire to roast their flesh. He passed around the meat to the other plowmen, and they all had a great feast. Then he went with Elijah as his assistant.

17. Conflict Between Ben-hadad and Ahab

King Ben-hadad of Syria now mobilized his army and with 32 allied nations and their hordes of chariots and horses besieged Samaria, the Israeli capital. He sent this message into the city to King Ahab of Israel: "Your silver and gold are mine, as are your prettiest wives and the best of your children!"

"All right, my lord," Ahab replied. "All that I have is yours!"

Soon Ben-hadad's messengers returned again with another message: "You must not only give me your silver, gold, wives and children, but about this time tomorrow I will send my men to search your palace and the homes of your people, and they will take away whatever they like!"

Then Ahab summoned his advisers. "Look what this man is doing," he complained to them. "He is stirring up trouble despite the fact that I have already told him he could have my wives and children and silver and gold, just as he demanded."

"Don't give him anything more," the elders advised.

So he told the messengers from Ben-hadad, "Tell my lord the king, 'I will give you everything you asked for the first time, but your men may not search the palace and the homes of the people.' " So the messengers returned to Ben-hadad.

The Syrian king then sent this message to Ahab: "May the gods do more to me than I am going to do to you if I don't turn Samaria into handfuls of dust!"

The king of Israel retorted, "Don't count your chickens before they hatch!"

So he mustered the troops from the 232 provinces together with the rest of his army of seven thousand men. About noontime, as Ben-hadad and the 32 allied kings were still drinking themselves drunk, the first of Ahab's troops marched out of the city. As they approached, Ben-hadad's scouts reported to him, "Some troops are coming!"

"Take them alive," Ben-hadad commanded, "whether they have come for truce or for war."

By now Ahab's entire army had joined the attack. Each one killed a Syrian soldier, and suddenly the entire Syrian army panicked and fled. The Israelis chased them, but King Ben-hadad and a few others escaped on horses. However, the great bulk of the horses and chariots were captured, the most of the Syrian army was killed in a great slaughter.

Then the prophet approached King Ahab and said, "Get ready for another attack by the king of Syria." For after their defeat, Ben-hadad's officers said to him, "The Israeli God is a god of the hills; that is why they won. But we can beat them easily on the plains."

The following year he called up the Syrian army and marched out against Israel again, this time at Aphek. Israel then mustered its army, set up supply lines and moved into the battle. But the Israeli army looked like two little flocks of baby goats in comparison to the vast Syrian forces that filled the countryside!

Then a prophet went to the king of Israel with this message from the Lord: "Because the Syrians have declared, 'The Lord is a God of the hills and not of the plains,' I will help you defeat this vast army, and you shall know that I am indeed the Lord."

The two armies camped opposite each other for seven days, and on the seventh day the battle began. And the Israelis killed a hundred thousand Syrian infantrymen that first day. The rest fled.

18. Ahab and Naboth's Vineyard

Naboth, a man from Jezreel, had a vineyard on the outskirts of the city near King Ahab's palace. One day the king talked to him about selling him this land. "I want it for a garden," the king explained, "because it's so convenient to the palace." He offered cash or, if Naboth preferred, a piece of better land in trade.

But Naboth replied, "Not on your life! That land has been in my family for generations." So Ahab went back to the palace angry and sullen. He refused to eat and went to bed with his face to the wall!

"What in the world is the matter?" his wife Jezebel asked him. "Why aren't you eating? What has made you so upset and angry?"

"I asked Naboth to sell me his vineyard or to trade it, and he refused!" Ahab told her.

"Are you the king of Israel or not?" Jezebel demanded. "Get up and eat and don't worry about it. I'll get you Naboth's vineyard!" So she wrote letters in Ahab's name, sealed them with his seal, and addressed them to the civic leaders of Jezreel where Naboth lived. In her letters she commanded: "Call the citizens together for fasting and prayer. Then summon Naboth, and find two scoundrels who will accuse him of cursing God and the king. Then take him out and execute him."

The city fathers followed the queen's instructions. They called the meeting and put Naboth on trial. Then two men who had no conscience accused him of cursing God and the king; and he was dragged outside the city and stoned to death. The city officials then sent word to Jezebel that Naboth was dead.

When Jezebel heard the news, she said to Ahab, "You know the vineyard Naboth wouldn't sell you? Well, you can have it now! He's dead!" So Ahab went down to the vineyard to claim it.

But the Lord said to Elijah, "Go to Samaria to meet King Ahab. He will be at Naboth's vineyard, taking possession of it. Give him this message from Me: 'Isn't killing Naboth bad enough? Must you rob him too? Because you have done this, dogs shall lick your blood outside the city just as they licked the blood of Naboth!' "

"So my enemy has found me!" Ahab exclaimed to Elijah.

"Yes," Elijah answered, "I have come to place God's curse upon you because you have sold yourself to the devil. The Lord is going to bring great harm to you and sweep you away; He will not let a single one of your male descendants survive! He is going to destroy your family as He did the family of King Jeroboam and the family of King Baasha, for you have made Him very angry and have led all of Israel into sin. The Lord has also told me that the dogs of Jezreel shall tear apart the body of your wife Jezebel. The members of your family who die in the city shall be eaten by dogs and those who die in the country shall be eaten by vultures."

No one else was so completely sold out to the devil as Ahab, for his wife Jezebel encouraged him to do every sort of evil. He was especially guilty because he worshiped idols just as the Amorites did—the people whom the Lord had chased out of the land to make room for the people of Israel.

19. Ahab's Death

For three years there was no war between Syria and Israel. But during the third year while King Jehoshaphat of Judah was visiting King Ahab of Israel, Ahab said to his officials, "Do you realize that the Syrians are still occupying our city of

Ramoth-gilead? And we're sitting here without doing a thing about it!" Then he turned to Jehoshaphat and asked him, "Will you send your army with mine to recover Ramoth-gilead?"

And King Jehoshaphat of Judah replied, "Of course! You and I are brothers; my people are yours to command, and my horses are at your service.

"But," he added, "we should ask the Lord first, to be sure of what He wants us to do."

So King Ahab summoned his 400 heathen prophets and asked them, "Shall I attack Ramoth-gilead or not?"

And they all said, "Yes, go ahead, for God will help you conquer it."

But Jehoshaphat asked, "Isn't there a prophet of the Lord here? I'd like to ask him too."

"Well, there's one," King Ahab replied, "but I hate him, for he never prophesies anything good. He always has something gloomy to say. His name is Micaiah, the son of Imlah."

"Oh, come now!" Jehoshaphat replied, "Don't talk like that!"

So King Ahab called to one of his aides, "Go get Micaiah. Hurry!" Meanwhile all the prophets continued prophesying before the two kings who were dressed in their royal robes and were sitting on thrones placed on the threshing floor near the city gate.

The messenger who went to get Micaiah told him what the other prophets were saying and urged him to say the same thing. But Micaiah told him, "This I vow, that I will say only what the Lord tells me to!"

When he arrived the king asked him, "Micaiah, shall we attack Ramoth-gilead or not?"

"Why, of course! Go right ahead!" Micaiah told him. "You will have a great victory, for the Lord will cause you to conquer!"

"How many times must I tell you to speak only what the Lord tells you to?" the king demanded.

Then Micaiah told him, "I saw all Israel scattered upon the mountains as sheep without a shepherd. And the Lord said, 'Their king is dead; send them to their homes.' "

Turning to Jehoshaphat, Ahab complained, "Didn't I tell you this would happen? He *never* tells me anything good. It's *always* bad."

Then King Ahab ordered Micaiah's arrest. "Take him to Amon, the mayor of the city, and to my son Joash. Tell them, 'The king says to put this fellow in jail and feed him with bread and water—and only enough to keep him alive—until I return in peace.'"

"If you return in peace," Micaiah replied, "it will prove that the Lord has not spoken through me." Then he turned to the people standing nearby and said, "Take note of what I've said."

So King Ahab of Israel and King Jehoshaphat of Judah led their armies to Ramoth-gilead. Ahab said to Jehoshaphat, "You wear your royal robes, but I'll not wear mine!"

So Ahab went into the battle disguised in an ordinary soldier's uniform. For the king of Syria had commanded his 32 chariot captains to fight no one except King Ahab himself. When they saw King Jehoshaphat in his royal robes, they thought, "That's the man we're after." So they wheeled around to attack him. But when Jehoshaphat shouted out to identify himself, they turned back!

However, an arrow shot at random struck King Ahab between the joints of his armor. "Take me out of the battle for I am badly wounded," he groaned to his chariot driver.

The battle became more and more intense as the day wore on; and King Ahab went back in, propped up in his chariot with the blood from his wound running down onto the floorboards. Finally, toward evening he died. Just as the sun was going down the cry ran through his troops. "It's all over—return home! The king is dead!" And his body was taken to Samaria and buried there.

When his chariot and armor were washed beside the pool of Samaria where the prostitutes bathed, dogs came and licked the king's blood just as the Lord had said would happen.

The rest of Ahab's history, including the story of the ivory palace and the cities he built, is written in *The Annals of the Kings of Israel.* So Ahab was buried among his ancestors, and Ahaziah his son became the new king of Israel.

20. Jehoshaphat's Prayer for Deliverance

Jehoshaphat reigned in Jerusalem for 25 years. He did as his father Asa had done, obeying the Lord in all but one thing: he did not destroy the shrines on the hills, so the people sacrificed and burned incense there. He built great freighters to sail to Ophir for gold but they never arrived, for they were wrecked at Ezion-geber.

Jehoshaphat made no more trips to Israel, but remained quietly at Jerusalem. Later he went out again among the people, traveling from Beer-sheba to the hill country of Ephraim to encourage them to worship the God of their ancestors.

He appointed judges throughout the nation in all the larger cities, and instructed them: "Watch your step—I have not appointed you—God has; and He will stand beside you and help you give justice in each case that comes before you. Be very much afraid to give any other decision than what God tells you to."

Later on word reached Jehoshaphat, "A vast army is marching against you from beyond the Salt Sea, from Syria." He was badly shaken by this news and determined to beg help from the Lord; so he announced that all the people of Judah should go without food for a time, in penitence and intercession before the Lord.

People from all across the nation came to Jerusalem to plead unitedly with Him. Jehoshaphat stood among them and prayed this prayer: "O Lord God of our fathers—You are so powerful, so mighty! Who can stand against You? We truly believe that in a time like this—whenever we are faced with any calamity such as war, disease or famine—that You will hear us and rescue us. And now see what the armies of Ammon, Moab and Mount Seir are doing. O our God, won't You stop them? We have no way to protect ourselves against this mighty army. We don't know what to do; but we are looking to You."

Then the Spirit of the Lord came upon one of the men standing there. "Listen to me, all you people of Judah!" he exclaimed. "The Lord says, 'Don't be afraid! Tomorrow go down and attack them! But you will not need to fight! Take your places; stand quietly and see the incredible rescue operation God will perform for you.' "

After consultation with the leaders of the people Jehoshaphat determined that there should be a choir leading the march, clothed in sanctified garments and singing the song "His Loving-kindness Is Forever." And at the moment they began to sing and to praise, the Lord caused the armies of Ammon, Moab and Mount Seir to begin fighting among themselves, and they destroyed each other!

King Jehoshaphat became king of Judah when he was 35 years old and reigned 25 years in Jerusalem. He was buried with his ancestors in the city of his forefather, David; and his son Jehoram took the throne.

21. Elijah's Successor

Now the time came for the Lord to take Elijah to heaven—by means of a whirlwind! Elijah said to Elisha as they left Gilgal, "Stay here, for the Lord has told me to go to Bethel."

But Elisha replied, "I swear to God that I won't leave you!" So they went on together to Bethel.

Then Elijah said to Elisha, "Please stay here, for the Lord has sent me to the Jordan River."

But Elisha replied as before, "I swear to God that I won't leave you."

So they went on together and stood beside the Jordan River as fifty of the young prophets watched from a distance. Then Elijah folded his cloak together and struck the water with it. The river divided and they went across on dry ground! When they arrived on the other side Elijah said to Elisha, "What wish shall I grant you before I am taken away?"

Elisha replied, "Please grant me twice as much prophetic power as you have had."

"You have asked a hard thing," Elijah replied. "If you see me when I am taken from you, then you will get your request. But if not, then you won't."

As they were walking along talking, suddenly a chariot of

fire drawn by horses of fire appeared and drove between them, separating them, and Elijah was carried by a whirlwind into heaven. Elisha saw it and cried out, "My father! My father! The chariot of Israel and the charioteers!"

As they disappeared from sight he tore his robe. Then he picked up Elijah's cloak, returned to the bank of the Jordan River and struck the water with it. "Where is the Lord God of Elijah?" he cried out. And the water parted and Elisha went across!

When the young prophets of Jericho saw what had happened, they exclaimed, "The spirit of Elijah rests upon Elisha!" And they went to meet him and greeted him respectfully.

Now a delegation of the city officials of Jericho visited Elisha. "We have a problem," they told him. "This city is located in beautiful natural surroundings, as you can see; but the water is bad, and causes our women to have miscarriages."

"Well," he said, "bring me a new bowl filled with salt." So they brought it to him. Then he went out to the city well and threw the salt in and declared, "The Lord has healed these waters. They shall no longer cause death or miscarriage." And sure enough! The water was purified just as Elisha had said.

22. Elisha and Naaman's Leprosy

The king of Syria had high admiration for Naaman the commander-in-chief of his army, for he had led his troops to many glorious victories. So he was a great hero, but he was a leper. Bands of Syrians had invaded the land of Israel and among their captives was a little girl who had been given to Naaman's wife as a maid. One day the little girl said to her mistress, "I wish my master would go to see the prophet in Samaria. He would heal him of his leprosy!"

Naaman told the king what the little girl had said. "Go and visit the prophet," the king told him. "I will send a letter of introduction for you to carry to the king of Israel."

So Naaman started out, taking gifts of twenty thousand dollars in silver, sixty thousand dollars in gold and ten suits of clothing. The letter to the king of Israel said: "The man bringing this letter is my servant Naaman; I want you to heal him of his leprosy."

When the king of Israel read it, he tore his clothes and said, "This man sends me a leper to heal! Am I God, that I can kill and give life? He is only trying to get an excuse to invade us again."

But when Elisha the prophet heard about the king of Israel's plight, he sent this message to him: "Why are you so upset? Send Naaman to me, and he will learn that there is a true prophet of God here in Israel."

So Naaman arrived with his horses and chariots and stood at the door of Elisha's home. Elisha sent a messenger out to tell him to go and wash in the Jordan River seven times and he would be healed of every trace of his leprosy! But Naaman was angry and stalked away. "Look," he said, "I thought at least he would come out and talk to me! I expected him to wave his hand over the leprosy and call upon the name of the Lord his God and heal me! Aren't the Abana River and Pharpar River of Damascus better than all the rivers of Israel put together? If it's rivers I need, I'll wash at home and get rid of my leprosy." So he went away in a rage.

But his officers tried to reason with him and said, "If the prophet had told you to do some great thing, wouldn't you have done it? So you should certainly obey him when he says simply to go and wash and be cured!" So Naaman went down to the Jordan River and dipped himself seven times as the prophet had told him to. And his flesh became as healthy as a little child's and he was healed!

Then he and his entire party went back to find the prophet; they stood humbly before him and Naaman said, "I know at last that there is no God in all the world except in Israel; now please accept my gifts."

But Elisha replied, "I swear by Jehovah my God that I will not accept them." Naaman urged him to take them, but he absolutely refused.

But Gehazi, Elisha's servant, said to himself, "My master shouldn't have let this fellow get away without taking his gifts. I will chase after him and get something from him." So Gehazi caught up with him. When Naaman saw him coming, he jumped down from his chariot and ran to meet him.

"Is everything all right?" he asked.

"Yes," he said, "but my master has sent me to tell you that two young prophets from the hills of Ephraim have just arrived, and he would like two thousand dollars in silver and two suits to give to them."

"Take four thousand dollars," Naaman insisted. He gave him two expensive robes, tied up the money in two bags, and gave them to two of his servants to carry back with Gehazi. But when they arrived at the hill where Elisha lived, Gehazi took the bags from the servants and sent the men back. Then he hid the money in his house.

When he went in to his master, Elisha asked him, "Where have you been, Gehazi?"

"I haven't been anywhere," he replied.

But Elisha asked him, "Don't you realize that I was there in thought when Naaman stepped down from his chariot to meet you? Is this the time to receive money and clothing and olive farms and vineyards and sheep and oxen and servants? Because you have done this, Naaman's leprosy shall be upon you and upon your children and your children's children forever." And Gehazi walked from the room a leper, his skin as white as snow.

23. Famine in Samaria

Later on, however, King Ben-hadad of Syria mustered his entire army and besieged Samaria. As a result there was a great famine in the city. After a long while even a donkey's head sold for fifty dollars and a pint of dove's dung brought three dollars!

One day as the king of Israel was walking along the wall of the city, a woman called to him, "Help, my lord the king!"

"If the Lord doesn't help you, what can I do?" he retorted. "I have neither food nor wine to give you. However, what's the matter?"

She replied, "This woman proposed that we eat my son one

day and her son the next. So we boiled my son and ate him, but the next day when I said, 'Kill your son so we can eat him,' she hid him."

When the king heard this he tore his clothes. The people watching noticed through the rip he tore in them that he was wearing an inner robe made of sackcloth next to his flesh. "May God kill me if I don't execute Elisha this very day," the king vowed.

Elisha was sitting in his house at a meeting with the elders of Israel when the king sent a messenger to summon him. But before the messenger arrived Elisha said to the elders, "This murderer has sent a man to kill me. When he arrives, shut the door and keep him out, for his master will soon follow him." While Elisha was still saying this, the messenger arrived, followed by the king.

The prophet declared, "The Lord says that by this time tomorrow two gallons of flour or four gallons of barley grain will be sold in the markets of Samaria for a dollar!"

The officer assisting the king said, "That couldn't happen if the Lord made windows in the sky!"

But Elisha replied, "You will see it happen, but you won't be able to buy any of it!"

Now there were four lepers sitting outside the city gates. "Why sit here until we die?" they asked each other. "We will starve if we stay here and we will starve if we go back into the city; so we might as well go out and surrender to the Syrian army. If they let us live so much the better; but if they kill us we would have died anyway."

So that evening they went out to the camp of the Syrians, but there was no one there! For the Lord had made the whole Syrian army hear the clatter of speeding chariots and a loud galloping of horses and the sounds of a great army approaching. "The king of Israel has hired the Hittites and Egyptians to attack us," they cried out. So they panicked and fled into the night, abandoning their tents, horses, donkeys and everything else.

When the lepers arrived at the edge of the camp they went into one tent after another, eating, drinking wine and carrying out silver and gold and clothing and hiding them. Finally they said to each other, "This isn't right. This is wonderful news and we aren't sharing it with anyone! Even if we wait until morning, some terrible calamity will certainly fall upon us; come on, let's go back and tell the people at the palace."

So they went back to the city and told the watchmen what had happened: They had gone out to the Syrian camp and no one was there! The horses and donkeys were tethered and the tents were all in order, but there was not a soul around! Then the watchmen shouted the news to those in the palace.

The king got out of bed and told his officers, "I know what has happened. The Syrians know we are starving, so they have left their camp and have hidden in the fields, thinking that we will be lured out of the city. Then they will attack us and make slaves of us and get in."

One of his officers replied, "We'd better send out scouts to see. Let them take five of the remaining horses—if something happens to the animals it won't be any greater loss than if they stay here and die with the rest of us!"

Four chariot horses were found and the king sent out two charioteers to see where the Syrians had gone. They followed a trail of clothing and equipment all the way to the Jordan River —thrown away by the Syrians in their haste. The scouts returned and told the king, and the people of Samaria rushed out and plundered the camp of the Syrians. So it was true that two gallons of flour and four gallons of barley were sold that day for one dollar, just as the Lord had said! The king appointed his special assistant to control the traffic at the gate, but he was knocked down and trampled and killed as the people rushed out. This is what Elisha had predicted on the previous day when the king had come to arrest him.

24. Ahab's Family Destroyed

Meanwhile Elisha had summoned one of the young prophets. "Get ready to go to Ramoth-gilead," he told him. "Take this vial of oil with you, and find Jehu (the son of Jehoshaphat, the son of Nimshi). Call him into a private room away from his friends, and pour the oil over his head. Tell him that the Lord has anointed him to be the king of Israel; then run for your life!"

So the young prophet did as he was told. When he arrived in Ramoth-gilead, he found Jehu sitting around with the other army officers. "I have a message for you, sir," he said.

"For which one of us?" Jehu asked.

"For you," he replied.

So Jehu left the others and went into the house, and the young man poured the oil over his head and said, "The Lord God of Israel says, 'I anoint you king of the Lord's people, Israel. You are to destroy the family of Ahab; you will avenge the murder of My prophets and of all My other people who were killed by Jezebel.'"

Jehu went back to his friends and one of them asked him, "What did that crazy fellow want? Is everything all right?"

"You know very well who he was and what he wanted," Jehu replied.

"No, we don't," they said. "Tell us."

So he told them what the man had said and that he had been anointed king of Israel! They quickly carpeted the bare steps with their coats and blew a trumpet, shouting, "Jehu is king!"

"Since you want me to be king," Jehu told the men who were with him, "don't let anyone escape to Jezreel to report what we have done."

Then Jehu jumped into a chariot and rode to Jezreel himself to find King Joram who was lying there wounded. King Ahaziah of Judah was there too, for he had gone to visit him. The watchman on the Tower of Jezreel saw Jehu and his company approaching and shouted, "Someone is coming."

"Send out a rider and find out if he is friend or foe," King Joram shouted back.

So a soldier rode out to meet Jehu. "The king wants to know whether you are friend or foe," he demanded. "Do you come in peace?"

Jehu replied, "What do you know about peace? Get behind me!"

The watchman called out to the king that the messenger

had met them but was not returning. So the king sent out a second rider. He rode up to them and demanded in the name of the king to know whether their intentions were friendly or not.

Jehu answered, "What do you know about friendliness? Get behind me!"

"He isn't returning either!" the watchman exclaimed. "It must be Jehu, for he is driving so furiously."

"Quick! Get my chariot ready!" King Joram commanded.

Then he and King Ahaziah of Judah rode out to meet Jehu. They met him at the field of Naboth, and King Joram demanded, "Do you come as a friend, Jehu?"

Jehu replied, "How can there be friendship as long as the evils of your mother Jezebel are all around us?"

Then King Joram reined the chariot horses around and fled, shouting to King Ahaziah, "There is treachery, Ahaziah! Treason!" Then Jehu drew his bow with his full strength and shot Joram between the shoulders. The arrow pierced his heart, and he sank down dead in his chariot.

When Jezebel heard that Jehu had come to Jezreel, she painted her eyelids and fixed her hair and sat at a window. As Jehu entered the gate of the palace, she shouted at him, "How are you today, you murderer! You son of a Zimri who murdered his master!"

He looked up and saw her at the window and shouted, "Who is on my side?" And two or three eunuchs looked out at him. "Throw her down!" he yelled.

So they threw her out the window, and her blood spattered against the wall and on the horses; and she was trampled by the horses' hoofs. Then Jehu went into the palace for lunch. Afterwards he said, "Someone go and bury this cursed woman, for she is the daughter of a king." But when they went out to bury her, they found only her skull, her feet and her hands.

25. Temple Repairs

It was seven years after Jehu had become the king of Israel

that Joash became king of Judah. He reigned in Jerusalem for 40 years. All his life Joash did what was right because Jehoiada the high priest instructed him.

One day King Joash said to Jehoiada, "The Temple building needs repairing. Whenever anyone brings a contribution to the Lord, whether it is a regular assessment or some special gift, use it to pay for whatever repairs are needed."

But in the twenty-third year of his reign the Temple was still in disrepair. So Joash called for Jehoiada and the other priests and asked them, "Why haven't you done any thing about the Temple? Now don't use any more money for your own needs; from now on it must all be spent on getting the Temple into good condition."

So the priests agreed to set up a special repair fund that would not go through their hands lest it be diverted to care for their personal needs. Jehoiada the priest bored a hole in the lid of a large chest and set it on the right-hand side of the altar at the Temple entrance. The doorkeepers put all of the peoples' contributions into it. Whenever the chest became full, the king's financial secretary and the high priest counted it, put it into bags and gave it to the construction superintendents to pay the carpenters, stonemasons, quarrymen, timber dealers and stone merchants, and to buy the other materials needed to repair the Temple of the Lord. Thus the repairs were completed.

26. Elisha's Death

When Elisha was in his last illness, King Joash visited him and wept over him. "My father! My father! You are the strength of Israel!" he cried.

Elisha told him, "Get a bow and some arrows," and he did. "Open that eastern window," he instructed. Then he told the king to put his hand upon the bow, and Elisha laid his own hands upon the king's hands. "Shoot!" Elisha commanded, and he did. Then Elisha proclaimed, "This is the Lord's arrow, full of victory over Syria; for you will completely conquer the Syrians at Aphek. Now pick up the other arrows and strike them against the floor."

So the king picked them up and struck the floor three times.

But the prophet was angry with him. "You should have struck the floor five or six times," he exclaimed, "for then you would have beaten Syria until they were entirely destroyed; now you will be victorious only three times." So Elisha died and was buried.

27. The Reign of Jeroboam II

Historical Note: It was during the reign of Jeroboam II that Amos and Hosea appeared, prophets to the Northern Kingdom of Israel. Jonah also "prophesied" during this period. See II Kings 14:25.

Meanwhile over in Israel Jeroboam II had become king during the fifteenth year of the reign of Amaziah (son of Joash), king of Judah. Jeroboam's reign lasted 41 years. But he was as evil as Jeroboam I (the son of Nebat) who had led Israel into the sin of worshiping idols.

Jeroboam II recovered the lost territories of Israel between Hamath and the Dead Sea just as the Lord God of Israel had predicted through Jonah (son of Amittai) the prophet from Gath-hepher. For the Lord saw the bitter plight of Israel—that she had no one to help her, and He had not said that He would blot out the name of Israel—so He used King Jeroboam II to save her.

When Jeroboam II died he was buried with the other kings of Israel and his son Zechariah became the new king of Israel. The rest of Jeroboam's biography is recorded in *The Annals of the Kings of Israel*—all that he did, and his great power, and his wars, and how he recovered Damascus and Hamath which had been captured by Judah.

28. End of the Kingdom of Israel

New king of Israel: Hoshea
Father's name: Elah
Length of his reign: nine years in Samaria

217

> Character of his reign: evil—but not as bad as some
> of the other kings of Israel.
> Reigning in Judah at this time: King Ahaz who had
> been the king there for twelve years.

King Shalmaneser of Assyria attacked and defeated King Hoshea, so Israel had to pay heavy annual taxes to Assyria. Then Hoshea conspired against the king of Assyria by asking King So of Egypt to help him shake free of Assyria's power, but this treachery was discovered. At the same time he refused to pay the annual tribute to Assyria. So the king of Assyria put him in prison and in chains for his rebellion.

Now the land of Israel was filled with Assyrian troops for three years, besieging Samaria the capital city of Israel. Finally in the ninth year of King Hoshea's reign Samaria fell and the people of Israel were exiled to Assyria. They were placed in colonies in the city of Halah and along the banks of the Habor River in Gozan, and among the cities of the Medes.

This disaster came upon the nation of Israel because the people worshiped other gods, thus sinning against the Lord their God who had brought them safely out of their slavery in Egypt. They had followed the evil customs of the nations which the Lord had cast out from before them.

Again and again the Lord had sent prophets to warn both Israel and Judah to turn from their evil ways; He had warned them to obey His commandments which He had given to their ancestors through these prophets, but Israel wouldn't listen.

Even Judah refused to obey the commandments of the Lord their God: they too walked in the same evil paths as Israel had, so the Lord rejected all the descendants of Jacob. He punished them by delivering them to their attackers until they were destroyed. For Israel split off from the kingdom of David and chose Jeroboam I (the son of Nebat) as its king. Then Jeroboam drew Israel away from following the Lord. He made them sin a great sin, and the people of Israel never quit doing the evil things that Jeroboam led them into until the Lord finally swept them away, just as all His prophets had warned would happen.

So Israel was carried off to the land of Assyria where they remain to this day. And the king of Assyria transported colonies of people from Babylon, Cuthah, Avva, Hamath and Sepharvaim and resettled them in the cities of Samaria, replacing the people of Israel. So the Assyrians took over Samaria and the other cities of Israel.

29. The Reign of Uzziah

Historical Note: It was during the reign of Uzziah that Isaiah began his prophetic ministry in Jerusalem.

The people of Judah now crowned 16-year-old Uzziah as their new king. After his father's death he rebuilt the city of Eloth and restored it to Judah. In all, he reigned fifty-two years in Jerusalem. His mother's name was Jecoliah from Jerusalem. He followed in the footsteps of his father Amaziah and was, in general, a good king so far as the Lord's opinion of him was concerned. While Zechariah was alive Uzziah was always eager to please God. Zechariah was a man who had special revelations from God. And as long as the king followed the paths of God, he prospered, for God blessed him.

The Ammonites paid annual tribute to him. His fame spread even to Egypt, for he was very powerful. He built fortified towers in Jerusalem at the Corner Gate, and the Valley Gate and at the turning of the wall. He also constructed forts in the Negeb, and made many water reservoirs for he had great herds of cattle out in the valleys and on the plains. He was a man who loved the soil and had many farms and vineyards, both on the hillsides and in the fertile valleys. And he produced engines of war to shoot arrows and huge stones from the towers and battlements, invented by brilliant men and manufactured in Jerusalem. So he became very famous, for the Lord helped him wonderfully until he was very powerful.

But at that point he became proud—and corrupt. He sinned against the Lord his God by entering the forbidden sanctuary of the Temple and personally burning incense upon the altar. Azariah the high priest went in after him with eighty other priests, all brave men, and demanded that he get out.

"It is not for you, Uzziah, to burn incense," they declared. "That is the work of the priest alone, the sons of Aaron who are consecrated to this work. Get out, for you have trespassed, and the Lord is not going to honor you for this!"

Uzziah was furious, and refused to set down the incense burner he was holding. But look! Suddenly—leprosy appeared in his forehead! When Azariah and the others saw it, they rushed him out; in fact, he himself was as anxious to get out as they were to get him out, because the Lord had struck him.

So King Uzziah was a leper until the day of his death and lived in isolation, but cut off from his people and from the Temple. When Uzziah died, he was buried in the royal cemetery even though he was a leper, and his son Jotham became the new king.

30. Hezekiah and the Great Revival

Hezekiah was 25 years old when he became the king of Judah, and he reigned 29 years in Jerusalem. His mother's name was Abijah, the daughter of Zechariah. His reign was a good one in the Lord's opinion, just as his ancestor David's had been.

In the very first month of the first year of his reign, he reopened the doors of the Temple and repaired them. He organized Levites at the Temple into an orchestral group, using cymbals, psalteries and harps. This was in accordance with the directions of David and the prophets Gad and Nathan, who had received their instructions from the Lord. The priests formed a trumpet corps. Then Hezekieh ordered the burnt offering to be placed upon the altar. As the sacrifice began, the instruments of music began to play the songs of the Lord, accompanied by the trumpets.

King Hezekiah ordered the Levites to sing before the Lord some of the psalms of David and of the prophet Asaph. They gladly did this, bowed their heads and worshiped. "The consecration ceremony is now ended," Hezekiah said. "Now bring your sacrifices and thank offerings." So the people from every part of the nation brought their sacrifices and thank offerings. Those who wished to brought burnt offerings too. There was an abundance of burnt offerings and the usual drink offering with each, and many peace offerings. So it was that the Temple was restored to service and the sacrifices offered again. And Hezekiah and all the people were very happy because of what God had accomplished so quickly.

King Hezekiah now sent letters throughout all of Israel, Judah, Ephraim and Manasseh, inviting everyone to come to the Temple at Jerusalem for the annual Passover celebration. "Come back to the Lord God of Abraham, Isaac and Israel," the king's letter said, "so that He will return to us who have escaped from the power of the kings of Assyria."

And so it was that a very large crowd assembled at Jerusalem in the month of May for the Passover celebration. Thus the people of Israel celebrated the Passover at Jerusalem for seven days with great joy. Meanwhile the Levites and priests praised the Lord with music and cymbals day after day. King Hezekiah spoke very appreciatively to the Levites of their excellent music. So for seven days the observance continued, peace offerings were sacrificed and the people confessed their sins to the Lord God of their fathers.

The enthusiasm continued, so it was unanimously decided to prolong the observance for another seven days. King Hezekiah gave the people a thousand young bulls for offerings and seven thousand sheep; and the princes donated a thousand young bulls and ten thousand sheep. And at this time another large group of priests stepped forward and sanctified themselves. Then the people of Judah together with the priests, the Levites, the foreign residents and the visitors from Israel were filled with deep joy. For Jerusalem hadn't seen a celebration like this one since the days of King David's son Solomon. Then the priests and Levites stood and blessed the people, and the Lord heard their prayers from His holy Temple in heaven.

31. Jerusalem Delivered from Assyria

In the fourteenth year of King Hezekiah's reign, Sennacherib, king of Assyria, came to fight against the walled cities of Judah and conquered them. Next he sent his personal representative with a great army from Lachish to confer with King Hezekiah in Jerusalem. He camped near the outlet of the upper pool along the road going past the field where cloth is bleached. Then Eliakim (Hilkiah's son) who was the prime minister of Israel, and Shebna the king's scribe, and Joah (Asaph's son) the royal secretary formed a truce team and went out of the city to meet with him.

The Assyrian ambassador told them to go and say to Hezekiah, "The mighty king of Assyria says you are a fool to think that the king of Egypt will help you. What are the Pharaoh's promises worth? Mere words won't substitute for strength, yet you rely on him for help and have rebelled against me! Egypt is a dangerous ally. She is a sharpened stick that will pierce your hand if you lean on it. That is the experience of everyone who has ever looked to her for help.

"But perhaps you say, 'We are trusting in the Lord our God!' Oh? Isn't He the one your king insulted, tearing down His temples and altars in the hills and making everyone in Judah worship only at the altars here in Jerusalem? My master, the king of Assyria, wants to make a little bet with you!— that you don't have two thousand men left in your entire army! If you do, he will give you two thousand horses for them to ride on! With that tiny army, how can you think of proceeding against even the smallest and worst contingent of my master's troops? For you'll get no help from Egypt."

Then he shouted in Hebrew to the Jews listening on the wall, "Hear the words of the great king, the king of Assyria: Don't let Hezekiah fool you—nothing he can do will save you. Don't let him talk you into trusting in the Lord by telling you the Lord won't let you be conquered by the king of Assyria. Don't listen to Hezekiah, for here is the king of Assyria's offer to you: Give me a present as a token of surrender; open the gates and come out, and I will let you each have your own farm and garden and water, until I can arrange to take you to a country very similar to this one—a country where there are bountiful harvests of grain and grapes, a land of plenty.

"Don't let Hezekiah deprive you of all this by saying the Lord will deliver you from my armies. Has any other nation's

gods ever gained victory over the armies of the king of Assyria? Don't you remember what I did to Hamath and
Arpad? Did their gods save them? And what about Sepharvaim and Samaria? Where are their gods now? Of all the gods
of these lands, which one has ever delivered their people from
my power? Name just one! And do you think this God of
yours can deliver Jerusalem from me? Don't be ridiculous!"

But the people were silent and answered not a word, for Hezekiah had told them to say nothing in reply.

Then Eliakim (son of Hilkiah) the prime minister, and
Shebna the royal scribe and Joah (son of Asaph) the royal secretary went back to Hezekiah with clothes ripped to shreds as a
sign of their despair and told him all that had happened.

King Hezekiah went over to the Temple and prayed, saying,
"O Lord of Hosts, God of Israel enthroned above the cherubim, You alone are God of all the kingdoms of the earth. You
alone made heaven and earth. Listen as I plead; see me as I
pray; look at this letter from King Sennacherib, for he has
mocked the Living God. It is true, O Lord, that the kings of
Assyria have destroyed all those nations. And thrown their
gods into the fire; for they weren't gods at all, but merely idols
carved by men from wood and stone. Of course the Assyrians
could destroy them. O Lord our God, save us so that all the
kingdoms of the earth will know that You are God, and You
alone."

Then Isaiah the son of Amoz sent this message to King Hezekiah: "The Lord God of Israel says, 'This is My answer to
your prayer against Sennacherib, Assyria's king. The Lord
says to him: My people—the helpless virgin daughter of
Zion—laughs at you and scoffs and shakes her head at you in
scorn. Who is it you scoffed against and mocked? Whom did
you revile? At whom did you direct your violence and pride?
It was against the Holy One of Israel! But I know you well—
your comings and goings and all you do—and the way you
have raged against Me. Because of your anger against the
Lord—and I heard it all!—I have put a hook in your nose
and a bit in your mouth and led you back to your own land by
the same road you came.' "

Then God said to Hezekiah, "Here is the proof that I am the

One who is delivering this city from the king of Assyria: This year he will abandon his siege. He will return to his own country by the road he came on, and will not enter this city, says the Lord. For My own honor I will defend it, and in memory of My servant David."

That night the Angel of the Lord went out to the camp of the Assyrians and killed 185,000 soldiers; when the living wakened the next morning, all these lay dead before them. Then Sennacherib, king of Assyria, returned to his own country, to Nineveh. And one day while he was worshiping in the temple of Nisroch his god, his sons Adrammelech and Sharezer killed him with their swords; then they escaped into the land of Ararat, and Esarhaddon his son became king.

32. Hezekiah's Last Years

Hezekiah now became deathly sick, and Isaiah the prophet went to visit him. "Set your affairs in order and prepare to die," Isaiah told him. "The Lord says you won't recover."

Hezekiah turned his face to the wall. "O Lord," he pleaded, "remember how I've always tried to obey You and to please You in everything I do . . ." Then he broke down and cried.

So before Isaiah had left the courtyard, the Lord spoke to him again. "Go back to Hezekiah, the leader of My people, and tell him that the Lord God of his ancestor David has heard his prayer and seen his tears. I will heal him. Three days from now he will be out of bed and at the Temple! I will add fifteen years to his life and save him and this city from the king of Assyria. And it will all be done for the glory of My own name and for the sake of My servant David."

Isaiah then instructed Hezekiah to boil some dried figs and to make a paste of them and spread it on the boil. And he recovered!

At that time Merodach-baladan (the son of King Baladan of Babylon) learned of his sickness and sent ambassadors with greetings and a present to Hezekiah. Hezekiah welcomed them and showed them all his treasures—the silver, gold, spices, aromatic oils, the armory—everything.

Then Isaiah went to King Hezekiah and asked him, "What did these men want? Where are they from?"

"From far away in Babylon," Hezekiah replied.

"What have they seen in your palace?" Isaiah asked.

And Hezekiah replied, "Everything. I showed them all my treasures."

Then Isaiah said to Hezekiah, "Listen to the word of the Lord: The time will come when everything in this palace shall be carried to Babylon. All the treasures of your ancestors will be taken—nothing shall be left. Some of your own sons will be taken away and made into eunuchs who will serve in the palace of the king of Babylon."

"All right," Hezekiah replied, "if this is what the Lord wants, it is good." But he was really thinking, "At least there will be peace and security during the remainder of my own life!"

Hezekiah became very wealthy and was highly honored. He had to construct special treasury buildings for his silver, gold, precious stones, spices, shields and gold bowls. He also built many storehouses for his grain, new wine and olive oil, with many stalls for his animals and folds for the great flocks of sheep and goats he purchased. He acquired many towns, for God had given him great wealth. He damned up the upper spring of Gihon and brought the water down through an aqueduct to the west side of the City of David sector in Jerusalem. He prospered in everything he did. When Hezekiah died he was buried in the royal hillside cemetery among the other kings, and all Judah and Jerusalem honored him at his death.

33. Josiah's Great and Good Reign

Josiah was only 8 years old when he became king. He reigned 31 years in Jerusalem. His was a good reign, as he carefully followed the good example of his ancestor King David. For when he was 16 years old in the eighth year of his reign, he began to search for the God of his ancestor David. Four years later he began to clean up Judah and Jerusalem, destroying the heathen altars and the shame-idols on the hills. He went out personally to watch as the altars of Baal were knocked apart, the obelisks above the altars chopped down, and the shame-idols ground into dust and scattered over the graves of those who had sacrificed to them. He broke down the heathen altars, ground to powder the shame-idols, and chopped down the obelisks. He did this everywhere throughout the whole land of Israel before returning to Jerusalem.

One day when Hilkiah the high priest was at the Temple recording the money collected at the gates, he found an old scroll which turned out to be the laws of God as given to Moses! "Look!" Hilkiah exclaimed to Shaphan, the king's secretary, "See what I have found in the Temple! These are the laws of God!"

When the king heard what these laws required of God's people, he ripped his clothing in despair, and summoned Hilkiah. "Go to the Temple and plead with the Lord for me!" the king told them. "Pray for all that remnant of Israel and Judah! For this scroll says that the reason the Lord's great anger has been poured out upon us is that our ancestors have not obeyed these laws that are written here."

Then the king summoned all the elders of Judah and Jerusalem, and the priests and Levites and all the people great and small to accompany him to the Temple. There the king read the scroll to them—the covenant of God that was found in the Temple. As the king stood before them, he made a pledge to the Lord to follow His commandments with all his heart and soul and to do what was written in the scroll. And he required everyone in Jerusalem and Benjamin to subscribe to this pact with God and all of them did.

Josiah also exterminated the mediums and wizards and every kind of idol worship both in Jerusalem and throughout the land. For Josiah wanted to follow all the laws which were written in the book that Hilkiah the priest had found in the Temple. There was no other king who so completely turned to the Lord and followed all the laws of Moses; and no king since the time of Josiah has approached his record of obedience.

Afterwards King Neco of Egypt led his army intending to fight the Assyrians at Carchemish on the Euphrates River, and

Josiah declared war on him. But King Neco sent ambassadors to Josiah with this message: "I don't want a fight with you, O king of Judah! I have come only to fight the king of Assyria! Leave me alone! God has told me to hurry! Don't meddle with God or He will destroy you, for He is with me."

But Josiah refused to turn back. Instead he led his army into the battle at the Valley of Megiddo. (He laid aside his royal robes so that the enemy wouldn't recognize him.) Josiah refused to believe that Neco's message was from God. The enemy archers struck King Josiah with their arrows and fatally wounded him. "Take me out of the battle," he exclaimed to his aides.

So they lifted him out of his chariot and placed him in his second chariot and brought him back to Jerusalem where he died. He was buried there in the royal cemetery. And all Judah and Jerusalem, including even Jeremiah the prophet, mourned for him, as did the Temple choirs. To this day they still sing sad songs about his death, for these songs of sorrow were recorded among the official lamentations.

34. End of the Kingdom of Judah

Josiah's son Jehoahaz was selected as the new king. He was 23 years old when he began to reign, but lasted only three months. Then he was deposed by the king of Egypt, who demanded an annual tribute from Judah of $250,000. The king of Egypt now appointed Eliakim, the brother of Jehoahaz, as the new king of Judah, and Eliakim's name was changed to Jehoiakim. Jehoahaz was taken to Egypt as a prisoner.

Jehoiakim was 25 years old when he became king, and he reigned 11 years in Jerusalem. But the reign was an evil one. Finally Nebuchadnezzar, king of Babylon, conquered Jerusalem and took away the king in chains to Babylon. Nebuchadnezzar also took some of the golden bowls and other items from the Temple, placing them in his own temple in Babylon. The rest of the deeds of Jehoiakim and all the evil he did are written in *The Annals of the Kings of Judah*. His son Jehoiachin became the new king.

Jehoiachin was 18 years old when he ascended the throne. But he lasted only three months and ten days, and it was an evil reign as far as the Lord was concerned. During his reign the armies of King Nebuchadnezzar of Babylon besieged the city of Jerusalem. Nebuchadnezzar himself arrived during the siege, and King Jehoiachin, all of his officials and the queen mother surrendered to him. The surrender was accepted, and Jehoiachin was imprisoned in Babylon during the eighth year of Nebuchadnezzar's reign. The Babylonians carried home all the treasures from the Temple and the royal palace; and they cut apart all the gold bowls which King Solomon of Israel had placed in the Temple at the Lord's directions.

King Nebuchadnezzar took ten thousand captives from Jerusalem, including King Jehoiachin, his wives, the queen mother and all the princes and officials, the best of the soldiers, craftsmen and smiths. So only the poorest and least skilled people were left in the land. Then the king of Babylon appointed King Jehoiachin's great-uncle, Mattaniah, to be the next king; and he changed his name to Zedekiah.

But King Zedekiah rebelled against the king of Babylon. Then Jeremiah said to Zedekiah, "The Lord, the God of Hosts, the God of Israel, says: If you will surrender to Babylon, you and your family shall live and the city will not be burned. If you refuse to surrender, this city shall be set afire by the Babylonian army and you will not escape."

But when Shephatiah (son of Mattan) and Gedaliah (son of Pashur) and Jucal (son of Shelemiah) and Pashur (son of Malchiah) heard what Jeremiah had been telling the people— that everyone remaining in Jerusalem would die by sword, starvation or disease, but anyone surrendering to the Babylonians would live; and that the city of Jerusalem would surely be captured by the king of Babylon—they went to the king and said: "Sir, this fellow must die. That kind of talk will undermine the morale of the few soldiers we have left, and of all the people too. This man is a traitor."

So King Zedekiah agreed. "All right," he said. "Do as you like—I can't stop you." They took Jeremiah from his cell and lowered him by ropes into an empty cistern in the prison yard. (It belonged to Malchiah, a member of the royal family.) There was no water in it, but there was a thick layer of mire at the bottom, and Jeremiah sank down into it.

When Ebedmelech the Ethiopian, an important palace official, heard that Jeremiah was in the cistern, he rushed out to the Gate of Benjamin where the king was holding court. "My lord the king," he said, "these men have done a very evil thing in putting Jeremiah into the cistern. He will die of hunger, for almost all the bread in the city is gone."

Then the king commanded Ebedmelech to take thirty men with him and pull Jeremiah out before he died. So Ebedmelech took 30 men and went to a discarded supply depot in the palace where used clothing was kept. There he found some old rags and discarded garments which he took to the cistern and lowered to Jeremiah on a rope.

Ebedmelech called down to Jeremiah, "Use these rags under your armpits to protect you from the ropes." Then, when Jeremiah was ready, they pulled him out and returned him to the palace prison where he remained.

One day King Zedekiah sent for Jeremiah to meet him at the side entrance of the Temple. "I want to ask you something," the king said, "and don't try to hide the truth."

Jeremiah said, "If I tell you the truth, you will kill me. And you won't listen to me anyway."

So King Zedekiah swore before Almighty God his Creator that he would not kill Jeremiah or give him to the men who were after his life. "I am afraid to surrender," the king said, "for the Babylonians will hand me over to the Jews who have defected to them, and who knows what they will do to me?"

Jeremiah replied, "You won't get into their hands if only you will obey the Lord; your life will be spared and all will go well for you."

Now King Nebuchadnezzar of Babylon mobilized his entire army and laid siege to Jerusalem, arriving on March 25 of the ninth year of the reign of King Zedekiah of Judah. The siege continued into the eleventh year of his reign. The last food in the city was eaten on July 24, and that night the king and his troops made a hole in the inner wall and fled out toward the Arabah through a gate that lay between the double walls near the king's garden. The Babylonian troops surrounding the city took out after him and captured him in the plains of Jericho, and all his men scattered. He was taken to Riblah where he was tried and sentenced before the king of Babylon. He was forced to watch as his sons were killed before his eyes. Then his eyes were put out and he was bound with chains and taken away to Babylon.

General Nebuzaradan, the captain of the royal bodyguard, arrived at Jerusalem from Babylon on July 22 of the nineteenth year of the reign of King Nebuchadnezzar. He burned down the Temple, the palace, and all the other houses of any worth. He then supervised the Babylonian army in tearing down the walls of Jerusalem. The remainder of the people in the city and the Jewish deserters who had declared their allegiance to the king of Babylon were all taken as exiles to Babylon. But the poorest of the people were left to farm the land.

The Babylonians broke up the bronze pillars of the Temple and the bronze tank and its bases and carried all the bronze to Babylon. They also took all the pots, shovels, firepans, snuffers, spoons and other bronze instruments used for the sacrifices. The gold and silver bowls and all the rest of the gold and silver were melted down to bullion. Then King Nebuchadnezzar appointed Gedaliah (the son of Ahikam and grandson of Shaphan) as governor over the people left in Judah.

35. Jeremiah Freed

Meanwhile King Nebuchadnezzar had told Nebuzaradan to find Jeremiah. "See that he isn't hurt," he said. "Look after him well and give him anything he wants." So Nebuzaradan the captain of the guard, and Nebushazban the chief of the eunuchs, and Nergalsharezer the king's adviser and all the officials took steps to do as the king had commanded. They sent soldiers to bring Jeremiah out of the prison and put him into the care of Gedaliah.

The captain called for Jeremiah and said, "The Lord your

God has brought this disaster on this land, just as He said He would. For these people have sinned against the Lord. That is why it happened. Now I am going to take off your chains and let you go. If you want to come with me to Babylon, fine; I will see that you are well cared for. But if you don't want to come, don't. The world is before you—go where you like. If you decide to stay, then return to Gedaliah who has been appointed as governor of Judah by the king of Babylon and stay with the remnant he rules. But it's up to you; go where you like."

Then Nebuzaradan gave Jeremiah some food and money and let him go. He chose to return to Gedaliah and lived in Judah with the people left in the land.

36. The Babylonian Captivity

The Jews in Moab, and among the Ammonites, and in Edom and other nearby countries heard that a few people were still left in Judah, that the king of Babylon had not taken them all away and that Gedaliah was the governor. Then they all began to return to Judah from the many places to which they had fled. They stopped at Mizpah to discuss their plans with Gedaliah and then went out to the deserted farms and gathered a great harvest of wine grapes and other crops. But seven months later, Ishmael, a member of the royal line, went to Mizpah with ten men and killed Gedaliah and his court—both the Jews and the Babylonians. Then all the men of Judah and the guerrilla leaders fled in panic to Egypt, for they were afraid of what the Babylonians would do to them.

The number of captives taken to Babylon in the seventh year of Nebuchadnezzar's reign was 3,023. Eleven years later he took 832 more; five years after that he sent Nebuzaradan, his captain of the guard, and took 745—a total of 4,600 captives in all.

Jehovah the God of their fathers sent His prophets again and again to warn them, for He had compassion on His people and on His Temple. But the people mocked these messengers of God and despised their words, scoffing at the prophets until the anger of the Lord could no longer be restrained, and there was no longer any remedy.

Then the Lord brought the king of Babylon against them who killed their young men, even going after them right into the Temple; he had no pity upon them, killing even young girls and old men. The Lord used the king of Babylon to destroy them completely.

He also took home with him all the items great and small used in the Temple, and treasures from both the Temple and the palace, and took with him all the royal princes. Then his army burned the Temple and broke down the walls of Jerusalem and burned all the palaces and destroyed all the valuable Temple utensils. Those who survived were taken away to Babylon as slaves to the king and his sons until the kingdom of Persia conquered Babylon.

Thus the word of the Lord spoken through Jeremiah came true.

LAMENTATIONS

The book of Lamentations is an elegy of sorrow and lament over the fall of Jerusalem and the destruction of the Temple. The terrible suffering and distress of the people during the final siege are described in vivid detail.

1. Lament for Jerusalem

Jerusalem's streets once thronged with people are silent now. Like a widow broken with grief, she sits alone in her mourning. She, once queen of nations, is now a slave. She sobs through the night; tears run down her cheeks. Among all her lovers, there is none to help her. All her friends are now her enemies. Why is Judah led away a slave? Because of all the wrong she did to others, making them her slaves. Now she sits in exile far away. There is no rest, for those she persecuted have turned and conquered her. The roads to Zion mourn, no longer filled with joyous throngs who come to celebrate the Temple feasts; the city gates are silent; her priests groan; her virgins have been dragged away. Bitterly she weeps.

And now in the midst of all Jerusalem's sadness she remembers happy bygone days. She thinks of all the precious joys she had before her mocking enemy struck her down— and there was no one to give her aid. For Jerusalem sinned so horribly; therefore she is tossed away like dirty rags. All who honored her despise her now, for they have seen her stripped naked and humiliated. She groans and hides her face. Her enemies have plundered her completely, taking everything precious she owns. She has seen foreign nations violate her sacred Temple—foreigners You had forbidden even to enter.

Her people groan and cry for bread; they have sold all they have for food to give a little strength. "Look, O Lord," she prays, "and see how I'm despised."

Is it nothing to you, all you who pass by? Look and see if there is any sorrow like my sorrow, because of all the Lord has done to me in the day of His fierce wrath. For all these things I weep; tears flow down my cheeks. My Comforter is far away— He who alone could help me. My children have no future; we are a conquered land. Jerusalem pleads for help but no one comforts her. For the Lord has spoken: "Let her neighbors be her foes! Let her be thrown out like filthy rags!"

And the Lord is right; for we rebelled. And yet, O people everywhere, behold and see my anguish and despair; for my sons and daughters are taken far away as slaves to distant lands.

2. Anguish of the City

I have cried until the tears no longer come; my heart is broken, my spirit poured out, as I see what has happened to my people; little children and tiny babies are fainting and dying in the streets. "Mamma, Mamma, we want food," they cry, and then collapse upon their mothers' shrunken breasts. Their lives ebb away like those wounded in battle.

In all the world has there ever been such sorrow? O Jerusalem, what can I compare your anguish to? How can I comfort you? For your wound is deep as the sea. Who can heal you? Your prophets have said so many foolish things, false to the core. They have not tried to hold you back from slavery by pointing out your sins. They lied and said that all was well.

All who pass by scoff and shake their heads and say, "Is this the city called 'Most Beautiful in All the World,' and 'Joy of All the Earth'?"

Then the people wept before the Lord. O walls of Jerusalem, let tears fall down upon you like a river; give yourselves no rest from weeping day or night. Rise in the night and cry to your God. Pour out your hearts like water to the Lord; lift up your hands to Him; plead for your children as they faint with hunger in the streets.

3. Prayer for Mercy

O Lord, all peace and all prosperity have long since gone for You have taken them away. I have forgotten what enjoyment is. All hope is gone; my strength has turned to water, for the Lord has left me. Oh, remember the bitterness and suffering You have dealt to me! For I can never forget these awful years; always my soul will live in utter shame.

Yet there is one ray of hope: His compassion never ends. It is only the Lord's mercies that have kept us from complete destruction. Great is His faithfulness; His loving-kindness begins afresh each day. My soul claims the Lord as my inheritance; therefore I will hope in Him. The Lord is wonderfully good to those who wait for Him, to those who seek for Him. It is good both to hope and wait quietly for the salvation of the Lord.

It is good for a young man to be under discipline, for it causes him to sit apart in silence beneath the Lord's demands, to lie face downward in the dust; then at last there is hope for him. Let him turn the other cheek to those who strike him, and let him accept their awful insults, for the Lord will not abandon him forever. Although God gives him grief, yet He will show compassion too, according to the greatness of His loving-kindness. For He does not enjoy afflicting men and causing sorrow.

Let us examine ourselves and repent and turn again to the Lord. Let us lift our hearts and hands to Him.

4. The Ravages of Famine

How the finest gold has lost its luster! For the inlaid Temple walls are scattered in the streets! The cream of our youth—the finest of the gold—are treated as earthenware pots.

Even the jackals feed their young, but not my people Israel.

They are like cruel desert ostriches, heedless of their babies' cries. The children's tongues stick to the roofs of their mouths for thirst, for there is not a drop of water left. Babies cry for bread but no one can give them any. Those who used to eat fastidiously are begging in the streets for anything at all. Those brought up in palaces now scratch in garbage pits for food. For the sin of my people is greater than that of Sodom where utter disaster struck in a moment without the hand of man.

Our princes were lean and tanned, the finest specimens of men; but now their faces are as black as soot. No one can recognize them. Their skin sticks to their bones; it is dry and hard and withered. Those killed by the sword are far better off than those who die of slow starvation.

5. Prayer for Restoration

O Lord, remember all that has befallen us; see what sorrows we must bear! Our homes, our nation now are filled with foreigners. We are orphans—our fathers dead, our mothers widowed. We must even pay for water to drink; our fuel is sold to us at the highest of prices. We bow our necks beneath the victors' feet; unending work is now our lot.

The old men sit no longer in the city gates; the young no longer dance and sing. The joy of our hearts has ended; our dance has turned to death. Our glory is gone. The crown is fallen from our head. Woe upon us for our sins. Our hearts are faint and weary; our eyes grow dim. Jerusalem and the Temple of the Lord are desolate, deserted by all but wild animals lurking in the ruins.

O Lord, forever You remain the same! Your throne continues from generation to generation. Why do You forget us forever? Why do You forsake us for so long? Turn us around and bring us back to You again! That is our only hope! Give us back the joys we used to have! *Or have You utterly rejected us? Are You angry with us still?*

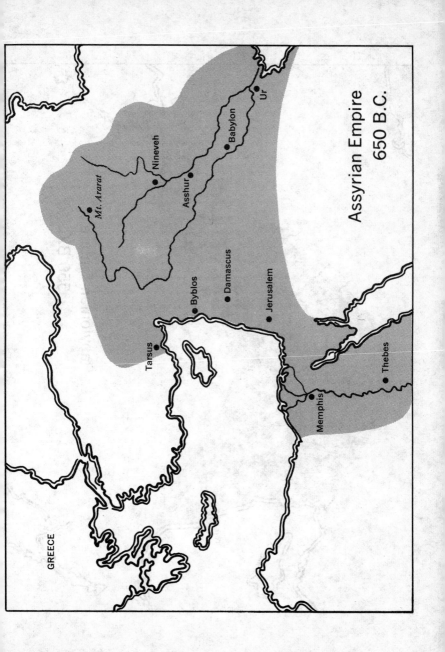

GREECE

Mt. Ararat

Nineveh

Asshur

Babylon

Ur

Byblos

Damascus

Jerusalem

Tarsus

Memphis

Thebes

Assyrian Empire
650 B.C.

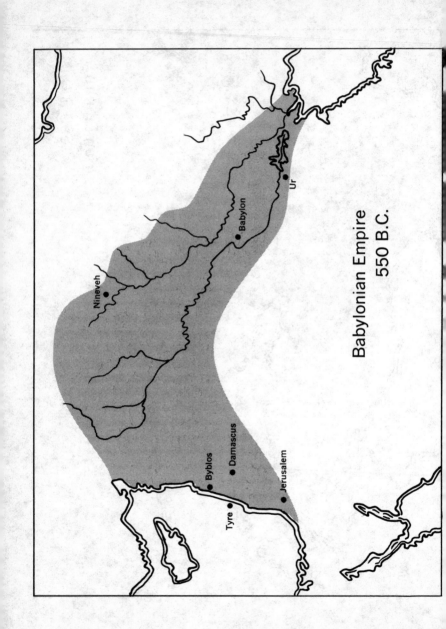

Babylonian Empire
550 B.C.

Nineveh

Babylon

Ur

Byblos

Damascus

Tyre

Jerusalem

PART 5 Stories of Jews Near and Far

JONAH

Selections from Jonah, Daniel, Esther, Ezra and Nehemiah. The events in this part embrace a period of around 350 years —from 760 to 432 B.C.

According to 2 Kings 14:27 Jonah "prophesied" during the reign of Jeroboam II, about 780-740 B.C. Nineveh, the city to which Jonah was sent, was capital of Assyria, a brutal and militaristic nation hated and feared by other peoples of western Asia including Israel. This empire stood for some 300 years but was finally conquered and Nineveh destroyed in 612 B.C. (Compare Jonah with the later book of Nahum.)

1. Jonah's Disobedience

THE Lord sent this message to Jonah the son of Amittai: "Go to the great city of Nineveh and give them this announcement from the Lord: 'I am going to destroy you; for your wickedness rises before Me; it smells to highest heaven.'"

But Jonah was afraid to go and ran away from the Lord. He went down to the seacoast to the port of Joppa where he found a ship leaving for Tarshish. He bought a ticket, went on board and climbed down into the dark hold of the ship to hide there from the Lord. But as the ship was sailing along, suddenly the Lord flung a terrific wind over the sea, causing a great storm that threatened to send them to the bottom. Fearing for their lives, the desperate sailors threw the cargo overboard to lighten the ship and shouted to their gods for help. And all this time Jonah was sound asleep down in the hold.

So the captain went down after him. "What do you mean," he roared, "sleeping at a time like this? Get up and cry to your God and see if He will have mercy on us and save us!"

Then the crew decided to draw straws to see which of them had offended the gods and caused this terrible storm, and Jonah drew the short one. "What have you done," they asked, "to bring this awful storm upon us? Who are you? What is your work? What country are you from? What is your nationality?"

And he said, "I am a Jew; I worship Jehovah, the God of heaven who made the earth and sea." Then he told them he was running away from the Lord.

The men were terribly frightened when they heard this. "Oh, why did you do it?" they shouted; and what should we do to you to stop the storm?" For it was getting worse and worse.

"Throw me out into the sea," he said, "and it will become calm again. For I know this terrible storm has come because of me."

Then they picked up Jonah and threw him overboard into the raging sea—and the storm stopped! Now the Lord had arranged for a huge fish to swallow Jonah. And Jonah was inside the fish three days and three nights.

2. Jonah Inside the Fish

Then Jonah prayed to the Lord his God from inside the fish:

"In my great trouble I cried to the Lord and He answered me; from the depths of death I called, and Lord, You heard me! You threw me into the ocean depths; I sank down into the floods of waters and was covered by Your wild and stormy waves.

"When I had lost all hope, I turned my thoughts once more to the Lord. And my earnest prayer went to You in Your holy Temple. I will never worship anyone but You! For how can I thank You enough for all You have done? I will surely fulfill my promises. For my deliverance comes from the Lord alone."

And the Lord ordered the fish to spit up Jonah on the beach, and it did.

3. The Repentance of Nineveh

Then the Lord spoke to Jonah again: "Go to that great city Nineveh," He said, "and warn them of their doom, as I told you to before!"

So Jonah obeyed and went to Nineveh. Now Nineveh was a very large city with extensive suburbs—so large that it would take three days to walk around it. But the very first day when Jonah entered the city and began to preach, the people repented. Jonah shouted to the crowds that gathered around him, "Forty days from now Nineveh will be destroyed!" And they believed him and declared a fast. From the king on down everyone put on sackcloth, the rough, coarse garments worn at times of mourning. And the king and his nobles sent this message throughout the city: "Let no one, not even the animals, eat anything at all, nor even drink any water. Everyone must wear sackcloth and cry mightily to God; and let everyone turn from his evil ways, from his violence and robbing. Who can tell? Perhaps even yet God will decide to let us live, and will hold back His fierce anger from destroying us."

And when God saw that they had put a stop to their evil ways, He abandoned His plan to destroy them and didn't carry it through.

4. Jonah's Rebuke

This change of plans made Jonah very angry. He complained to the Lord about it: "This is exactly what I thought You'd do, Lord, when I was there in my own country and You first told me to come here. That's why I ran away to Tarshish. For I knew You were a gracious God, merciful, slow to get angry, and full of kindness; I knew how easily You could cancel Your plans for destroying these people."

Then the Lord said, "Is it right to be *angry* about *this?*"

So Jonah went out and sat sulking on the east side of the city, and he made a leafy shelter to shade him as he waited there to see if anything would happen to the city. And when the leaves of the shelter withered in the heat, the Lord arranged for a vine to grow up quickly and spread its broad leaves over Jonah's head to shade him. This made him comfortable and very grateful.

But God also prepared a worm! The next morning the worm ate through the stem of the plant so that it withered away and died. Then when the sun was hot, God ordered a scorching east wind to blow on Jonah, and the sun beat down upon his head until he grew faint and wished to die. He said, "Death is better than this!"

And God said to Jonah, "Is it right for you to be angry because the plant died?"

"Yes," Jonah said, "it is; it is right for me to be angry enough to die!"

Then the Lord said, "You feel sorry for yourself when your shelter is destroyed—though you did no work to put it there—and it is at best short-lived. And why shouldn't I feel sorry for a great city like Nineveh with its 120,000 people in utter spiritual darkness and with all its cattle?"

DANIEL

The events recorded in this book cover a period of more than 70 years. Daniel and his three friends were among the captives brought to Babylon from Jerusalem at the command of Nebuchadnezzar a short time before it was destroyed.

1. The Courage of Daniel and His Friends

Three years after King Jehoiakim began to rule in Judah, Babylon's King Nebuchadnezzar attacked Jerusalem with his armies and the Lord gave him victory over Jehoiakim. When he returned to Babylon, he took along some of the sacred cups from the Temple of God and placed them in the treasury of his god in the land of Shinar.

Then he ordered Ashpenaz who was in charge of his palace personnel to select some of the Jewish youths brought back as captives—young men of the royal family and nobility of Judah—and to teach them the Chaldean language and literature. "Pick strong, healthy, good-looking lads," he said; "those who have read widely in many fields, are well informed, alert and sensible and have enough poise to look good around the palace."

The king assigned them the best of food and wine from his own kitchen during their three-year-training period, planning to make them his counselors when they graduated. Daniel, Hananiah, Mishael and Azariah were four of the young men chosen, and all from the tribe of Judah. However, their superintendent gave them Babylonian names as follows: Daniel was called Belteshazzar; Hananiah was called Shadrach; Mishael was called Meshach; Azariah was called Abednego.

But Daniel made up his mind not to eat the food and wine given to them by the king. He asked the superintendent for permission to eat other things instead. Now as it happened, God had given the superintendent a special appreciation for Daniel and sympathy for his predicament. But he was alarmed by Daniel's suggestion. "I'm afraid you will become pale and thin compared with the other youths your age," he said, "and then the king will behead me for neglecting my responsibilities."

Daniel talked it over with the steward who was appointed by the superintendent to look after them and suggested a ten-day diet of only vegetables and water; then, at the end of this trial period the steward could see how they looked in comparison with the other fellows who ate the king's rich food and decided whether or not to let them continue their diet. The steward finally agreed to the test.

Well, at the end of the ten days, Daniel and his three friends looked healthier and better nourished than the youths who had been eating the food supplied by the king! So after that the steward fed them only vegetables and water without the rich foods and wines!

God gave these four youths great ability to learn and they soon mastered all the literature and science of the time; and God gave to Daniel special ability in understanding the meanings of dreams and visions. When the three-year-training period was completed, the superintendent brought all the young men to the king for oral exams, as he had been ordered to do. King Nebuchadnezzar had long talks with each of them, and none of them impressed him as much as Daniel, Hananiah, Mishael and Azariah. So they were put on his regular staff of advisers. And in all matters requiring information and balanced judgment, the king found these young men's advice ten times better than that of all the skilled magicians and wise astrologers in his realm. Daniel held this appointment as the king's counselor until the first of the reign of King Cyrus.

2. Nebuchadnezzar's Dream

One night in the second year of his reign, Nebuchadnezzar had a terrifying nightmare and awoke trembling with fear. And to make matters worse, he couldn't remember his dream! He immediately called in all his magicians, conjurers, sorcerers and astrologers and demanded that they tell him what his dream had been. "I've had a terrible nightmare," he said as they stood before him, "and I can't remember what it was. Tell me, for I fear some tragedy awaits me."

Then the astrologers speaking in Aramaic said to the king, "Sir, tell us the dream and then we can tell you what it means."

But the king replied, "I tell you, the dream is gone—I can't remember it. And if you won't tell me what it was and what it means, I'll have you torn limb from limb and your houses made into heaps of rubble! But I will give you many wonderful gifts and honors if you tell me what the dream was and what it means. So begin!"

The Chaldeans replied to the king, "There isn't a man alive who can tell others what they have dreamed! And there isn't a king in all the world who would ask such a thing! This is an impossible thing the king requires. No one except the gods can tell you your dream, and they are not here to help."

Upon hearing this the king was furious, and sent out orders to execute all the wise men of Babylon. And Daniel and his companions were rounded up with the others to be killed.

That night in a vision God told Daniel what the king had dreamed. Then Daniel praised the God of heaven, saying, "Blessed be the name of God forever and ever, for He alone has all wisdom and all power. World events are under His control. He removes kings and sets others on their thrones. He gives wise men their wisdom and scholars their intelligence. He reveals profound mysteries beyond man's understanding. He knows all hidden things for He is light, and darkness is no obstacle to Him. I thank and praise You, O God of my fathers, for You have given me wisdom and glowing health; and now even this vision of the king's dream and the understanding of what it means."

Then Daniel went in to see Arioch who had been ordered to execute the wise men of Babylon, and he said, "Don't kill them. Take me to the king and I will tell him what he wants to know."

Then Arioch hurried Daniel to the king and said, "I've found one of the Jewish captives who will tell you your dream!"

The king said to Daniel, "Is this true? Can you tell me what my dream was and what it means?"

Daniel replied, "No wise man, astrologer, magician or wizard can tell the king such things, but there is a God in heaven who reveals secrets, and He has told you in your dream what will happen in the future. This was your dream:

"Oh, King, you saw a huge and powerful statue of a man, shining brilliantly, frightening and terrible. The head of the statue was made of purest gold, its chest and arms were of silver, its belly and thighs of brass, its legs of iron, its feet part iron and part clay. But as you watched a Rock was cut from the mountainside by supernatural means. It came hurtling towards the statue and crushed the feet of iron and clay, smashing them to bits. Then the whole statue collapsed into a heap of iron, clay, brass, silver and gold; its pieces were crushed as small as chaff, and the wind blew them all away. But the Rock that knocked the statue down became a great mountain that covered the whole earth.

"That was the dream; now for its meaning: Your Majesty, you are a king over many kings, for the God of heaven has given you your kingdom, power, strength and glory. You rule the farthest provinces, and even animals and birds are under your control, as God decreed. You are that head of gold.

"But after your kingdom has come to an end, another world power will arise to take your place. This empire will be inferior to yours. And after that kingdom has fallen, yet a third great power represented by the bronze belly of the statue will rise to rule the world.

"Following it, the fourth kingdom will be strong as iron—smashing, bruising and conquering. The feet and toes you saw —part iron and part clay—show that later on this kingdom will be divided. Some parts of it will be as strong as iron and some as weak as clay. This mixture of iron with clay also shows that these kingdoms will try to strengthen themselves by forming alliances with each other through intermarriage of their rulers; but this will not succeed, for iron and clay don't mix.

"During the reigns of those kings, the God of heaven will set up a kingdom that will never be destroyed; no one will ever conquer it. It will shatter all these kingdoms into nothingness; but it shall stand forever, indestructible. That is the meaning of the Rock cut from the mountain without human hands—the Rock that crushed to powder all the iron and brass, the clay, the silver and the gold. Thus the great God has shown what will happen in the future; and this interpretation of your dream is as sure and certain as my description of it."

Then the king made Daniel very great; he gave him many costly gifts and appointed him to be ruler over the whole province of Babylon, as well as chief over all his wise men. At Daniel's request, the king appointed Shadrach, Meshach and Abednego as Daniel's assistants to be in charge of all the affairs of the province of Babylon; Daniel served as chief magistrate in the king's court.

3. Nebuchadnezzar's Humiliation

All these things happened to Nebuchadnezzar: Twelve months after this dream, he was strolling on the roof of the royal palace in Babylon, and saying, "I, by my own mighty power, have built this beautiful city as my royal residence and as the capital of my empire."

While he was still speaking these words, a voice called down from heaven, "Oh, King Nebuchadnezzar, this message is for you: You are no longer ruler of this kingdom. You will be forced out of the palace to live with the animals in the fields and to eat grass like the cows for seven years until you finally realize that God parcels out the kingdoms of men and gives them to anyone He chooses."

That very same hour this prophecy was fulfilled. Nebuchadnezzar was chased from his palace and ate grass like the cows, and his body was wet with dew. His hair grew long as eagles' feathers, and his nails were like birds' claws.

"At the end of seven years I, Nebuchadnezzar, looked up to heaven, and my sanity returned, and I praised and worshiped the Most High God and honored Him who lives forever, whose rule is everlasting, His kingdom evermore. All the people of the earth are nothing when compared to Him, He does whatever He thinks best among the hosts of heaven, as well as here among the inhabitants of earth. No one can stop Him or challenge Him, saying, 'What do You mean by doing these things?'

"When my mind returned to me, so did my honor and glory and kingdom. My counselors and officers came back to me and I was reestablished as head of my kingdom with even greater honor than before. Now I, Nebuchadnezzar, praise and glorify and honor the King of Heaven, the Judge of all, whose every act is right and good; for He is able to take those who walk proudly and push them into the dust!"

4. The Fiery Furnace

King Nebuchadnezzar made a gold statue ninety feet high and nine feet wide and set it up on the Plain of Dura in the province of Babylon; then he sent messages to all the princes, governors, captains, judges, treasurers, counselors, sheriffs and rulers of all the provinces of his empire to come to the dedication of his statue. When they had all arrived and were standing before the monument, a herald shouted out, "Oh, people of all nations and languages, this is the king's command: When the band strikes up, you are to fall flat on the ground to worship King Nebuchadnezzar's golden statue; anyone who refuses to obey will immediately be thrown into a flaming furnace."

So when the band began to play, everyone—whatever his nation, language or religion—fell to the ground and worshiped the statue. But some officials went to the king and accused Daniel and his friends of refusing to worship! Then Nebuchadnezzar in a terrible rage ordered Shadrach, Meshach and Abednego to be brought in before him.

"Is it true, oh Shadrach, Meshach and Abednego," he asked, "that you are refusing to serve my gods or to worship the golden statue I set up? I'll give you one more chance. When the music plays, if you fall down and worship the statue all will be well. But if you refuse you will be thrown into a flaming furnace within the hour. And what god can deliver you out of my hands then?"

Shadrach, Meshach and Abednego replied, "Oh, Nebuchadnezzar, we are not worried about what will happen to us. If we are thrown into the flaming furnace, our God is able to deliver us; and He will deliver us out of your hand, Your Majesty. But if He doesn't, please understand, sir, that even then we will never under any circumstance serve your gods or worship the golden statue you have erected."

Then Nebuchadnezzar was filled with fury and his face became dark with anger at Shadrach, Meshach and Abednego. He commanded that the furnace be heated up seven times hotter than usual, and called for some of the strongest men of his army to bind Shadrach, Meshach and Abednego and throw them into the fire. So they bound them tight with ropes and threw them into the furnace, fully clothed. But suddenly as he was watching, Nebuchadnezzar jumped up in amazement and exclaimed to his advisers, "Didn't we throw three men into the furnace?"

"Yes," they said, "we did indeed, Your Majesty."

"Well, look!" Nebuchadnezzar shouted. "I see *four* men, unbound, walking around in the fire, and they aren't even hurt by the flames! And the fourth looks like a god!"

Then Nebuchadnezzar came as close as he could to the open door of the flaming furnace and yelled: "Shadrach, Meshach and Abednego, servants of the Most High God! Come out! Come here!" So they stepped out of the fire. Then the princes, governors, captains and counselors crowded around them and saw that the fire hadn't touched them—not a hair of their heads was singed. Their coats were unscorched and they didn't even smell of smoke!

Then Nebuchadnezzar said, "Blessed be the God of Shadrach, Meshach and Abednego, for He sent His angel to deliver His trusting servants when they defied the king's commandment and were willing to die rather than serve or worship any god except their own."

Then the king gave promotions to Shadrach, Meshach and Abednego, so that they prospered greatly there in the province of Babylon.

5. The Handwriting on the Wall

Belshazzar the king invited a thousand of his officers to a great feast where the wine flowed freely. While he was drinking he was reminded of the gold and silver cups taken long before from the Temple in Jerusalem during Nebuchadnezzar's reign and brought to Babylon. Belshazzar ordered that these sacred cups be brought in to the feast; and when they arrived he and his princes, wives and concubines drank toasts from them to their idols made of gold and silver, brass and iron, wood and stone.

Suddenly as they were drinking from these cups, they saw the fingers of a man's hand writing on the plaster of the wall opposite the lampstand. The king himself saw the fingers as they wrote. His face blanched with fear, and such terror gripped him that his knees knocked together and his legs gave way beneath him. "Bring the magicians and astrologers!" he screamed. "Bring the Chaldeans! Whoever reads that writing on the wall and tells me what it means will be dressed in purple robes of royal honor with a gold chain around his neck and will become the third ruler in the kingdom!"

But when they came, none of them could understand the writing or tell him what it meant. The king grew more and more hysterical; his face reflected the terror he felt, and his officers too were shaken.

So Daniel was rushed in to see the king. The king asked him, "Are you the Daniel that King Nebuchadnezzar brought from Israel as a Jewish captive? I have heard that you have the spirit of the gods within you and that you are filled with enlightenment and wisdom. My wise men and astrologers have tried to read that writing on the wall and tell me what it means, but they can't. I am told that you can solve all kinds of mysteries. If you can tell me the meaning of those words, I will clothe you in purple robes with a golden chain around your neck and make you the third ruler in the kingdom."

Daniel answered, "Keep your gifts, or give them to someone else; but I will tell you what is meant by *Mene, Mene, Tekel, Parsin*.

"*Mene* means 'numbered'—God has numbered the days of your reign, and they are ended.

"*Tekel* means 'weighed'—You have been weighed in God's balances and have failed the test.

"*Parsin* means 'divided'—Your kingdom will be divided and given to the Medes and Persians."

Then at Belshazzar's command Daniel was robed in purple and a golden chain was hung around his neck, and he was proclaimed third ruler in the kingdom.

That very night Belshazzar, the Chaldean king, was killed; and Darius the Mede entered the city and began reigning at the age of 62.

6. Daniel in the Lions' Den

Darius divided the kingdom into 120 provinces, each under a governor. The governors were accountable to three presidents (Daniel was one of them) so that the king could administer the kingdom efficiently. Daniel soon proved himself more capable than all the other presidents and governors, for he had great ability. The king began to think of placing him over the entire empire as his administrative officer. This made the other presidents and governors very jealous, and they began searching for some fault in the way Daniel was handling his affairs so that they could complain to the king about him. But they couldn't find anything to criticize! He was faithful and honest and made no mistakes. So they concluded, "Our only chance is his religion!"

They decided to go to the king and say, "King Darius, live forever! We presidents, governors, counselors and deputies have unanimously decided that you should make a law, irrevocable under any circumstance, that for the next 30 days anyone who asks a favor of God or man—except from you, Your Majesty—shall be thrown to the lions."

King Darius signed the law, but though Daniel knew about it, he went home and knelt down as usual in his upstairs bedroom with its windows open towards Jerusalem and prayed three times a day, just as he always had, giving thanks to his God.

Then the men thronged to Daniel's house and found him praying there, asking favors of his God. They rushed back to the king and reminded him about his law. "Haven't you signed a decree," they said, "that permits no petitions to any God or man—except you— for 30 days? And anyone disobeying will be thrown to the lions?"

"Yes," the king replied, "it is a law of the Medes and Persians that cannot be altered or revoked."

Then they told the king, "That fellow Daniel, one of the Jewish captives, is paying no attention to you or your law. He is asking favors of his God three times a day."

Reluctantly the king gave the order for Daniel's arrest, and he was taken to the den of lions. The king said to him, "May your God whom you worship continually deliver you." And then they threw him in.

Very early the next morning the king hurried out to the lions' den and called out in anguish, "Oh, Daniel, servant of the Living God, was your God whom you worship continually able to deliver you from the lions?"

Then he heard a voice! "Your Majesty, live forever!" It was Daniel! "My God has sent His angel," he said, "to shut the lions' mouths so that they can't touch me; for I am innocent before God; nor, sir, have I wronged you."

The king was beside himself with joy and ordered that Daniel be lifted from the den. And not a scratch was found on him, because he believed in his God.

So Daniel prospered in the reign of Darius and in the reign of Cyrus the Persian.

ESTHER

Ahasuerus or Xerxes was king of Persia from 482 to 465 B.C. Thus the story of his wife Esther must fit somewhere between those two dates. From a strictly chronological viewpoint this story belongs after Ezra, but as the setting is in Persia and because the books of Daniel and Esther show a similar spiritual courage it seems proper to place the two together.

1. Vashti Deposed

It was the third year of the reign of King Ahasuerus, emperor of vast Media-Persia with its 127 provinces stretching from India to Ethiopia. This was the year of the great celebration at Shushan Palace to which the emperor invited all his governors, aides and army officers, bringing them in from every part of Media-Persia for the occasion. The celebration lasted six months, a tremendous display of the wealth and glory of his empire. When it was all over, the king gave a special party for the palace servants and officials—janitors and cabinet officials alike—for seven days of revelry, held in the courtyard of the palace garden. Drinks were served in golden goblets of many designs, and there was an abundance of royal wine for the king was feeling very generous.

On the final day, when the king was feeling high, half-drunk from wine, he told the seven eunuchs who were his personal aides—Mehuman, Biztha, Harbona, Bigtha, Abagtha, Zethar, and Carcas—to bring Queen Vashti to him with the royal crown upon her head so that all the men could gaze upon her beauty, for she was a very beautiful woman. But when they conveyed the emperor's order to Queen Vashti, she refused to come.

The king was furious, but first consulted his lawyers, for he did nothing without their advice. They were men of wisdom who knew the temper of the times as well as Persian law and justice, and the king trusted their judgment. These men were Carshena, Shethar, Admatha, Tarshish, Meres, Marsena and Memucan, seven high officials of Media-Persia. They were his personal friends as well as being the chief officers of the government.

"What shall we do about this situation?" he asked them. "What penalty does the law provide for a queen who refuses to obey the king's orders properly sent through his aides?"

Memucan answered for the others, "Queen Vashti has wronged not only the king but every official and citizen of your empire. We suggest that, subject to your agreement, you issue a royal edict, a law of the Medes and Persians that can never be changed, that Queen Vashti be forever banished from your presence and that you choose another queen more worthy than she." The king and all his aides thought this made good sense, so he followed Memucan's counsel.

2. Esther Crowned Queen

After King Ahasuerus' anger had cooled, he began brooding over the loss of Vashti, realizing that he would never see her again. So his aides suggested, "Let us go and find the most beautiful girls in the empire and bring them to the king for his pleasure. We will appoint agents in each province to select young lovelies for the royal harem. Hegai, the eunuch in charge, will see that they are given beauty treatments, and after that, the girl who pleases you most shall be the queen instead of Vashti." This suggestion naturally pleased the king very much, and he put the plan into immediate effect.

Now there was a certain Jew at the palace named Mordecai (son of Jair, son of Shimei, son of Kish, a Benjaminite). He had been captured when Jerusalem was destroyed by King Nebuchadnezzar and had been exiled to Babylon along with King Jeconiah of Judah and many others. This man had a beautiful and lovely young cousin, Hadassah (also called Esther), whose father and mother were dead and whom he had adopted into his family and raised as his own daughter. So now as a result of the king's decree, Esther was brought to the king's harem at Shushan Palace, along with many other young girls. Hegai, who was responsible for the harem, was very much impressed with her and did his best to make her happy; he ordered a special menu for her, favored her for the beauty treatments, gave her seven girls from the palace as her maids, and gave her the most luxurious apartment in the harem. Esther hadn't told anyone that she was a Jewess, for Mordecai had said not to.

When it was Esther's turn to go to the king, she accepted the advice of Hegai, the eunuch in charge of the harem, dressing according to his instructions. And all the other girls exclaimed with delight when they saw her. So Esther was taken to the palace of the king in January of the seventh year of his reign.

Well, the king loved Esther more than any of the other girls. He was so delighted with her that he set the royal crown on her head and declared her queen instead of Vashti.

3. Haman's Cruel Plot

One day as Mordecai was on duty at the palace, two of the king's eunuchs, Bigthan and Teresh who were guards at the palace gate, became angry at the king and plotted to assassinate him. Mordecai heard about it and passed on the information to Queen Esther who told the king, crediting Mordecai with the information. An inquisition was held, the two men found guilty and impaled alive. This was all duly recorded in the book of the history of King Ahasuerus' reign.

Soon afterwards King Ahasuerus appointed Haman (son of Hammedatha the Agagite) as prime minister. He was the most powerful official in the empire next to the king himself. Now all the king's officials bowed before him in deep reverence whenever he passed by, for so the king had commanded. But Mordecai refused to bow.

"Why are you disobeying the king's commandment?" the others demanded day after day, but he still refused. Finally they spoke to Haman about it. Haman decided, however, not to lay hands on Mordecai alone, but to move against all of Mordecai's people, the Jews, and destroy all of them throughout the whole kingdom of Ahasuerus. The most propitious time for this action was determined by throwing dice. This was done in April of the twelfth year of the reign of Ahasuerus and February of the following year was the date indicated.

Haman now approached the king about the matter. "There is a certain race of people scattered through all the provinces of your kingdom," he began, "and their laws are different from those of any other nation, and they refuse to obey the king's laws; therefore it is not in the king's interest to let them live. If it please the king, issue a decree that they be destroyed, and I will pay $20 million into the royal treasury for the expenses involved in this purge."

The king agreed, confirming his decision by removing his ring from his finger and giving it to Haman, telling him, "Keep the money, but go ahead and do as you like with these people—whatever you think best."

Two or three weeks later, Haman called in the king's secretaries and dictated letters to the governors and officials throughout the empire, to each province in its own languages and dialects. These letters were signed in the name of King Ahasuerus and sealed with his ring. They were then sent by messengers into all the provinces of the empire, decreeing that the Jews—young and old, women and children—must all be killed on the thirteenth day of February of the following year and their property given to those who killed them.

4. Esther's Heroic Decision

When Mordecai learned what had been done, he tore his clothes, put on sackcloth and ashes and went out into the city, crying with a loud and bitter wail. Then he stood outside the gate of the palace, for no one was permitted to enter in mourning clothes. Mordecai also gave Hathach a copy of the king's decree dooming all Jews, telling him to show it to Esther, letting her know what was happening and to ask her to go to the king to plead for her people.

So Hathach returned to Esther with Mordecai's message. Esther told Hathach to go back and say to Mordecai, "All the world knows that anyone, whether man or woman, who goes into the king's inner court without his summons is doomed to die unless the king holds out his golden scepter; and the king has not called for me to come to him in more than a month." So Hathach gave Esther's message to Mordecai.

This was Mordecai's reply to Esther: "Do you think you will escape there in the palace when all other Jews are killed? If you keep quiet at a time like this, God will deliver the Jews from some other source, but you and your relatives will die. What's more, who can say but that God has brought you into the palace for just such a time as this?"

Then Esther said to tell Mordecai: "Go and gather together all the Jews of Shushan and fast for me; do not eat or drink for three days, night or day; and I and my maids will do the same. Then, though it is strictly forbidden, I will go in to see the king; and if I perish, I perish."

5. Gallows for Mordecai

Three days later Esther put on her royal robes and entered the inner court just beyond the royal hall of the palace where the king was sitting upon his royal throne. And when he saw Queen Esther standing there in the inner court, he welcomed her, holding out the golden scepter to her. So Esther approached and touched its tip. Then the king asked her, "What do you wish, Queen Esther? What is your request? I will give it to you, even if it is half the kingdom!"

And Esther replied, "If it please Your Majesty, I want you and Haman to come to a banquet I have prepared for you today."

The king turned to his aides. "Tell Haman to hurry!" he said. So the king and Haman came to Esther's banquet.

During the wine course the king said to Esther, "Now tell me what you really want, and I will give it to you, even if it is half of the kingdom!"

Esther replied, "My request, my deepest wish, is that if Your Majesty loves me and wants to grant my request, that you come again with Haman tomorrow to the banquet I shall prepare for you. And tomorrow I will explain what this is all about."

What a happy man was Haman as he left the banquet! But when he saw Mordecai there at the gate, not standing up or trembling before him, he was furious. However, he restrained himself and went on home and gathered together his friends and Zeresh his wife, and told them of the banquet and of Mordecai.

"Well," suggested Zeresh his wife and all his friends, "Get ready a 75-foot-high gallows, and in the morning ask the king to let you hang Mordecai on it; and when this is done you can go on your merry way with the king to the banquet." This pleased Haman immensely and he ordered the gallows built.

6. Haman's Humiliation

That night the king had trouble sleeping and decided to read awhile. He ordered the historical records of his kingdom from the library, and in them he came across the item telling how Mordecai had exposed the plot of Bigthan and Teresh, two of the king's eunuchs, serving as watchmen at the palace gates, who had plotted to assassinate him.

"What reward did we ever give Mordecai for this?" the king asked.

"Nothing!" his courtiers replied.

"Who is on duty in the outer court?" the king inquired. Now as it happened Haman had just arrived in the outer court. of the palace to ask the king to hang Mordecai from the gallows he was building.

So the courtiers replied to the king, "Haman is out there."

"Bring him in," the king ordered.

So Haman came in and the king said to him, "What should I do to honor a man who truly pleases me?"

Haman thought to himself, "Who would he want to honor more than me?" So he replied, "Bring out some of the royal robes the king himself has worn, the king's own horse and the royal crown, and instruct one of the king's most noble princes to robe the man and to lead him through the streets on the king's own horse, shouting before him, 'This is the way the king honors those who truly please him!' "

"Excellent!" the king said to Haman. "Hurry and take these robes and my horse, and do just as you have said—to Mordecai the Jew, who works at the Chancellery. Follow every detail you have suggested."

So Haman took the robes and put them on Mordecai, mounted him on the king's own steed and led him through the streets of the city, shouting "This is the way the king honors those he delights in." Afterwards Mordecai returned to his job, but Haman hurried home utterly humiliated.

7. Haman's Execution

Later that day the king and Haman came to Esther's banquet. And again during the wine course the king asked her, "What is your petition, Queen Esther? What do you wish? Whatever it is I will give it to you, even if it is half of my kingdom!"

At last Queen Esther replied, "If I have won your favor, O king, and if it please Your Majesty, save my life and the lives of my people. For I and my people have been sold to those who will destroy us. We are doomed to destruction and slaughter. If we were only to be sold as slaves perhaps I could remain quiet, though even then there would be incalculable damage to the king that no amount of money would begin to cover."

"What are you talking about?" King Ahasuerus demanded. "Who would dare touch you?"

Esther replied, "This wicked Haman is our enemy." Then Haman grew pale with fright before the king and queen. The king jumped to his feet and went out into the palace garden as Haman stood up to plead for his life to Queen Esther, for he knew that he was doomed. In despair he fell upon the couch where Queen Esther was reclining, just as the king returned from the palace garden.

"Will he even rape the queen right here in the palace before my very eyes?" the king roared. Instantly the death veil was placed over Haman's face.

Then Harbona, one of the king's aides, said, "Sir, Haman has just ordered a 75-foot gallows constructed to hang Mordecai, the man who saved the king from assassination! It stands in Haman's courtyard."

"Hang Haman on it," the king ordered. So they did, and the king's wrath was pacified.

8. Plot Against Jews Foiled

On that same day King Ahasuerus gave the estate of Haman, the Jews' enemy, to Queen Esther. Then Mordecai was brought before the king, for Esther had told the king that he was her cousin and stepfather. The king took off his ring—which he had taken back from Haman—and gave it to Mordecai, appointing him prime minister, and Esther appointed Mordecai to be in charge of Haman's estate.

And now once more Esther came before the king, falling down at his feet and begging him with tears to stop Haman's plot against the Jews.

Then King Ahasuerus said to Queen Esther and Mordecai the Jew, "I have given Esther the palace of Haman and he has been hanged upon the gallows because he tried to destroy you. Now go ahead and send a message to the Jews, telling them whatever you want to in the king's name. Seal it with the king's ring so that it can never be reversed."

This decree gave the Jews everywhere permission to unite in the defense of their lives and their families, to destroy all the forces opposed to them and to take their property.

And in every city and province, as the king's decree arrived, the Jews were filled with joy and had a great celebration and declared a holiday.

So on the twenty-eighth day of February, the day the two decrees of the king were to be put into effect—the day the Jews' enemies had hoped to vanquish them, though it turned out quite to the contrary—the Jews gathered in their cities throughout all the king's provinces to defend themselves against any who might try to harm them; but no one tried, for they were greatly feared. And all the rulers of the provinces—the governors, officials and aides—helped the Jews for fear of Mordecai; for Mordecai was a mighty name in the king's palace and his fame was known throughout all the provinces; for he had become more and more powerful.

9. Feast of Purim Inaugurated

Mordecai wrote a history of all these events, and sent letters to the Jews near and far throughout all the king's provinces, encouraging them to declare an annual holiday on the fourteenth and fifteenth of March to celebrate with feasting, gladness and the giving of gifts this historic day when the Jews were saved from their enemies, when their sorrow was turned to gladness and their mourning into happiness.

The Jews adopted Mordecai's suggestion and began this annual custom, as a reminder of the time when Haman (son of Hammedatha the Agagite), the enemy of all the Jews, had plotted to destroy them at the time determined by a throw of the dice; and to remind them that when the matter came before the king, he issued a decree causing Haman's plot to boomerang, and Haman and his sons were hanged on the gallows. That is why this celebration is called "Purim," because the word for "throwing dice" in Persian is "pur."

All the Jews throughout the realm agreed to inaugurate this tradition and to pass it on to their descendants and to all who became Jews; they declared they would never fail to celebrate these two days at the appointed time each year. It would be an annual event from generation to generation, celebrated by every family throughout the countryside and cities of the empire, so that the memory of what had happened would never perish from the Jewish race.

Meanwhile, Queen Esther had written a letter throwing her full support behind Mordecai's letter inaugurating this annual feast of Purim. Thus the commandment of Esther confirmed these dates and it was recorded as law.

EZRA

Ezra covers approximately 78 years. Zerubbabel led the first group of exiles back to their homeland in 537 B.C. Ezra led the second in 458 B.C. The reconstruction of the Temple was finally completed in 516 B.C. For the ministry of Haggai and Zechariah in connection with the rebuilding of the Temple, see Book II pages 387-393.

1. First Return of the Exiles

During the first year of the reign of King Cyrus of Persia, the Lord fulfilled Jeremiah's prophecy by giving King Cyrus the desire to send this proclamation throughout his empire (he also put it into the permanent records of the realm):

"Cyrus, King of Persia, hereby announces that Jehovah, the God of heaven who gave me my vast empire, has now given me the responsibility of building Him a Temple in Jerusalem in the land of Judah. All Jews throughout the kingdom may now return to Jerusalem to rebuild this Temple of Jehovah who is the God of Israel and of Jerusalem. May His blessings rest upon you. Those Jews who do not go should contribute toward the expenses of those who do and also supply them with clothing, transportation, supplies for the journey and a freewill offering for the Temple."

Then God gave a great desire to the leaders of the tribes of Judah and Benjamin, and to the priests and Levites, to return to Jerusalem at once to rebuild the Temple. And all the Jewish exiles who chose to remain in Persia gave them whatever assistance they could, as well as gifts for the Temple.

King Cyrus himself donated the gold bowls and other valuable items which King Nebuchadnezzar had taken from the Temple at Jerusalem and had placed in the temple of his own gods. He instructed Mithredath, the treasurer of Persia, to present these gifts to Shesh-bazzar, the leader of the exiles returning to Judah. The items Cyrus donated included:

- 1,000 gold trays
- 1,000 silver trays
- 29 censers
- 30 bowls of solid gold
- 2,410 silver bowls (of various designs)
- 1,000 miscellaneous items.

In all there were 5,469 gold and silver items turned over to Shesh-bazzar to take back to Jerusalem.

A total of 42,360 persons returned to Judah, in addition to 7,337 slaves and 200 choir members, both men and women. They took with them 736 horses, 245 mules, 435 camels and 6,720 donkeys. Some of the leaders were able to give generously toward the rebuilding of the Temple, and each gave as much as he could. The total value of their gifts amounted to $300,000 of gold, $170,000 of silver and 100 robes for the priests.

So the priests and Levites and some of the common people settled in Jerusalem and its nearby villages; and the singers, the gatekeepers, the Temple workers and the rest of the people returned to the other cities of Judah from which they had come.

2. Foundation of the Temple Completed

During the month of September everyone who had returned to Judah came to Jerusalem from their homes in the other towns. Then Jeshua (son of Jozadak) with his fellow priests, and Zerubbabel (son of Shealtiel) and his clan, rebuilt the altar of the God of Israel and sacrificed burnt offerings upon it as instructed in the laws of Moses, the man of God. The altar was rebuilt on its old site, and it was used immediately to sacrifice morning and evening burnt offerings to the Lord.

It was on the fifteenth day of September that the priests began sacrificing the burnt offerings to the Lord. (This was before they began building the foundation of the Temple.) Then they hired masons and carpenters and bought cedar logs from the people of Tyre and Sidon, paying for them with food, wine and olive oil. The logs were brought down from the Lebanon Mountains and floated along the coast of the Mediterranean Sea to Joppa, for King Cyrus had included this provision in his grant.

The actual construction of the Temple began in June of the second year of their arrival at Jerusalem. The supervision of the entire project was given to Jeshua, Kadmi-el, Henadad and their sons and relatives, all of whom were Levites. When the builders completed the foundation of the Temple, the priests put on their priestly robes and blew their trumpets; and the descendants of Asaph crashed their cymbals to praise the Lord in the manner ordained by King David. They sang rounds of praise and thanks to God, singing this song: "He is good, and His love and mercy toward Israel will last forever." Then all the people gave a great shout praising God because the foundation of the Temple had been laid.

But many of the priests and Levites and other leaders—the old men who remembered Solomon's beautiful Temple—wept aloud while others were shouting for joy! So the shouting and the weeping mingled together in a loud commotion that could be heard from far away!

3. The Temple Rebuilt

When the enemies of Judah and Benjamin heard that the exiles had returned and were rebuilding the Temple, they approached Zerubbabel and the other leaders and suggested, "Let us work with you, for we are just as interested in your God as you are; we have sacrificed to Him ever since King Esar-haddon of Assyria brought us here."

But Zerubbabel and Jeshua and the other Jewish leaders replied, "No, you may have no part in this work. The Temple of the God of Israel must be built by the Israelis, just as King Cyrus has commanded."

Then the local residents tried to discourage and frighten them by sending agents to tell lies about them to King Cyrus. This went on during his entire reign and lasted until King Darius took the throne. Following is the letter which Governor Tattenai, Shethar-bozenai and the other officials sent to King Darius:

"To King Darius:

"Greetings! We wish to inform you that we went to the construction site of the Temple of the great God of Judah. It is being built with huge stones, and timber is being laid in the city walls. The work is going forward with great energy and success. We asked the leaders, 'Who has given you permission to do this?' And we demanded their names so that we could notify you.

"But they insist that King Cyrus of Babylon during the first year of his reign issued a decree that the Temple should be rebuilt, and they say King Cyrus returned the gold and silver bowls which Nebuchadnezzar had taken from the Temple in Jerusalem and had placed in the temple of Babylon. They say these items were delivered into the safekeeping of a man named Shesh-bazzar, whom King Cyrus appointed as governor of Judah. The king instructed him to return the bowls to Jerusalem and to let the Temple of God be built there as before.

"So Shesh-bazzar came and laid the foundations of the Temple at Jerusalem; and the people have been working on it ever since, though it is not yet completed. We request that you search in the royal library of Babylon to discover whether King Cyrus ever made such a decree; and then let us know your pleasure in this matter."

So King Darius issued orders that a search be made in the Babylonian archives where documents were stored. Eventually the record was found in the palace at Ecbatana in the province of Media. This is what it said:

"In this first year of the reign of King Cyrus, a decree has been sent out concerning the Temple of God at Jerusalem where the Jews offer sacrifices. It is to be rebuilt, and the foundations are to be strongly laid. The height will be 90 feet and the width will be 90 feet. There will be three layers of huge stones in the foundation, topped with a layer of new timber. All expenses will be paid by the king. And the gold and silver bowls which were taken from the Temple of God by Nebuchadnezzar shall be taken back to Jerusalem and put into the Temple as they were before."

So King Darius sent this message to Governor Shethar-bozenai and the other officials west of the Euphrates: "Do not disturb the construction of the Temple. Let it be rebuilt on its former site, and don't molest the governor of Judah and the other leaders in their work. Moreover, I decree that you are to pay the full construction costs without delay from my taxes collected in your territory."

Governor Tattenai, Shethar-bozenai and their companions complied at once with the command of King Darius. So the Jewish leaders continued in their work; and they were greatly encouraged by the preaching of the prophets Haggai and Zechariah (son of Iddo).

The Temple was finally finished, as had been commanded by God and decreed by Cyrus, Darius and Artaxerxes, the kings of Persia. The completion date was February eighteenth in the sixth year of the reign of King Darius. The Temple was then dedicated with great joy by the priests, the Levites and all the people. Then the priests and Levites were divided into their various service corps to do the work of God as instructed in the laws of Moses.

The Passover was celebrated on the first day of April. For by that time many of the priests and Levites had consecrated themselves. And some of the heathen people who had been re-located in Judah turned from their immoral customs and joined the Israelis in worshiping the Lord God. They, with the entire nation, ate the Passover feast and celebrated the Feast of Unleavened Bread for seven days. There was great joy throughout the land because the Lord had caused the king of Assyria to be generous to Israel and to assist in the construction of the Temple.

4. Second Return Led by Ezra

As a Jewish religious leader, Ezra was well versed in Jehovah's laws which Moses had given to the people of Israel. He asked to be allowed to return to Jerusalem, and the king granted his request; for the Lord his God was blessing him. Many ordinary people as well as priests, Levites, singers, gatekeepers and Temple workers traveled with him. They left Babylon in the middle of March in the seventh year of the reign of Artaxerxes and arrived at Jerusalem in the month of August, for the Lord gave them a good trip. This was because Ezra had determined to study and obey the laws of the Lord and to become a Bible teacher, teaching those laws to the people of Israel.

King Artaxerxes presented this letter to Ezra the priest, the student of God's commands:

"From: Artaxerxes, the king of kings.

"To: Ezra, the priest, the teacher of the laws of the God of heaven. I decree that any Jew in my realm, including the priests and Levites, may return to Jerusalem with you. And take with you the gold bowls and other items we are giving you for the Temple of your God at Jerusalem. If you run short of money for the construction of the Temple or for any similar needs, you may requisition funds from the royal treasury.

"I, Artaxerxes the king, send this decree to all the treasurers in the provinces west of the Euphrates River: 'You are to give Ezra whatever he requests of you (for he is a priest and teacher of the laws of the God of heaven), up to $200,000 in silver; 1,255 bushels of wheat; 990 gallons of wine; any amount of salt; and whatever else the God of heaven demands for His Temple; for why should we risk God's wrath against the king and his sons? I also decree that no priest, Levite, choir member, gatekeeper, Temple attendant or other worker in the Temple shall be required to pay taxes of any kind.'

"And you, Ezra, are to use the wisdom God has given you to select and appoint judges and other officials to govern all the people west of the Euphrates River; if they are not familiar with the laws of your God, you are to teach them. Anyone refusing to obey the law of your God and the law of the king shall be punished immediately by death, banishment, confiscation of goods or imprisonment."

Then Ezra gave thanks, speaking these words:

"Praise the Lord God of our ancestors who made the king want to beautify the Temple of the Lord in Jerusalem! And praise God for demonstrating such loving-kindness to me by honoring me before the king and his Council of Seven and before all of his mighty princes! I was given great status because the Lord my God was with me; and I persuaded some of the leaders of Israel to return with me to Jerusalem.

"We assembled at the Ahava River and camped there for three days while I went over the lists of the people and the priests who had arrived. Then I declared a fast while we were at the Ahava River so that we would humble ourselves before our God; and we prayed that He would give us a good journey and protect us, our children and our goods as we traveled. For I was ashamed to ask the king for soldiers and cavalry to accompany us and protect us from the enemies along the way. After all, we had told the king that our God would protect all those who worshiped Him, and that disaster could come only to those who had forsaken Him! So we fasted and begged God to take care of us. And He did.

"We broke camp at the Ahava River at the end of March and started off to Jerusalem; and God protected us and saved us from enemies and bandits along the way. So at last we arrived safely at Jerusalem. On the fourth day after our arrival the silver, gold and other valuables were weighed in the Temple by Meremoth (the son of Uriah the priest), Eleazar (son of Phinehas), Jozabad (son of Jeshua), and Noadiah (son of Binnui)—all of whom were Levites. A receipt was given for each item, and the weight of the gold and silver was noted. Then everyone in our party sacrificed burnt offerings to the God of Israel."

But then the Jewish leaders came to tell me that many of the Jewish people and even some of the priests and Levites had taken up the horrible customs of the heathen people who lived in the land—the Canaanites, Hittites, Perizzites, Jebusites, Ammonites, Moabites, Egyptians and Amorites: the men of Israel had married girls from these heathen nations and had taken them as wives for their sons. So the holy people of God were being polluted by these mixed marriages; and the political leaders were some of the worst offenders.

When I heard this, I tore my clothing and pulled hair from my head and beard and sat down utterly baffled. Then many who feared the God of Israel because of this sin of His people came and sat with me until the time of the evening burnt offering.

Finally I stood before the Lord in great embarrassment; then I fell to my knees and lifted my hands to the Lord and cried out, "O my God, I am ashamed; I blush to lift up my face to You, for our sins are piled higher than our heads and our guilt is as boundless as the heavens. Our whole history has been one of sin; that is why we and our kings and our priests were slain by the heathen kings—we were captured, robbed and disgraced, just as we are today. But now we have been given a moment of peace, for You have permitted a few of us to return to Jerusalem from our exile. You have given us a moment of joy and new life in our slavery.

"And now, O God, what can we say after all of this? For once again we have abandoned You and broken Your laws! The prophets warned us that the land we would possess was totally defiled by the horrible practices of the people living there. From one end to the other it is filled with corruption. You told us not to let our daughters marry their sons, not to let our sons marry their daughters and not to help those nations in any way. You warned us that only if we followed this rule could we become a prosperous nation and forever leave that prosperity to our children as an inheritance. And now even after our punishment in exile because of our wickedness (and we have been punished far less than we deserved), and even though You have let some of us return, we have broken Your commandments again and intermarried with people who do these awful things. Surely Your anger will destroy us now until not even this little remnant escapes.

"O Lord God of Israel, You are a just God; what hope can we have if You give us justice as we stand here before You in our wickedness?"

As I lay on the ground in front of the Temple weeping and praying and making this confession, a large crowd of men, women and children gathered around and cried with me. Then I, Ezra the priest, arose and addressed them:

"You have sinned, for you have married heathen women; now we are even more deeply under God's condemnation than we were before. Confess your sin to the Lord God of your fathers and do what He demands: separate yourselves from the heathen people about you and from these women."

Then all the men spoke up and said, "We will do what you have said."

Then Shecaniah (the son of Jehiel of the clan of Elam) said to me, "We acknowledge our sin against our God, for we have married these heathen women. But there is hope for Israel in spite of this. For we agree before our God to divorce our heathen wives and to send them away with our children; we will follow your commands and the commands of the others who fear our God. We will obey the laws of God. Take courage and tell us how to proceed in setting things straight, and we will fully cooperate."

So I stood up and demanded that the leaders of the priests and the Levites and all the people of Israel swear that they would do as Shecaniah had said. And they all agreed.

NEHEMIAH

Nehemiah was cupbearer to Artaxerxes, king of Persia. His journey to Jerusalem, in 445 B.C., to lead a crusade to rebuild its walls, occurred almost 100 years after the first return of the exiles recorded in Ezra.

1. Nehemiah's Grief

The Autobiography of Nehemiah, the Son of Hacaliah:

In December of the twentieth year of the reign of King Artaxerxes of Persia, when I was at the palace at Shushan, one of my fellow Jews named Hanani came to visit me with some men who had arrived from Judah. I took the opportunity to inquire about how things were going in Jerusalem. "How are they getting along?" I asked, "—the Jews who returned to Jerusalem from their exile here?"

"Well," they replied, "things are not good; the wall of Jerusalem is still torn down, and the gates are burned." When I heard this I sat down and cried. In fact I refused to eat for several days, for I spent the time in prayer to the God of heaven.

"O Lord God," I cried out, "O great and awesome God who keeps His promises and is so loving and kind to those who love and obey Him! O Lord, please hear my prayer! Heed the prayers of those of us who delight to honor You. Please help me now as I go in and ask the king for a great favor—put it into his heart to be kind to me." (I was the king's cupbearer.)

2. Nehemiah's Request

One day in April four months later, as I was serving the king his wine he asked me, "Why so sad? You aren't sick, are you? You look like a man with deep troubles." (For until then I had always been cheerful when I was with him.)

I was badly frightened, but I replied, "Sir, why shouldn't I be sad? For the city where my ancestors are buried is in ruins, and the gates have been burned down."

"Well, what should be done?" the king asked.

With a quick prayer to the God of heaven I replied, "If it please Your Majesty and if you look upon me with your royal favor, send me to Judah to rebuild the city of my fathers!"

Then I added this to my request: "If it please the king, give me letters to the governors west of the Euphrates River instructing them to let me travel through their countries on my way to Judah; also a letter to Asaph, the manager of the king's forest, instructing him to give me timber for the beams and gates of the fortress near the Temple, for the city walls and for a house for myself." The king granted these requests, for God was being gracious to me.

Three days after my arrival at Jerusalem I stole out during the night, taking only a few men with me; for I hadn't told a soul about the plans for Jerusalem which God had put into my heart. I was mounted on my donkey and the others were on foot. Then we went to the Fountain Gate and to the King's Pool, but my donkey couldn't get through the rubble. So we circled the city, and I followed the brook, inspecting the wall. I entered again at the Valley Gate.

The city officials did not know I had been out there, or why, for as yet I had said nothing to anyone about my plans—not to the political or religious leaders, or even to those who would be doing the work.

But now I told them, "You know full well the tragedy of our city; it lies in ruins and its gates are burned. Let us rebuild the wall of Jerusalem and rid ourselves of this disgrace!" Then I told them about the desire God had put into my heart, of my conversation with the king and the plan to which he had agreed.

They replied at once, "Good! Let's rebuild the wall!" And so the work began. But when Sanballat (the Horonite) and Tobiah (an Ammonite who was a government official) heard of my arrival, they were very angry that anyone was interested in helping Israel.

3. Walls of the City Rebuilt

Sanballat, when he learned that we were rebuilding the wall, flew into a rage and insulted and mocked us and laughed at us, and so did his friends and the Samaritan army officers. "What does this bunch of poor, feeble Jews think they are doing?" he scoffed. "Do they think they can build the wall in a day if they offer enough sacrifices? And look at those charred stones they are pulling out of the rubbish and using again!"

Tobiah who was standing beside him remarked, "If even a fox walked along the top of their wall, it would collapse!"

Then I prayed, "Hear us, O Lord God, for we are being mocked. May their scoffing fall back upon their own heads, and may they themselves become captives in a foreign land! Do not ignore their sin. Do not blot it out, for they have despised You in despising us who are building Your wall."

At last the wall was completed to half its original height around the entire city, for the workers worked hard. But when Sanballat and Tobiah and the Arabians, Ammonites and Ashdodites heard that the work was going right ahead and that the breaks in the wall were being repaired, they became furious. They plotted to lead an army against Jerusalem to bring about riots and confusion. But we prayed to our God and guarded the city day and night to protect ourselves.

Our enemies learned that we knew of their plot, and that God had exposed and frustrated their plan. Now we all returned to our work on the wall; but from then on, only half worked while the other half stood guard behind them. And the masons and laborers worked with weapons within easy reach beside them or with swords belted to their sides. The trumpeter stayed with me to sound the alarm. I told everyone living outside the walls to move into Jerusalem so that their servants could go on guard duty as well as work during the day. During this period none of us—I, nor my brothers, nor the servants, nor the guards who were with me—ever took off our clothes. And we carried our weapons with us at all times.

The wall was finally finished in early September, just 52 days after we had begun! When our enemies and the surrounding nations heard about it, they were frightened and humiliated. Then they realized that the work had been done with the help of our God.

4. Ezra Reads the Law

After the wall was finished and we had hung the doors in the gates and had appointed the gatekeepers, singers and Levites, I gave the responsibility of governing Jerusalem to my brother Hanani and to Hananiah, the commander of the fortress, a very faithful man who revered God more than most people do. I issued instructions to them not to open the Jerusalem gates until well after sunrise and to close and lock them while the guards were still on duty. I also directed that the guards be residents of Jerusalem, that they must be on duty at regular times and that each homeowner who lived near the wall must guard the section of wall next to his own home. For the city was large, but the population was small; and only a few houses were scattered throughout the city.

The priests, the Levites, the gatekeepers, the choir members, the Temple attendants and the rest of the people now returned home to their own towns and villages throughout Judah. But during the month of September they came back to Jerusalem.

Now, in mid-September, all the people assembled at the plaza in front of the Water Gate and requested Ezra, their religious leader, to read to them the law of God which He had given to Moses. So Ezra the priest brought out to them the scroll of Moses' laws. He stood on a wooden stand made especially for the occasion so that everyone could see him as he read. He faced the square in front of the Water Gate and read from early morning until noon. Everyone stood up as he opened the scroll. And all who were old enough to understand paid close attention. Then Ezra blessed the Lord, the great God, and all the people said, "Amen" and lifted their hands toward heaven; then they bowed and worshiped the Lord with their faces toward the ground.

All the people began sobbing when they heard the commands of the law. Then Ezra the priest and I as governor, and the Levites who were assisting me, said to them, "Don't cry on such a day as this! For today is a sacred day before the Lord your God—It is a time to celebrate with a hearty meal and to send presents to those in need, for the joy of the Lord is your strength. You must not be dejected and sad!"

And the Levites, too, quieted the people, telling them, "That's right! Don't weep! For this is a day of holy joy, not of sadness." So the people went away to eat a festive meal and to send presents; it was a time of great and joyful celebration because they could hear and understand God's words. Ezra read from the scroll on each of the seven days of the feast; and on the eighth day there was a solemn closing service as required by the laws of Moses.

5. Ezra's Prayer of Confession

On October 10 the people returned for another observance; this time they fasted and clothed themselves with sackcloth and sprinkled dirt in their hair. And the Israelis separated themselves from all foreigners. The laws of God were read aloud to them for two or three hours, and for several more hours they took turns confessing their own sins and those of their ancestors. And everyone worshiped the Lord their God.

Then the Levite leaders called out to the people, "Stand up and praise the Lord your God, for He lives from everlasting to everlasting. Praise His glorious name! It is far greater than we can think or say."

Then Ezra prayed, "You alone are God. You have made the skies and the heavens, the earth and the seas, and everything in them. And now, O great and awesome God, You who keep Your promises of love and kindness—do not let all the hardships we have gone through become as nothing to You. Great trouble has come upon us and upon our kings and princes and priests and prophets and ancestors from the days when the kings of Assyria first triumphed over us until now. Every time You punished us You were being perfectly fair; we have sinned so greatly that You gave us only what we deserved.

"Our kings, princes, priests and ancestors didn't obey Your laws or listen to Your warnings. They did not worship You despite the wonderful things You did for them and the great goodness You showered upon them. You gave them a large, fat land, but they refused to turn from their wickedness. So now we are slaves here in the land of plenty which You gave to our ancestors! Slaves among all this abundance! The lush yield of this land passes into the hands of the kings whom You have allowed to conquer us because of our sins. They have power over our bodies and our cattle, and we serve them at their pleasure and are in great misery. Because of all this, we again promise to serve the Lord! And we and our princes and Levites and priests put our names to this covenant."

Many sacrifices were offered on that joyous day, for God had given us cause for great joy. The women and children rejoiced too, and the joy of the people of Jerusalem was heard far away!

6. Nehemiah's Reforms

One day I was on a farm and saw some men treading winepresses on the Sabbath, hauling in sheaves, and loading their donkeys with wine, grapes, figs and all sorts of produce which they took that day into Jerusalem. So I opposed them publicly. There were also some men from Tyre bringing in fish and all sorts of wares and selling them on the Sabbath to the people of Jerusalem.

I asked the leaders of Judah, "Why are you profaning the Sabbath? Wasn't it enough that your fathers did this sort of thing and brought the present evil days upon us and upon our city? And now you are bringing more wrath upon the people of Israel by permitting the Sabbath to be desecrated in this way."

So from then on I commanded that the gates of the city be shut as darkness fell on Friday evenings and not be opened until the Sabbath had ended; and I sent some of my servants to guard the gates so that no merchandise could be brought in on the Sabbath day. The merchants and tradesmen camped outside Jerusalem once or twice.

But I spoke sharply to them and said, "What are you doing out here camping around the wall? If you do this again, I will arrest you." And that was the last time they came on the Sabbath. I commanded the Levites to purify themselves and to guard the gates in order to preserve the sanctity of the Sabbath. Remember this good deed, O my God! Have compassion upon me in accordance with Your great goodness.

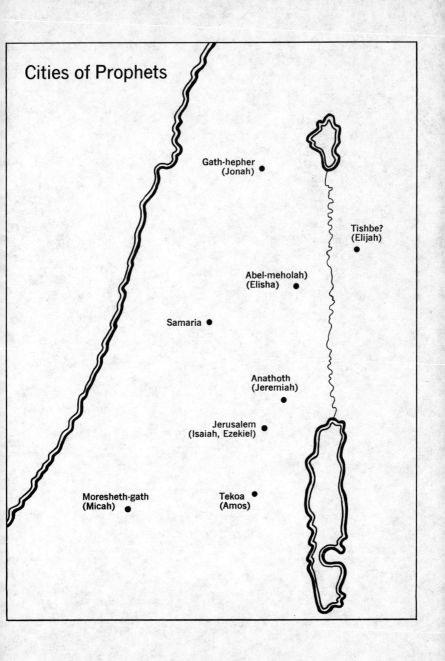

Cities of Prophets

Gath-hepher
(Jonah)

Tishbe?
(Elijah)

Abel-meholah)
(Elisha)

Samaria

Anathoth
(Jeremiah)

Jerusalem
(Isaiah, Ezekiel)

Moresheth-gath
(Micah)

Tekoa
(Amos)

Book II

HIGHLIGHTS
FROM
PROPHECY

Selections from Joel, Amos, Hosea, Isaiah,
Micah, Nahum, Zephaniah, Habakkuk, Jeremiah,
Obadiah, Ezekiel, Haggai, Zechariah, Malachi

JOEL

Although there are striking similarities between Joel and Amos, it is not possible to date Joel precisely. His style is forceful and vivid; his message deals largely with a locust "invasion" which he declares God will send as judgment upon Israel and as a warning of the possibility of even greater judgment in the future.

1. Locusts on the March

This message came from the Lord to Joel, son of Pethuel: Listen, you aged men of Israel! Everyone, listen! In all your lifetime, yes, in all your history, have you ever heard of such a thing as I am going to tell you? In years to come, tell your children about it; pass the awful story down from generation to generation. For after the cutter-locusts finish eating your crops, the swarmer-locusts will take what's left! After them will come the hopper-locusts! And then the stripper-locusts too!

Sound the alarm in Jerusalem! Let the blast of the warning trumpet be heard upon My holy mountain! Let everyone tremble in fear, for the day of the Lord's judgment approaches. It is a day of darkness and gloom, of black clouds and thick darkness. What a mighty army! It covers the mountains like night! How great, how powerful these "people" are! The likes of them have not been seen before and never will again throughout the generations of the world! Fire goes before them and follows them on every side! Ahead of them the land lies fair as Eden's garden in all its beauty, but they destroy it to the ground; not one thing escapes. They look like tiny horses and they run as fast.

Look at them leaping along the tops of the mountain! Listen to the noise they make, like the rumbling of chariots or the roar of fire sweeping across a field; and like a mighty army moving into battle. Fear grips the waiting people; their faces grow pale with fright. These soldiers charge like infantry; they scale the walls like picked and trained commandos. Straight forward they march, never breaking ranks. They never crowd each other. Each is right in place. No weapon can stop them.

Wake up and weep, you drunkards; for all the grapes are ruined and all your wine is gone!

A vast army of locusts covers the land. It is a terrible army too numerous to count with teeth as sharp as those of lions! They have ruined My vines and stripped the bark from the fig trees, leaving trunks and branches white and bare. They swarm upon the city; they run up on the walls; they climb up into the houses, coming like thieves through the windows. The earth quakes before them and the heavens tremble. The sun and moon are obscured and the stars are hid. The Lord leads them with a shout. This is His mighty army and they follow His orders. The day of the judgment of the Lord is an awesome, terrible thing. Who can endure it?

2. Time to Pray

Announce a fast; call a solemn meeting. Gather the elders and all the people into the Temple of the Lord your God and weep before Him there. Well may you farmers stand so shocked and stricken; well may you vinedressers weep. Weep for the wheat and the barley too, for they are gone. The grapevines are dead; the fig trees are dying; the pomegranates wither; the apples shrivel on the trees; all joy has withered with them. O priests, robe yourselves in sackcloth. O ministers of my God, lie all night before the altar, weeping. For there are no more offerings of grain and wine for you.

The Lord says, "Turn to Me now while there is time. Give

Me all your hearts. Come with fasting, weeping, mourning. Let your remorse tear at your hearts and not your garments." Return to the Lord your God, for He is gracious and merciful. He is not easily angered; He is full of kindness and anxious not to punish you. Who knows? Perhaps even yet He will decide to let you alone and give you a blessing instead of His terrible curse. Perhaps He will give you so much that you can offer your grain and wine to the Lord as before!

Sound the trumpet in Zion! Call a fast and gather all the people together for a solemn meeting. Bring everyone—the elders, the children and even the babies. Call the bridegroom from his quarters and the bride from her privacy. The priests, the ministers of God, will stand between the people and the altar, weeping; and they will pray, "Spare Your people, O our God; don't let the heathen rule them, for they belong to You. The seed rots in the ground; the barns and granaries are empty; the grain has dried up in the fields. The cattle groan with hunger; the herds stand perplexed for there is no pasture for them; the sheep bleat in misery. Lord, help us! For the heat has withered the pastures and burned up all the trees. Even the wild animals cry to You for help, for there is no water for them. The creeks are dry and the pastures are scorched. Don't let thy people be disgraced by the taunts of the heathen who say, 'Where is this God of theirs? How weak and helpless He must be!'"

3. God's Answer

Then the Lord will pity His people and be indignant for the honor of His land! He will reply, "See, I am sending you much corn and wine and oil to fully satisfy your need. No longer will I make you a laughingstock among the nations. I will remove these armies from the north and send them far away; I will turn them back into the parched wastelands where they will die; half shall be driven into the Dead Sea and the rest into the Mediterranean. Their rotting stench will rise upon the land. The Lord has done a mighty miracle for you.

"Fear not, My people; be glad now and rejoice, for He has

done amazing things for you. Let the flocks and herds forget their hunger: the pastures will turn green again. The trees will bear their fruit: the fig trees and grapevines will flourish once more. Rejoice, O people of Jerusalem, rejoice in the Lord your God! For the rains He sends are tokens of forgiveness. Once more the autumn rains will come, as well as those of spring. The threshing floors will pile high again with wheat, and the presses overflow with olive oil and wine. And I will give you back the crops the locusts ate!—My great destroying army that I sent against you. And you will know that I am here among My people Israel, and that I alone am the Lord your God. And My people shall never again be dealt a blow like this. After I have poured out My rains again, I will pour out My Spirit upon all of you! Your sons and daughters will prophesy; your old men will dream dreams, and your young men see visions.

"Multitudes, multitudes waiting in the valley for the verdict of their doom! For the Day of the Lord is near in the Valley of Judgment. The sun and moon will be darkened and the stars withdraw their light. The Lord shouts from His Temple in Jerusalem and the earth and sky begin to shake. But to His people Israel, the Lord will be very gentle. He is their refuge and strength. Then you shall know at last that I am the Lord your God in Zion, My holy mountain. Jerusalem shall be Mine forever; the time will come when no foreign armies will pass through her any more. Sweet wine will drip from the mountains, and the hills shall flow with milk. Water will fill the dry stream beds of Judah, and a fountain will burst forth from the temple of the Lord to water Acacia Valley. Israel will prosper forever, and Jerusalem will thrive as generations pass. For My home is in Jerusalem with My people."

AMOS

Amos prophesied to the Northern Kingdom of Israel during the reign of Jeroboam II, approximately 780-740 B.C. (See page 217 or II Kings 14:23-29.) He was a stern and courageous spokesman for social justice, exposing and denouncing moral rottenness: greed, immorality and oppression of the poor.

1. Judgment Against Nearby Nations

Amos was a herdsman living in the village of Tekoa. All day long he sat on the hillsides watching the sheep, keeping them from straying. One day in a vision God told him some of the things that were going to happen to His nation Israel. This vision came to him at the time Uzziah was king of Judah and while Jeroboam, son of Joash, was king of Israel—two years before the earthquake. This is his report of what he saw and heard:

The Lord roared like a ferocious lion from his lair from His Temple on Mount Zion. And suddenly the lush pastures of Mount Carmel withered and dried, and all the shepherds mourned.

The Lord says, "The people of Damascus have sinned again and again, and I will not forget it. I will not leave her unpunished any more. For they have threshed My people in Gilead like grain is threshed with iron rods."

The Lord says, "Gaza has sinned again and again, and I will not forget it. I will not leave her unpunished any more. For she sent My people into exile, selling them as slaves in Edom."

The Lord says, "The people of Tyre have sinned again and again and I will not forget it. I will not leave them unpunished any more. For they broke their treaty with their brother, Israel; they attacked and conquered him and led him into slavery to Edom."

The Lord says, "Edom has sinned again and again, and I will not forget it. I will not leave him unpunished any more. For he chased his brother, Israel, with the sword; he was pitiless in unrelenting anger."

The Lord says, "The people of Ammon have sinned again and again, and I will not forget it. I will not leave them unpunished any more. For in their wars in Gilead to enlarge their borders, they committed cruel crimes, ripping open pregnant women with their swords."

The Lord says, "The people of Moab have sinned again and again, and I will not forget it. I will not leave them unpunished any more. For they desecrated the tombs of the kings of Edom with no respect for the dead."

The Lord says, "The people of Judah have sinned again and again, and I will not forget it. I will not leave them unpunished any more. For they have rejected the laws of God, refusing to obey Him. They have hardened their hearts and sinned as their fathers did."

2. Judgment Against Israel

The Lord says, "The people of Israel have sinned again and again, and I will not forget it. I will not leave them unpunished any more. For they have perverted justice by accepting bribes and sold into slavery the poor who can't repay their debts; they trade them for a pair of shoes. They trample the poor in the dust and kick aside the meek. And a man and his father defile the same temple-girl, corrupting My holy name. At their religious feasts they lounge in clothing stolen from their debtors, and in My own Temple they offer sacrifices of wine they purchased with stolen money.

"Yet think of all I did for them! I chose your sons to be Nazirites and prophets—can you deny this, Israel?" asks the Lord. "But you caused the Nazirites to sin by urging them to drink your wine, and you silenced My prophets, telling them, 'Shut up!' Therefore I will make you groan as a wagon groans that is loaded with sheaves. Your swiftest warriors will stumble in flight. The strong will all be weak, and the great ones can no longer save themselves. The archer's aim will fail, the swiftest runners won't be fast enough to flee. Even the best of horsemen can't outrun the danger then. The most courageous of your mighty men will drop their weapons and run for their lives that day." The Lord God has spoken.

"Listen! This is your doom! It is spoken by the Lord against both Israel and Judah—against the entire family I brought from Egypt:

"Of all the peoples of the earth, I have chosen you alone. That is why I must punish you the more for all your sins. For how can we walk together with your sins between us? Would I be roaring as a lion unless I had a reason? The fact is I am getting ready to destroy you. But always, first of all, I warn you through My prophets. This I now have done."

The Lion has roared—tremble in fear. The Lord God has sounded your doom—I dare not refuse to proclaim it. "My people have forgotten what it means to do right," says the Lord. "Their beautiful homes are full of the loot from their thefts and banditry. Therefore," the Lord God says, "an enemy is coming! He is surrounding them and will shatter their forts and plunder those beautiful homes."

The Lord says, "A shepherd tried to rescue his sheep from a lion, but it was too late: he snatched from the lion's mouth two legs and a piece of ear. So it will be when the Israeli in Samaria are finally rescued—all they will have left is half a chair and a tattered pillow.

"Listen to this announcement and publish it throughout all Israel," says the Lord, the God of Hosts. "On the same day that I punish Israel for her sins, I will also destroy the idol altars at Bethel. The horns of the altar will be cut off and fall to the ground. And I will destroy the beautiful homes of the wealthy—their winter mansions and their summer houses too —and demolish their ivory palaces."

Listen, you merchants who rob the poor, trampling on the needy; you who long for the Sabbath to end and the religious holidays to be over so you can get out and start cheating again —using your weighted scales and undersized measures; you who make slaves of the poor, buying them for their debt of a piece of silver or a pair of shoes, or selling them your moldy wheat—the Lord, the Pride of Israel, has sworn: "I won't forget your deeds! The land will tremble as it awaits its doom, and everyone will mourn. It will rise up like the River Nile at floodtime, toss about and sink again. At that time I will make the sun go down at noon and darken the earth in the daytime. And I will turn your parties into times of mourning, and your songs of joy will be turned to cries of despair. You will wear funeral clothes and shave your heads as signs of sorrow, as if your only son had died; bitter, bitter will be that day.

"I destroyed some of your cities, as I did Sodom and Gomorrah; those left are like half-burned firebrands snatched away from fire. And still you won't return to Me," says the Lord. "Therefore I will bring upon you all these further evils I have spoken of. Prepare to meet your God in judgment, Israel. For you are dealing with the One who formed the mountains and made the winds and knows your every thought; He turns the morning to darkness and crushes down the mountains underneath His feet: Jehovah, the Lord, the God of Hosts, is His name."

3. What God Wants

The Lord says to the people of Israel, "Seek Me—and live. Don't seek the idols of Bethel, Gilgal or Beer-sheba; for the people of Gilgal will be carried off to exile, and those of Bethel shall surely come to grief." Seek the Lord and live, or else He will sweep like fire through Israel and consume her, and none of the idols in Bethel can put it out. Oh, evil men, you make "justice" a bitter pill for the poor and oppressed. "Righteousness" and "fair play" are meaningless fictions to you!

Seek Him who created the Seven Stars and the constellation Orion; who turns darkness into morning and day into night; who calls forth the water from the ocean and pours it out as rain upon the land. The Lord, Jehovah, is His name. With blinding speed and violence He brings destruction on the strong, breaking all defenses. How you hate honest judges! How you despise people who tell the truth! You trample the poor and steal their smallest crumb by all your taxes, fines and usury; therefore you will never live in the beautiful stone houses you are building, nor drink the wine from the lush vineyards you are planting. For many and great are your sins. I know them all so well. You are the enemies of everything good; you take bribes; you refuse justice to the poor.

Therefore the Lord God of Hosts says this: "There will be crying in all the streets and every road. Call for the farmers to weep with you too; call for professional mourners to wail and lament. There will be sorrow and crying in every vineyard. For I will pass through and destroy. You say, 'If only the day of the Lord were here, for then God would deliver us from all our foes.' But you have no idea what you ask. For that day will *not* be light and prosperity but darkness and doom! How terrible the darkness will be for you; not a ray of joy or hope will shine. In that day you will be as a man who is chased by a lion—and met by a bear; or a man in a dark room who leans against a wall—and puts his hand on a snake. Yes, that will be a dark and hopeless day for you. I hate your show and pretense—your hypocrisy of 'honoring' Me with your religious feasts and solemn assemblies. I will not accept your burnt offerings and thank offerings. Away with your hymns of praise —they are mere noise to My ears. I will not listen to your music, no matter how lovely it is. I want to see a mighty flood of justice—a torrent of doing good."

4. Amos Ordered to Leave

This is what the Lord God showed me in a vision: the Lord was standing beside a wall built with a plumbline, checking it with a plumbline to see if it was straight. And the Lord said to me, "Amos, what do you see?"

I answered, "A plumbline."

And He replied, "I will test My people with a plumbline. I will no longer turn away from punishing. The idol altars and temples of Israel will be destroyed; and I will destroy the dynasty of King Jeroboam by the sword."

But when Amaziah, the priest of Bethel, heard what Amos was saying, he rushed a message to Jeroboam, the king, "Amos is a traitor to our nation and is plotting your death. This is intolerable. It will lead to rebellion all across the land. He says you will be killed, and Israel will be sent far away into exile and slavery."

Then Amaziah sent orders to Amos, "Get out of here, you prophet, you! Flee to the land of Judah and do your prophesying there! Don't bother us here with your visions; not here in the capital where the king's chapel is!"

But Amos replied, "I am not really one of the prophets. I do not come from a family of prophets. I am just a herdsman and fruit picker. But the Lord took me from caring for the flocks and told me, 'Go and prophesy to My people Israel.'

"Now therefore listen to this message to you from the Lord. You say, 'Don't prophesy against Israel.' The Lord's reply is this, 'Because of your interference, your wife will become a prostitute in this city, and your sons and daughters will be killed and your land divided up. You yourself will die in a heathen land, and the people of Israel will certainly become slaves in exile, far from their land.' "

5. Restoration Promised

Woe to those lounging in luxury at Jerusalem and Samaria, so famous and popular among the people of Israel. You push away all thought of punishment awaiting you, but by your deeds you bring the Day of Judgment near. You lie on ivory beds surrounded with luxury, eating the meat of the tenderest lambs and the choicest calves. You sing idle songs to the sound of the harp and fancy yourselves to be as great musicians as King David was. You drink wine by the bucketful and perfume yourselves with sweet ointments, caring nothing at all that your brothers need your help. Therefore you will be the first to be taken as slaves; suddenly your revelry will end.

Jehovah, the Lord God of Hosts, has sworn by His own name, "I despise the pride and false glory of Israel. I hate their beautiful homes. I will turn over this city and everything in it to her enemies." Therefore those who are wise will not try to interfere with the Lord in the dread day of your punishment. Be good, flee evil—and live! Then the Lord God of Hosts will truly be your helper, as you have claimed He is. Hate evil and love the good; remodel your courts into true halls of justice. Perhaps even yet the Lord God of Hosts will have mercy on His people who remain.

"The eyes of the Lord God are watching Israel, that sinful nation, and I will root her up and scatter her across the world. Yet I have promised that this rooting out will not be permanent. For I have commanded that Israel be sifted by the other nations as grain is sifted in a sieve, yet not one true kernel will be lost. But all these sinners who say, 'God will not touch us,' will die by the sword.

"Then, at that time, I will rebuild the City of David, which is now lying in ruins, and return it to its former glory, and Israel will possess what is left of Edom, and of all the nations that belong to me." For so the Lord, who plans it all, has said. "The time will come when there will be such abundance of crops that the harvest time will scarcely end before the farmer starts again to sow another crop, and the terraces of grapes upon the hills of Israel will drip sweet wine! I will restore the fortunes of My people Israel, and they shall rebuild their ruined cities and live in them again. They shall plant vineyards and gardens and eat their crops and drink their wine. I will firmly plant them there upon the land that I have given them; they shall not be pulled up again," says the Lord your God.

HOSEA

Hosea was a contemporary of Amos, so for a fuller understanding of Hosea's ministry, see the selections from Amos and
their introduction. However, Hosea was less severe though not
less grieved by the sins of Israel. Amos has been called "the
prophet of judgment"; Hosea, "the prophet of grace." Fittingly,
his name—the same as Joshua and Jesus—means "saviour."

1. Warning of Judgment

Hear the word of the Lord, O people of Israel. The Lord
has filed a lawsuit against you listing the following charges:

There is no faithfulness, no kindness, no knowledge of God
in your land. You swear and lie and kill and steal and commit
adultery. There is violence everywhere with one murder after
another. That is why your land is not producing; it is filled
with sadness. All living things grow sick and die; the animals,
the birds, and even the fish begin to disappear. Don't point
your finger at someone else and try to pass the blame to him!

The more My people multiplied, the more they sinned
against Me. They exchanged the glory of God for the disgrace
of idols. For they are asking a piece of wood to tell them what
to do. "Divine truth" comes to them through tea leaves! Longing after idols has made them foolish. For they have played the
harlot, serving other gods, deserting Me. They sacrifice to
idols on the tops of mountains; they go up into the hills to burn
incense beneath the pleasant shade of oaks and poplars and
terebinth trees. There your daughters turn to prostitution and
your brides commit adultery.

The priests rejoice in the sins of the people; they lap it up
and lick their lips for more! And thus it is like priest, like
people—because the priests are wicked the people are too.

Therefore I will punish both priests and people for all their wicked deeds. Listen to this, you priests and all of Israel's leaders; listen, all you men of the royal family: you are doomed! For you have deluded the people with idols at Mizpah and Tabor, and dug a deep pit to trap them at Acacia. But never forget—I will settle up with all of you for what you've done. I have seen your evil deeds. Israel, you have left Me as a harlot does her husband; you are utterly defiled.

My people mingle with the heathen, picking up their evil ways; thus they become as good-for-nothing as a half-baked cake! Worshiping foreign gods has sapped their strength, but they don't know it. Ephraim's hair is turning gray, and he doesn't even realize how weak and old he is. His pride in other gods has openly condemned him; yet he doesn't return to his God, nor even try to find Him. Ephraim is a silly, witless dove calling to Egypt, flying to Assyria. But as she flies, I throw My net over her and bring her down like a bird from the sky; I will punish her for all her evil ways.

Woe to my people for deserting Me; let them perish, for they have sinned against Me. I wanted to redeem them but their hard hearts would not accept the truth. They lie there sleepless with anxiety, but won't ask My help. Instead they worship heathen gods, asking them for crops and for prosperity. I have helped them and made them strong; yet now they turn against Me. They look everywhere except to heaven, to the Most High God.

Sound the alarm! They are coming! Like a vulture the enemy descends upon the people of God because they have broken My treaty and revolted against My laws. Now Israel pleads with Me and says, "Help us, for You are our God!"

But it is too late! Israel has thrown away her chance disdainfully and now her enemies will chase her. She has appointed kings and princes, but not with My consent. They have cut themselves off from My help by worshiping the idols that they made from their silver and gold. O Samaria, I reject this calf —this idol you have made. My fury burns against you. How long will it be before one honest man is found among you? When will you admit this calf you worship was made by human hands! It is not God! Therefore, it must be smashed to bits. They have sown the wind and they will reap the whirl-wind. Their cornstalks stand there barren, withered, sickly, with no grain; if it has any, foreigners will eat it.

Ephraim has built many altars, but they are not to worship Me! They are altars of sin! Even if I gave her ten thousand laws, she'd say they weren't for her—that they applied to someone far away. Her people love the ritual of their sacrifice, but to Me it is meaningless! I will call for an accounting of their sins and punish them; they shall return to Egypt. Israel has built great palaces; Judah has constructed great defenses for her cities; but they have forgotten their Maker. Therefore I will send down fire upon those palaces and burn those for-tresses.

The people of Samaria tremble lest their calf-god idols at Bethaven should be hurt; the priests and people, too, mourn over the departed honor of their shattered gods. This idol—this calf-god thing—will be carted with them when they go as slaves to Assyria, a present to the great king there. Ephraim will be laughed at for trusting in this idol; Israel will be put to shame. As for Samaria her king shall disappear like a chip of wood upon an ocean wave. And the idol altars of Aven at Bethel where Israel sinned will crumble. Thorns and thistles will grow up to surround them. And the people will cry to the mountains and hills to fall upon them and crush them. The time of Israel's punishment has come; the day of recompense is almost here and soon Israel will know it all too well. "The prophets are crazy; the inspired men are mad." Yes, so they mock, for the nation is weighted with sin and shows only hatred for those who love God. I will come against you for your disobedience; I will gather the armies of the nations against you to punish you for your heaped-up sins. My God will destroy the people of Israel because they will not listen or obey. They will be wandering Jews, homeless among the na-tions.

2. Rejected and Reclaimed

Hosea married Gomer, daughter of Diblaim, and she conceived and bore him a son. And the Lord said, "Name the child Jezreel, for in the valley of Jezreel I am about to punish King Jehu's dynasty to avenge the murders he committed."

Soon Gomer had another child—this one a daughter. And God said to Hosea, "Name her Lo-Ruhamah (meaning 'no more mercy') for I will have no more mercy upon Israel to forgive her again. But I *will* have mercy on the tribe of Judah. I will personally free her from her enemies without any help from her armies or her weapons."

After Gomer had weaned Lo-Ruhamah, she again conceived and this time gave birth to a son. And God said, "Call him Lo-Ammi (meaning 'not mine'), for Israel is not Mine and I am not her God."

Some time later God said, "O Jezreel, rename your brother and sister. Call your brother Ammi (which means 'now you are Mine'); name your sister Ruhamah ('Pitied'), for now God will have mercy on her!"

Plead with your mother, for she has become another man's wife—I am no longer her husband. Beg her to stop her harlotry and quit giving herself to others. And I will not give special favors to her children as I would to my own, for they are not my children; they belong to other men. For their mother has committed adultery. She doesn't realize that all she has, has come from Me. But I will court her again, bring her into the wilderness and speak to her tenderly there. There I will give back her vineyards to her, and transform her Valley of Troubles into a Door of Hope. She will respond to me there, singing with joy as in days long ago in her youth after I had freed her from captivity in Egypt. In that coming day, says the Lord, she will call me "My Husband" instead of "My Master."

O Israel, I will cause you to forget your idols, and their names will not be spoken any more. At that time I will make a treaty between you and the wild animals, birds and snakes not to fear each other any more; and I will destroy all weapons, and all wars will end. Then you will lie down in peace and safety, unafraid; and I will bind you to Me forever with chains of righteousness and justice and love and mercy. I will betroth you to Me in faithfulness and love, and you will really know Me then as you never have before.

Then the Lord said to me, "Go and get your wife again and bring her back to you and love her, even though she loves adultery. For the Lord still loves Israel though she has turned to other gods and offered them choice gifts."

So I bought her back from her slavery for a couple of dollars and eight bushels of barley, and I said to her, "You must live alone for many days; do not go out with other men nor be a harlot; and I will wait for you."

This illustrates the fact that Israel will be a long time without a king or prince and without an altar, temple, priests or even idols! Afterwards they will return to the Lord their God, and to the Messiah, their king; and they shall come trembling, submissive to the Lord and to His blessings.

3. Divine Grace

How prosperous Israel is—a luxuriant vine all filled with fruit! But the more wealth I give her, the more she pours it on the altars of her heathen gods; the richer the harvests I give her, the more beautiful the statues and idols she erects. I wanted to forgive Israel, but her sins were far too great—no one can even live in Samaria without being a liar, thief and bandit! Her people never seem to recognize that I am watching them. Their sinful deeds give them away on every side; I see them all. Yes, I have seen a horrible thing in Israel—Ephraim chasing other gods, Israel utterly defiled.

O Judah, for you also there is a plentiful harvest of punishment waiting—and I wanted so much to bless you! I will abandon them and return to My home until they admit their guilt and look to Me for help again; for as soon as trouble comes, they will search for Me and say: "Come, let us return to the Lord; it is He who has torn us—He will heal us. He has wounded—He will bind us up. In just a couple of days, or three at the most, He will set us on our feet again, to live in His kindness! Oh that we might know the Lord! Let us press on to know Him, and He will respond to us as surely as the coming of dawn or the rain of early spring."

When Israel was a child I loved him as a son and brought him out of Egypt. But the more I called to him, the more he rebelled, sacrificing to Baal and burning incense to idols. I trained him from infancy: I taught him to walk, I held him in My arms. But he doesn't know or even care that it was I who raised him. As a man would lead his favorite ox, so I led Israel with My ropes of love. I loosened his muzzle so he could eat. I myself have stopped and fed him.

Oh, how can I give you up, My Ephraim? How can I let you go? How can I forsake you like Admah and Zeboiim? My heart cries out within Me; how I long to help you! No, I will not punish you as much as My fierce anger tells Me to. This is the last time I will destroy Ephraim. For I am God and not man; I am the Holy One living among you and I did not come to destroy. For the people shall walk after the Lord. I shall roar as a lion at their enemies and My people shall return trembling from the west. Like a flock of birds they will come from Egypt—like doves flying from Assyria.

O Israel, how well I remember those first delightful days when I led you through the wilderness! How refreshing was your love! How satisfying like the early figs of summer in their first season! But then you deserted Me for Baal-peor, to give yourselves to other gods, and soon you were as foul as they.

But I will court her again, and bring her into the wilderness, and speak to her tenderly there. There I will give back her vineyards to her, and transform her Valleys of Troubles into a Door of Hope. She will respond to me there, singing with joy as in days long ago in her youth, after I had freed her from captivity in Egypt.

In that coming day, says the Lord, she will call me "My Husband" instead of "My Master."

And I will bind you to Me forever with chains of righteousness and justice and love and mercy. I will betroth you to Me in faithfulness and love, and you will really know Me then as you never have before.

4. Salvation Offered

O Israel, return to the Lord, your God, for you have been crushed by your sins. Bring your petition. Come to the Lord and say, "O Lord, take away our sins; be gracious to us and receive us, and we will offer you the sacrifice of praise. Assyria cannot save us, nor can our strength in battle; never again will we call the idols we have made 'our gods'; for in You alone, O Lord, the fatherless find mercy."

Then I will cure you of idolatry and faithlessness, and My love will know no bounds, for My anger will be forever gone! I will refresh Israel like the dew from heaven; she will blossom as the lily and root deeply in the soil like cedars in Lebanon. Her branches will spread out as beautiful as olive trees, fragrant as the forests of Lebanon. Her people will return from exile far away and rest beneath My shadow. They will be a watered garden and bloom like grapes and be as fragrant as the wines of Lebanon.

In that day, says the Lord, I will answer the pleading of the sky for clouds, to pour down water on the earth in answer to its cry for rain. Then the earth can answer the parched cry of the grain, the grapes, and the olive trees for moisture and for dew—and the whole grand chorus shall sing together that "God sows!" He has given all! At that time I will sow a crop of Israelis and raise them for Myself! I will pity those who are not pitied, and I will say to those who are not My people, "Now you are My people." They will reply, "You are our God!"

O Ephraim! Stay away from idols! I am living and strong! I look after you and care for you. I am like an evergreen tree yielding My fruit to you throughout the year. My mercies never fail. Plant the good seeds of righteousness and you will reap a crop of My love; plow the hard ground of your hearts, for now is the time to seek the Lord that He may come and shower salvation upon you. Whoever is wise let him understand these things. Whoever is intelligent let him listen. For the paths of the Lord are true and right and good men walk along them. But sinners trying it will fail.

ISAIAH

MESSAGES IN JUDAH

Isaiah's prophetic ministry to the Southern Kingdom (Judah) began in the year King Uzziah died and continued through the reigns of Jotham, Ahaz and Hezekiah. It was centered in Jerusalem and lasted about 50 years from around 740-690 B.C. For historical background, see Book I, Part 4, pages 219-225.

These are the messages that came to Isaiah, son of Amoz, in the visions he saw during the reigns of King Uzziah, King Jotham, King Ahaz and King Hezekiah—all kings of Judah. In these messages God showed him what was going to happen to Judah and Jerusalem in the days ahead.

1. Isaiah's Vision and Call

The year King Uzziah died I saw the Lord! He was sitting on a lofty throne, and the Temple was filled with His glory.

Hovering about Him were mighty, six-winged seraphs. With two of their wings they covered their faces, with two others they covered their feet and with two they flew. In a great antiphonal chorus they sang, "Holy, holy, holy is the Lord of Hosts; the whole earth is filled with His glory." Such singing it was! It shook the Temple to its foundations, and suddenly the entire sanctuary was filled with smoke.

I said, "My doom is sealed, for I am a foulmouthed sinner, a member of a sinful, foulmouthed race; and I have looked upon the King, the Lord of heaven's armies."

Then one of the seraphs flew over to the altar and with a pair of tongs picked out a burning coal. He touched my lips with it and said, "Now you are pronounced 'Not guilty' because this coal has touched your lips. Your sins are all forgiven."

Then I heard the Lord asking, "Whom shall I send as a messenger to My people? Who will go?"

And I said, "Lord, I'll go! Send *me*."

And He said, "Yes, go. But tell My people that though they hear My words repeatedly, they won't understand them. Though they watch and watch as I perform My miracles, still they won't know what they mean. So dull their understanding, close their ears and shut their eyes. I don't want them to see or to hear or to understand, or to turn to Me to heal them."

Then I said, "Lord, how long will it be before they are ready to listen?"

And He replied, "Not until their cities are destroyed— without a person left—and the whole country is an utter wasteland, and they are all taken away as slaves to other countries far away and all the land of Israel lies deserted! Yet a tenth—a remnant—will survive; and though Israel is invaded again and again and destroyed, yet Israel will be like a tree cut down whose stump still lives to grow again."

2. Call to Repentance

Listen, O heaven and earth, to what the Lord is saying: The children I raised and cared for so long and tenderly have turned against Me. Even the animals—the donkey and the ox —know their owner and appreciate his care for them, but not My people Israel. No matter what I do for them, they still don't care. Oh, what a sinful nation they are! They walk bent-backed beneath their load of guilt. Their fathers before them were evil too. Born to be bad, they have turned their backs upon the Lord and have despised the Holy One of Israel. They have cut themselves off from My help. O, my people, haven't you had enough of punishment?

Listen, you leaders of Israel, you men of Sodom and Gomorrah, as I call you now. Listen to the Lord. Hear what He is telling you! I am sick of your sacrifices. Don't bring Me any more of them. I don't want your fat rams; I don't want to see the blood from your offerings. Who wants your sacrifices when you have no sorrow for your sins? The incense you bring Me is a stench in my nostrils. Your holy celebrations of the new moon and the sabbath, and your special days for fasting— even your most pious meetings—all are frauds! I want nothing more to do with them. I hate them all; I can't stand the sight of them.

Oh wash yourselves! Be clean! Let Me no longer see you doing all these wicked things; quit your evil ways. Learn to do good, to be fair and to help the poor, the fatherless and widows. Come, let's talk this over! No matter how deep the stain of your sins, I can take it out and make you as clean as freshly fallen snow. Even if you are stained as red as crimson, I can make you white as wool! If you will only let Me help you, if you will only obey, then I will make you rich! But if you keep on turning your backs and refusing to listen to Me, you will be killed by your enemies; I, the Lord, have spoken.

3. God's Case Against His People

In the last days Jerusalem and the Temple of the Lord will become the world's greatest attraction and people from many lands will flow there to worship the Lord. "Come," everyone will say, "let us go up the mountain of the Lord, to the Temple of the God of Israel; there He will teach us His laws and we will obey them." For in those days the world will be ruled from Jerusalem. The Lord will settle international disputes; all the nations will convert their weapons of war into implements of peace. Then at the last all wars will stop and all military training will end.

O Israel, come, let us walk in the light of the Lord and be obedient to His laws! For the day is coming when your proud looks will be brought low; the Lord alone will be exalted. On that day the Lord of Hosts will move against the proud and haughty and bring them to the dust. All the glory of mankind will bow low; the pride of men will lie in the dust, and the Lord alone shall be exalted. And all idols shall be utterly abolished and destroyed.

O My people! Can't you see what fools your rulers are? Weak as women! Foolish as little children playing king! True leaders? No, misleaders! Leading you down the garden path to destruction. The Lord stands up! He is the great prosecuting attorney presenting His case against His people! First to feel His wrath will be the elders and the princes, for they have defrauded the poor. They have filled their barns with grain extorted from the helpless peasants. "How dare you grind My people in the dust like that?" the Lord of Hosts will demand of them.

Next, He will judge the haughty Jewish women who mince along—noses in the air, tinkling bracelets on their ankles—with wanton eyes that rove among the crowds to catch the glances of the men. Gone shall be their scarves and veils, headbands; ankle chains, earrings and perfumes; their rings and jewels; their ornate combs and mirrors; purses and party clothes, capes, beautiful dresses, negligees and lovely lingerie. All their beauty shall be gone; all that will be left to them is shame and disgrace.

Woe to you who get up early in the morning to go on long drinking bouts that last till late at night—woe to you drunken bums. You furnish lovely music at your grand parties; the orchestras are superb! But for the Lord you have no thought or care. They say that what is right is wrong, and what is wrong is right; that black is white and white is black; bitter is sweet and sweet is bitter. Woe to those who are wise and shrewd in their own eyes! Woe to those who are "heroes" when it comes to drinking, and boast about the liquor they can hold. They take bribes to pervert justice, letting the wicked go free and putting innocent men in jail. Therefore God will deal with them and burn them. They will disappear like straw on fire. Their roots will rot and their flowers wither, for they have thrown away the laws of God and despised the Word of the Holy One of Israel.

4. Parable of the Vineyard

Now I will sing a song about His vineyard to the One I love. *My Beloved has a vineyard on a very fertile hill. He plowed it and took out all the rocks and planted His vineyard with the choicest vines. He built a watchtower and cut a winepress in the rocks. Then He waited for the harvest, but the grapes that grew were wild and sour and not at all the sweet ones He expected.*

Now men of Jerusalem and Judah, you have heard the case! You be the judges! What more could I have done? Why did My vineyard give Me wild grapes instead of sweet? I will tear down the fences and let My vineyeard go to pasture to be trampled by cattle and sheep. I won't prune it or hoe it, but let it be overgrown with briars and thorns. I will command the clouds not to rain on it any more.

I have given you the story of God's people. They are the vineyard that I spoke about. Israel and Judah are His pleasant acreage! He expected them to yield a crop of justice, but found bloodshed instead. He expected righteousness, but the cries of deep oppression met His ears.

5. Messages to Ahaz

During the reign of Ahaz (the son of Jotham and grandson of Uzziah), Jerusalem was attacked by King Rezin of Syria and King Pekah of Israel (the son of Remaliah). But it was not taken; the city stood. However, when the news came to the royal court, "Syria is allied with Israel against us!" the hearts of the king and his people trembled with fear as the trees of a forest shake in a storm.

Then the Lord said to Isaiah, "Go out to meet King Ahaz, you and Shear-jashub, your son. You will find him at the end of the aqueduct which leads from Gihon Spring to the upper reservoir, near the road that leads down to the bleaching field. Tell him to quit worrying," the Lord said. "Tell him he needn't be frightened by the fierce anger of those two has-beens, Rezin and Pekah. Yes, the kings of Syria and Israel are coming against you. They say that they will invade Judah and throw her people into panic. Then they will fight their way into Jerusalem and install the son of Tabeel as their king. But the Lord God says their plan will not succeed."

Not long after this, the Lord sent this further message to King Ahaz: "Ask Me for a sign, Ahaz, to prove that I will indeed crush your enemies as I have said. Ask anything you like, in heaven or on earth."

But the king refused. "No," he said, "I'll not bother the Lord with anything like that."

Then Isaiah said: O house of David, you aren't satisfied to exhaust *my* patience; you exhaust the Lord's as well! All right then, the Lord Himself will choose the sign—a child shall be born to a virgin! And she shall call Him Immanuel (meaning "God is with us"). By the time this child is weaned and knows right from wrong, the two kings you fear so much—the kings of Israel and Syria—will both be dead. But later on, the Lord will bring a terrible curse on you and on your nation and your family. There will be terror such as has not been known since the division of Solomon's empire into Israel and Judah— the mighty king of Assyria will come with his great army! When they finally stop plundering, the whole nation will be a pastureland; whole flocks and herds will be destroyed, and a farmer will be fortunate to have a cow and two sheep left. At that time the lush vineyards will become patches of briars. All the land will be one vast thornfield, a hunting ground overrun by wildlife. No one will go to the fertile hillsides where once the gardens grew, for thorns will cover them; cattle, sheep and goats will graze there.

6. A Deliverer Promised

Nevertheless, that time of darkness and despair shall not go on forever. Though soon the land of Zebulon and Naphtali will be under God's contempt and judgment, yet in the future these very lands, Galilee and Northern Transjordan, where lies the road to the Sea, will be filled with glory. The people who walk in darkness shall see a great Light—a Light that will shine on all those who live in the land of the shadow of death. For Israel will again be great, filled with joy like that of reapers when the harvest time has come, and like that of men dividing up the plunder they have won. For God will break the chains that bind His people and the whip that scourges them, just as He did when He destroyed the vast host of the Midianites by Gideon's little band. In that glorious day of peace there will no longer be the issuing of battle gear; no more the bloodstained uniforms of war; all such will be burned.

For unto us a child is born; unto us a Son is given; and the government shall be upon His shoulder. These will be His royal titles: "Wonderful," "Counselor," "The Mighty God," "The Everlasting Father," "The Prince of Peace." His ever-expanding peaceful government will never end. He will rule with perfect fairness and justice from the throne of His father David. He will bring true justice and peace to all the nations of the world. This is going to happen because the Lord of heaven's armies has dedicated Himself to do it! And the Spirit of the Lord shall rest upon Him, the Spirit of wisdom, understanding, counsel and might; the Spirit of knowledge and of the fear of the Lord. His delight will be obedience to the Lord. He will not judge by appearance, false evidence or hearsay, but will defend the poor and the exploited. He will rule against the wicked who oppress them. For He will be clothed with fairness and with truth.

In that day the wolf and the lamb will lie down together, and the leopard and goats will be at peace. Calves and fat cattle will be safe among lions, and a little child shall lead them all. The cows will graze among bears; cubs and calves will lie down together, and lions will eat grass like the cows. Babies

307

will crawl safely among poisonous snakes, and a little child who puts his hand in a nest of deadly adders will pull it out unharmed. Nothing will hurt or destroy in all My holy mountain; for as the waters fill the sea, so shall the earth be full of the knowledge of the Lord. In that day He who created the royal dynasty of David will be a banner of salvation to all the world. The nations will rally to Him, for the land where He lives will be a glorious place. This is My plan for the whole earth—I will do it by My mighty power that reaches everywhere around the world.

7. Songs of Thanksgiving

On that day you will say, "Praise the Lord! He was angry with me, but now He comforts me! See, God has come to save me! I will trust and not be afraid, for the Lord is my strength and song; He is my salvation! Oh, the joy of drinking deeply from the Fountain of Salvation!" In that wonderful day you will say, "Thank the Lord! Praise His name! Tell the world about His wondrous love! How mighty He is!" Let all the people of Jerusalem shout His praise with joy! For great and mighty is the Holy One of Israel, who lives among you!

O Lord, I will honor and praise Your name, for You are my God; You do such wonderful things! You planned them long ago, and now You have accomplished them, just as You said! You turn mighty cities into heaps of ruins. The strongest forts are turned to rubble. Beautiful palaces in distant lands disappear and never will be rebuilt. Therefore strong nations will shake with fear before You; ruthless nations will obey and glorify Your name.

But to the poor, O Lord, You are a refuge from the storm, a shadow from the heat, a shelter from merciless men who are like a driving rain that melts down an earthen wall. As a hot, dry land is cooled by clouds, You will cool the pride of ruthless nations.

Here on Mount Zion in Jerusalem, the Lord of Hosts will spread a wondrous feast for everyone around the world—a delicious feast of good food with clear, well-aged wine and choice beef. At that time He will remove the cloud of gloom, the pall of death that hangs over the earth; He will swallow up death forever; the Lord God will wipe away all tears and take away forever all insults and mockery against His land and people. The Lord has spoken—He will surely do it! In that day the people will proclaim, "This is our God, in whom we trust, for whom we waited. Now at last He is here." What a day of rejoicing!

Listen to them singing! In that day the whole land of Judah will sing this song:

Our city is strong! We are surrounded by the walls of His salvation! Open the gates to everyone, for all may enter in who love the Lord. He will keep in perfect peace all those who trust in Him, whose thoughts turn often to the Lord! Trust in the Lord God always, for in the Lord Jehovah is your everlasting strength. He humbles the proud and brings the haughty city to the dust; its walls come crashing down. He presents it to the poor and needy for their use. But for good men the path is not uphill and rough! God does not give them a rough and treacherous path, but smooths the road before them. O Lord, we love to do Your will! Our hearts' desire is to glorify Your name.

In that day (of Israel's freedom) let this anthem be their song:

Israel is My vineyard; I the Lord will tend the fruitful vines; every day I'll water them, and day and night I'll watch to keep all enemies away. My anger against Israel is gone. If I find thorns and briers bothering her, I will burn them up unless these enemies of Mine surrender and beg for peace and My protection. The time will come when Israel will take root and bud and blossom and fill the whole earth with her fruit! Then at last the Lord of Hosts himself will be their crowning glory, the diadem of beauty to His people.

8. Zion's Future Glory

Even the wilderness and desert will rejoice in those days; the desert will blossom with flowers. Yes, there will be an abundance of flowers and singing and joy! The deserts will become as green as the Lebanon Mountains, as lovely as Mount Carmel's pastures and Sharon's meadows; for the Lord will display His glory there, the excellency of our God.

With this news bring cheer to all discouraged ones. Encourage those who are afraid. Tell them, "Be strong, fear not, for your God is coming to destroy your enemies. He is coming to save you." And when He comes, He will open the eyes of the blind and unstop the ears of the deaf. The lame man will leap up like a deer, and those who could not speak will shout and sing! Springs will burst forth in the wilderness and streams in the desert. The parched ground will become a pool with springs of water in the thirsty land. Where desert jackals lived there will be reeds and rushes!

A main road will go through that once-deserted land; it will be named "the Holy Highway." No evilhearted men may walk upon it. God will walk there with you; even the most stupid cannot miss the way. No lion will lurk along its course nor will there be any other dangers; only the redeemed will travel there. These, the ransomed of the Lord, will go home along that road to Zion, singing the songs of everlasting joy. For them all sorrow and all sighing will be gone forever; only joy and gladness will be there.

9. The Folly of Trusting Egypt

Woe to those who run to Egypt for help, trusting their mighty cavalry and chariots instead of looking to the Holy One of Israel and consulting Him. Woe to my rebellious children, says the Lord. You ask advice from everyone but Me and decide to do what I don't want you to do. You yoke yourselves with unbelievers, thus piling up your sins. For without consulting Me you have gone down to Egypt to find aid and have put your trust in Pharaoh for his protection. But in trusting Pharaoh, you will be disappointed, humiliated and disgraced, for he can't deliver on his promises to save you. For though his power extends to Zoan and Hanes, yet it will all turn out to your shame—he won't help one little bit! See them moving slowly across the terrible desert to Egypt—donkeys and camels laden down with treasure to pay for Egypt's aid. On through the badlands they go, where lions and swift venomous snakes live—and Egypt will give you nothing in return! For Egypt's promises are worthless! "The reluctant dragon," I call her!

For the Lord God, the Holy One of Israel, says: Only in returning to Me and waiting for Me will you be saved. In quietness and confidence is your strength, but you'll have none of this. "No," you say. "We will get our help from Egypt; they will give us swift horses for riding to battle." But the only swiftness you are going to see is the swiftness of your enemies chasing you! One of them will chase a thousand of you! Five of them will scatter you until not two of you are left together. You will be like lonely trees in the distant mountain tops.

Yet the Lord still waits for you to come to Him, so He can show you His love; He will conquer you to bless you, just as He said. For the Lord is faithful to His promises. Blessed are all those who wait for Him to help them.

10. God's Protection

The Lord has told me this: When a lion, even a young one, kills a sheep he pays no attention to the shepherd's shouts and noise. He goes right on and eats. In such manner the Lord will come and fight upon Mount Zion. He will not be frightened away! He, the Lord of Hosts, will hover over Jerusalem as birds hover round their nests, and He will defend the city and deliver it.

Therefore, O my people, though you are such wicked rebels, come, return to God. I know the glorious day will come when every one of you will throw away his golden idols and silver images—which in your sinfulness you have made. And the Assyrians will be destroyed but not by swords of men. The sword of God will smite them. They will panic and flee, and the strong young Assyrians will be taken away as slaves. Even their generals will quake with terror and flee when they see the battle flags of Israel, says the Lord. For the flame of God burns brightly in Jerusalem.

The Lord is very great and lives in heaven. He will make Jerusalem the home of justice and goodness and righteousness. An abundance of salvation is stored up for Judah in a safe place, along with wisdom and knowledge and reverence for God. He will shelter Israel from the storm and wind. He will refresh her as a river in the desert and as the cooling shadow of a mighty rock within a hot and weary land. Then at last the eyes of Israel will open wide to God; His people will listen to His voice.

Special Note: For the historical events which followed these preceding messages, see Book I, Part 4, pages 221-225.

MESSAGES IN BABYLON

The primary purpose of Isaiah's messages in Babylon (pages 312-328) was to comfort the exiles in Babylon and to inspire them to return to their native land, rebuild the Temple and re-establish their worship in Jerusalem. Those messages will therefore be best understood with a picture of the expatriate Jews in Babylon—including the writings of Ezekiel and the Daniel stories—in mind. The language is vivid and compassionate, marked by poetic outbursts of sublime grandeur.

11. Good News for Jerusalem

Comfort, Oh comfort My people, says your God. Speak tenderly to Jerusalem and tell her that her sad days are gone. Her sins are pardoned, and the Lord will give her twice as many blessings as He gave her punishment before.

Listen! I hear the voice of someone shouting, "Make a road

for the Lord through the wilderness; make Him a straight, smooth road through the desert. Fill the valleys; level the hills; straighten out the crooked paths and smooth off the rough spots in the road. The glory of the Lord will be seen by all mankind together." The Lord has spoken—it shall be.

The voice says, "Shout!"

"What shall I shout?" I asked.

"Shout that man is like the grass that dies away, and all his beauty fades like dying flowers. The grass withers, the flower fades beneath the breath of God. And so it is with fragile man. The grass withers, the flowers fade, but the Word of our God shall stand forever."

O crier of good news, shout to Jerusalem from the mountain tops! Shout louder—don't be afraid—tell the cities of Judah, "Your God is coming!" Yes, the Lord God is coming with mighty power; He will rule with awesome strength. See, His reward is with Him, to each as he has done. He will feed His flock like a shepherd; He will carry the lambs in His arms and gently lead the ewes with young.

The Spirit of the Lord God is upon me because the Lord has anointed me to bring good news to the suffering and afflicted. He has sent me to comfort the brokenhearted, to announce liberty to captives and to open the eyes of the blind. He has sent me to tell those who mourn that the time of God's favor to them and the day of His wrath to their enemies has come. To all who mourn in Israel He will give:

Beauty for ashes;

Joy instead of mourning;

Praise instead of heaviness.

Who else has held the oceans in His hands and measured off the heavens with His ruler? Who else knows the weight of all the earth and weighs the mountains and the hills? Who can. advise the Spirit of the Lord or be His teacher or give Him counsel? Has He ever needed anyone's advice? Did He need instruction as to what is right and best?

No, for all the peoples of the world are nothing in comparison with Him—they are but a drop in the bucket, dust on the scales. He picks up the islands as though they had no weight at all. All of Lebanon's forests do not contain sufficient fuel to consume a sacrifice large enough to honor Him, nor are all its animals enough to offer to our God. All the nations are as nothing to Him; in His eyes they are less than nothing—mere emptiness and froth.

Are you so ignorant? Are you so deaf to the words of God —the words He gave before the worlds began? Have you never heard nor understood? It is God who sits above the circle of the earth. (The people below must seem to Him like grasshoppers!) He is the One who stretches out the heavens like a curtain and makes His tent from them. He dooms the great men of the world and brings them all to naught. They hardly get started, barely take root, when He blows on them and their work withers. The wind carries them off like straw.

"With whom will you compare Me? Who is My equal?" asks the Holy One. Look up into the heavens! Who created all these stars? As a shepherd leads his sheep calling each by its pet name, and counts them to see that none are lost or strayed, so God does with stars and planets! O Jacob, O Israel, how can you say that the Lord doesn't see your troubles and isn't being fair? Don't you yet understand? Don't you know by now that the everlasting God, the Creator of the farthest parts of the earth, never grows faint or weary? No one can fathom the depths of His understanding. He gives power to the tired and worn-out and strength to the weak. Even the youths shall be exhausted, and the young men will all give up. But they that wait upon the Lord shall renew their strength; they shall mount up with wings like eagles; they shall run and not be weary; they shall walk and not faint.

12. Assurance of God's Help

As for you, O Israel, you are Mine, My chosen one; for you are Abraham's family, and he was My friend. I have called you back from the ends of the earth and said that you must serve but Me alone, for I have chosen you and will not throw you away. Fear not for I am with you. Do not be dismayed; I am your God. I will strengthen you; I will help you; I will uphold you with My victorious right hand. I am holding you by your right hand—I, the Lord your God—and I say to you, Don't be afraid. I am here to help you. Despised though you are, fear not, O Israel, for I will help you. I am the Lord, your Redeemer; I am the Holy One of Israel.

When the poor and needy seek water and there is none and their tongues are parched from thirst, then I will answer when they cry to Me. I, Israel's God, will never forsake them. I will open up rivers for them on high plateaus! I will give them fountains of water in the valleys! In the deserts will be pools of water and rivers fed by springs shall flow across the dry, parched ground. I will plant trees—cedars, myrtle, olive trees, the cypress, fir and pine on barren land. Everyone will see this miracle and understand that it is God who did it, Israel's Holy One.

13. A Righteous Ruler Promised

See My Servant, whom I uphold; My Chosen One, in whom I delight. I have put My Spirit upon Him; He will reveal justice to the nations of the world. He will be gentle—He will not shout nor quarrel in the streets. He will not break the bruised reed nor quench the dimly burning flame. He will encourage the fainthearted, those tempted to despair. He will see full justice given to all who have been wronged. He won't be satisfied until truth and righteousness prevail throughout the earth, nor until even distant lands beyond the seas have put their trust in Him.

The Lord God who created the heavens and stretched them out and created the earth and everything in it, and gives life and breath and spirit to everyone in all the world, He is the One who says (to His servant, the Messiah), "I the Lord have called You to demonstrate My righteousness. I will guard and support You, for I have given You to My people as the personal confirmation of My covenant with them. You shall also be a light to guide the nations unto Me. You will open the eyes of the blind, and release those who sit in prison darkness and despair. I am the Lord! That is My name, and I will not give My glory to anyone else; I will not share My praise with carved idols. Everything I prophesied came true and now I will prophesy again. I will tell you the future before it happens."

Sing a new song to the Lord; sing His praises, all you who live in earth's remotest corners! Sing, O sea! Sing, all you who live in distant lands beyond the sea!

14. God's All-Sufficient Power

But now the Lord who created you, O Israel, says, Don't be afraid, for I have ransomed you; I have called you by name; you are Mine. When you go through deep waters and great trouble, I will be with you. When you go through rivers of difficulty you will not drown! When you walk through the fire of oppression you will not be burned up—the flames will not consume you. For I am the Lord your God, your Saviour, the Holy One of Israel. I gave Egypt and Ethiopia and Seba (to Cyrus) in exchange for your freedom, as your ransom. Others died that you might live; I traded their lives for yours because you are precious to Me and honored, and I love you.

Don't be afraid, for I am with you. I will gather you from east and west, from north and south. I will bring My sons and daughters back to Israel from the farthest corners of the earth. All who claim Me as their God will come, for I have made them for My glory; I created them.

I have witnesses, O Israel, says the Lord! You are My witnesses and My servants, chosen to know and to believe Me and to understand that I alone am God. There is no other God; there never was and never will be. I am the Lord, and there is no other Saviour. Whenever you have thrown away your idols, I have shown you My power. With one word I have saved you. You have seen Me do it; you are My witnesses that it is true. From eternity to eternity I am God. No one can oppose what I do. I, yes, I alone am He who blots away your sins for My own sake and will never think of them again. Listen to Me, all Israel who are left; I have created you and cared for you since you were born. I will be your God through all your lifetime, yes, even when your hair is white with age. I made you and I will care for you. I will carry you along and be your Saviour.

15. God's Faithfulness

Listen to Me, O My servant Israel, O My chosen ones: The Lord who made you, who will help you, says, O servant of Mine, don't be afraid. O Jerusalem, My chosen ones, don't be afraid. For I will give you abundant water for your thirst and for your parched fields. And I will pour out My Spirit and My blessings on your children. They shall thrive like watered grass, like willows on a river bank. "I am the Lord's," they'll proudly say, or "I am a Jew," and tattoo upon their hands the name of God or the honored name of Israel.

The Lord, the King of Israel, says—yes, it is Israel's Redeemer, the Lord of Hosts who says it—I am the First and Last; there is no other God. Who else can tell you what is going to happen in the days ahead? Let them tell you if they can. Let them prove their power. Let them do as I have done since ancient times. Don't, don't be afraid. Haven't I proclaimed from ages past that I would save you? You are My witnesses—is there any other God? No! None that I know about! There is no other Rock! Pay attention, Israel, for you are My servant; I made you and I will not forget to help you. I've blotted out your sins; they are gone like morning mist at noon! Oh, return to Me, for I have paid the price to set you free.

Sing, O heavens, for the Lord has done this wondrous thing. Shout, O earth; break forth into song, O mountains and forests, yes, and every tree; for the Lord redeemed Jacob and is glorified in Israel! The Lord your Redeemer, the Holy One of Israel, says, I am the Lord your God, who punishes you for your own good and leads you along the paths that you should follow. Oh, that you had listened to My laws! Then you would have had peace flowing like a gentle river and great waves of righteousness. Then you would have become as numerous as the sands along the seashores of the world, too many to count, and there would have been no need for your destruction.

Yet even now be free from your captivity! Leave Babylon, singing as you go; shout to the ends of the earth that the Lord has redeemed His servants. Sing for joy, O heavens; shout, O earth; break forth with song, O mountains; for the Lord has comforted His people and will have compassion upon them in their sorrow. Yet they say, "My Lord has deserted us; He has forgotten us."

Never! Can a mother forget her little child and not have love for her own son? Yet even if that should be, I will not forget you. See, I have tattooed your name upon My palm and ever before Me is a picture of Jerusalem's walls. The time will come when God's redeemed will all come home again. They shall come with singing to Jerusalem, filled with joy and ever-lasting gladness; sorrow and mourning will all disappear. I, even I, am He who comforts you and gives you all this joy.

16. God's Message to Cyrus

The Lord, your Redeemer who made you, says, All things were made by Me; I alone stretched out the heavens. By Myself I made the earth and everything in it. When I speak to the rivers and say, "Be dry!" they shall be dry. When I say of Cyrus, "He is My shepherd," he will certainly do as I say; and Jerusalem will be rebuilt and the Temple restored, for I have spoken it.

This is the Lord's message to Cyrus, God's anointed, whom He has chosen to conquer many lands. God shall empower his right hand and he shall crush the strength of mighty kings. God shall open the gates of Babylon to him; the gates shall not be shut against him any more. I will go before you, Cyrus, and level the mountains and smash down the city gates of brass and iron bars. And I will give you treasures hidden in the darkness, secret riches; and you will know that I am doing this—I the Lord, the God of Israel, the One who calls you by your name. And why have I named you for this work? For the sake of Jacob, My servant—Israel, My chosen. I called you by name when you didn't know Me. I am the Lord; there is no other God. I will strengthen you and send you out to victory even though you don't know Me, and all the world from east to west will know there is no other God. I am the Lord and there is no one else. I alone am God.

I form the light and make the dark. I send good times and bad. I the Lord am He who does these things. I have made the earth and created man upon it. With My hands I have stretched out the heavens and commanded all the vast myriads of stars. I have raised up Cyrus to fulfill My righteous purpose, and I will direct all his paths. He shall restore My city and free My captive people—and not for a reward!

Truly, O God of Israel, Saviour, You work in strange, mysterious ways.

17. The Doom of Babylon

The idols of Babylon, Bel and Nebo, are being hauled away on ox carts! But look! The beasts are stumbling! The cart is turning over! The gods are falling out onto the ground! Is that the best that they can do? If they cannot even save themselves from such a fall, how can they save their worshipers from Cyrus? You thought your reign would never end, queen kingdom of the world. You didn't care a whit about My people or think about the fate of those who do them harm.

O pleasure-mad kingdom, living at ease, bragging as the greatest in the world—listen to the sentence of My court upon your sins. You say, "I'll never be a widow; I'll never lose my children." Well, those two things shall come upon you in one moment, in full measure in one day: widowhood and the loss of your children despite all your witchcraft and magic. You felt secure in all your wickedness. "No one sees me," you said. Your wisdom and knowledge have caused you to turn away from God and claim greatness above anyone in all the world. That is why disaster shall overtake you suddenly—so suddenly that you won't know where it comes from. And there will be no atonement then to cleanse away your sins.

O Babylon, the unconquered, come sit in the dust; for your

days of glory, pomp and honor are ended. O daughter of Chaldea, never again will you be the lovely princess, tender and delicate. Take heavy millstones and grind the corn; remove your veil; strip off your robe; expose yourself to public view. You shall be in nakedness and shame. I will take vengeance upon you and will not repent. So speaks our Redeemer who will save Israel from Babylon's mighty power; the Lord of Hosts is His name, the Holy One of Israel. Sit in darkness and silence, O Babylon; never again will you be called "the queen of kingdoms."

18. Deliverance Promised

Wake up, wake up, Jerusalem, and clothe yourself with strength from God. Put on your beautiful clothes, O Zion, Holy City; for sinners—those who turn from God—will no longer enter your gates. Rise from the dust, Jerusalem; take off the slave bands from your neck, O captive daughter of Zion. I will reveal My name to My people and they shall know the power in that name. Then at last they will recognize that it is I—yes, I—who speaks to them.

How beautiful upon the mountains are the feet of those who bring the happy news of peace and salvation, the news that the God of Israel reigns. The watchmen shout and sing with joy, for right before their eyes they see the Lord God bring His people home again. Let the ruins of Jerusalem break into joyous song, for the Lord has comforted His people; He has redeemed Jerusalem. The Lord has bared His holy arm before the eyes of all the nations; the ends of the earth shall see the salvation of our God. Go now, leave your bonds and slavery. Put Babylon and all it represents far behind you—it is unclean to you. You are the holy people of the Lord; you shall not leave in haste, running for your lives; for the Lord will go ahead of you. He, the God of Israel, will protect you from behind.

Listen to Me, all who hope for deliverance, who seek the Lord! Consider the quarry from which you were mined, the rock from which you were cut! Yes, think about your ances-

tors Abraham and Sarah from whom you came. You worry at
being so small and few, but Abraham was only *one* when I
called him. But when I blessed him, he became a great nation.
And the Lord shall bless Israel again and make her deserts
blossom; her barren wilderness shall become as beautiful as
the Garden of Eden. Joy and gladness shall be found there,
thanksgiving and lovely songs. Listen to Me, My people; listen, O Israel, for I will see that right prevails.

My mercy and justice are coming soon; your salvation is on
the way. I will rule the nations; they shall wait for Me and long
for Me to come. Soon, soon you slaves shall be released;
dungeon, starvation and death are not your fate. For I am the
Lord your God, the Lord of Hosts, who dried a path for you
right through the sea between the roaring waves. And I have
put My words in your mouth and hidden you safe within My
hand. I planted the stars in place and molded all the earth. I
am the One who says to Israel, You are Mine. Fear not; you
will no longer live in shame. The shame of your youth and the
sorrows of widowhood will be remembered no more, for your
Creator will be your husband. The Lord of Hosts is His name;
He is your Redeemer, the Holy One of Israel, the God of all
the earth. For the Lord has called you back from your grief—
a young wife abandoned by her husband. For a brief moment
I abandoned you. But with great compassion I will gather you.

In a moment of anger I turned My face a little while; but
with everlasting love I will have pity on you, says the Lord,
your Redeemer. Just as in the time of Noah I swore that I
would never again permit the waters of a flood to cover the
earth and destroy its life, so now I swear that I will never again
pour out My anger on you as I have during this exile. For the
mountains may depart and the hills disappear, but My kindness shall not leave you. My promise of peace for you will
never be broken, says the Lord who has mercy upon you.

19. God's Suffering Servant

See, My Servant shall prosper; He shall be highly exalted.

Yet many shall be amazed when they see Him—yes, even far-off foreign nations and their kings; they shall stand dumbfounded, speechless in His presence. For they shall see and understand what they had not been told before. They shall see My Servant beaten and bloodied, so disfigured one would scarcely know it was a person standing there. So shall He cleanse many nations.

But, oh, how few believe it! Who will listen? To whom will God reveal His saving power? In God's eyes He was like a tender green shoot, sprouting from a root in dry and sterile ground. But in our eyes there was no attractiveness at all, nothing to make us want Him. We despised Him and rejected Him—a man of sorrows, acquainted with bitterest grief. We turned our backs on Him and looked the other way when He went by. He was despised and we didn't care.

Yet it was *our* grief He bore, *our* sorrows that weighed Him down. And we thought His troubles were a punishment from God, for His *own* sins!

But He was wounded and bruised for *our* sins. He was chastised that we might have peace; He was lashed—and we were healed. *We* are the ones who strayed away like sheep! *We,* who left God's paths to follow our own. Yet God laid on *Him* the guilt and sins of every one of us!

He was oppressed and He was afflicted, yet He never said a word. He was brought as a lamb to the slaughter; and as a sheep before her shearers is dumb, so He stood silent before the ones condemning Him. From prison and trial they led Him away to His death. But who among the people of that day realized it was for their sins that He was dying—that He was suffering their punishment? He was buried like a criminal in a rich man's grave; but He had done no wrong and had never spoken an evil word.

Yet it was the Lord's good plan to bruise Him and fill Him with grief. But when His soul has been made an offering for sin, then He shall have a multitude of children, many heirs. He shall live again and God's program shall prosper in His hands. And when He sees all that is accomplished by the anguish of

His soul, He shall be satisfied; and because of what He has experienced, My righteous Servant shall make many to be counted righteous before God, for He shall bear all their sins. Therefore I will give Him the honors of one who is mighty and great, because He has poured out His soul unto death. He was counted as a sinner. He bore the sins of many, and He pled with God for sinners.

20. Mercy Offered to All

Say there! Is anyone thirsty? Come and drink—even if you have no money! Come, take your choice of wine and milk—it's all free! Why spend your money on foodstuffs that don't give you strength? Why pay for groceries that don't do you any good? Listen and I'll tell you where to get good food that fattens up the soul! Come to me with your ears wide open. Listen, for the life of your soul is at stake. I am ready to make an everlasting covenant with you, to give you all the unfailing mercies and love that I had for King David. You also will command the nations and they will come running to obey, not because of your own power or virtue but because I, the Lord your God, have glorified you.

Seek the Lord while you can find Him. Call upon Him now while He is near. Let men cast off their wicked deeds; let them banish from their minds the very thought of doing wrong! Let them turn to the Lord that He may have mercy upon them, and to our God, for He will abundantly pardon! This plan of Mine is not what you would work out, neither are My thoughts the same as yours! For just as the heavens are higher than the earth, so are My ways higher than yours, and My thoughts than yours.

As the rain and snow come down from heaven and stay upon the ground to water the earth and cause the grain to grow and to produce seed for the farmer and bread for the hungry. So also is My Word. I send it out and it always produces fruit. It shall accomplish all I want it to and prosper everywhere I send it.

You will live in joy and peace. The mountains and hills, the

trees of the field—all the world around you—will rejoice.
Where once were thorns, fir trees will grow; where briers grew,
the myrtle trees will sprout up. This miracle will make the
Lord's name very great and be an everlasting sign of God's
power and love.

21. Gentiles to Be Included.

Be just and fair to all, the Lord God says. Do what's right
and good, for I am coming soon to rescue you. Blessed is the
man who refuses to work during My Sabbath days of rest, but
honors them; and blessed is the man who checks himself from
doing wrong. And My blessings are for Gentiles, too, when
they accept the Lord; don't let them think that I will make
them second-class citizens.

As for the Gentiles, the outsiders who join the people of the
Lord and serve Him and love His name, and are His servants
and don't desecrate the Sabbath, and have accepted His covenant and promises, I will bring them also to My holy mountain
of Jerusalem, and make them full of joy within My house of
prayer. I will accept their sacrifices and offerings, for My Temple shall be called a house of prayer for all people! For the Lord
God who brings back the outcasts of Israel says, I will bring
others too besides My people Israel.

I will say, Rebuild the road! Clear away the rocks and
stones. Prepare a glorious highway for My people's return
from captivity. The high and lofty One who inhabits eternity,
the Holy One, says this: I live in that high and holy place
where those with contrite, humble spirits dwell: and I refresh
the humble and give new courage to those with repentant
hearts.

22. False Piety and True

Shout with the voice of a trumpet blast; tell My people of
their sins! Yet they act so pious! They come to the Temple
every day and are so delighted to hear the reading of My laws
—just as though they would obey them—just as though they

don't despise the commandments of their God! How anxious they are to worship correctly; oh, how they love the Temple services!

Heaven is My throne and the earth is My footstool: what temple can you build for Me as good as that? My hand has made both earth and skies, and they are Mine. Yet I will look with pity on the man who has a humble and a contrite heart who trembles at My word. But those who choose their own ways, delighting in their sins, are cursed. God will not accept their offerings. When such men sacrifice an ox on the altar of God, it is no more acceptable to Him than human sacrifice. If they sacrifice a lamb, or bring an offering of grain, it is as loathsome to God as putting a dog or the blood of a swine on His altar! When they burn incense to Him, He counts it the same as though they blessed an idol.

"We have fasted before You," they say. "Why aren't You impressed? Why don't You see our sacrifices? Why don't You hear our prayers? We have done much penance, and You don't even notice it!" I'll tell you why! Because you are living in evil pleasure even while you are fasting, and you keep right on oppressing your workers. Look, what good is fasting when you keep on fighting and quarreling? This kind of fasting will never get you anywhere with Me. Is this what I want, this doing of penance and bowing like reeds in the wind and putting on sackcloth and covering yourselves with ashes? Is that what you call fasting?

No, the kind of fast I want is that you stop oppressing those who work for you and treat them fairly and give them what they earn. I want you to share your food with the hungry and bring right into your own homes those who are helpless, poor and destitute. Clothe those who are cold and don't hide from relatives who need your help. If you do these things, God will shed His own glorious light upon you. He will heal you; your godliness will lead you forward; and goodness will be a shield before you, and the glory of the Lord will protect you from behind. Then when you call, the Lord will answer. "Yes, I am here," He will quickly reply. All you need to do is to stop oppressing the weak, and to stop making false accusations and spreading vicious rumors!

Feed the hungry! Help those in trouble! Then your light will shine out from the darkness, and the darkness around you shall be as bright as day. And the Lord will guide you continually, and satisfy you with all good things, and you will be like a well-watered garden, like an everflowing spring.

23. Future Glory of Zion

Arise, My people! Let your light shine for all the nations to see! For the glory of the Lord is streaming from you. Darkness as black as night shall cover all the peoples of the earth, but the glory of the Lord will shine from you. All nations will come to your light; mighty kings will come to see the glory of the Lord upon you. Lift up your eyes and see! For your sons and daughters are coming home to you from distant lands. Your eyes will shine with joy, your hearts will thrill, for merchants from around the world will flow to you, bringing you the wealth of many lands.

Though once despised and hated and rebuffed by all, you will be beautiful forever, a joy for all the generations of the world; for I will make you so. Powerful kings and mighty nations shall provide you with the choicest of their goods to satisfy your every need, and you will know at last and really understand that I, the Lord, am your Saviour and Redeemer, the Mighty One of Israel. I will exchange your brass for gold, your iron for silver, your wood for brass, your stones for iron. Peace and righteousness shall be your taskmasters!

Violence will disappear out of your land—all war will end. Your walls will be "Salvation" and your gates "Praise." No longer will you need the sun or moon to give you light, for the Lord your God will be your everlasting light, and He will be your glory. Your sun shall never set; the moon shall not go down—for the Lord will be your everlasting light; your days of mourning all will end. All your people will be good. They will possess their land forever, for I will plant them there with My own hands; this will bring Me glory. The smallest family shall multiply into a clan; the tiny group shall be a mighty nation. I, the Lord, will bring it all to pass when it is time.

Because I love Zion, because my heart yearns for Jerusalem, I will not cease to pray for her or to cry out to God on her behalf until she shines forth in His righteousness and is glorious in His salvation. The nations shall see your righteousness. Kings shall be blinded by your glory; and God will confer on you a new name. He will hold you aloft in His hands for all to see—a splendid crown for the King of kings. Never again shall you be called "the Godforsaken Land" or the "Land that God Forgot." Your new name will be "the Land of God's Delight" and "the Bride," for the Lord delights in you and will claim you as His own.

Go out! Go out! Prepare the roadway for My people to return! Build the roads, pull out the boulders, raise the flag of Israel. See, the Lord has sent His messengers to every land and said, "Tell My people, I, the Lord your God, am coming to save you and will bring you many gifts." And they shall be called "the Holy People" and "the Lord's Redeemed," and Jerusalem shall be called "the Land of Desire" and "the City God Has Blessed."

24. Promise for the Future

I am creating new heavens and a new earth—so wonderful that no one will even think about the old ones anymore. Be glad; rejoice forever in My creation. Look! I will recreate Jerusalem as a place of happiness and her people shall be a joy! And I will rejoice in Jerusalem, and in My people; and the voice of weeping and crying shall not be heard there any more. No longer will babies die when only a few days old; no longer will men be considered old at 100! Only sinners will die that young!

In those days when a man builds a house, he will keep on living in it—it will not be destroyed by invading armies as in the past. My people will plant vineyards and eat the fruit themselves—their enemies will not confiscate it. For My people will live as long as trees and will long enjoy their hard won gains. Their harvests will not be eaten by their enemies; their children will not be born to be cannon fodder; for they are the children of those the Lord has blessed; and their children too shall be blessed. I will answer them before they even call to Me. While they are still talking to Me about their needs, I will go ahead and answer their prayers! The wolf and lamb shall feed together, the lion shall eat straw as the ox does, and poisonous snakes shall strike no more! In those days nothing and no one shall be hurt or destroyed in all My holy mountain, says the Lord.

Rejoice with Jerusalem; be glad with her, all you who love her, you who mourned for her. Delight in Jerusalem; drink deep of her glory even as an infant at a mother's generous breasts. Prosperity shall overflow Jerusalem like a river, says the Lord, for I will send it; the riches of the Gentiles will flow to her. Her children shall be nursed at her breasts, carried on her hips and dandled on her knees. I will comfort you there as a little one is comforted by its mother. When you see Jerusalem, your heart will rejoice; vigorous health will be yours. All the world will see the good hand of God upon His people.

"As for Me, this is My promise to them," says the Lord: "My Holy Spirit shall not leave them, and they shall want the good and hate the wrong—they and their children and their children's children forever."

MICAH

Micah was a contemporary of Isaiah, and like him, a prophet to Judah. Isaiah was primarily a court prophet, an adviser to kings; while Micah was from the country and concerned himself more with ethics and morality than with politics. His influence extended over a long period, around 740-690 B.C.

1. Sins of Israel and Judah

These are messages from the Lord to Micah, who lived in the town of Moresheth during the reigns of King Jotham, King Ahaz and King Hezekiah, all kings of Judah. The messages were addressed to both Samaria and Judah and came to Micah in the form of visions.

Attention! Let all the peoples of the world listen. For the Lord in His holy temple has made accusations against you! Look! He is coming! He leaves His throne in heaven and comes to earth, walking on the mountain tops which melt beneath His feet and flow into the valleys like wax in fire, like water pouring down a hill.

And why is this happening?

Because of the sins of Israel and Judah.

What sins?

The idolatry and oppression centering in the capital cities, Samaria and Jerusalem!

Therefore the entire city of Samaria will crumble into a heap of rubble and become an open field, her streets plowed up for planting grapes! The Lord will tear down her walls and her forts, exposing their foundations. He will pour their stones into the valleys below.

Woe is me! It is as hard to find an honest man as grapes and figs when harvest days are over. Not a cluster to eat, not a single early fig however much I long for it! The good men have disappeared from the earth; not one fair-minded man is left. They are all murderers, turning against even their own brothers. They go at their evil deeds with both hands; and how skilled they are in using them! The governor and judge alike demand bribes. The rich man pays them off and tells them whom to ruin. Justice is twisted between them.

Even the best of them are prickly as briers; the straightest is more crooked than a hedge of thorns. But your judgment day is coming swiftly now; your time of punishment is almost here; confusion, destruction and terror will be yours. Don't trust anyone, not your best friend—not even your wife! For the son despises his father; the daughter defies her mother; the bride curses her mother-in-law. Yes, a man's enemies will be found in his own home.

2. Sins of the False Prophets

Listen, you leaders of Israel—you are supposed to know right from wrong, yet you are the very ones who hate good and love evil; you skin My people and strip them to the bone. You devour them, flog them, break their bones and chop them up like meat for the cooking pot—and then you plead with the Lord for His help in times of trouble! Do you really expect Him to listen? He will look the other way! You false prophets! You who lead His people astray! You who cry "Peace" to those who give you food and threaten those who will not pay! This is God's message to you: The night will close about you and cut off all your visions; darkness will cover you, with never a word from God. The sun will go down upon you and your day will end.

Listen to me, you leaders of Israel who hate justice and love unfairness, and fill Jerusalem with murder and sin of every kind—you leaders who take bribes; you priests and prophets who won't preach and prophesy until you're paid. (And yet you fawn upon the Lord and say, "All is well—the Lord is here among us. No harm can come to us.") It is because of you that Jerusalem will be plowed like a field and become a heap of rubble; the mountain top where the Temple stands will be overgrown with brush.

The Lord's voice calls out to all Jerusalem—listen to the Lord if you are wise! The armies of destruction are coming; the Lord is sending them. For your sins are very great—is there to be no end of getting rich by cheating? The homes of the wicked are full of ungodly treasures and lying scales. Shall I say "Good!" to all your merchants with their bags of false, deceitful weights? How could God be just while saying that? Your rich men are wealthy through extortion and violence; your citizens are so used to lying that their tongues can't tell the truth! Therefore I will wound you! I will make your hearts miserable for all your sins.

3. What God Wants

O mountains, listen to the Lord's complaint! For He has a case against His people Israel! He will prosecute them to the full. O My people, what have I done that makes you turn away from Me? Tell Me why your patience is exhausted! Answer Me! For I brought you out of Egypt and cut your chains of slavery; and I gave you Moses, Aaron and Miriam to help you.

"How can we make up to You for what we've done?" you ask. "Shall we bow before the Lord with offerings of yearling calves?" Oh, no! For if you offered Him thousands of rams and ten thousands of rivers of olive oil, would that please Him? Would He be satisfied? If you sacrificed your oldest child, would that make Him glad? Then would He forgive your sins? Of course not!

No, He has told you what He wants, and this is all it is: to be fair and just and merciful, and to walk humbly with your God.

4. Zion's Future Glory

But in the last days Mount Zion will be the most renowned of all the mountains of the world, praised by all nations; people from all over the world will make pilgrimages there. "Come," they will say to one another, "let us visit the mountain of the Lord, and see the Temple of the God of Israel; He will tell us what to do, and we will do it." For in those days the whole world will be ruled by the Lord from Jerusalem! He will issue His laws and announce His decrees from there.

He will arbitrate among the nations and dictate to strong nations far away. They will beat their swords into plowshares and their spears into pruninghooks; nations shall no longer fight each other, for all war will end. There will be universal peace, and all the military academies and training camps will be closed down. Everyone will live quietly in his own home in peace and propserity, for there will be nothing to fear. The Lord Himself has promised this. Therefore we will follow the Lord our God forever and ever, even though all the nations around us worship idols!

In that coming day, the Lord says that He will bring back His punished people—sick and lame and dispossessed—and make them strong again in their own land, a mighty nation. And the Lord Himself shall be their King from Mount Zion forever. O Jerusalem—the watchtower of God's people—your royal might and power will come back to you again, just as before.

5. Small But Famous

O Bethlehem Ephratah, you are but a small Judean village, yet you will be the birthplace of My King who is alive from everlasting ages past! God will abandon His people to their enemies until the time of Israel's spiritual rebirth, then at last the exile remnants of Israel will rejoin their brethren in their own land. And He shall stand and feed His flock in the strength of the Lord, in the majesty of the name of the Lord His God; and His people shall remain there undisturbed, for He will be greatly honored all around the world. He will be our peace. Then the nation of Israel will refresh the world like a gentle dew or the welcome showers of rain.

O Lord, come and rule Your people; lead Your flock; make them live in peace and prosperity; let them enjoy the fertile pastures of Bashan and Gilead as they did long ago.

"Yes," replies the Lord, "I will do mighty miracles for you, like those when I brought you out of slavery in Egypt."

Where is another God like You who pardons the sins of the survivors among His people? You cannot stay angry with Your people, for You love to be merciful. Once again You will have compassion on us. You will tread our sins beneath Your feet; You will throw them into the depths of the ocean! You will bless us as You promised Jacob long ago. You will set Your love upon us, as You promised our father Abraham!

NAHUM

Subject: As God of the nations, Jehovah decrees judgment upon Nineveh, a world capital. Nahum's prophetic description of the siege and fall of the city (in 606 B.C.) is unforgettably graphic.

Author: Nahum, a prophet of Elkosh.

When: Between 664 and 606 B.C.

Note: See *Jonah* for a different picture of Nineveh in another period of history.

1. The Doom of Nineveh

This is the vision God gave to Nahum who lived in Elkosh concerning the impending doom of Nineveh:

Nineveh, you are finished! You are already surrounded by enemy armies! Sound the alarm! Man the ramparts! Muster your defenses full force, and keep a sharp watch for the enemy attack to begin! Shields flash red in the sunlight! The attack begins! See their scarlet uniforms! See their glittering chariots moving forward side by side, pulled by prancing steeds! Your own chariots race recklessly along the streets and through the squares, darting like lightning, gleaming like torches. The king shouts for his officers; they stumble in their haste, rushing to the walls to set up their defenses. But too late! The river gates are open! The enemy has entered! The palace is in panic!

Listen! Hear the crack of the whips as the chariots rush forward against her—wheels rumbling, horses' hoofs pounding and chariots clattering as they bump wildly through the streets! See the flashing swords and glittering spears in the upraised arms of the cavalry! The dead are lying in the streets —bodies, heaps of bodies, everywhere. Men stumble over them, scramble to their feet and fall again. All this because Nineveh sold herself to the enemies of God. The beautiful and faithless city, mistress of deadly charms, enticed the nations with her beauty, then taught them all to worship her false gods, bewitching people everywhere.

Merchants, numerous as stars, filled your city with vast wealth, but your enemies swarm like locusts and carry it away. Your princes and officials crowd together like grasshoppers in the hedges in the cold; but all of them will flee away and disappear like locusts when the sun comes up and warms the earth. O Assyrian king, your princes lie dead in the dust; your people are scattered across the mountains; there is no shepherd now to gather them. There is no healing for your wound—it is far too deep to cure. All who hear your fate will clap their hands for joy; for where can one be found who has not suffered from your cruelty?

Nineveh is like a leaking water tank! Her soldiers slip away, deserting her; she cannot hold them back. "Stop, stop," she shouts, but they keep on running. Loot the silver! Loot the gold! There seems to be no end of treasures. Her vast, uncounted wealth is stripped away. Soon the city is an empty shambles; hearts melt in horror; knees quake; her people stand aghast, pale-faced and trembling. Where now is that great Nineveh, lion of the nations, full of fight and boldness, where even the old and feeble, as well as the young and tender, lived unafraid?

O Nineveh, once mighty lion! You crushed your enemies to feed your children and your wives, and filled your city and your homes with captured goods and slaves. But now the Lord of Hosts has turned against you. He destroys your weapons. Your chariots stand there, silent and unused. Your finest youth lie dead. Never again will you bring back slaves from conquered nations; never again will you rule the earth.

See the messengers come running down the mountains with glad news: "The invaders have been wiped out and we are safe!" O Judah, proclaim a day of thanksgiving and worship only the Lord as you have vowed. For this enemy from Nineveh will never come again. He is cut off forever; he will never be seen again. God is jealous over those He loves; that is why He takes vengeance on those who hurt them. The Lord is good. When trouble comes, He is the place to go! And He knows everyone who trusts in Him!

ZEPHANIAH

Subject: A message from the Lord—the approaching judgment upon Jerusalem unless her people repent.

Author: Zephaniah, a contemporary of King Josiah.

When: Between 640 and 610 B.C.

1. Warning to Jerusalem

Woe to filthy, sinful Jerusalem, city of violence and crime. In her pride she won't listen even to the voice of God. No one can tell her anything; she refuses all correction. She does not trust the Lord nor seek for God. Her leaders are like roaring lions hunting for their victims—out for everything that they can get. Her judges are like ravenous wolves at evening time, who by dawn have left no trace of their prey. Her prophets are liars seeking their own gain; her priests defile the Temple by their disobedience to God's laws. But the Lord is there within the city, and He does no wrong. Day by day His justice is more evident but no one heeds—the wicked know no shame.

"I will sweep away everything in all your land," says the Lord. "I will destroy it to the ground. And I will destroy those who no longer worship the Lord and those who never loved Him and never wanted to.

"On that Day of Judgment I will punish the leaders and princes of Judah and all others wearing heathen clothing. Yes, I will punish those who follow heathen customs and who rob and kill to fill their masters' homes with evil gain of violence and fraud. A cry of alarm will begin at the farthest gate of Jerusalem, coming closer and closer until the noise of the advancing army reaches the very top of the hill where the city is built. Wail in sorrow, you people of Jerusalem. All your greedy businessmen, all your loan sharks—all will die. I will search with lanterns in Jerusalem's darkest corners to find and punish those who sit contented in their sins, indifferent to God, thinking He will let them alone. They are the very ones whose property will be plundered by the enemy, whose homes will be ransacked; they will never have a chance to live in the new homes they have built. They will never drink wine from the vineyards they have planted." That terrible day is near. Swiftly it comes—a day when strong men will weep bitterly.

2. Answered Prayer

Gather together and pray, you shameless nation, while there still is time—before judgment begins, and your opportunity is blown away like chaff; before the fierce anger of the Lord falls and the terrible day of His wrath begins. Beg Him to save you, all who are humble—all who have tried to obey. Walk humbly and do what is right; perhaps even yet the Lord will protect you from His wrath in that day of doom.

Sing, O daughter of Zion; shout, O Israel; be glad and rejoice with all your heart, O daughter of Jerusalem. For the Lord will remove His hand of judgment and disperse the armies of your enemy. And the Lord Himself, the King of Israel, will live among you! At last your troubles will be over—you need fear no more.

On that day the announcement to Jerusalem will be, "Cheer up, don't be afraid. For the Lord your God has arrived to live among you. He is a mighty Saviour. He will give you victory. He will rejoice over you in great gladness; He will love you and not accuse you."

Is that a joyous choir I hear? No, it is the Lord Himself exulting over you in happy song, "I have gathered your wounded and taken away your reproach. And I will deal severely with all who have oppressed you. I will save the weak and helpless ones and bring together those who were chased away. I will give glory to My former exiles, mocked and shamed. At that time I will gather you together and bring you home again and give you a good name—a name of distinction among all the peoples of the earth; and they will praise you when I restore your fortunes before your very eyes," says the Lord. "They will live quietly, in peace, and lie down in safety, and no one will make them afraid."

HABAKKUK

This short book has exerted an influence in inverse proportion to its size. Habakkuk wrestles with this problem: Why does God allow a godless nation—the Chaldeans—to invade and devastate the land where His chosen people live?

The Chaldeans began to assert themselves in 626 B.C. and in 605 B.C. at Carchemish they defeated Egypt and Judah's King Josiah died, a victim of this power struggle.

1. Habakkuk's Complaint

This is the message that came to the prophet Habakkuk in a vision from God: O Lord, how long must I call for help before You will listen? I shout to You in vain; there is no answer. "Help! Murder!" I cry, but no one comes to save. Must I forever see this sin and sadness all around me? Wherever I look there is oppression and bribery and men who love to argue and to fight. The law is not enforced and there is no justice given in the courts. The wicked far outnumber the righteous. Bribes and trickery prevail.

The Lord replied: "Look! and be amazed! You will be astounded at what I am about to do! For I am going to do something in your own lifetime that you will have to see to believe. I am raising a new force on the world scene—the Chaldeans, a cruel and violent nation who will march across the world and conquer it. They are notorious for their cruelty. They do as they like, and no one can interfere. Their horses are swifter than leopards. They are a fierce people, more fierce than wolves at dusk. They scoff at kings and princes and scorn their forts. They simply heap up dirt against their walls and capture them! They sweep past like wind and are gone; but their guilt is deep, for they claim their power is from their gods."

O Lord my God, my Holy One, You who are eternal—is Your plan in all of this to wipe us out? Surely not! O God our rock. You have decreed the rise of these Chaldeans to chasten and correct us for our awful sins. We are wicked, but they far more! Will You, who cannot allow sin in any form, stand idly by while they swallow us up? Should You be silent while the wicked destroy those who are better than they? Are we but fish to be caught and killed? Are we but creeping things that have no leader to defend them from their foes? Must we be strung up on their hooks and dragged out in their nets while they rejoice? Then they will worship their nets and burn incense before them! "These are the gods who make us rich," they'll say. Will You let them get away with this forever? Will they succeed forever in their heartless wars?

2. God's Answer

I will climb my watchtower now and wait to see what answer God will give to my complaint.

Then the Lord said to me: Write My answer on a billboard large and clear, so that anyone can read it at a glance and rush to tell the others. But these things I plan won't happen right away. Slowly, steadily, surely, the time approaches when the vision will be fulfilled. If it seems slow do not despair, for these things will surely come to pass. Just be patient! They will not be overdue a single day! Note this: Wicked men trust themselves alone as these Chaldeans do—and fail; but the righteous man trusts in Me—and lives! What's more, these arrogant Chaldeans are betrayed by all their wine, for it is treacherous. In their greed they have collected many nations, but like death and hell, they are never satisfied.

The time is coming when all their captives will taunt them, saying: You robbers! At last justice has caught up with you! Now you will get your just desserts for your oppression and extortion! Suddenly your debtors will rise up in anger and turn on you and take all you have, while you stand trembling and helpless.

Woe to you for getting rich by evil means, attempting to live beyond the reach of danger. By the murders you commit, you have shamed your name and forfeited your lives. The very stones in the walls of your homes cry out against you, and the beams in the ceilings echo what they say. Woe to you who build cities with money gained from murdering and robbery! Woe to you for making your neighboring lands reel and stagger like drunkards beneath your blows, and then gloating over their nakedness and shame. Soon your own glory will be replaced by shame. Drink down God's judgment on yourselves. Stagger and fall! You cut down the forests of Lebanon—now you will be cut down! You terrified the wild animals you caught in your traps—now terror will strike you because of all your murdering and violence in cities everywhere. Woe to those who command their lifeless wooden idols to arise and save them, who call out to the speechless stone to tell them what to do. Can images speak for God? They are overlaid with gold and silver, but there is no breath at all inside!

But the Lord is in His holy temple; let all the earth be silent before Him. Has not the Lord decreed that godless nations' gains will turn to ashes in their hands? They work so hard, but all in vain! The time will come when all the earth is filled, as the waters fill the sea, with an awareness of the glory of the Lord.

3. Habakkuk's Prayer

This is the prayer of triumph that Habakkuk sang before the Lord:

O Lord, now I have heard Your report and I worship You in awe for the fearful things You are going to do. In this time of our deep need begin again to help us, as You did in years gone by. Show us Your power to save us. In Your wrath remember mercy. I see God moving across the deserts from Mount Sinai. His brilliant splendor fills the earth and sky; His glory fills the heavens, and the earth is full of His praise! What a wonderful God He is! From His hands flash rays of brilliant light. He rejoices in His awesome power.

Was it in anger, Lord, You smote the rivers and parted the sea? Were You displeased with them? No, You were sending Your chariots of salvation! All saw Your power! Then springs burst forth upon the earth at Your command! The mountains watched and trembled. Onward swept the raging water. The mighty deep cried out, announcing its surrender to the Lord. The lofty sun and moon began to fade, obscured by brilliance from Your arrows and the flashing of Your glittering spear. You marched across the land in awesome anger and trampled down the nations in Your wrath. Your horsemen marched across the sea; the mighty waters piled high. I tremble when I hear all this; my lips quiver with fear. My legs give way beneath me and I shake in terror. I will quietly wait for the day of trouble to come upon the people who invade us.

Even though the fig trees are all destroyed, and there is neither blossom left nor fruit; and though the olive crops all fail, and the fields lie barren; even if the flocks die in the fields and the cattle barns are empty, yet I will rejoice in the Lord; I will be happy in the God of my salvation. The Lord God is my strength, and He will give me the speed of a deer and bring me safely over the mountains.

JEREMIAH

Jeremiah's prophetic ministry began around 627 B.C. when he was only 20 years of age and continued for over 50 years. He lived and prophesied during the decline, dissolution and fall of the Southern Kingdom of Judah. (Jerusalem was captured and laid waste by Nebuchadnezzar in 586 B.C.) He saw the end coming and advised surrender to Babylon, instead of resistance. For this reason he was hated and persecuted as a traitor. For the historical background of his ministry see Book I, Part 4, pages 227-236.

1. Jeremiah's Call

These are God's messages to Jeremiah the priest (the son of Hilkiah) who lived in the town of Anathoth in the land of Benjamin. The first of these messages came to him in the thirteenth year of the reign of Amon's son Josiah, king of Judah. Others came during the reign of Josiah's son Jehoiakim, king of Judah, and at various other times until July of the eleventh year of the reign of Josiah's son Zedekiah, king of Judah, when Jerusalem was captured and the people were taken away as slaves.

The Lord said to me: "I knew you before you were formed within your mother's womb; before you were born I sanctified you and appointed you as My spokesman to the world."

"O Lord God," I said. "I can't do that! I'm far too young! I'm only a youth!"

"Don't say that," He replied, "for you will go wherever I send you and speak whatever I tell you to. And don't be afraid of the people, for I the Lord will be with you and see you through."

Then He touched my mouth and said, "See, I have put My words in your mouth! Today your work begins, to warn the nations and the kingdoms of the world. In accord with My words spoken through your mouth I will tear down some and destroy them, and plant others and nurture them and make them strong and great."

2. Two Visions of Judgment

The Lord said to me, "Look, Jeremiah! What do you see?"

I replied, "I see a whip made from the branch of an almond tree."

And the Lord replied, "That's right, and it means that I will surely carry out My threats of punishment." Then the Lord asked me, "What do you see now?"

And I replied, "I see a pot of boiling water, tipping southward, spilling over Judah."

"Yes," He said, "for terror from the north will boil out upon all the people of this land. I am calling the armies of the kingdoms of the north to come to Jerusalem and set their thrones at the gates of the city and all along its walls and in all the other cities of Judah. This is the way I will punish My people for deserting Me and for worshiping other gods—yes, idols they themselves have made! Get up and dress and go out and tell them whatever I tell you to say. Don't be afraid of them, or else I will make a fool of you in front of them. For see, today I have made you impervious to their attacks. They cannot harm you. You are strong like a fortified city that cannot be captured, like an iron pillar and heavy gates of brass. All the kings of Judah and its officers and priests and people will not be able to prevail against you. They will try, but they will fail. For I am with you," says the Lord. "I will deliver you."

3. Israel's Idolatry

O Israel, says the Lord, why did your fathers desert Me? What sin did they find in Me that turned them away and changed them into fools who worship idols? They ignore the fact that it was I the Lord who brought them safely out of Egypt and led them through the barren wilderness, a land of deserts and rocks, of drought and death where no one lives or even travels. And I brought them into a fruitful land to eat of its bounty and goodness, but they made it into a land of sin and corruption and turned My inheritance into an evil thing.

Look around you and see if you can find another nation anywhere that has traded in its old gods for new ones—even though their gods are nothing. Send to the west to the island of Cyprus; send to the east to the deserts of Kedar. See if anyone there has ever heard so strange a thing as this. And yet My people have given up their glorious God for silly idols! The heavens are shocked at such a thing and shrink back in horror and dismay. For My people have done two evil things: They have forsaken Me, the fountain of life-giving water; and they have built for themselves broken cisterns that can't hold water!

Like a thief, the only shame that Israel knows is getting caught. Kings, princes, priests and prophets—all are alike in this. They call a carved-up wooden post their father, and for their mother they have an idol chiseled out from stone. Yet in time of trouble they cry to Me to save them! Why don't you call on these gods you have made? When danger comes, let *them* go out and save you if they can! For you have as many gods as there are cities in Judah. Don't come to Me—you are all rebels, says the Lord. I have punished your children but it did them no good; they still will not obey. And you yourselves have killed my prophets as a lion kills its prey.

O My people, listen to the words of God, "Have I been unjust to Israel? Have I been to them a land of darkness and of evil? Why then do My people say, 'At last we are free from God; we won't have anything to do with Him again!' How can you disown your God like that? Can a girl forget her jewels? What bride will seek to hide her wedding dress? Yet for years on end My people have forgotten Me—the most precious of their treasures. And yet you say, 'I haven't done a thing to anger God. I'm sure He isn't angry!' I will punish you severely because you say, 'I haven't sinned!' You say to Me, 'O Father, You have always been my friend; surely You won't be angry about such a little thing! Surely You will just forget it!' So you talk, and keep on doing all the evil that you can."

4. Call to Repentance

This message from the Lord came to me during the reign of King Josiah:

Have you seen what Israel does? Like a wanton wife who gives herself to other men at every chance, so Israel has worshiped other gods on every hill, beneath every shady tree. I thought that someday she would return to Me and once again be Mine, but she didn't come back. And her faithless sister Judah saw the continued rebellion of Israel. Yet she took no heed even though she saw that I divorced faithless Israel. But now Judah too has left Me and given herself to harlotry, for she has gone to other gods to worship them. In fact, faithless Israel is less guilty than treacherous Judah!

The Lord is saying to the men of Judah and Jerusalem, "Plow up the hardness of your hearts; otherwise the good seed will be wasted among the thorns. Cleanse your minds and hearts, not just your bodies, or else My anger will burn you to a crisp because of all your sins. And no one will be able to put the fire out."

Shout to Jerusalem and to all Judea, telling them to sound the alarm throughout the land. "Run for your lives! Flee to the fortified cities!" Send a signal from Jerusalem: "Flee now, don't delay! For I the Lord am bringing vast destruction on you from the north." A lion—a destroyer of nations—stalks from his lair; and he is headed for your land. Your cities will lie in ruin without inhabitant. Put on clothes of mourning and weep with broken hearts, for the fierce anger of the Lord has not stopped yet.

O Jerusalem, cleanse your hearts while there is time. You can yet be saved by casting out your evil thoughts. From Dan and from Mount Ephraim your doom has been announced. Warn the other nations that the enemy is coming from a distant land and they shout against Jerusalem and the cities of Judah. They surround Jerusalem like shepherds moving in on some wild animal! For my people have rebelled against Me, says the Lord. Your ways have brought this down upon you. It is a bitter dose of your own medicine.

My heart, my heart—I writhe in pain; my heart pounds within me. I cannot be still because I have heard, O my soul, the blast of the enemies' trumpets and the enemies' battle cries. Wave upon wave of destruction rolls over the land, until it lies in utter ruin. Suddenly, in a moment, every house is crushed. How long must this go on? How long must I see war and death surrounding me? Until My people leave their foolishness, for they refuse to listen to Me; they are dull retarded children who have no understanding. They are smart enough at doing wrong, but for doing right they have no talent, none at all.

I hear voices high upon the windswept mountains crying, crying. It is the sons of Israel who have turned their backs on God and wandered far away. O My rebellious children, come back to Me again and I will heal you from your sins.

5. Sin and Punishment

The message to Jeremiah from the Lord:

Run up and down through every street in all Jerusalem; search high and low and see if you can find one fair and honest man! Search every square, and if you find just one, I'll not destroy the city! Even under oath, men lie.

Then I said, "But what can we expect from the poor and ignorant? They don't know the ways of God. How can they obey Him? I will go now to their leaders, the men of importance, and speak to them, for they know the ways of the Lord and the judgment that follows sin. But they too have utterly rejected their God."

So I will send upon them the wild fury of the lion from the forest; the desert wolves shall pounce upon them, and a leopard shall lurk around their cities so that all who go out shall be torn apart. For their sins are very many; their rebellion against Me is great. For the people of Israel and Judah are full of treachery against Me, says the Lord. They have lied and said, "He won't bother us! No evil will come upon us! There will be neither famine nor war! God's prophets are windbags full of words with no divine authority. Their claims of doom will fall upon themselves, not us!"

Therefore this is what the Lord God of Hosts says to His prophets: Because of talk like this I'll take your words and prophecies and turn them into raging fire and burn up these people like kindling wood. See, I will bring a distant nation against you, O Israel, says the Lord; a mighty nation, an ancient nation whose language you don't understand. Their weapons are deadly; the men are all mighty. And they shall eat your harvest and your children's bread, and your flocks of sheep and herds of cattle, yes, and your grapes and figs; and they shall sack your walled cities that you think are safe.

But I will not completely blot you out, so says the Lord. And when your people ask, "Why is it that the Lord is doing this to us?" then you shall say, "You rejected Him and gave yourselves to other gods while in your land; now you must be slaves to foreigners in their lands."

Make this announcement to Judah and to Israel: "Listen, O foolish, senseless people—you with the eyes that do not see and the ears that do not listen—have you no respect at all for Me? Should I sit back and act as though nothing is going on?" the Lord God asks. "Shouldn't I punish a nation such as this? A horrible thing has happened in this land—the priests are ruled by false prophets, and My people like it so! But your doom is certain."

6. God's Final Warning to Jerusalem

This is your last warning, O Jerusalem. If you don't listen, I will let you know when trouble comes." But you said, "No! Even the few who remain in Israel shall be gleaned again, the Lord of Hosts has said; for as a grape-picker checks each vine to pick what he has missed, so the remnant of My people shall be destroyed again. But who will listen when I warn them? Their ears are closed and they refuse to hear. The word of God has angered them; they don't want it at all.

Yet the Lord pleads with you still: Ask where the good road is, the godly paths where you walked in the days of long ago. Travel there, and you will find rest for your souls. But you reply, "No, that is not the road we want!" I set watchmen over you who warned you: "Listen for the sound of the trumpet! It will let you know when trouble comes." But you said, "No! We won't pay any attention!" This, then, is My decree against My people: (Listen to it, distant lands; listen to it, O My people in Jerusalem; listen to it, all the earth!) I will bring evil upon this people; it will be the fruit of their own sin because they will not listen to Me. They reject My law. There is no use now in burning sweet incense from Sheba before Me! Keep your expensive perfumes! I cannot accept your offerings; they have no sweet fragrance for Me.

Even if Moses and Samuel stood before Me pleading for these people, even then I wouldn't help them—away with them! Get them out of My sight! And if they say to you, "But where can we go?" tell them the Lord says, "Those who are destined for death, to death; those who must die by the sword, to the sword; those doomed to starvation, to famine; and those for captivity, to captivity."

I will appoint over them four kinds of destroyers—the sword to kill, the dogs to tear, and the vultures and wild animals to finish up what's left. Because of the wicked things that Manasseh, son of Hezekiah king of Judah, did in Jerusalem, I will punish you so severely that your fate will horrify the peoples of the world. Who will feel sorry for you, Jerusalem? Who will weep for you? Who will even bother to ask how you are? You have forsaken Me and turned your backs upon Me. Therefore I will clench My fists against you to destroy you. I am tired of always giving you another chance. O Jerusalem, pride of My people, put on mourning clothes and sit in ashes and weep bitterly as for an only son. For suddenly the destroying armies will be upon you.

Jeremiah, I have made you an assayer of metals, that you may test this My people and determine their value. Listen to what they are saying and watch what they are doing. Are they not the worst of rebels, full of evil talk against the Lord? They are insolent as brass, hard and cruel as iron. The bellows blow fiercely; the refining fire grows hotter, but it can never cleanse them, for there is no pureness in them to bring out. Why continue the process longer? All is dross. No matter how hot the fire, they continue in their wicked ways. I must label them "impure, rejected silver," and I have discarded them.

7. Hypocrisy in Life

Then the Lord said to Jeremiah: Go over to the entrance of the Temple of the Lord and give this message to the people:

O Judah, listen to this message from God. Listen to it, all of you who worship here. The Lord of Hosts, the God of Israel says: Even yet if you quit your evil ways I will let you stay in your own land. But don't be fooled by those who lie to you and say that since the Temple of the Lord is here, God will never let Jerusalem be destroyed.

You may remain under these conditions only: If you stop your wicked thoughts and deeds and are fair to others; and stop exploiting orphans, widows and foreigners. And stop your murdering. And stop worshiping idols as you do now, for it causes your own hurt. Then, and only then, will I let you stay in this land that I gave to your fathers to keep forever.

You think that because the Temple is here, you will never suffer? Don't fool yourselves! Do you really think that you can steal, murder, commit adultery, lie, worship Baal and all of those new gods of yours, and then come here and stand before Me in My Temple and chant "God will save us!"—only to go right back to all these evil things again?

The Lord of Hosts, the God of Israel says, Away with your offerings and sacrifices! It wasn't offerings and sacrifices I wanted from your fathers when I led them out of Egypt. That was not the point of My command. But what I told them was: *Obey* Me and I will be your God and you shall be My people; only do as I say and all shall be well! But they wouldn't listen; they kept on doing whatever they wanted to, following their

351

own stubborn, evil thoughts. They went backwards instead of forwards. Ever since the day your fathers left Egypt until now I have kept on sending them My prophets, day after day. But they wouldn't listen to them or even try to hear. They are hard and stubborn and rebellious—worse even than their fathers were.

Once again give them this message from the Lord: When a person falls, he jumps up again; when he is on the wrong road and discovers his mistake, he goes back to the fork where he made the wrong turn. But these people keep on along their evil path, even though I warn them. I listen to their conversation and what do I hear? Is anyone sorry for sin? Does anyone say, "What a terrible thing I have done?" No, all are rushing pell-mell down the path of sin as swiftly as a horse rushing to the battle!

The stork knows the time of her migration, as does the turtledove, and the crane and the swallow. They all return at God's appointed time each year; but not My people! They don't accept the laws of God! How can you say, "We understand His laws," when your teachers have twisted them up to mean a thing I never said? They give useless medicine for My people's grievous wounds, for they assure them all is well when that isn't so at all! Are they ashamed because they worship idols? No, not in the least; they don't even know how to blush!

8. Jeremiah's Grief

My grief is beyond healing; my heart is broken. Listen to the weeping of my people all across the land. "Where is the Lord?" they ask. "Has God deserted us?"

"Oh, why have they angered Me with their carved idols and strange evil rites?" the Lord replies.

"The harvest is finished; the summer is over and we are not saved." I weep for the hurt of my people; I stand amazed, silent, dumb with grief. Is there no medicine in Gilead? Is there no physician there? Why doesn't God do something? Why doesn't He help? Oh, that my eyes were a fountain of tears, I would weep forever; I would sob day and night for the slain of my people! Oh, that I could go away and forget them and live in some wayside shack in the desert, for they are all adulterous, treacherous men.

"They bend their tongues like bows to shoot their arrows of untruth. They care nothing for right and go from bad to worse; they care nothing for Me," says the Lord. "Should not I punish them for such things as this?" asks the Lord. "Shall not My soul be avenged on such a nation as this? Sobbing and weeping, I point to their mountains and pastures, for now they are desolate without a living soul. Gone is the lowing of cattle, gone the birds and wild animals. All have fled. And I will turn Jerusalem into heaps of ruined houses where jackals have their dens. The cities of Judah shall be ghost towns with no one living in them."

Who is wise enough to understand all this? Where is the Lord's messenger to explain it? Why is the land a wilderness so that no one dares even to travel through?

"Because," the Lord replies, "My people have forsaken My commandments and not obeyed My laws."

9. Wisdom and Folly Contrasted

The Lord says: Let not the wise man bask in his wisdom, nor the mighty man in his might, nor the rich man in his riches. Let them boast in this alone: That they truly know Me and understand that I am the Lord of justice and of righteousness whose love is steadfast; and that I love to be this way to My people.

O Lord, there is no other God like You. For You are great and Your name is full of power. Who would not fear You, O King of nations?—and that title belongs to You alone! Among all the wise men of the earth and in all the kingdoms of the world there isn't anyone like You. The wisest of men who worship idols are altogether stupid and foolish. They bring beaten sheets of silver from Tarshish and gold from Uphaz and give them to skillful goldsmiths who make their idols; then they clothe these gods in kingly purple robes that expert tailors make. But the Lord is the only true God, the living God, the everlasting King. The whole earth shall tremble at His anger; the world shall hide before His displeasure.

Say to those who worship other gods that their so-called gods who have not made the heavens and earth shall vanish from the earth, but our God formed the earth by His power and wisdom, and by His intelligence He hung the stars in space and stretched out the heavens. It is His voice that echoes in the thunder of the storm clouds. He causes mist to rise upon the earth; He sends the lightning and brings the rain; and from His treasuries He brings the wind. But foolish men without knowledge of God bow before their idols. It is a shameful business that these men are in, for what they make are frauds, gods without life or power in them. All are worthless, silly; they will be crushed when their makers perish. But the God of Jacob is not like these foolish idols. He is the Creator of all, and Israel is His chosen nation. The Lord of Hosts is His name.

The shepherds of my people have lost their senses; they no longer follow God nor ask His will. Therefore they perish and their flocks are scattered. O Lord, I know it is not within the power of man to map his life and plan his course—so You correct me, Lord. But please be gentle. Don't do it in Your anger for I would die.

10. Jeremiah and His Enemies

Jeremiah said, "What sadness is mine, my mother; oh, that I had died at birth! For I am hated everywhere I go. I am neither a creditor soon to foreclose nor a debtor refusing to pay—yet they all curse me. Well, let them curse! Lord, You know how I have pled with You on their behalf—how I have begged You to spare these enemies of mine.

"Lord, You know it is for Your sake that I am suffering. They are persecuting me because I have proclaimed Your word to them. Don't let them kill me! Rescue me from their clutches, and give them what they deserve! Your words are what sustain me; they are food to my hungry soul. They bring joy to my sorrowing heart and delight me. How proud I am to bear Your name, O Lord. I have not joined the people in their merry feasts. I sit alone beneath the hand of God. I burst with indignation at their sins. Yet You have failed me in my time of need! You have let them keep right on with all their persecutions. Will they never stop hurting me? Your help is as uncertain as a seasonal mountain brook—sometimes a flood, sometimes as dry as a bone."

The Lord replied: "Stop this foolishness and talk some sense! Only if you return to trusting Me will I let you continue as My spokesman. You are to influence *them,* not let them influence *you!* They will fight against you like a besieging army against a high city wall. But they will not conquer you for I am with you to protect and deliver you, says the Lord. Yes, I will certainly deliver you from these wicked men and rescue you from their ruthless hands."

11. The Cost of Sin

My people sin as though commanded to, as though their evil were laws chiseled with an iron pen or diamond point upon their stony hearts or on the corners of their altars. Their youths do not forget to sin, worshiping idols beneath each tree, high in the mountains or in the open country down below. And so I will give all your treasures to your enemies as the price that you must pay for all your sins. And the wonderful heritage I reserved for you will slip out of your hand; and I will send you away as slaves to your enemies in distant lands. For you have kindled a fire of My anger that shall burn forever.

The Lord says: Cursed is the man who puts his trust in mortal man and turns his heart away from God. He is like a stunted shrub in the desert with no hope for the future; he lives on the salt-encrusted plains in the barren wilderness; good times pass him by forever. But blessed is the man who trusts in the

Lord and has made the Lord his hope and confidence. He is like a tree planted along a riverbank, with its roots reaching deep into the water—a tree not bothered by the heat nor worried by long months of drought. Its leaves stay green and it goes right on producing all its luscious fruit. The heart is the most deceitful thing there is. It is desperately wicked. No one can really know how bad it is! Only the Lord knows! He searches all hearts and examines deepest motives so He can give to each person his right reward, according to his deeds— how he has lived.

Like a partridge filling her nest with young she has not hatched and which will soon fly away and desert her, so is the man who gets his wealth by unjust means. Sooner or later he will lose his riches and at the end of his life become a poor old fool. But our refuge is Your throne, eternal, high and glorious. O Lord the Hope of Israel, all who turn away from You shall be disgraced and shamed; they are registered for earth and not for glory, for they have forsaken the Lord, the fountain of living waters.

Lord, You alone can heal me. You alone can save, and my praises are for You alone. Men scoff at me and say, "What is this word of the Lord you keep talking about? If these threats of yours are really from God, why don't they come true?" Lord, I don't want the people crushed by terrible calamity. The plan is Yours, not mine. It is *Your* message I've given them, not my own. *I* don't want them doomed! Lord, don't desert me now! You alone are my hope.

12. Jeremiah's Prayers

O Lord God! You have made the heavens and earth by Your great power; nothing is too hard for You! You are loving and kind to thousands, yet children suffer for their fathers' sins; You are the great and mighty God, the Lord of Hosts. You have all wisdom and do great and mighty miracles; for Your eyes are open to all the ways of men, and You reward everyone according to his life and deeds. You have done incredible things in the land of Egypt—things still remembered to this day. And You have continued to do great miracles in Israel and all around the world. You have made Your name very great, as it is today. You brought Israel out of Egypt with mighty miracles and great power and terror.

You gave Israel this land that You promised their fathers long ago—a wonderful land that flows with milk and honey. Our fathers came and conquered it and lived in it, but they refused to obey You or to follow Your laws; they have hardly done one thing You told them to. That is why You have sent all this terrible evil upon them. See how the siege mounds have been built against the city walls; and the Babylonians shall conquer the city by sword, famine and disease. Everything has happened just as You said—as You determined it should!

Then the people said, "Come, let's get rid of Jeremiah. We have our own priests and wise men and prophets—we don't need his advice. Let's silence him that he may speak no more against us, nor bother us again."

O Lord, help me! See what they are planning to do to me! Should they repay evil for good? They have set a trap to kill me, yet I spoke well of them to You and tried to defend them from Your anger. Now, Lord, let their children starve to death and let the sword pour out their blood! Let their wives be widows and be bereft of all their children! Let their men die in epidemics and their youths die in battle! Let screaming be heard from their homes as troops of soldiers come suddenly upon them. For they have dug a pit for me to fall in, and they have hidden traps along my path. Lord, You know all their murderous plots against me. Don't forgive them, don't blot out their sin, but let them perish before You; deal with them in Your anger.

Then I said, O Lord, You deceived me when You promised me Your help. I have to give them Your messages because You are stronger than I am, but now I am the laughingstock of the city, mocked by all. You have never once let me speak a word of kindness to them; always it is disaster and horror and destruction. No wonder they scoff and mock and make my name a household joke. And I can't quit! For if I say I'll never again mention the Lord—never more speak in His name— then His Word in my heart is like fire that burns in my bones, and I can't hold it any longer. Yet on every side I hear their whispered threats and am afraid. "We will report you," they say. Even those who were my friends are watching me, waiting for a fatal slip. "He will trap himself," they say, "and then we will get our revenge on him."

But the Lord stands beside me like a great warrior, and before Him, the Mighty, Terrible One, they shall stumble. They cannot defeat me; they shall be shamed and thoroughly humiliated, and they shall have a stigma upon them forever. O Lord of Hosts, who knows those who are righteous and examines the deepest thoughts of hearts and minds, let me see Your vengeance on them. For I have committed my cause to You.

I will sing out in thanks to the Lord! Praise Him! For He has delivered me, poor and needy, from my oppressors. Yet, cursed be the day that I was born! Cursed be the man who brought my father the news that a son was born. Let that messenger be destroyed like the cities of old which God overthrew without mercy. Terrify him all day long with battle shouts, because he did not kill me at my birth! Oh that I had died within my mother's womb, that it had been my grave! Why was I ever born? For my life has been but trouble and sorrow and shame. Bring confusion and trouble on all who persecute me; but give me peace.

13. God's Sovereign Power

Here is another message to Jeremiah from the Lord: Go down to the shop where clay pots and jars are made and I will talk to you there. I did as He told me and found the potter working at his wheel. But the jar that he was forming didn't turn out as he wished, so he kneaded it into a lump and started again.

Then the Lord said, "O Israel, can't I do to you as this potter has done to his clay? As the clay is in the potter's hand, so are you in My hand. Whenever I announce that a certain nation or kingdom is to be taken up and destroyed, if that nation renounces its evil ways, I will not destroy it as I had planned. And if I announce that I will make a certain nation strong and great, but that nation changes its mind and turns to evil and refuses to obey Me, then I too will change My mind and not bless that nation as I had said I would."

Therefore go and warn all Judah and Jerusalem, saying: Hear the word of the Lord, He is planning evil against you now instead of good; turn back from your evil paths and do what is right.

"Don't waste your breath," they replied. "We have no intention whatever of doing what God says. We will continue to live as we want to, free from any restraint, full of stubbornness and wickedness!"

Then the Lord said: Even among the heathen, no one has ever heard of such a thing! My people have done something too horrible to understand. The snow never melts high up in the Lebanon Mountains. The cold flowing streams from the crags of Mount Hermon never run dry. These can be counted on. But not My people! For they have deserted Me and turned to foolish idols. They have turned away from the ancient highways of good and walk the muddy paths of sin. Therefore their land shall become desolate, so that all who pass by will gasp and shake their heads in amazement at its utter desolation. I will scatter My people before their enemies as the east wind scatters dust; and in all their trouble I will turn My back on them and refuse to notice their distress.

Israel has forsaken Me and turned this valley into a place of shame and wickedness. The people burn incense to idols—idols that neither this generation nor their forefathers nor the kings of Judah have worshiped before—and they have filled this place with the blood of innocent children. They have built high altars to Baal and there they burn their sons in sacrifice—a thing I never commanded them nor even thought of! The day is coming, says the Lord, when this valley shall no longer be called Topheth or Ben-Hinnom Valley, but the Valley of Slaughter. And now, Jeremiah, as these men watch, smash the jar you brought with you and say to them, "This is the message to you from the Lord of Hosts. As this jar lies shattered, so I will shatter the people of Jerusalem; and as this jar cannot be mended, neither can they."

As Jeremiah returned from Topheth where he had delivered

this message, he stopped in front of the Temple of the Lord and said to all the peope, "The Lord of Hosts, the God of Israel, says: I will bring upon this city and her surrounding towns all the evil I have promised, because you have stubbornly refused to listen to the Lord."

14. Warning to Jehoiakim

Then the Lord said to me: Go over and speak directly to the king of Judah and say, Listen to this message from God, O king of Judah, sitting on David's throne. Let your servants and your people listen too. The Lord says: Be fair-minded. Do what is right! Help those in need of justice! Quit your evil deeds! Protect the rights of aliens and immigrants, orphans and widows; stop murdering the innocent! If you put an end to all these terrible deeds you are doing, then I will deliver this nation and once more give kings to sit on David's throne, and there shall be prosperity for all. But if you refuse to pay attention to this warning, I swear by My own name, says the Lord, that this palace shall become a shambles. Instead of leading My flock to safety, you have deserted them and driven them to destruction. And now I will pour out judgment upon you for the evil you have done to them.

And woe to you, King Jehoiakim, for you are building your great palace with forced labor. By not paying wages you are building injustice into its walls and oppression into its doorframes and ceilings. You say, "I will build a magnificent palace with huge rooms and many windows, panelled throughout with fragrant cedar and painted a lovely red." But a beautiful palace does not make a great king! Why did your father Josiah reign so long? Because he was just and fair in all his dealings. That is why God blessed him. He saw to it that justice and help was given the poor and the needy and all went well for him. This is how a man lives close to God. But you! You are full of selfish greed and all dishonesty! You murder the innocent, oppress the poor and reign with ruthlessness.

Therefore this is God's decree of punishment against King

Jehoiakim who succeeded his father Josiah on the throne: His family will not weep for him when he dies. His subjects will not even care that he is dead. For the time is coming, says the Lord, when I will place a righteous Branch upon King David's throne. He shall be a King who shall rule with wisdom and justice and cause righteousness to prevail everywhere throughout the earth. And this is His name: THE LORD OUR RIGHTEOUSNESS. At that time Judah will be saved and Israel will live in peace.

15. False Prophets Denounced

My heart is broken for the false prophets, full of deceit. I awake with fear and stagger as a drunkard does from wine because of the awful fate awaiting them, for God has decreed holy words of judgment against them. I knew the prophets of Samaria were unbelievably evil, for they prophesied by Baal and led My people Israel into sin; but the prophets of Jerusalem are even worse! The things they do are horrible; they commit adultery and love dishonesty. They encourage and compliment those who are doing evil instead of turning them back from their sins. These prophets are as thoroughly depraved as the men of Sodom and Gomorrah were.

Therefore the Lord of Hosts says: I will feed them with bitterness and give them poison to drink. For it is because of them that wickedness fills this land. This is My warning to My people, says the Lord of Hosts. Don't listen to these false prophets when they prophesy to you, filling you with futile hopes. They are making up everything they say. They do not speak for Me! They keep saying to these rebels who despise Me, "Don't worry! All is well." And to those who live the way they want to they say, "The Lord has said you shall have peace!" But can you name even one of these prophets who lives close enough to God to hear what He is saying? Has even one of them cared enough to listen? See, the Lord is sending a furious whirlwind to sweep away these wicked men. The terrible anger of the Lord will not abate until it has carried out the

361

full penalty He decrees against them. When Jerusalem has fallen you will see what I mean.

I have not sent these prophets, yet they claim to speak for Me; I gave them no message, yet they say their words are Mine. If they were Mine, they would try to turn My people from their evil ways. Am I a God who is only in one place and cannot see what they are doing? Can anyone hide from Me? Am I not everywhere in all of heaven and earth?

If they are prophets, they are prophets of deceit, inventing everything they say. By telling these false dreams they are trying to get My people to forget Me in the same way as did their fathers who turned away to the idols of Baal. Let these false prophets tell their dreams and let My true messengers faithfully proclaim My every word. There is a difference between chaff and wheat! Does not My word burn like fire? asks the Lord. Is it not like a mighty hammer that smashed the rock to pieces? So I stand against these prophets who get their messages from each other—these smooth-tongued prophets who say, "This message is from God!" Their made-up dreams are flippant lies that lead My people into sin. I did not send them and they have no message at all for My people, says the Lord.

When one of the people or one of these prophets or priests asks you, "Well, Jeremiah, what is the sad news from the Lord today?" you shall reply, "What sad news? You are the sad news, for the Lord has cast you away!"

And as for the false prophets and priests and people who joke about "today's sad news from God," I will punish them and their families for saying this. You can ask each other, "What's God's message? What is He saying?" But stop using this term, "God's sad news." For what is sad is you and your lying. You are twisting My words and inventing "messages from God" that I didn't speak. You may respectfully ask Jeremiah, "What is the Lord's message? What has He said to you?" But if you ask him about "today's sad news from God," when I have warned you not to mock like that, then I, the Lord God, will unburden Myself of the burden you are to Me. I will cast you out of My presence, you and this city I gave to you and your fathers. And I will bring reproach upon you and your name shall be infamous through the ages.

16. Parable of the Baskets of Figs

After Nebuchadnezzar, king of Babylon, had captured, enslaved and exiled Jeconiah (son of Jehoiakim), king of Judah, to Babylon along with the princes of Judah and the skilled tradesmen—the carpenters and blacksmiths—the Lord gave me this vision: I saw two baskets of figs placed in front of the Temple in Jerusalem. In one basket there were fresh, just-ripened figs, but in the other the figs were spoiled and moldy, too rotten to eat. Then the Lord said to me, "What do you see, Jeremiah?"

I replied, "Figs, some very good and some very bad."

Then the Lord said, "The good figs represent the exiles sent to Babylon. I have done it for their good. I will see that they are well-treated and I will bring them back here again. I will help them and not hurt them; I will plant them and not pull them up. I will give them hearts that respond to Me. They shall be My people and I will be their God, for they shall return to Me with great joy.

"But the rotten figs represent Zedekiah, king of Judah, his officials, all the others of Jerusalem left here in this land and those who live in Egypt. I will treat them like spoiled figs, too bad to use. I will make them repulsive to every nation of the earth, and they shall be mocked and taunted and cursed wherever I compel them to go. And I will send massacre and famine and disease among them until they are destroyed from the land of Israel which I gave to them and to their fathers."

17. Jeremiah's Final Message

This message for all the people of Judah came from the Lord to Jeremiah during the fourth year of the reign of King Jehoiakim of Judah (son of Josiah). This was the year Nebuchadnezzar, king of Babylon, began his reign. "For the past 23 years," Jeremiah said, "from the thirteenth year of the reign of Josiah (son of Amon), king of Judah, until now, God has been sending me His messages. I have faithfully passed them on to you, but you haven't listened. Again and again down through the years, God has sent you His prophets, but you have refused to hear. Each time the message was this: Turn from the evil road you are traveling and from the evil things you are doing. Only then can you continue to live here in this land which the Lord gave to you and to your ancestors forever.

"Don't anger Me by worshiping idols; but if you are true to Me, then I'll not harm you." But you won't listen; you have made Him furious with your idols. So you have brought upon yourselves all the evil that has come your way. And now the Lord God of Hosts says:

"Because you have not listened to Me, I will gather together all the armies of the north under Nebuchadnezzar, king of Babylon (I have appointed him as My deputy), and I will bring them all against this land and its people and against the other nations near you, and I will utterly destroy you and make you a byword of contempt forever. I will take away your joy, your gladness and your wedding feasts; your businesses shall fail and all your homes shall lie in silent darkness. This entire land shall become a desolate wasteland; all the world will be shocked at the disaster that befalls you. Israel and her neighboring lands shall serve the king of Babylon for seventy years."

18. Restoration Promised

This is another of the Lord's messages to Jeremiah: The Lord God of Israel says, Write down for the record all that I have said to you. For the time is coming when I will restore the fortunes of My people, Israel and Judah, and I will bring them home to this land that I gave to their fathers; they shall possess it and live here again. For on that day, says the Lord of Hosts, I will break the yoke from their necks and snap their chains, and foreigners shall no longer be their masters! For they shall serve the Lord their God, and David their king, whom I will raise up for them, says the Lord.

So don't be afraid, O Jacob My servant; don't be dismayed, O Israel; for I will bring you home again from distant lands, and your children from their exile. They shall have rest and quiet in their own land, and no one shall make them afraid. I will give you back your health again and heal your wounds. Now you are called "the Outcast" and "Jerusalem, the place nobody wants."

But, says the Lord, when I bring you home again from your captivity and restore your fortunes, Jerusalem will be rebuilt upon her ruins; the palace will be reconstructed as it was before. The cities will be filled with joy and great thanksgiving, and I will multiply My people and make of them a great and honored nation. Their children shall prosper as in David's reign; their nation shall be established before Me, and I will punish anyone who hurts them. They will have their own ruler again. He will not be a foreigner. And I will invite him to be a priest at My altars—for who would dare to come unless invited—and he shall approach Me and You shall be My people and I will be your God.

At that time, says the Lord, all the families of Israel shall recognize Me as the Lord; they shall act like My people. I will care for them as I did those who escaped from Egypt, to whom I showed My mercies in the wilderness, when Israel sought for rest. For long ago the Lord had said to Israel: I have loved you, O My people, with an everlasting love; with loving kindness I have drawn you to Me. I will rebuild your nation, O virgin of Israel. You will again be happy and dance merrily with the timbrels. Again you will plant your vineyards upon the mountains of Samaria and eat from your own gardens there.

The day shall come when watchmen on the hills of Ephraim will call out and say, "Arise, and let us go up to Zion to the Lord our God."

For the Lord says, Sing with joy for all that I will do for Israel, the greatest of the nations! Shout out with praise and joy, "The Lord has saved His people, the remnant of Israel." For I will bring them from the north and from earth's farthest ends, not forgetting their blind and lame, young mothers with their little ones, those ready to give birth. It will be a great company who comes.

19. Homecoming Celebration

The Lord spoke to me again, saying: In Ramah there is bitter weeping, Rachel is weeping for her children and she cannot be comforted, for they are gone.

But the Lord says: Don't cry any longer; for I have heard your prayers and you will see them again; they will come back to you from the distant land of the enemy. There is hope for your future, says the Lord, and your children will come again to their own land. They shall come home and sing songs of joy upon the hills of Zion, and they shall be radiant over the goodness of the Lord—the good crops, the wheat and the wine and the oil, and the healthy flocks and herds. Their life shall be like a watered garden, and all their sorrows shall be gone. The young girls will dance for joy, and menfolk—old and young —will take their part in all the fun; for I will turn their mourning into joy and I will comfort them and make them rejoice, for their captivity with all its sorrows will be behind them.

The people shall no longer quote this proverb—"Children pay for their fathers' sins." For everyone shall die for his own sins—the person eating sour grapes is the one whose teeth are set on edge.

The day will come, says the Lord, when I will make a new contract with the people of Israel and Judah. It won't be like the one I made with their fathers when I took them by the hand to bring them out of the land of Egypt—a contract they broke, forcing me to reject them, says the Lord. But this is the new contract I will make with them: I will inscribe My laws upon their hearts so that they shall want to honor Me. Then they shall truly be My people and I will be their God. At that time it will no longer be necessary to admonish one another to know the Lord. For everyone both great and small shall really know Me then, says the Lord, and I will forgive and forget their sins.

The Lord who gives us sunlight in the daytime and the moon and stars to light the night and who stirs the sea to make the roaring waves—His name is Lord of Hosts—says this: I am as likely to reject My people Israel as I am to do away with these laws of nature! Not until the heavens can be measured and the foundations of the earth explored will I consider casting them away forever for their sins!

For the time is coming, says the Lord, when all Jerusalem shall be rebuilt for the Lord, when the whole topic of conversation will be that God is bringing His people home from the countries of the north where He had sent them as slaves for punishment. You will look back no longer to the time I brought you out from slavery in Egypt. That mighty miracle will scarcely be mentioned any more. Yes, I will bring you back again, says the Lord, to this same land I gave your fathers. And I will cleanse away all their sins against Me and pardon them. Then this city will be an honor to Me, and it will give Me joy and be a source of praise and glory to Me before all the nations of the earth! The people of the world will see the good I do for My people and will tremble with awe!

The Lord declares that the happy voices of bridegrooms and of brides and the joyous song of those bringing thanksgiving offerings to the Lord will be heard again in this doomed land. The people will sing: "Praise the Lord! For He is good and His mercy endures forever!" For I will make this land happier and more prosperous than it has ever been before. This land—though every man and animal and city is doomed —will once more see shepherds leading sheep and lambs. Once again their flocks will prosper in the mountain villages, in the cities east of the Philistine plain, in all the cities of the Negeb, in the land of Benjamin, in the vicinity of Jerusalem and in all the cities of Judah.

Yes, the day will come, says the Lord, when I will do for Israel and Judah all the good I promised them. At that time I will bring to the throne the true Son of David, and He shall rule justly. In that day the people of Judah and Jerusalem shall live in safety and their motto will be, "The Lord is our righteousness!"

OBADIAH

Obadiah calls for divine judgment upon the Edomites for their inhuman treatment of Judah. Because Edom attacked her at various times in her history, it is not possible to date this prophecy exactly. It could be as early as 586 B.C. or later than 575 B.C.

1. Divine Judgment upon Edom

In a vision, the Lord God showed Obadiah the future of the land of Edom. A report has come from the Lord, he said that God has sent an ambassador to the nations with this message: Attention! You are to send your armies against Edom and destroy her!

I will cut you down to size among the nations, Edom, making you small and despised. You are proud because you live in those high, inaccessible cliffs. "Who can ever reach us way up here!" you boast. Don't fool yourselves! Though you soar as high as eagles and build your nest among the stars, I will bring you plummeting down, says the Lord. Far better it would be for you if thieves had come at night to plunder you—for they would not take everything! or if your vineyards were robbed of all their fruit—for at least the gleanings would be left! Every nook and cranny will be searched and robbed, and every treasure found and taken.

And why? Because of what you did to your brother Israel. Now your sins will be exposed for all to see; ashamed and defenseless, you will be cut off forever. For you deserted Israel in his time of need. You stood aloof, refusing to lift a finger to help him when invaders carried off his wealth and divided Jerusalem among them by lot; you were as one of his enemies. You yourselves went into the land of Israel in the day of his calamity and looted him. You made yourselves rich at his expense. You stood at the crossroads and killed those trying to escape; you captured the survivors and returned them to their enemies in that terrible time of his distress.

You should not have done it. You should not have gloated when they took him far away to foreign lands; you should not have rejoiced in the day of his misfortune; you should not have mocked in his time of need. As you have done to Israel, so will it be done to you. Your acts will boomerang upon your heads.

EZEKIEL

As a young man Ezekiel was captured and carried captive to Babylon, ten years before Jerusalem was totally destroyed. Thus it was in Babylon that he exercised his prophetic ministry, between 592 and 570 B.C. Not only did he relate to his fellow exiles, but often addressed messages to Jerusalem before its fall in 586 B.C. Following that catastrophic event, he became a messenger of hope speaking with assurance of God's continuing devotion to His people and predicting their ultimate restoration.

1. Ezekiel's Vision and Call

Ezekiel was a priest—the son of Buzi—who lived with the Jewish exiles beside the Chebar Canal in Babylon. One day late in June when I was 30 years old, the heavens were suddenly opened to me and I saw visions from God.

I saw in this vision a great storm coming towards me from the north, driving before it a huge cloud glowing with fire, with a mass of fire inside that flashed continually; and in the fire there was something that shone like polished brass. Then from the center of the cloud, four strange forms appeared that looked like men, except that each had four faces and two pairs of wings! Their legs were those of men, but their feet were cloven like calves' feet and shone like burnished brass. And beneath each of their wings I could see human hands. The four living beings were joined wing to wing, and they flew straight forward without turning.

The sky spreading out above them looked as though it were made of crystal; it was inexpressibly beautiful. Each being's wings stretched straight out to touch the others' wings, and each had two wings covering his body. And as they flew their wings roared like waves against the shore, or like the voice of God, or like the shouting of a mighty army. When they stopped they let down their wings. And every time they stopped, there came a voice from the crystal sky above them.

For high in the sky above them was what looked like a throne made of beautiful blue sapphire stones; and upon it sat Someone who appeared to be a Man. From His waist up He seemed to be all glowing bronze, dazzling like fire; from His waist down He seemed to be entirely flame; and there was a glowing halo like a rainbow all around Him. That was the way the glory of the Lord appeared to me. And when I saw it, I fell face downward on the ground and heard the voice of Someone speaking to me:

"Son of dust," He said, "I am sending you to the nation of Israel, to a nation rebelling against Me. They and their fathers have kept on sinning against Me until this very hour. For they are a hardhearted, stiff-necked people. But I am sending you to give them My messages—the messages of the Lord God. And whether they listen or not (for remember, they are rebels), they will at least know they have had a prophet among them. Son of dust, don't be afraid of them; don't be frightened even though their threats are sharp and barbed and sting like scorpions. Don't be dismayed by their dark scowls. For remember, they are rebels!

"But see, I have made you hard and stubborn too—as tough as they are. I have made your forehead as hard as rock. So don't be afraid of them, or fear their sullen, angry looks, even though they are such rebels."

Then He added, "Son of dust, let all My words sink deep into your own heart first; listen to them carefully for yourself. Then afterward, go to your people in exile and whether or not they will listen, tell them: This is what the Lord God says!"

2. Ezekiel's Vision of Exiles

Then the Spirit lifted me up and the glory of the Lord began to move away, accompanied by the sound of a great earthquake. It was the noise of the wings of the living beings as they touched against each other and the sound of their wheels beside them. The Spirit lifted me up and took me away to Tel-abib, another colony of Jewish exiles beside the Chebar River. I went in bitterness and anger, but the hand of the Lord was strong upon me. And I sat among them, overwhelmed, for seven days.

At the end of the seven days, the Lord said to me: "Son of dust, I have appointed you as a watchman for Israel; whenever I send My people a warning, pass it on to them at once. If you refuse to warn the wicked when I want you to tell them, 'You are under the penalty of death, therefore repent and save your life'—they will die in their sins but I will punish you! I will demand your blood for theirs. But if you warn them and they keep on sinning and refuse to repent, they will die in their sins, but you are blameless—you have done all you could.

"And if a good man becomes bad, and you refuse to warn him of the consequences, and the Lord destroys him, his previous good deeds won't help him—he shall die in his sin. But I will hold you responsible for his death and punish you. But if you warn him and he repents, he shall live and you have saved your own life too."

3. Ezekiel's Vision of Jerusalem

Then late in August of the sixth year of King Jehoiachin's captivity, as I was talking with the elders of Judah in my home, the power of the Lord God fell upon me. I saw what appeared to be a Man; from His waist down, He was made of fire; from His waist up, He was all amber-colored brightness. He put out what seemed to be a hand and took me by the hair. And the Spirit lifted me up into the sky and seemed to transport me to Jerusalem, to the entrance of the north gate, where the large idol was that had made the Lord so angry.

Suddenly the glory of the God of Israel was there, just as I had seen it before in the valley. He said to me, "Son of dust, look toward the north." So I looked and sure enough, north of the altar gate in the entrance, stood the idol. And He said: "Son of dust, do you see what they are doing? Do you see what great sins the people of Israel are doing here, pushing Me from My Temple? But come, and I will show you greater sins than these!"

Then He brought me to the door of the Temple court where I made out an opening in the wall. "Now dig into the wall," He said. I did and uncovered a door to a hidden room. "Go on in," He said, "and see the wickedness going on in there!" So I went in. The walls were covered with pictures of all kinds of snakes, lizards, and hideous creatures, besides all the various idols worshiped by the people of Israel. Seventy elders of Israel were standing there along with Jaazaniah, son of Shaphan, worshiping the pictures. Each of them held a censer of burning incense, so there was a thick cloud of smoke above their heads. Then the Lord said to me: "Son of dust, have you seen what the elders of Israel are doing in their minds? For they say, 'The Lord doesn't see us; He has gone away!' " Then he added, "Come, and I will show you greater sins than these!"

He brought me to the north gate of the Temple, and there sat women weeping for Tammuz, their god. "Have you seen this?" He asked. "But I will show you greater evils than these!" Then He brought me into the inner court of the Temple and there at the door between the porch and the bronze altar were about twenty-five men standing with their backs to the Temple of the Lord, facing east, worshiping the sun! "Have you seen this?" He asked. "Is it nothing to the people of Judah that they commit these terrible sins, leading the whole nation into idolatry, thumbing their noses at Me and arousing My fury against them? Therefore I will deal with them in fury. I will neither pity nor spare. And though they scream for mercy, I will not listen.

"Even King Zedekiah shall go out at night through a hole in the wall, taking only what he can carry with him. His face will be muffled, and he won't be able to see. I will capture him in My net and bring him to Babylon, the land of the Chaldeans; but he shall not see it. He shall die there. I will scatter his servants and guards to the four winds and send the sword after them. And when I scatter them among the nations, then they shall know I am the Lord.

"Son of dust, when the people of this land sin against Me, then I will crush them with My fist and break off their food supply and send famine to destroy both man and beast. If Noah, Daniel and Job were all living today, they alone would be saved by their righteousness, and I would destroy the remainder of Israel," says the Lord God.

"Son of dust, the remnant left in Jerusalem are saying about your brother exiles: 'It is because they were so wicked that the Lord has deported them. Now the Lord has given us their land!' But tell the exiles that the Lord God says: Although I have scattered you in the countries of the world, yet I will be a sanctuary to you for the time that you are there, and I will gather you back from the nations where you are scattered and give you the land of Israel again. And when you return you will remove every trace of all this idol worship. I will give you one heart and a new spirit; I will take from you your hearts of stone and give you tender hearts of love for God, so that you can obey My laws and be My people, and I will be your God. But as for those now in Jerusalem, who long for idols, I will repay them fully for their sins," the Lord God says.

Then the cherubim lifted their wings and rose into the air with their wheels beside them; and the glory of the God of Israel stood above them. Then the glory of the Lord rose from over the city and stood above the mountain on the east side. Afterwards the Spirit of God carried me back again to Babylon to the Jews in exile there. And so ended the vision of my visit to Jerusalem. And I told the exiles everything the Lord had shown me.

4. False Prophets Denounced

Again the Lord said to me, "Son of dust, prophesy against the false prophets of Israel who are inventing their own visions and claiming to have messages from Me when I have never told them anything at all. Woe upon them!"

Then this message came to me: "O Israel, these 'prophets' of yours are as useless as foxes for rebuilding your walls! O evil prophets, what have you ever done to strengthen the walls of Israel against her enemies—by strengthening Israel in the Lord? Instead you have lied when you said, 'My message is from God!' God did not send you. And yet you expect Him to fulfill your prophecies. Can you deny that you have claimed to see 'visions' you never saw and that you have said, 'This message is from God,' when He never spoke to you at all?"

Therefore the Lord God says: "I will destroy you for these visions and lies. My hand shall be against you, and you shall be cut off from among the leaders of Israel; I will blot out your names and you will never see your own country again. And you shall know I am the Lord. For these evil men deceive My people by saying God will send peace, when that is not My plan at all! My people build a flimsy wall and these prophets praise them for it—and cover it with whitewash! Tell these evil builders that their wall will fall. A heavy rainstorm will undermine it; great hailstones and mighty winds will knock it down. And when the wall falls, the people will cry out, 'Why didn't you tell us that it wasn't good enough? Why did you whitewash it and cover up its faults?' Yes, it will surely fall."

The Lord God says: "I will sweep it away with a storm of indignation and with a great flood of anger and with hailstones of wrath. I will break down your whitewashed wall, it will fall on you and crush you, and you shall know I am the Lord. For they were lying prophets, claiming Jerusalem will have peace when there is no peace, says the Lord God."

5. Allegory of the Useless Vine

Then this message came to me from the Lord: "Son of dust, what good are vines from the forest? Are they as useful as trees? Are they even as valuable as a single branch? No, for vines can't be used even for making pegs to hang up pots and pans! All they are good for is fuel—and even so, they burn but poorly! So they are useless both before and after being put in the fire!

"This is what I mean: The people of Jerusalem are like the vines of the forest—useless before being burned and certainly useless afterwards! And I will set Myself against them to see to it that if they escape from one fire, they will fall into another. Then you shall know I am the Lord. And I will make the land desolate because they worship idols," says the Lord God.

6. Allegory of the Unfaithful Wife

Then again a message came to me. "Son of dust," the Lord said, "speak to Jerusalem about her loathsome sins. Tell her!" And these are the words He spoke:

You are no better than the people of Canaan—your father must have been an Amorite and your mother a Hittite! When you were born, no one cared for you. When I first saw you, your umbilical cord was uncut, and you had been neither washed nor rubbed with salt nor clothed. No one had the slightest interest in you; no one pitied you or cared for you. On that day when you were born, you were dumped out into a field and left to die, unwanted.

But I came by and saw you there, covered with your own blood, and I said, "Live! Thrive like a plant in the field!" And you did! You grew up and became tall, slender and supple, a jewel among jewels.

Later when I passed by and saw you again, you were old enough for marriage; and I wrapped My cloak around you to legally declare My marriage vow. I signed a covenant with you, and you became Mine. Then when the marriage had taken place, I gave you beautiful clothes of embroidered linens and silk, and sandals made of dolphin hide. I gave you lovely ornaments, bracelets and beautiful necklaces, a ring for your nose and two more for your ears, and a lovely tiara for your head. And so you were made beautiful with gold and silver; and your clothes were silk and linen and beautifully embroidered. You ate the finest foods and became more beautiful than ever. You looked like a queen, and so you were!

Your reputation was great among the nations for your beauty; it was perfect because of all the gifts I gave you, says the Lord God.

But you thought you could get along without Me—you trusted in your beauty instead; and you gave yourself as a harlot to every man who came along. Your beauty was his for the asking. You used the lovely things I gave you for making idol shrines and to decorate your bed of harlotry. Unbelievable! There has never been anything like it before! You took the very jewels and gold and silver ornaments I gave to you and made statues of men and worshiped them. This is adultery against Me. You used the beautifully embroidered clothes I gave you—to cover your idols! And used My oil and incense to worship *them!* You set before them—imagine it—the fine flour and oil and honey I gave you; you used it as a lovely sacrifice to *them!* And you took My sons and daughters you had borne to Me, sacrificed them to your gods and they are gone. Wasn't it enough that you should be a harlot? Must you also slay My children in the fires of strange altars? And in all these years of adultery and sin you have not thought of those days long ago when you were naked and covered with blood.

The Lord God says: Because I see your filthy sins, your adultery with your lovers—your worshiping of idols—and the slaying of your children as sacrifices to your gods, this is what I am going to do: I will punish you as a murderess is punished and as a woman breaking wedlock living with other men. I will give you to your lovers—these many nations—to destroy. They will knock down your brothels and idol altars, strip you and take your beautiful jewels and leave you naked and ashamed. They will burn your homes, punishing you before the eyes of many women. And I will see to it that you stop your adulteries with other gods and end your payments to your allies for their love. Then at last My fury against you will die away; My jealousy against you will end, and I will be quiet and not be angry with you any more.

For the Lord God says: You lightly broke your solemn vows to Me, yet I will keep the pledge I made to you when you were young. I will establish an everlasting covenant with you forever. And you will remember with shame all the evil you have done. You will be overcome by My favor when I take your sisters, Samaria and Sodom, and make them your daughters for you to rule over. You will know you don't deserve this gracious act, for you did not keep My covenant. I will reaffirm My covenant with you, and you will know I am the Lord. Despite all you have done, I will be kind to you again; you will cover your mouth in silence and in shame when I forgive you all that you have done, says the Lord God.

7. In Defense of God's Justice

Then the Lord's message came to me again:

Why do people use this proverb about the land of Israel: "The children are punished for their fathers' sins"? As I live, says the Lord God, you will not use this proverb any more in Israel, for all souls are Mine to judge, fathers and sons alike, and My rule is this: It is for a man's own sins that he will die.

But if a man is just and does what is lawful and right, and obeys My laws, that man is just, says the Lord, and he shall surely live. But if that man has a son who is a robber or murderer who fulfills none of his responsibilities, who refuses to obey the laws of God, loves idols and worships them on the mountains, commits adultery, oppresses the poor and needy, robs his debtors by refusing to let them redeem what they have given him in pledge, shall that man live? No! He shall surely die, and it is his own fault.

But if this sinful man has, in turn, a son who sees all his father's wickedness so that he fears God and decides against that kind of life, and if he helps the poor and does not loan money at interest and obeys My laws—he shall not die because of his father's sins; he shall surely live. But his father shall die for his own sins because he is cruel and robs and does wrong.

"What?" you ask. "Doesn't the son pay for his father's sins?" No! For if the son does what is right and keeps My laws, he shall surely live. The one who sins is the one who dies. The son shall not be punished for his father's sins, nor the father for his son's. The righteous person will be rewarded for his own goodness and the wicked person for his wickedness.

But if a wicked person turns away from all his sins and begins to obey My laws and do what is just and right, he shall surely live and not die. All his past sins will be forgotten; and he shall live because of his goodness. Do you think I like to see the wicked die? asks the Lord. Of course not! I only want him to turn from his wicked ways and live. However, if a righteous person turns to sinning and acts like any other sinner, should he be allowed to live? No, of course not. All his previous goodness will be forgotten and he shall die for his sins.

Yet you say: "The Lord isn't being fair!" Listen to Me, O people of Israel. Am I the One who is unfair or is it you? When a good man turns away from being good and begins sinning and dies in his sins, he dies for the evil he has done. And if a wicked person turns away from his wickedness, obeys the law and does right, he shall save his soul, for he has thought it over and decided to turn from his sins and live a good life. He shall surely live—he shall not die. And yet the people of Israel keep saying: "The Lord is unfair!" O people of Israel, it is you who are unfair, not I. I will judge each of you, O Israel, and punish or reward each according to your own actions. Oh, turn from your sins while there is yet time. Put them behind you and receive a new heart and a new spirit. For why will you die, O Israel? I do not enjoy seeing you die, the Lord God says. Turn, turn and live!

8. Allegory of the Prodigal Daughters

The Lord's message came to me again:

There were two sisters who as young girls became prostitutes in Egypt. The older girl was named Oholah; her sister was Oholibah. (I am speaking of Samaria and Jerusalem!) I married them, and they bore Me sons and daughters. But then Oholibah turned to other gods instead of Me and gave her love to the Assyrian, her neighbors who were all attractive young men, captains and commanders in handsome blue, dashing about on their horses. And so she sinned with them—the choicest men of Assyria—worshiping their idols, defiling herself. And so I delivered her into the evil clutches of the Assyrians whose gods she loved so much. They stripped her and killed her and took away her children as their slaves. Her name was known to every woman in the land as a sinner who had received what she deserved.

But when Oholibah (Jerusalem) saw what had happened to her sister she went right ahead in the same way and sinned even more than her sister. She fawned over her Assyrian neighbors, those handsome young men on fine steeds, those army officers in handsome uniforms—all of them desirable! I saw the way she was going, following right along behind her older sister. She was in fact more debased than Samaria, for she fell in love with pictures she saw painted on a wall! They were pictures of Babylonian military officers, outfitted in striking red uniforms with handsome belts and flowing turbans on their heads. When she saw these paintings she longed to give herself to the men pictured; so she sent messengers to Chaldea to invite them to come to her. And they came and committed adultery with her, defiling her in the bed of love; but afterwards she hated them and broke off all relations with them.

And now the Lord God says that He will raise against you, O Oholibah (Jerusalem), those very nations from which you turned away, disgusted. For the Babylonians will come, and with them all the Chaldeans from Pekod and Shoa and Koa and all the Assyrians—handsome young men of high rank, riding their steeds. They will come against you from the north with chariots and wagons and a great army fully prepared for attack. They will surround you on every side with armored men and I will let them at you, to do with you as they wish. Four great punishments await Jerusalem to destroy life: war, famine, ferocious beasts, plague. You brought all this upon yourself by worshiping the gods of other nations, defiling yourself with all their idols. You have followed in your sister's footsteps, so I will punish you with the same terrors that destroyed her. Yes, the terrors that fell upon her will fall upon you—and the cup from which she drank was full and large. And all the world will mock you for your woe. You will reel like a drunkard beneath the awful blows of sorrow and distress, just as your sister Samaria did. In deep anguish you will drain that cup of terror to the very bottom and will lick the inside to get every drop. For I have spoken, says the Lord. Because you have forgotten Me and turned your backs upon Me, therefore you must bear the consequence of all your sin.

Son of dust, you must accuse Jerusalem and Samaria of all their awful deeds. For they have committed both adultery and murder; they have worshiped idols and murdered My children whom they bore to Me, burning them as sacrifices on their altars. On the same day they defiled My Temple and ignored My Sabbaths, for when they had murdered their children in front of their idols, then even that same day they actually came into My Temple to worship! That is how much regard they have for Me! But just persons everywhere will judge them for what they really are—adulteresses and murderers. They will mete out to them the sentences the law demands.

The Lord God says: Bring an army against them and hand them out to be crushed and despised. For their enemies will stone them and kill them with swords; they will butcher their sons and daughters and burn their homes. Thus will I make lewdness and idolatry to cease from the land. My judgment will be a lesson againt idolatry for all to see. For you will be fully repaid for all your harlotry, your worshiping of idols. You will suffer the full penalty; and you will know that I alone am God.

Calamity upon calamity will befall you; woe upon woe, disaster upon disaster! You will long for a prophet to guide you, but the priests and elders and the kings and princes will stand helpless, weeping in despair. The people will tremble with fear, for I will do to them the evil they have done, and give them all their just deserts. They shall learn that I am the Lord.

9. A Refugee's Report

"Son of dust, on the day I finish taking from them in Jerusalem the joy of their hearts and their glory and joys—their wives and their sons and their daughters—on that day a refugee from Jerusalem will start on a journey to come to you in Babylon to tell you what has happened."

And sure enough, in the eleventh year of our exile, one who escaped from Jerusalem arrived to tell me, "The city has fallen!"

Then this message came to me: "Son of dust, the scattered remnants of Judah living among the ruined cities keep saying, 'Abraham was only one man and yet he got possession of the whole country! We are many, so we should certainly be able to get it back!' But the Lord God says: You are powerless, for you do evil! You eat meat with the blood; you worship idols and murder. Do you suppose I'll let you have the land? Murderers! Idolators! Adulterers! Should you possess the land? Tell them the Lord God says: As I live, surely those living in the ruins shall die by the sword. Those living in the open fields shall be eaten by wild animals, and those in the forts and caves shall die of disease. I will desolate the land and her pride. Her power shall come to an end. And the mountain villages of Israel shall be so ruined that no one will even travel through them. When I have ruined the land because of their sins then they shall know I am the Lord!"

10. Hypocrites at Worship

"Son of dust, your people are whispering behind your back. They talk about you in their houses and whisper about you at the doors saying, 'Come on, let's have some fun! Let's go hear him tell us what the Lord is saying!' So they come as though they are sincere and sit before you listening. But they have no intention of doing what I tell them to; they talk very sweetly about loving the Lord, but with their hearts they are loving their money. You are very entertaining to them, like someone who sings lovely songs with a beautiful voice or plays well on an instrument. They hear what you say but don't pay any attention to it! But when all these terrible things happen to them—as they will—then they will know a prophet has been among them."

11. Leaders Denounced

Then this message came to me from the Lord: Son of dust, prophesy against the shepherds, the leaders of Israel.

The Lord God says to you: Woe to the shepherds who feed

themselves instead of their flocks. Shouldn't shepherds feed the sheep? You eat the best food and wear the finest clothes, but you let your flocks starve. You haven't taken care of the weak nor tended the sick nor bound up the broken bones nor gone looking for those who have wandered away and are lost. Instead you have ruled them with force and cruelty. So they were scattered, without a shepherd. They have become a prey to every animal that comes along. My sheep wandered through the mountains and hills and over the face of the earth, and there was no one to search for them or care about them.

Therefore I am against the shepherds, and I will hold them responsible for what has happened to My flock. I will take away their right to feed the flock—and take away their right to eat. I will save My flock from being taken for their food. For the Lord God says: I will search and find My sheep. I will be like a shepherd looking for his flock. I will find My sheep and rescue them from all the places they were scattered in that dark and cloudy day. And I will bring them back from among the people and nations where they were, back home to their own land of Israel, and I will feed them upon the mountains of Israel and by the rivers where the land is fertile and good. Yes, I will give them good pasture on the high hills of Israel. There they will lie down in peace and feed in luscious mountain pastures.

"I Myself will be the shepherd of My sheep and cause them to lie down in peace," the Lord God says. "I will seek My lost ones, those who strayed away, and bring them safely home again. I will put splints and bandages upon their broken limbs and heal the sick. And I will destroy the powerful, fat shepherds; I will feed them, yes—feed them punishment! I will surely judge between these fat shepherds and their scrawny sheep."

I Myself will save My flock; no more will they be picked on and destroyed. And I will notice which is plump and which is thin, and why! And I will set one shepherd over all My people, even My servant David. He shall feed them and be a shepherd to them. And I the Lord will be their God, and My servant David shall be a Prince among My people. I the Lord have spoken it.

I will make a peace pact with them and drive away the dangerous animals from the land so that My people can safely camp in the wildest places and sleep safely in the woods. I will make My people and their homes around My hill a blessing. And there shall be showers, showers of blessing, for I will not shut off the rains but send them in their seasons. Their fruit trees and fields will yield bumper crops, and everyone will live in safety. When I have broken off their chains of slavery and delivered them from those who profiteered at their expense, they shall know I am the Lord. No more will other nations conquer them nor wild animals attack. They shall live in safety and no one shall make them afraid.

And I will raise up a notable vine in Israel so that My people will never again go hungry nor be shamed by heathen conquest. In this way they will know that I, the Lord their God, am with them, and that they, the people of Israel, are My people, says the Lord God. "You are My flock, the sheep of My pasture. You are My men and I am your God," so says the Lord.

12. Divine Promise of Restoration

Then this further word came to me from the Lord:

Son of dust, when the people of Israel were living in their own country, they defiled it by their evil deeds. To Me their worship was as foul as filthy rags. They polluted the land with murder and with the worshiping of idols, so I poured out My fury upon them. And I exiled them to many lands; that is how I punished them for the evil way they lived. But when they were scattered out among the nations, then they were a blight upon My holy name because the nations said, "These are the people of God and He couldn't protect them from harm!" I am concerned about My reputation that was ruined by My people throughout the world.

Therefore say to the people of Israel: The Lord God says, "I am bringing you back again, but not because you deserve it; I am doing it to protect My holy name which you tarnished among the nations. I will honor My great name that you defiled, and the people of the world shall know I am the Lord. I will be honored before their eyes by delivering you from exile among them. For I will bring you back home again to the land of Israel. Then it will be as though I had sprinkled clean water on you, for you will be clean—your filthiness will be washed away, your idol worship gone.

"And I will give you a new heart—I will give you new and right desires—and put a new spirit within you. I will take out your stony hearts of sin and give you new hearts of love. And I will put My Spirit within you so that you will obey My laws and do whatever I command. And you shall live in Israel, the land which I gave your fathers long ago. And you shall be My people and I will be your God. I will cleanse away your sins. I will abolish crop failures and famine. I will give you huge harvests from your fruit trees and fields, and never again will the surrounding nations be able to scoff at your land for its famines. Then you will remember your past sins and loathe yourselves for all the evils you did. But always remember this: It is not for your own sakes that I will do this, but for Mine, O My people Israel.

"Thus will I show My greatness and bring honor upon My name; and all the nations of the world will hear what I have done, and know that I am God!"

13. Dry Bones

The power of the Lord was upon me and I was carried away by the Spirit of the Lord to a valley full of old, dry bones that were scattered everywhere across the ground. He led me around among them, and then He said to me: "Son of dust, can these bones become people again?"

I replied, "Lord, You alone know the answer to that."

Then He told me to speak to the bones and say: "O dry bones, listen to the words of God, for the Lord God says: See! I am going to make you live and breathe again! I will replace the flesh and muscles on you and cover you with skin. I will put breath into you, and you shall live and know I am the Lord."

So I spoke these words from God, just as He told me to.

Suddenly there was a rattling noise from all across the valley, and the bones of each body came together and attached to each other as they used to be. Then as I watched, the muscles and flesh formed over the bones, and skin covered them. But the bodies had no breath. Then He told me to call to the wind and say: "The Lord God says: Come from the four winds, O Spirit, and breathe upon these slain bodies that they may live again." I spoke to the winds as He commanded me and the bodies began breathing. They lived, and stood up—a very great army.

Then He told me what the vision meant: "These bones," He said, "represent all the people of Israel. They say: 'We have become a heap of dried out bones—all hope is gone.' But tell them, the Lord God says: My people, I will open your graves of exile and cause you to rise again and return to the land of Israel. And then at last, O My people, you will know I am the Lord. I will put My Spirit into you, and you shall live and return home again to your own land. Then you will know that I, the Lord, have done just what I promised you."

For the Lord God says: "I am gathering the people of Israel from among the nations, and bringing them home from around the world to their own land, to unify them into one nation. One king shall be king of them all; no longer shall they be divided into two nations. They shall stop polluting themselves with idols and their other sins; for I will save them from all this foulness. Then they shall truly be My people and I their God. And David, My servant shall be their king, their only shepherd; and they shall obey My laws and all My wishes. They shall live in the land of Israel where their fathers lived, the land I gave My servant Jacob. They and their children and their grandchildren after them shall live there for all generations. And My servant David shall be their Prince forever. And I will make a covenant of peace with them, an everlasting pact. I will bless them and multiply them and put My Temple among them forever. And I will make My home among them. Yes, I will be their God and they shall be My people."

HAGGAI

Haggai was one of 42,360 Jewish exiles who returned to Jerusalem from Babylon under the leadership of Zerubbabel in about 536 B.C. Both he and his contemporary, Zechariah, were concerned for the rebuilding of the Temple. Its foundations had been laid in 536 B.C., but hostile neighbors and indifference among the Jews had delayed its completion. As a direct result of the preaching of Haggai and Zechariah, the work was resumed, and finally completed in 515 B.C. For historical background, see Book I, Part 5, pages 263-271.

1. Rebuild My Temple

Subject: A message from the Lord. To: Haggai the prophet, who delivered it to Zerubbabel (son of Shealtiel), governor of Judah; and to Joshua (son of Josedech), the high priest—for it was addressed to them. When: In late August of the second year of the reign of King Darius I.

"Why is everyone saying it is not the right time for rebuilding My Temple?" asks the Lord.

His reply to them is this, "Is it then the right time for you to live in luxurious homes when the Temple lies in ruins? Look at the result: You plant much but harvest little. You have scarcely enough to eat or drink and not enough clothes to keep you warm. Your income disappears as though you were putting it into pockets filled with holes!

"Think it over," says the Lord of Hosts. "Consider how you have acted and what has happened as a result! Then go up into the mountains and bring down timber, and rebuild My Temple; and I will be pleased with it and appear there in My glory," says the Lord.

Then Zerubbabel (son of Shealtiel), the governor of Judah, and Joshua (son of Josedech), the high priest, and the few people remaining in the land obeyed Haggai's message from the Lord their God; they began to worship Him in earnest. Then the Lord told them (again sending the message through Haggai, His messenger), "I am with you; I will bless you." And the Lord gave them a desire to rebuild His Temple; so they all gathered in early September of the second year of King Darius' reign and volunteered their help.

Another message came to Haggai from the Lord that same day: "Tell Zerubbabel, the governor of Judah, that I am about to shake the heavens and the earth, and to overthrow thrones and destroy the strength of the kingdoms of the nations. I will overthrow their armed might, and brothers and companions will kill each other. But when that happens, I will take you, O Zerubbabel My servant, and honor you like a signet ring upon My finger, for I have specially chosen you," says the Lord of Hosts.

"But take courage, O Zerubbabel and Joshua and all the people; take courage and work, for I am with you," says the Lord of Hosts, "for I promised when you left Egypt that My Spirit would remain among you; so don't be afraid." For the Lord of Hosts says, "In just a little while I will begin to shake the heavens and earth—and the oceans, too, and the dry land—I will shake all nations; and the Desire of All Nations shall come to this Temple; and I will fill this place with My glory," says the Lord of Hosts.

ZECHARIAH

Zechariah's style is symbolic and picturesque in contrast with that of Haggai's which is plain and direct. But the setting is the same. (See the introduction to Haggai.)

1. The City's Future

These messages from the Lord were given to Zechariah (son of Berechiah and grandson of Iddo the prophet) in early November of the second year of the reign of King Darius:

The Lord of Hosts was very angry with your fathers. But He will turn again and favor you if only you return to Him. Don't be like your fathers were! The earlier prophets pled in vain with them to turn from all their evil ways. "Come, return to Me," the Lord God said. But no, they wouldn't listen; they paid no attention at all. Your fathers and their prophets are now long dead, but remember the lesson they learned, that *God's word endures!* It caught up with them and punished them. Then at last they repented. "We have gotten what we deserved from God," they said. "He has done just what He warned us He would."

The following February this vision came in the night:

When I looked around me again, I saw a man carrying a yardstick in his hand. "Where are you going?" I asked.

"To measure Jerusalem," he said; "I want to see whether it is big enough for all the people!"

Then the angel who was talking to me went over to meet another angel coming towards him. "Go tell this young man," said the other angel, "that Jerusalem will some day be so full of people that she won't have room enough for all! Many will live outside the city walls with all their many cattle—and yet they will be safe. For the Lord Himself will be a wall of fire protecting them and all Jerusalem; He will be the glory of the city."

"Come, flee from the land of the north, from Babylon," says the Lord to all His exiles there. "I scattered you to the winds but I will bring you back again. Escape, escape to Zion now!" says the Lord.

Again the Lord of Hosts says, "I am greatly concerned—yes, furiously angry—because of all that Jerusalem's enemies have done to her. Now I am going to return to My land and I Myself will live within Jerusalem; and Jerusalem shall be called the faithful city, and the holy mountain, and the mountain of the Lord of Hosts. And after that," the Lord of Hosts declares, "you will all live in peace and prosperity and each of you will own a home of your own where you can invite your neighbors."

2. Zerubbabel Commended and Encouraged

Then the angel who had been talking with me woke me, as though I had been asleep. "What do you see now?" he asked.

I answered, "I see a golden lampstand holding seven lamps, and at the top there is a reservoir for the olive oil that feeds the lamps, flowing into them through seven tubes."

Then he said, "This is God's message to Zerubbabel: 'Not by might nor by power, but by My Spirit, says the Lord of Hosts—you will succeed because of My Spirit, though you are few and weak.' Therefore no mountain however high can stand before Zerubbabel! For it will flatten out before him! And Zerubbabel will finish building this Temple with mighty shouts of thanksgiving for God's mercy, declaring that all was done by grace alone. Do not despise this small beginning, for the eyes of the Lord rejoice to see the work begin, to see the plumbline in the hand of Zerubbabel. For these seven lamps represent the eyes of the Lord that see everywhere around the world."

The Lord of Hosts says, "Get on with the job and finish it! You have been listening long enough! For since you began laying the foundation of the Temple, the prophets have been telling you about the blessings that await you when it's finished. Before the work began there were no jobs, no wages, no security; if you left the city, there was no assurance you would ever return, for crime was rampant. But it is all so different now!" says the Lord of Hosts. "For I am sowing peace and prosperity among you. Your crops will prosper; the grapevines will be weighted down with fruit; the ground will be fertile with plenty of rain; all these blessings will be given the people left in the land. 'May you be as poor as Judah,' the heathen used to say to those they cursed! But no longer! For now Judah is a word of blessing, not a curse. 'May you be as prosperous and happy as Judah is,' they'll say. So don't be afraid or discouraged! Get on with rebuilding the Temple! If you do, I will certainly bless you. And don't think that I might change My mind. I did what I said I would when your fathers angered Me and I promised to punish them; and I won't change this decision of Mine to bless you.

"And I will surround My Temple like a guard to keep invading armies from entering Israel. I am closely watching their movements and I will keep them away; no foreign oppressors will again overrun My people's land. Rejoice greatly, O My people! Shout with joy! For look—your King is coming! He is the righteous One, the victor! Yet He is lowly, riding on a donkey's colt! I will disarm all peoples of the earth including My people in Israel, and He shall bring peace among the nations. His realm shall stretch from sea to sea, from the river to the ends of the earth."

The Lord their God will save His people in that day, as a shepherd caring for His sheep. They shall shine in His land as glittering jewels in a crown. How wonderful and beautiful all shall be! The abundance of grain and wine will make the young men and girls flourish; they will be radiant with health and happiness.

3. God and His People Reunited

I saw a man sitting on a red horse that was standing among the myrtle trees beside a river. Behind him were other horses, red and bay and white, each with its rider. An angel stood beside me, and I asked him, "Sir, what are all those horses for?"

"I'll tell you," he replied.

Then the rider on the red horse—he was the angel of the Lord—answered me, "The Lord has sent them to patrol the earth for Him." Then the other riders reported to the angel of the Lord, "We have patrolled the whole earth, and everywhere there is prosperity and peace."

Upon hearing this, the angel of the Lord prayed this prayer, "O Lord of Hosts, for 70 years Your anger has raged against Jerusalem and the cities of Judah. How long will it be until You again show mercy to them?" And the Lord answered the angel who stood beside me, speaking words of comfort and assurance.

Then the angel said, "Shout out this message from the Lord of Hosts: Don't you think I care about what has happened to Judah and Jerusalem? I am as jealous as a husband for his captive wife. I am very angry with the heathen nations sitting around at ease; for I was only a little displeased with My people, but the nations afflicted them far beyond My intentions. Therefore the Lord declares: I have returned to Jerusalem filled with mercy; My Temple will be rebuilt, says the Lord of Hosts and so will all Jerusalem. The Lord of Hosts declares that Jerusalem will have peace and prosperity so long that there will once again be aged men and women hobbling through her streets on canes; and the streets will be filled with boys and girls at play."

The Lord says, "This seems unbelievable to you—a remnant, small, discouraged as you are—but it is no great thing for Me. You can be sure that I will rescue My people from east and west, wherever they are scattered. I will bring them home again to live safely in Jerusalem; and they will be My people, and I will be their God, just and true and yet forgiving them their sins!"

Life-giving waters will flow out from Jerusalem, half towards the Dead Sea and half towards the Mediterranean, flowing continuously both in winter and in summer. And the Lord shall be King over all the earth. In that day there shall be one Lord—His name alone will be worshiped. "Sing, Jerusalem, and rejoice! For I have come to live among you," says the Lord. "At that time many nations will be converted to the Lord, and they too shall be My people; I will live among them all. And Judah shall be the Lord's inheritance in the Holy Land, for God shall once more choose to bless Jerusalem." Be silent, all mankind, before the Lord; for He has come to earth from heaven, from His holy home.

MALACHI

Malachi's name means "my messenger." He lived about one hundred years after Zechariah—between 450 and 400 B.C. The walls of Jerusalem had been rebuilt and the Temple services resumed, but times were hard due to drought and blighted crops. People were lazy, indifferent and spiritually listless. Divorce was common and the priests corrupt. Such were the conditions which confronted the last of the Old Testament prophets.

1. Priests Rebuked

Here is the Lord's message to Israel given through the prophet Malachi: "A son honors his father, a servant honors his master. I am your Father and Master, yet you don't honor Me, O priests, but you despise My name."

"Who? We?" you say. "When did we ever despise Your name?"

"When you offer polluted sacrifices on My altar."

"Polluted sacrifices? When have we ever done a thing like that?"

"Every time you say, 'Don't bother bringing anything very valuable to offer to God!' You tell the people that lame animals are all right to offer on the altar of the Lord—yes, even the sick and the blind ones. And you claim this isn't evil? Try it on your governor sometime—give him gifts like that—and see how pleased he is! 'God have mercy on us,' you recite; 'God be gracious to us!' But when you bring that kind of gift, why should He show you any favor at all?

"Oh, to find one priest among you who would shut the doors and refuse this kind of sacrifice. Priests' lips should flow with the knowledge of God so the people will learn God's laws. The priests are the messengers of the Lord of Hosts, and men should come to them for guidance. But not to you! For you have left God's paths. Your guidance has caused many to stumble in sin. You have distorted the covenant of Levi and made it into a grotesque parody," says the Lord of Hosts. "Therefore I have made you contemptible in the eyes of all the people: for you have not obeyed Me, but you let your favorites break the law without rebuke. For My name shall be great among the nations," says the Lord of Hosts.

"But you dishonor it, saying that My altar is not important and encouraging people to bring cheap, sick animals to offer to Me on it. You say, 'Oh, it's too difficult to serve the Lord and do what He asks.' And you turn up your noses at the rules He has given you to obey. Think of it! Stolen animals, lame and sick—as offerings to God! Should I accept such offerings as these?" asks the Lord. "Cursed is the man who promises a fine ram from his flock, and substitutes a sick one to sacrifice to God. For I am a great King," says the Lord of Hosts, "and My name is to be mightily revered among the Gentiles.

"Listen: I will send My messenger before Me to prepare the way. And then the Lord you are looking for will come suddenly to His Temple—the Messenger of God's promises, to bring you great joy. Yes, He is surely coming," says the Lord of Hosts. "But who can live when He appears? Who can endure His coming? For He is like a blazing fire refining precious metal and He can bleach the dirtiest garments! Like a refiner of silver He will sit and closely watch as the dross is burned away. He will purify the Levites, the ministers of God, refining them like gold or silver, so that they will do their work for God with pure hearts. Then once more the Lord will enjoy the offerings brought to Him by the people of Judah and Jerusalem, as He did before."

2. Divorce Deplored

We are children of the same father Abraham, all created by the same God. And yet we are faithless to each other, violating the covenant of our fathers! In Judah, in Israel and in Jerusalem there is treachery; for the men of Judah have defiled God's holy and beloved Temple by marrying heathen women who worship idols. May the Lord cut off from His covenant every last man, whether priest or layman, who has done this thing!

Yet you cover the altar with your tears because the Lord doesn't pay attention to your offerings anymore, and you receive no blessing from Him. "Why has God abandoned us?" you cry.

I'll tell you why: It is because the Lord has seen your treachery in divorcing your wives who have been faithful to you through the years, the companions you promised to care for and keep. You were united to your wife by the Lord. In God's wise plan, when you married, the two of you became one person in His sight. And what does He want? Godly children from your union. Therefore guard your passions! Keep faith with the wife of your youth.

3. Robbing God!

"Though you have scorned My laws from earliest time, yet you may still return to Me," says the Lord of Hosts. "Come and I will forgive you.

"But you say, 'We have never even gone away'

"Will a man rob God? Surely not! And yet you have robbed Me. 'What do you mean? When did we ever rob You?'

"You have robbed Me of the tithes and offerings due to Me. And so the awesome curse of God is cursing you, for your whole nation has been robbing Me.

"Bring all the tithes into the storehouse so that there will be food enough in My Temple; if you do, I will open up the windows of heaven for you and pour out a blessing so great you won't have room enough to take it in! Try it! Let Me prove it to you! Your crops will be large, for I will guard them from insects and plagues. Your grapes won't shrivel away before they ripen," says the Lord of Hosts. "And all nations will call you blessed, for you will be a land sparkling with happiness. These are the promises of the Lord of Hosts."

4. The Faithful

Then those who feared and loved the Lord spoke often of Him to each other. And He had a book of remembrance drawn up in which He recorded the names of those who feared Him and loved to think about Him. "They shall be Mine," says the Lord of Hosts, "in that day when I made up My jewels. And I will spare them as a man spares an obedient and dutiful son. Then you will see the difference between God's treatment of good men and bad, between those who serve Him and those who don't.

"For you who fear My name, the Sun of Righteousness will rise with healing in His wings. And you will go free, leaping with joy like calves let out to pasture. Then you will tread upon the wicked as ashes underfoot," says the Lord of Hosts.

"Remember to obey the laws I gave all Israel through Moses My servant on Mount Horeb. See, I will send you another prophet like Elijah before the coming of the great and dreadful Judgment Day of God. His preaching will bring fathers and children together again, to be of one mind and heart. For they will know that if they do not repent, I will come and utterly destroy their land."

O Israel, lift your eyes to see what God is doing all around the world; then you will say, "Truly, the Lord's great power goes far beyond our borders!"

"My name will be honored by the Gentiles from morning till night. All around the world they will offer sweet incense and pure offerings in honor of My name. For My name shall be great among the nations," says the Lord of Hosts.

Book III

HIGHLIGHTS FROM POETRY

Selections from Job, Psalms,
Proverbs, Ecclesiastes and the Song of Solomon

JOB

The book of Job is one of the great literary masterpieces of all time. In dialogue form, it moves with majestic sublimity from one speaker to another, seeking a philosophical answer to the age-long question, "Why do the righteous suffer?" Job rejects the dogmatic assertions of his friends that his misery is the result of some sin which he is hiding. He longs to lay his case before God Himself, and in the end, bows in humble acceptance of the Divine Will which neither he nor any other man can fully understand because of God's infinite and incomprehensible greatness.

1. Job's Prosperity

T HERE lived in the land of Uz a man named Job—a good man who feared God and stayed away from evil. He had a large family of seven sons and three daughters, and was immensely wealthy. He owned 7,000 sheep, 3,000 camels, 500 teams of oxen, 500 female donkeys and employed many servants. He was, in fact, the richest cattleman in that entire area. Every year when each of Job's sons had a birthday, he invited his brothers and sisters to his home for a celebration. On these occasions they would eat and drink with great merriment. When these birthday parties ended—and sometimes they lasted several days—Job would summon his children to him and sanctify them, getting up early in the morning and offering a burnt offering for each of them. For Job said, "Perhaps my sons have sinned and turned away from God in their hearts." This was Job's regular practice.

2. Job's Calamity

One day as the angels came to present themselves before the Lord, Satan the accuser came with them. "Where have you come from?" the Lord asked Satan.

Satan replied, "From patroling the earth."

Then the Lord asked Satan, "Have you noticed My servant Job? He is the finest man in all the earth—a good man who fears God and will have nothing to do with evil."

"Why shouldn't he, when You pay him so well?" Satan scoffed. "You have always protected him and his home and his property from all harm. You have prospered everything he does—look how rich he is! No wonder he worships You! But just take away his wealth, and You'll see him curse You to Your face!"

And the Lord replied to Satan, "You may do anything you like with his wealth, but don't harm him physically."

So Satan went away; and sure enough, not long afterwards when Job's sons and daughters were dining at the oldest brother's house, tragedy struck. A messenger rushed to Job's home with this news: "Your oxen were plowing with the donkeys feeding beside them, when the Sabeans raided us, drove away the animals and killed all the farmhands except me. I am the only one left."

While this messenger was still speaking, another arrived with more bad news: "The fire of God has fallen from heaven and burned up your sheep and all the herdsmen, and I alone have escaped to tell you."

Before this man finished, still another messenger rushed in, "Three bands of Chaldeans have driven off your camels and killed your servants, and I alone have escaped to tell you."

As he was still speaking, another arrived to say, "Your sons and daughters were feasting in their oldest brother's home, when suddenly a mighty wind swept in from the desert and engulfed the house so that the roof fell in on them and all are dead; and I alone escaped to tell you." Then Job stood up and tore his robe in grief and fell down upon the ground before God.

"I came naked from my mother's womb," he said, "and I shall have nothing when I die. The Lord gave me everything I had, and they were His to take away. Blessed be the name of the Lord." In all of this, Job did not sin or revile God.

3. Job's Pain

Now the angels came again to present themselves before the Lord, and Satan with them. "Where have you come from?" the Lord asked Satan.

"From patroling the earth," Satan replied.

"Well, have you noticed My servant Job?" the Lord asked. "He is the finest man in all the earth—a good man who fears God and turns away from all evil. And he has kept his faith in Me despite the fact that you persuaded Me to let you harm him without any cause."

"Skin for skin," Satan replied. "A man will give anything to save his life. Touch his body with sickness and he will curse You to Your face!"

"Do with him as you please," the Lord replied; "only spare his life." So Satan went out from the presence of the Lord and struck Job with a terrible case of boils from head to foot. Then Job took a broken piece of pottery to scrape himself; and he sat among the ashes.

His wife said to him, "Are you still trying to be godly when God has done all this to you? Curse Him and die."

But he replied, "You talk like some heathen woman. What? Shall we receive only pleasant things from the hand of God and never anything unpleasant?" So in all this Job said nothing wrong.

When three of Job's friends heard of all the tragedy that had befallen him, they got in touch with each other and traveled from their homes to comfort and console him. Their names were Eliphaz the Temanite, Bildad the Shuhite, and Zophar the Naamathite. Job was so changed that they could scarcely recognize him. Wailing loudly in despair, they tore their robes and threw dust into the air and put earth on their heads to demonstrate their sorrow. Then they sat upon the ground with him silently for seven days and nights, no one speaking a word; for they saw that his suffering was too great for words.

4. Job's Lament

At last Job spoke and cursed the day of his birth: Let the day of my birth be damned, and the night when I was conceived.

Let that day be forever forgotten. Let it be lost even to God, shrouded in eternal darkness. Why didn't I die at birth? Why did the midwife let me live? Why did she nurse me at her breasts? For if only I had died at birth, then I would be quiet now, asleep and at rest.

Oh, why should light and life be given to those in misery and bitterness who long for death and it won't come; who search for death as others search for food or money! What blessed relief when at last they die!

Why is a man allowed to be born if God is only going to give him a hopeless life of uselessness and frustration? I cannot eat for sighing; my groans pour out like water. What I always feared has happened to me. I was not fat and lazy, yet trouble struck me down.

5. Eliphaz's Counsel

A reply to Job from Eliphaz the Temanite:

Will you let me say a word? For who could keep from speaking out? In the past you have told many a troubled soul to trust in God and have encouraged those who are weak or falling, or lie crushed upon the ground or are tempted to despair. But now when trouble strikes you faint and are broken. At such a time as this should not trust in God still be your confidence? Shouldn't you believe that God will care for those who are good?

Stop and think! Have you ever known a truly good and innocent person who was punished? Experience teaches that it is those who sow sin and trouble who harvest the same. My advice to you is this: Go to God and confess your sins to Him.

How enviable the man whom God corrects! Oh, do not despise the chastening of the Lord when you sin. For though He wounds, He binds and heals again. He will deliver you again and again, so that no evil can touch you. He will keep you from death in famine and from the power of the sword in time of war. You will be safe from slander; no need to fear the future. You shall laugh at war and famine. Wild animals will leave you alone; dangerous animals will be at peace with you. You need not worry about your home while you are gone; nothing shall be stolen from your barns. Your sons shall become important men; your descendants shall be as numerous as grass! You shall live a long, good life; like standing grain you'll not be harvested until it's time! I have found from experience that all of this is true. For your own good, listen to my counsel.

6. Job's Answer to Eliphaz

Job's reply:

Oh that my sadness and troubles were weighed. For they are heavier than the sand of a thousand seashores. That is why I spoke so rashly. For the Lord has struck me down with His arrows; He has sent His poisoned arrows deep within my heart. All God's terrors are arrayed against me. Am I unfeeling like stone? Is my flesh made of brass? I am utterly helpless, without any hope.

One should be kind to a fainting friend, but you have accused me without the slightest fear of God. My brother, you have proved as unreliable as a brook; it floods when there is ice and snow, but in hot weather, disappears. The caravans turn aside to be refreshed, but there is nothing there to drink, and so they perish. When caravans from Tema and from Sheba stop for water, their hopes are dashed. And so my hopes in you are dashed—you turn away from me in terror and refuse to help. But why? Have I ever asked you for one slightest thing? Have I begged you for a present? Have I ever asked your help?

All I want is a reasonable answer—then I will keep quiet. Tell me, what have I done wrong? It is wonderful to speak the truth, but your criticisms are not based on fact. Are you going to condemn me just because I impulsively cried out in desperation? That would be like injuring a helpless orphan or selling a friend. Look at me! Would I lie to your face? Stop assuming my guilt, for I am righteous. Don't be so unjust. Don't I know the difference between right and wrong? Would I not admit it if I had sinned?

7. Job's Anguish

Ah, let me express my anguish. Let me be free to speak out of the bitterness of my soul.

O God, am I some monster, that You never let me alone? Even when I try to forget my misery in sleep, You terrify with nightmares. I would rather die of strangulation than go on and on like this. I hate my life. Oh, let me alone for these few remaining days.

What is mere man that You should spend Your time persecuting him? Must You be his inquisitor every morning and test him every moment of the day? Why won't You let me alone—even long enough to spit? Has my sin harmed You, O God, Watcher of Mankind? Why have You made me Your target and made my life so heavy a burden to me? Why not just pardon my sin and take it all away? For all so soon I'll lie down in the dust and die, and when You look for me, I shall be gone.

8. Bildad's Accusation

Bildad the Shuhite's reply to Job:

How long will you go on like this blowing words around like wind? Does God twist justice? If you were pure and good, He would hear your prayer, answer you and bless you with a happy home. And though you started with little, you would end with much.

Read the history books and see—for we were born but yesterday and know so little; our days here on earth are as transient as shadows. But the wisdom of the past will teach you. The experience of others will speak to you, reminding you that those who forget God have no hope. They are like rushes without any mire to grow in; or grass without water to keep it alive. Suddenly it begins to wither even before it is cut. A man without God is trusting in a spider's web. Everything he counts on will collapse.

But look! God will not cast away a good man, nor prosper evildoers. He will yet fill your mouth with laughter and your lips with shouts of joy. Those who hate you shall be clothed with shame, and the wicked destroyed.

9. Job's Answer to Bildad

Job's reply:

But how can a man be truly good in the eyes of God? If God decides to argue with him, can a man answer even one question of a thousand He asks? God is so wise and so mighty. Who has ever opposed Him successfully?

He made the Bear, Orion and the Pleiades, and the constellations of the southern Zodiac. He does incredible miracles, too many to count.

And who am I that I should try to argue with Almighty God, or even reason with Him? Even if I were sinless I wouldn't say a word. I would only plead for mercy.

Oh let Him stop beating me, so that I need no longer live in terror of His punishment. Then I could speak to Him without fear and tell Him boldly that I am not guilty.

I am weary of living. Let me complain freely. I will speak in my sorrow and bitterness. I will say to God, "Don't just condemn me—tell me *why* you are doing this to me. You have made me, and yet You destroy me. Oh please remember that I'm made of dust—will You change me back again to dust so soon? You have already poured me from bottle to bottle like milk and curdled me like cheese.

"Why did You even let me be born? Why didn't You let me die at birth? Then I would have been spared this miserable existence. I would have gone directly from the womb to the grave. Can't You see how little time I have left? Oh let me alone that I may have a little moment of comfort before I leave for the land of darkness and the shadow of death, never to return —a land as dark as midnight; a land of the shadow of death where only confusion reigns and where the brightest light is dark as midnight."

10. Zophar's Accusation

Zophar the Naamathite's reply to Job:

Shouldn't someone stem this torrent of words? Is a man proved right by all this talk? Should I remain silent while you boast? When you mock God, shouldn't someone make you ashamed? You claim you are pure in the eyes of God! Oh that God would speak and tell you what He thinks! Oh that He would make you truly see yourself, for He knows everything you've done. Listen! God is doubtless punishing you far less than you deserve!

Do you know the mind and purposes of God? Will long searching make them known to you? Are you qualified to judge the Almighty? Before you turn to God and stretch out your hands to Him, get rid of your sins and leave all iniquity behind you. Only then, without the spots of sin to defile you, can you walk steadily forward to God without fear. Only then can you forget your misery. It will all be in the past. And your life will be cloudless; any darkness will be as bright as morning!

11. Job's Answer to Zophar

Job's reply:

Yes, I realize you know everything! All wisdom will die with you! Well, I know a few things myself—you are no better than I am. And who doesn't know these things you've been saying?

Who doesn't know that the Lord does things like that? Ask the dumbest beast—he knows that it is so; ask the birds—they will tell you; or let the earth teach you, or the fish of the sea. For the soul of every living thing is in the hand of God, and the breath of all mankind.

Look, I have seen many instances like you describe. I know as much as you do. I'm not stupid. Oh how I long to speak directly to the Almighty. I want to talk this over with God Himself. For you are misinterpreting the whole thing. You are doctors who don't know what they are doing. Oh, please be quiet! That would be your highest wisdom.

Must you go on speaking for God when He never once has said the things that you are putting in His mouth? Does God want your help if you are going to twist the truth for Him? These tremendous statements you have made have about as much value as ashes. Your defense of God is as fragile as a clay vase! Be silent now and let me alone, that I may speak—and I am willing to face the consequences. Yes, I will take my life in my hand and say what I really think.

God may kill me for saying this—in fact, I expect Him to. Nevertheless I am going to argue my case with Him.

This is my case: *I know that I am righteous.*

"O God, there are two things I beg You not to do to me; only then will I be able to face You. Don't abandon me. And don't terrify me with Your awesome presence. Tell me, what have I done wrong? Point out my sin to me. Help me!"

How frail is man, how few his days, how full of trouble! He blossoms for a moment like a flower—and withers; as the shadow of a passing cloud, he quickly disappears. God has set mankind so brief a span of life—months is all He gives him! Not one bit longer may he live. For there is hope for a tree—if it's cut down it sprouts again and grows tender, new branches.

Though its roots have grown old in the earth and its stump decays, it may sprout and bud again at the touch of water, like a new seedling.

But when a man dies and is buried, where does his spirit go? If a man dies, shall he live again? This thought gives me hope, so that in all my anguish I eagerly await sweet death! He would call and I would come, and He would reward all I do. But now, instead, He gives me so few steps upon the stage of life, and notices every mistake I make.He bundles them all together as evidence against me.

Mountains wear away and disappear. Water grinds the stones to sand. Torrents tear away the soil. So every hope of man is worn away. Always God is against him, and then he passes off the scene. He makes him old and wrinkled, then sends him away, so he never knows it if his sons are honored; or they may fail and face disaster, but he knows it not. For him there is only sorrow and pain.

12. Eliphaz's Second Accusation

The answer of Eliphaz the Temanite:

You are supposed to be a wise man, and yet you give us all this foolish talk. You are nothing but a windbag! It isn't right to speak so foolishly. What good do such words do? Have you no fear of God? No reverence for Him? Your sins are telling your mouth what to say! Your words are based on clever deception, but why should I condemn you? Your own mouth does!

Are you the wisest man alive? Were you born before the hills were made? Have you heard the secret counsel of God? Are you called into His counsel room? Do you have a monopoly on wisdom? What do you know more than we do? What do you understand that we don't? What man in all the earth can be as pure and righteous as you claim to be? Why, God doesn't even trust the angels! Even the heavens can't be absolutely pure compared with Him! How much less someone like you who is corrupt and sinful, drinking in sin as a sponge soaks up water!

13. Job's Reaffirmation

Job's reply:

I have heard all this before. What miserable comforters all of you are. Won't you ever stop your flow of foolish words? What have I said that makes you speak so endlessly? But perhaps I'd sermonize the same as you—if you were I and I were you. I would spout off my criticisms against you and shake my head at you. But no! I would speak in such a way that it would help you. I would try to take away your grief. But now my grief remains no matter how I defend myself.

I am sick and near to death the grave is ready to receive me. I am surrounded by mockers. I see them everywhere. Will no one anywhere confirm my innocence? Only God has kept them back from understanding this. Oh, let them not triumph!

As for you—all of you please go away; for I do not find a wise man among you. My good days are in the past. My hopes have disappeared. My heart's desires are broken. They say that night is day and day is night; how they pervert the truth! If I die I go out into darkness, where I will call the grave my father and the worm my mother and my sister. Where then is my hope? Can anyone find any? No, my hope will go down with me to the grave. We shall rest together in the dust!

14. Bildad's Second Accusation

The reply of Bildad the Shuhite:

Who are you trying to fool? Speak some sense if you want us to answer! Have we become like animals to you, stupid and dumb? Just because you tear your clothes in anger, is this going to start an earthquake? Shall we all go and hide? The truth remains that if you do not prosper, it is because you are wicked. And your bright flame shall be put out. Yes, that is what happens to sinners, to those rejecting God.

The reply of Job:

How long are you going to trouble me and try to break me with your words? Ten times now you have declared I am a sinner. Why aren't you ashamed to deal with me so harshly? And if indeed I was wrong you have yet to prove it. You think yourselves so great? Then prove my guilt! The fact of the matter is that God has overthrown me and caught me in His net.

My relatives have failed me; my friends have all forsaken me. My own wife and brothers refuse to recognize me. My best friends abhor me. Those I loved have turned against me. I am skin and bones and have escaped death by the skin of my teeth. O my friends, pity me, for the angry hand of God has touched me. Why must you persecute me as God does? Why aren't you satisfied with my anguish?

Oh that I could write my plea with an iron pen in the rock forever. But as for me, I know that my Redeemer lives, and that He will stand upon the earth at last. And I know that after this body has decayed, this body shall see God. Then He will be on *my* side! Yes, I shall see Him not as a stranger but as a friend! What a glorious hope! How dare you go on persecuting me, as though I were proven guilty?

15. Zophar's Answer

The speech of Zophar the Naamathite:
I hasten to reply. For I have the answer for you. You have tried to make me feel ashamed of myself for calling you a sinner, but my spirit won't let me stop. Don't you realize that ever since man was first placed upon the earth, the triumph of the wicked has been short-lived, and the joy of the godless but for a moment?

He shall run into trouble at the peak of his powers. His treasures will be lost in deepest darkness. A raging fire will devour his goods, consuming all he has left. The heavens will reveal his sins, and the earth will give testimony against him. His wealth will disappear beneath the wrath of God. This is what awaits the wicked man, for God prepares it for him.
Job's reply:
Listen to me; let me speak, and afterwards, mock on. The truth is that the wicked live on to a good old age and become great and powerful. They live to see their children and their

grandchildren grow to maturity around them. Their homes are safe from every fear, and God does not punish them. Their cattle are productive; they have many happy children who spend their time singing and dancing. They are wealthy and need deny themselves nothing; they are prosperous to the end. All this despite the fact that they ordered God away and wanted no part of Him and His ways. Are they driven before the wind like straw and carried away by the storm? Not at all!

I know what you are going to say—You will tell me of rich and wicked men who came to disaster because of their sins. But I reply, Ask anyone who has been around and he can tell you the truth, that the evil man is usually spared in the day of calamity and allowed to escape. No one rebukes him openly. No one repays him for what he has done. And an honor-guard keeps watch at his grave. A great funeral procession precedes and follows him as the soft earth covers him. How can you comfort me when your whole premise is so wrong?

16. Eliphaz's Plea to Job

Another address from Eliphaz:

Is mere man of any worth to God? Even the wisest is of value only to himself! Is it any pleasure to the Almighty if you are righteous? Would it be any gain to Him if you were perfect? Is it because you are good that He is punishing you? Not at all! It is because of your wickedness! Your sins are endless! That is why you are now surrounded by traps and sudden fears, darkness and waves of horror.

Quit quarreling with God! Agree with Him and you will have peace at last! His favor will surround you if you will only admit that you were wrong. Listen to His instructions and store them in your heart. If you return to God and put right all the wrong in your home, then you will be restored. If you give up your lust for money and throw your gold away, then the Almighty Himself shall be your treasure; He will be your precious silver! Then you will delight yourself in the Lord and look up to God. You will pray to Him, and He will hear you, and you will fulfill all your promises to Him. Whatever you wish will happen! and the light of heaven will shine upon the road ahead of you.

The reply of Job:

My complaint today is still a bitter one, and my punishment far more severe than my fault deserves. Oh that I knew where to find God—that I could go to His throne and talk with Him there. I would tell Him all about my side of this argument, listen to His reply and understand what He wants. But I search in vain. I seek Him here, I seek Him there, and cannot find Him. I seek Him in His workshop in the north, but cannot find Him there; nor can I find Him in the south; there, too, He hides Himself.

He knows every detail of what is happening. Nevertheless, His mind concerning me remains unchanged, and who can turn Him from His purposes? Whatever He wants to do, He does. So He will do to me all He has planned, and there is more ahead. No wonder I am so terrified in His presence. When I think of it, terror grips me. God has given me a fainting heart; He, the Almighty, has terrified me with darkness all around me; thick, impenetrable darkness everywhere. Why doesn't God open the court and listen to my case? Why must the godly wait for Him in vain?

17. Bildad's Final Word

The further reply of Bildad the Shuhite:

God is powerful and dreadful. He enforces peace in heaven. Who is able to number His hosts of angels? And His light shines down on all the earth. How can mere man stand before God and claim to be righteous? Who in all the earth can boast that he is clean? God is so glorious that even the moon and stars are less than nothing as compared to Him. How much less is man, who is but a worm in His sight?

Job's reply:

What wonderful helpers you all are! And how you have encouraged me in my great need! How you have enlightened my stupidity! What wise things you have said! How did you ever think of all these brilliant comments? I will never, never agree that you are right; until I die I will vow my innocence. I am *not* a sinner—I repeat it again and again. My conscience is clear for as long as I live. Those who declare otherwise are my wicked enemies. They are evil men.

18. Search for True Wisdom

Men know how to mine silver and refine gold, to dig iron from the earth and melt copper from stone. Men know how to put light into darkness so that a mine shaft can be sunk into the earth and the earth searched and its deep secrets explored. Into the black rock, shadowed by death, men descend on ropes, swinging back and forth. Men know how to obtain food from the surface of the earth, while underneath there is fire. They know how to find sapphires and gold dust—treasures that no bird of prey can see, no eagle's eye observe—for they are deep within the mines. No wild animal has ever walked upon those treasures; no lion has set his paw there. Men know how to tear apart flinty rocks and how to overturn the roots of mountains. They drill tunnels in the rocks and lay bare precious stones. They dam up streams of water and pan the gold.

But though men can do all these things, they don't know where to find wisdom and understanding. They not only don't know how to get it, but, in fact, it is not to be found among the living. "It is not here," the oceans say; and the seas reply, "Nor is it here." It cannot be bought for gold or silver, not for all the gold of Ophir or precious onyx stones or sapphires. Wisdom is far more valuable than gold and glass. It cannot be bought for jewels mounted in fine gold. Coral or crystal is worthless in trying to get it; its price is far above rubies. Topaz from Ethiopia cannot purchase it, nor even the purest gold.

Then where can we get it? Where can it be found? God surely knows where it is to be found, for He looks throughout the whole earth, under all the heavens. He makes the winds blow and sets the boundaries of the oceans. He makes the laws of the rain and a path for the lightning. He knows where wisdom is and declares it to all who will listen. He established it and examined it thoroughly. And this is what He says to all mankind: "Look, to fear the Lord is true wisdom; to forsake evil is real understanding."

19. Job's Reminiscences

Job continued:

Oh, for the years gone by when God took care of me, when He lighted the way before me and I walked safely through the darkness; yes, in my early years, when the friendship of God was felt in my home; when the Almighty was still with me and my children were around me; when my projects prospered, and even the rock poured out streams of olive oil to me! I helped those who were ready to perish and they blessed me. And I caused the widows' hearts to sing for joy. All I did was just and honest, for righteousness was my clothing! I served as eyes for the blind and feet for the lame. I was as a father to the poor, and saw to it that even strangers received a fair trial. I thought, "Surely I shall die quietly in my nest after a long, good life." For everything I did prospered; the dew lay all night upon my fields and watered them. Fresh honors were constantly given me, and my abilities were constantly refreshed and renewed.

But now those younger than I deride me—young men whose fathers are less than my dogs. And now I have become the subject of their ribald song! I am a joke among *them! They* despise me, won't come near me and don't mind spitting in my face. For God has placed my life in jeopardy. These young men, having humbled me, now cast off all restraint before me. My heart is broken. Depression haunts my days. My weary nights are filled with pain as though something were relentlessly gnawing at my bones.

I cry to You, O God, but You don't answer me. I stand before You and You don't bother to look. You have become cruel toward me, and persecute me with great power and effect. You throw me into the whirlwind and dissolve me in the storm. My skin is black and peeling. My bones burn with fever. The voice of joy and gladness has turned to mourning.

20. Job's Introspection

God knows that I am innocent—if I have stepped off God's pathway, or if my heart has lusted for what my eyes have seen, or if I am guilty of any other sin, *then* let someone else reap the crops I have sown and let all that I have planted be rooted out. Or if I have longed for another man's wife, then may I die, and may my wife be in another man's home, and someone else become her husband. For lust is a shameful sin, a crime that should be punished. It is a devastating fire that destroys to hell, and would root out all I have planted.

If I have been unfair to my servants, how could I face God? What could I say when He questioned me about it? For God made me and my servant too. He created us both. If I have hurt the poor or caused widows to weep, or if I have taken advantage of an orphan because I thought I could get away with it—if I have done any of these things, then let my arm be torn from its socket! Let my shoulder be wrenched out of place!

If I have put my trust in money,

If my happiness depends on wealth,

If I have rejoiced at harm to an enemy—
But actually I have never cursed anyone nor asked for revenge —or if any or my servants have ever gone hungry—Actually I have never turned away even a stranger but have opened my doors to all—or if, like Adam, I have tried to hide my sins, this, too, must be punished by the judges. For if I had done such things, it would mean that I denied the God of heaven.

Oh that there were someone who would listen to me and try to see my side of this argument! Look, I will sign my signature to my defense; now let the Almighty show me that I am wrong; let *Him* approve the indictments made against me by my enemies. I would treasure it like a crown. Then I would tell Him exactly what I have done and why, presenting my defense as one He listens to—or if my land accuses me because I stole the fruit it bears, or if I have murdered its owners to get their land for myself, then let thistles grow on that land instead of wheat and weeds instead of barley.

Here Job's words are ended.

21. Elihu on "God's Moral Government"

The three men refused to reply further to Job because he kept insisting on his innocence. Then Elihu (son of Barachel the Buzite, of the Clan of Ram) became angry because Job refused to admit he had sinned and to acknowledge that God had just cause for punishing him. But he was also angry with Job's three friends because they had been unable to answer Job's arguments and yet had condemned him. Elihu had waited until now to speak because the others were older than he. But when he saw that they had no further reply, he spoke out angrily, and said, "I am young and you are old, so I held back and did not dare to tell you what I think, for those who are older are said to be wiser; but it is not mere age that makes men wise. Rather, it is the spirit in a man, the breath of the Almighty which makes him intelligent. So listen to me awhile and let me express my opinion. I have waited all this time, listening very carefully to your arguments, but not one of them has convinced Job that he is a sinner or has proved that he is.

"Please listen, Job, to what I have to say. I have begun to speak; now let me continue."

You have said it in my hearing, yes, you've said it again and again—"I am pure, I am innocent; I have not sinned." You say God is using a fine-toothed comb to try to find a single fault and so to count you as His enemy. "And He puts my feet in the stocks," you say, "and watches every move I make." All right, here is my reply: In this very thing you have sinned, by speaking of God that way. For God is greater than man. Why should you fight against Him just because He does not give account to you of what He does?

Who else is as arrogant as Job? He must have spent much time with evil men, for he said, "Why waste time trying to please God?" Listen to me, you with understanding. Surely everyone knows that *God doesn't sin!* Rather, He punishes the sinners. There is no truer statement than this: *God is never wicked or unjust.* He alone has authority over the earth and dispenses justice for the world. If God were to withdraw His Spirit, all life would disappear and mankind would turn again to dust.

Listen now and try to understand. Could God govern if He hated justice? Are you going to condemn the Almighty Judge? For God carefully watches the goings on of all mankind; He sees them all. No darkness is thick enough to hide evil men from His eyes; so there is no need to wait for some great crime before a man is called before God in judgment.

Why don't people exclaim to their God, "We have sinned, but we will stop"? Or, "We know not what evil we have done; only tell us, and we will cease at once." Must God tailor His justice to your demands? Must He change the order of the universe to suit your whims? The answer must be obvious even to you! Any one even half-bright will agree with me that you, Job, are speaking like a fool. You should be given the maximum penalty for the wicked way you have talked about God. For now you have added rebellion, arrogance and blasphemy to your other sins.

Let me go on and I will show you the truth of what I am saying. For I have not finished defending God! I will give you many illustrations of the righteousness of my Maker. I am telling you the honest truth, for I am a man of well-rounded knowledge. God is almighty and yet does not despise anyone! And He is perfect in His understanding. He does not reward the wicked with His blessings, but gives them their full share of punishment. He delivers by distress! This makes them listen to Him! How He wanted to lure you away from danger into a wide and pleasant valley and to prosper you there!

But you are too preoccupied with your imagined grievances against others. Watch out! Don't let your anger at others lead you into scoffing at God! Don't let your suffering embitter you at the only one who can deliver you. Do you really think that if you shout loudly enough against God, He will be ashamed and repent? Will this put an end to your chastisement? Do not desire the nighttime with its opportunities for crime. Turn back from evil, for it was to prevent you from getting into a life of evil that God sent this suffering.

22. Elihu on "God's Majestic Greatness"

Look, God is all-powerful. Who is a teacher like Him? Who can say that what He does is absurd or evil? Instead, glorify Him for His mighty works for which He is so famous. Everyone has seen these things from a distance. God is so great that we cannot begin to know Him. No one can begin to understand eternity. He draws up the water vapor and then distills it into rain which the skies pour down. Can anyone really understand the spreading of the clouds and the thunders within? See how He spreads the lightning around Him and blankets the tops of the mountains. By His fantastic powers in nature He punishes or blesses the people, giving them food in abundance.

He fills His hands with lightning bolts. He hurls each at its target. We feel His presence in the thunder. May all sinners be warned. Listen, listen to the thunder of His voice. It rolls across the heavens and His lightning flashes out in every direction. Afterwards comes the roaring of the thunder—the tremendous voice of His majesty. His voice is glorious in the thunder. We cannot comprehend the greatness of His power. For He directs the snow, the showers and storms to fall upon the earth. Man's work stops at such a time, so that all men everywhere may recognize His power. The wild animals hide in the rocks or in their dens. From the south comes the rain; from the north the cold. God blows upon the rivers, and even the widest torrents freeze. He loads the clouds with moisture and they send forth His lightning. The lightning bolts are directed by His hand. They do whatever He commands throughout the earth.

Listen, O Job, stop and consider the wonderful miracles of God. Do you know how God controls all nature and causes the lightning to flash forth from the clouds? Do you understand the balancing of the clouds with wonderful perfection and skill? Do you know why you become warm when the south wind is blowing and everything is still? Can you spread out the gigantic mirror of the skies as He does? You who think you know so much, teach the rest of us how we should approach God. For we are too dull to know! With your wisdom would we then dare to approach Him? Well, does a man wish to be swallowed alive? For as we cannot look at the sun for its brightness when the winds have cleared away the clouds, neither can we gaze at the terrible majesty of God breaking forth upon us from heaven, clothed in dazzling splendor. We cannot imagine the power of the Almighty, and yet He is so just and merciful that He does not destroy us. No wonder men everywhere fear Him! For He is not impressed by the world's wisest men!

23. God's Answer to Job

Then the Lord answered Job from the whirlwind:

Why are you using your ignorance to deny My providence? Now get ready to fight, for I am going to demand some answers from you, and you must reply.

Where were you when I laid the foundations of the earth? Tell me, if you know so much. Do you know how its dimensions were determined and who did the surveying? What supports its foundations, and who laid its cornerstone as the morning stars sang together and all the angels shouted for joy? Who decreed the boundaries of the seas when they gushed from the depths? Who clothed them with clouds and thick darkness and barred them by limiting their shores? And who said, "Thus far and no farther shall you come, and here shall your proud waves stop!"

Have you ever once commanded the morning to appear or caused the dawn to rise in the east? Have you ever told the daylight to spread to the ends of the earth, to end the night's wickedness? Have you ever robed the dawn in red, and disturbed the haunts of wicked men and stopped the arm raised to strike? Have you explored the springs from which the seas come or walked in the sources of their depths? Has the location of the gates of Death been revealed to you? Do you realize the extent of the earth? Tell Me about it if you know!

Where does the light come from, and how do you get there?

Or tell Me about the darkness. Where does it come from? Can you find its boundaries or go to its source? But of course you know all this! For you were born before it was all created, and you are so very experienced! Have you visited the treasuries of the snow or seen where hail is made and stored? For I have reserved it for the time when I will need it in war. Where is the path to the distribution point of light? Where is the home of the east wind? Who dug the valleys for the torrents of rain? Who laid out the path for the lightning, causing the rain to fall upon the barren deserts, so that the parched and barren ground is satisfied with water and tender grass springs up? Has the rain a father? Where does dew come from? Whose mother is the ice and frost? For the water changes and turns to ice, as hard as rock. Can you hold back the stars? Can you restrain Orion or Pleiades?

Can you ensure the proper sequence of the seasons or guide the constellation of the Bear with her satellites across the heavens? Do you know the laws of the universe and how the heavens influence the earth? Can you shout to the clouds and make it rain? Can you make lightning appear and cause it to strike as you direct it? Who gives intuition and instinct? Who is wise enough to number all the clouds? Who can tilt the water jars of heaven when everything is dust and clods?

Have you given the horse strength or clothed his neck with a quivering mane? Have you made him able to leap forward like a locust? His majestic snorting is something to hear! He paws the earth and rejoices in his strength. When he goes to war, he is unafraid and does not run away though the arrows or the flashing spear and javelin rattle against him. Fiercely he paws the ground and rushes forward into battle when the trumpet blows. At the sound of the bugle he shouts, "Aha!" He smells the battle when far away. He rejoices at the shouts of battle and the roar of the captain's commands.

Do you know how a hawk soars and spreads her wings to the south? Is it at your command that the eagle rises high upon the cliffs to make her nest? She lives upon the cliffs, making her home in her mountain fortress. From there she spies her prey from a very great distance. Her nestlings gulp down blood, for she goes wherever the slain are.

Then the Lord spoke to Job again from the whirlwind:

Stand up like a man and brace yourself for battle. Let Me ask you a question, and you give Me the answer. Are you going to discredit My justice and condemn Me, so that you can say you are right? Are you as strong as God?

Take a look at the behemoth! I made him too, just as I made you! He eats grass like an ox. See his powerful loins and the muscles of his belly. His tail is as straight as a cedar. The sinews of his thighs are tightly knit together. His vertebrae lie straight as a tube of brass. His ribs are like iron bars. How ferocious he is among all of God's creation, so let whoever hopes to master him bring a sharp sword! The mountains offer their best food to him—the other wild animals on which he preys. He lies down under the lotus plants, hidden by the reeds, covered by their shade among the willows there beside the stream. He is not disturbed by raging rivers, not even when the swelling Jordan rushes down upon him. No one can catch him off guard or put a ring in his nose and lead him away.

Can you catch leviathan with a hook and line? Or put a noose around his tongue? Can you tie him with a rope through the nose or pierce his jaw with a spike? Will he beg you to desist or try to flatter you from your intentions? Will he agree to let you make him your slave for life? Can you make a pet of him like a bird or give him to your little girls to play with? Do fishing partners sell him to the fishmongers? Will his hide be hurt by darts or his head with a harpoon? If you lay your hands upon him, you will long remember the battle that ensues, and you will never try it again! No, it's useless to try to capture him. It is frightening even to think about it!

When he stands up, the strongest are afraid. Terror grips them. No sword can stop him, nor spear nor dart nor pointed shaft. Iron is nothing but straw to him, and brass is rotten wood. Arrows cannot make him flee. Slingstones are as ineffective as straw. Clubs do no good and he laughs at the javelins hurled at him. His belly is covered with scales as sharp as shards; he drags across the ground like a steamroller! He makes the water boil with his commotion. He churns the depths. He leaves a shining wake of froth behind him. One would think the sea was made of froth! There is nothing else so fearless anywhere on earth. Of all the beasts, he is the proudest—monarch of all that he sees.

25. A Humble Man

Then Job replied to God:

I know that You can do anything and that no one can stop You. You ask who it is who has so foolishly denied Your providence. It is I. I was talking about things I knew nothing about and did not understand, things far too wonderful for me. You said, "Listen and I will speak! Let Me put the questions to you! See if you can answer them!"

But now I say, "I had heard about You before, but now I have seen You, and I loathe myself and repent in dust and ashes."

26. Restoration for Job

After the Lord had finished speaking with Job, He said to Eliphaz the Temanite: "I am angry with you and with your two friends, for you have not been right in what you have said about Me, as My servant Job was. Now take seven young bulls and seven rams and go to My servant Job and offer a burnt offering for yourselves. My servant Job will pray for you, and I will accept his prayer on your behalf and won't destroy you as I should because of your sin, your failure to speak rightly concerning My servant Job." So Eliphaz the Temanite, and Bildad the Shuhite, and Zophar the Naamathite did as the Lord commanded them. And the Lord accepted Job's prayer on their behalf.

Then when Job prayed for his friends, the Lord restored his wealth and happiness! In fact, the Lord gave him twice as much as before! All of his brothers, sisters and former friends arrived and feasted with him in his home, consoling him for all his sorrow, and comforting him because of all the trials the

Lord had brought upon him. And each of them brought him a gift of money and a gold ring.

So the Lord blessed Job at the end of his life more than at the beginning. For now he had fourteen thousand sheep, six thousand camels, one thousand teams of oxen and one thousand female donkeys. God also gave him seven more sons and three more daughters. These were the names of his daughters: Jemina, Kezia and Keren: In all the land there were no other girls as lovely as the daughters of Job; and their father put them into his will along with their brothers. Job lived 140 years after that, living to see his grandchildren and great-grandchildren too. Then at last he died, an old, old man, after living a long, good life.

PSALMS

The book of Psalms might be called the "Prayer Book of Old Testament Saints." The selections which follow have been chosen and captioned with the purpose of making them usable and profitable for personal meditation and family devotions.

1. Fruitful or Worthless

Oh, the joys of those who do not follow evil men's advice, who do not hang around with sinners, scoffing at the things of God. But they delight in doing everything God wants them to and day and night are always meditating on His laws and thinking about ways to follow Him more closely. They are like trees along a river bank bearing luscious fruit each season without fail. Their leaves shall never wither, and all they do shall prosper.

But for sinners, what a different story! They blow away like chaff before the wind! They are not safe on Judgment Day; they shall not stand among the godly. For the Lord watches over all the plans and paths of godly men, but the paths of the godless lead to doom.

2. God's Chosen Ruler

Jehovah said to my Lord the Messiah, "Rule as My regent— I will subdue your enemies and make them bow low before You." Jehovah has established Your throne in Jerusalem to rule over Your enemies. In that day of Your power Your people shall come to You willingly, dressed in holy altar robes. And Your strength shall be renewed day by day like morning dew. Jehovah has taken oath and will not rescind His vow that You are a priest forever like Melchizedek. God stands beside You to protect You.

What fools the nations are to rage against the Lord! How strange that men should try to outwit God! For a summit conference of the nations has been called to plot against the Lord and His Messiah, Christ the King. "Come, let us break His chains," they say, "and free ourselves from all this slavery to God." But God in heaven merely laughs! He is amused by all their puny plans. And then in fierce fury He rebukes them and fills them with fear. For the Lord declares, "This is the King of My choice, and I have enthroned Him in Jerusalem, My holy city."

His Chosen One replies, "I will reveal the everlasting purpose of God, for the Lord has said to Me, 'You are My Son. This is Your Coronation Day. Today I am giving You Your glory.' Only ask, and I will give you all the nations of the world.' "

O kings and rulers of the earth, listen while there is time. Serve the Lord with reverent fear; oh, the joys of those who put their trust in Him!

3. Evening Meditation

O God, You have always cared for me in my distress; now hear me as I call again. Have mercy on me. Hear my prayer. So many say that God will never help me. But Lord, You are my shield, my glory and my only hope. You alone can lift my head now bowed in shame. I cried out to the Lord, and He heard me from His Temple in Jerusalem. Then I lay down and slept in peace and woke up safely, for the Lord was watching over me.

Mark this well: The Lord has set apart the redeemed for Himself. Therefore He will listen to me and answer when I call to Him. Stand before the Lord in awe, and do not sin against

Him. Lie quietly upon your bed in silent meditation. Put your trust in the Lord, and offer Him pleasing sacrifices.

Many say that God will never help us. Prove them wrong, O Lord, by letting the light of Your face shine down upon us. Yes, the gladness You have given me is far greater than their joys at harvest time as they gaze at their bountiful crops. I will lie down in peace and sleep, for though I am alone, O Lord, You will keep me safely. For salvation comes from God. What joys He gives to all His people!

4. Morning Meditation

O Lord, hear me praying; listen to my plea, O God my King, for I will never pray to anyone but You. Each morning I will look to You in heaven and lay my requests before You, praying earnestly. I will come into Your Temple protected by Your mercy and Your love; I will worship You with deepest awe.

Lord, lead me as You promised me You would; otherwise my enemies will conquer me. Tell me clearly what to do, which way to turn. Make everyone rejoice who puts his trust in You. Keep them shouting for joy because You are defending them. Fill all who love You with Your happiness. For You bless the godly man, O Lord; You protect him with Your shield of love.

5. A Prayer for Healing

Pity me, O Lord, for I am weak. Heal me, for my body is sick, and I am upset and disturbed. My mind is filled with apprehension and with gloom. Oh, restore me soon. Come, O Lord, and make me well. In Your kindness save me. For if I die I cannot give You glory by praising You before my friends. I am worn out with pain; every night my pillow is wet with tears.

The Lord has heard my weeping and my pleading. He will answer all my prayers. I am depending on You, O Lord my God, to save me.

6. Message from Outer Space

The heavens are telling the glory of God; they are a marvelous display of His craftsmanship. Day and night they keep on telling about God. Without a sound or word, silent in the skies, their message reaches out to all the world. The sun lives in the heavens where God placed it and moves out across the skies as radiant as a bridegroom going to his wedding, or as joyous as an athlete looking forward to a race! The sun crosses the heavens from end to end, and nothing can hide from its heat.

O Lord our God, the majesty and glory of Your name fills all the earth and overflows the heavens. You have taught the little children to praise You perfectly. May their example shame and silence Your enemies! When I look up into the night skies and see the work of Your fingers—the moon and the stars You have made—I cannot understand how You can bother with mere puny man, to pay any attention to him!

And yet You have made him only a little lower than the angels and placed a crown of glory and honor upon his head. You have put him in charge of everything You made; everything is put under his authority:

All sheep and oxen and wild animals too,
The birds and fish and all the life in the sea.

O Jehovah, our Lord, the majesty and glory of Your name fills the earth.

7. Preparation for Worship

Lord, who may go and find refuge and shelter in Your tabernacle up on Your holy hill? Anyone who leads a blameless life and is truly sincere. Anyone who refuses to slander others, does not listen to gossip, never harms his neighbor; speaks out against sin, criticizes those committing it, commends the faithful followers of the Lord, keeps a promise even if it ruins him; does not crush his debtors with high interest rates, and refuses to testify against the innocent despite the bribes offered him—such a man shall stand firm forever.

The earth belongs to God! Everything in all the world is His! He is the One who pushed the oceans back to let dry land appear. Who may climb the mountain of the Lord and enter where He lives? Who may stand before the Lord? Only those with pure hands and hearts, who do not practice dishonesty and lying. They will receive God's own goodness as their blessing from Him, planted in their lives by God Himself, their Saviour. These are the ones who are allowed to stand before the Lord and worship the God of Jacob.

Open up, O ancient gates, and let the King of Glory in. Who is this King of Glory? The Lord, strong and mighty, invincible in battle. Yes, open wide the gates and let the King of Glory in. Who is this King of Glory? The Commander of all of heaven's armies!

8. Nearer My God to Thee

Save me, O God, because I have come to You for refuge. I said to Him, "You are my Lord; I have no other help but Yours." I want the company of the godly men and women in the land; they are the true nobility. Those choosing other gods shall all be filled with sorrow; I will not offer the sacrifices they do or even speak the names of their gods. The Lord Himself is my inheritance, my prize! He is my food and drink, my highest joy! He guards all that is mine. He sees that I am given pleasant brooks and meadows as my share! What a wonderful inheritance! I will bless the Lord who counsels me; He gives me wisdom in the night. He tells me what to do. I am always thinking of the Lord; and because He is so near, I never need to stumble or to fall. Heart, body, and soul are filled with joy.

Why am I praying like this? Because I know You will answer me, O God! Yes, listen as I pray. Show me Your strong love in wonderful ways, O Saviour of all those seeking Your help against their foes. Protect me as You would the pupil of Your eye; hide me in the shadow of Your wings as You hover over me. For You will not leave me among the dead; You will not allow Your beloved one to rot in the grave. You have let me experience the joys of life and the exquisite pleasures of

Your own eternal presence. My contentment is not in wealth but in seeing You and knowing all is well between us. And when I awake in heaven, I will be fully satisfied, for I will see You face-to-face.

9. God's Perfect Laws

God's laws are perfect. They protect us, make us wise and give us joy and light. God's laws are just and perfect. Reverence for God keeps us pure and leads us on to heaven. His laws are more desirable than gold. They are sweeter than honey dripping from a honeycomb. For they warn us away from harm and give success to those who obey them!

But how can I ever know what sins are lurking in my heart? Cleanse me from these hidden faults. And keep me from deliberate wrongs; help me to stop doing them. Only then can I be free of guilt and innocent of some great crime. May my spoken words and unspoken thoughts be pleasing even to You, O Lord my Rock and my Redeemer.

10. Prayer for a Friend

In your day of trouble, may the Lord be with you! May the God of Jacob keep you from all harm. May He send you aid from His sanctuary in Zion. May He remember with pleasure the gifts you have given Him, your sacrifices and burnt offerings. May He grant you your heart's desire and fulfill all your plans. May there be shouts of joy when we hear the news of your victory, flags flying with praise to God for all that He has done for you. May He answer all your prayers!

11. Man's Extremity, God's Opportunity

My God, my God, why have You forsaken me? Why do You refuse to help me or even to listen to my groans? Day and night I keep on weeping, crying for Your help, but there is no reply—for *You are holy*. The praises of our fathers surrounded Your throne; they trusted You and You delivered them. You heard their cries for help and saved them; they were never disappointed when they sought Your aid.

Lord, how You have helped me before! You took me safely from my mother's womb and brought me through the years of infancy. I have depended upon You since birth; You have always been my God. Don't leave me now, for trouble is near and no one else can possibly help. I am surrounded by fearful enemies, strong as the giant bulls from Bashan. They come at me with open jaws, like roaring lions attacking their prey. The enemy, this gang of evil men, circles me like a pack of dogs; they have pierced my hands and feet. They divide my clothes among themselves by a toss of the dice.

O Lord, don't stay away. O God my strength, hurry to my aid. Rescue me from death; spare my precious life from all these evil men. Save me from these lions' jaws and from the horns of these wild oxen; yes, God will answer me and rescue me. I will praise You to all my brothers; I will stand up before the congregation and testify of the wonderful things You have done. "Praise the Lord, each one of you who fears Him," I will say. "Each of you must fear and reverence His name. Let all Israel sing His praises, for He has not despised my cries of deep despair; He has not turned and walked away. When I cried to Him, He heard and came." Yes, I will stand and praise You before all the people. I will publicly fulfill my vows in the presence of all who reverence Your name.

12. The Good Shepherd

Because the Lord is my shepherd, I have everything I need! He lets me rest in the meadow grass and leads me beside the quiet streams. He restores my failing health. He helps me do what honors Him the most. Even when walking through the dark valley of death I will not be afraid, for You are close beside me, guarding, guiding all the way. You provide delicious food for me in the presence of my enemies. You have welcomed me as Your guest; blessings overflow! Your goodness and unfailing kindness shall be with me all of my life, and afterwards I will live with You forever in Your home.

13. Friendship with God

To You, O Lord, I pray! Don't fail me, Lord, for I am trusting You. Show me the path where I should go, O Lord; point out the right road for me to walk. Lead me; teach me; for You are the God who gives me salvation. I have no hope except in You. Overlook my youthful sins, O Lord! Look at me instead through eyes of mercy and forgiveness, through eyes of everlasting love and kindness.

The Lord is good and glad to teach the proper path to all who go astray; He will teach the ways that are right and best to those who humbly turn to Him. And when we obey Him, every path He guides us on is fragrant with His loving-kindness and His truth. But Lord, my sins! How many they are. Oh, pardon them for the honor of Your name. Where is the man who fears the Lord? God will teach him how to choose the best! He shall live within God's circle of blessing, and his children shall inherit the earth! Friendship with God is reserved for those who reverence Him. With them alone He shares the secrets of His promises.

My eyes are ever looking to the Lord for help, for He alone can rescue me. Come, Lord, and show me Your mercy, for I am helpless, overwhelmed, in deep distress; my problems go from bad to worse. Oh, save me from them all! See my sorrows; feel my pain; forgive my sins. Assign me godliness and integrity as my bodyguards, for I expect You to protect me. Oh, let it never be said that I trusted You in vain!

14. Waiting for the Lord

The Lord is my light and my salvation; whom shall I fear?

The one thing I want from God, the thing I seek most of all, is the privilege of meditating in His temple, living in His presence every day of my life, delighting in His incomparable perfections and glory. There I'll be when troubles come! He will hide me. He will set me on a high rock out of reach of all my enemies. Then I will bring Him sacrifices and sing His praises with much joy.

Listen to my pleading, Lord! Be merciful and send the help I need. My heart has heard You say, "Come and talk with Me, O My people." And my heart responds, "Lord, I am coming." Oh, do not hide Yourself when I am trying to find You. Do not angrily reject Your servant! You have been my help in all my trials before; don't leave me now. Don't forsake me, O God of my salvation. For if my father and mother should abandon me, You would welcome and comfort me. I am expecting the Lord to rescue me again, so that once again I will see His goodness to me here in the land of the living!

Don't be impatient! Wait for the Lord, and He will come and save you! Be brave, stouthearted and courageous. Yes, wait and He will help you.

15. God's Glory in the Storm

Praise the Lord, you angels of His; praise His glory and His strength. Praise Him for His majestic glory, the glory of His name. Come before Him clothed in sacred garments.

The voice of the Lord echoes from the clouds. The God of glory thunders through the skies. So powerful is His voice; so full of majesty. The voice of the Lord thunders through the lightning. It resounds through the deserts and shakes the wilderness of Kadesh. The voice of the Lord spins and topples the mighty oaks. It strips the forests bare! They whirl and sway beneath the blast. But in His temple all are praising, "Glory, glory to the Lord." At the Flood, the Lord showed His control of all creation. Now He continues to unveil His power. He will give His people strength. He will bless them with peace.

16. Thanksgiving for Healing

O Lord my God, I pled with You, and You gave me my health again. You brought me back from the brink of the grave, from death itself, and here I am alive! Oh, sing to Him you saints of His; give thanks to His holy name. His anger lasts a moment; His favor lasts for life! Weeping may go on all night, but in the morning there is joy.

In my prosperity I said, "This is forever; nothing can stop me now! The Lord has shown me His favor. He has made me steady as a mountain." Then, Lord, You turned Your face away from me and cut off Your river of blessings. Suddenly my courage was gone; I was terrified and panic-stricken. I cried to You, O Lord; oh, how I pled, "Hear me, Lord; oh, have pity and help me." Then He turned my sorrow into joy! He took away my clothes of mourning and gave me gay and festive garments to rejoice in so that I might sing glad praises to the Lord instead of lying in silence in the grave. O Lord my God, I will keep on thanking You forever!

17. God to the Rescue

O Lord, have mercy on me in my anguish. My eyes are red from weeping; my health is broken from sorrow. I am pining away with grief; my years are shortened, drained away because of sadness. My sins have sapped my strength; I stoop with sorrow and with shame. Answer quickly when I cry to You; bend low and hear my whispered plea. Be for me a great rock of safety from my foes. Yes, You are my rock and my fortress; honor Your name by leading me out of this peril. Pull me from the trap my enemies have set for me. For You alone are strong enough. Into Your hand I commit my spirit.

You have rescued me, O God who keeps His promises! For I worship only You; I am radiant with joy because of Your mercy, for You have listened to my troubles and have seen the crisis in my soul. Oh, how great is Your goodness to those who publicly declare that You will rescue them. For You have stored up great blessings for those who trust and reverence You. Hide Your loved ones in the shelter of Your presence, safe beneath Your hand, safe from all conspiring men.

Blessed is the Lord, for He has shown me that His never-failing love protects me like the walls of a fort! I spoke too hastily when I said, "The Lord has deserted me," for You listened to my plea and answered me. Oh, love the Lord all of you who are His people; for the Lord protects those who are loyal to Him, but harshly punishes all who haughtily reject Him. So cheer up! Take courage if you are depending on the Lord!

18. When I Confessed

What happiness for those whose guilt has been forgiven! What joys when sins are covered over! What relief for those who have confessed their sins and God has cleared their record. There was a time when I wouldn't admit what a sinner I was. But my dishonesty made me miserable and filled my days with frustration. All day and all night Your hand was heavy on me. My strength evaporated like water on a sunny day until I finally admitted all my sins to You and stopped trying to hide them. I said to myself, "I will confess them to the Lord." And You forgave me! All my guilt is gone!

After this experience, I say that every believer should confess his sins to God as soon as he becomes aware of them, while there is yet time to be forgiven. If he does this, judgment will not touch him. You are my hiding place from every storm of life; You even keep me from getting into trouble! You surround me with songs of victory. Abiding love surrounds those who trust in the Lord. So rejoice in Him, all those who are His, and shout for joy, all those who try to obey Him.

19. Wonderful Heritage

Let all the joys of the godly well up in praise to the Lord, for it is right to praise Him. Play joyous melodies of praise upon the lyre and on the harp! Compose new songs of praise to Him, accompanied skillfully on the harp; sing joyfully. For all God's words are right, and everything He does is worthy of our trust. He loves whatever is just and good; the earth is filled with His tender love. He merely spoke, and the heavens and all the galaxies of stars were formed. He made the oceans, pouring them into His vast reservoirs. Let everyone in all the world—men, women and children—fear the Lord and stand in awe of Him. For when He but spoke, the world began! It appeared at His command! His own plan stands forever. His intentions are the same for every generation. Blessed is the nation whose God is the Lord, whose people He has chosen as His own.

Here is my description of a truly happy land where Jehovah is God:

> Sons vigorous and tall as growing plants,
> Daughters of graceful beauty like the pillars
>   of a palace wall,
> Barns full to the brim with crops of every kind,
> Sheep by the thousands out in our fields,
> Oxen loaded down with produce,
> No enemy attacking the walls, but peace everywhere,
> And no crime in our streets.

Yes, happy are those whose God is Jehovah.

The Lord gazes down upon mankind from heaven where He lives. He has made their hearts and closely watches everything they do. The eyes of the Lord are watching over those who fear Him, who rely upon His steady love. He will keep them from death even in times of famine! We depend upon the Lord alone to save us. Only He can help us, He protects us like a shield. No wonder we are happy in the Lord! For we are trusting Him! We trust His holy name. Yes, Lord, let Your constant love surround us, for our hopes are in You alone.

20. Thanksgiving for Answered Prayer

I will praise the Lord no matter what happens. I will constantly speak of His glories and grace. I will boast of all His kindness to me. Let all who are discouraged take heart! Let us praise the Lord together and exalt His name. For I cried to Him and He answered me! He freed me from all my fears. Others too were radiant at what He did for them. Theirs was no downcast look of rejection! This poor man cried to the Lord—and the Lord heard him and saved him out of his troubles. For the Angel of the Lord guards and rescues all who reverence Him.

Oh, put God to the test and see how kind He is! See for yourself the way His mercies shower down on all who trust in Him! If you belong to the Lord, reverence Him; for everyone who does this has everything he needs. Even strong young lions sometimes go hungry, but those of us who reverence the Lord will never lack any good thing.

Sons and daughters, come and listen and let me teach you the importance of trusting and fearing the Lord. Do you want a long, good life? Then watch your tongue! Keep your lips from lying. Turn from all known sin and spend your time in doing good. Try to live in peace with everyone; work hard at it. For the eyes of the Lord are intently watching all who live good lives, and He gives attention when they cry to Him.

Yes, the Lord hears the good man when he calls to Him for help and saves him out of all his troubles. The Lord is close to those whose hearts are breaking; He rescues those who are humbly sorry for their sins. The good man does not escape all troubles—he has them too. But the Lord helps him in each and every one. As for those who serve the Lord, He will redeem them; everyone who takes refuge in Him will be freely pardoned.

21. The Fountain of Life

Your steadfast love, O Lord, is as great as all the heavens. Your faithfulness reaches beyond the clouds! Your justice is as solid as God's mountains. Your decisions are as full of wisdom as the oceans are with water. You are concerned for men and animals alike! How precious is Your constant love, O

God! All humanity takes refuge in the shadow of Your wings! You feed them with blessings from Your own table and let them drink from Your rivers of delight. For You are the Fountain of Life; our light is from Your Light. Pour out Your unfailing love on those who know You! Never stop giving Your salvation to those who long to do Your will.

22. Commitment and Trust

Never envy the wicked! Soon they fade away like grass and disappear. Trust in the Lord instead. Be kind and good to others; then you will live safely here in the land and prosper, feeding in safety. Be delighted with the Lord! Then He will give you all your heart's desires. Commit everything you do to the Lord. Trust Him to help you do it and He will. Your innocence will be clear to everyone. He will vindicate you with the blazing light of justice shining down as from the noonday sun. Rest in the Lord; wait patiently for Him to act. Don't be envious of evil men who prosper. Stop your anger! Turn off your wrath. Don't fret and worry—it only leads to harm.

The steps of good men are directed by the Lord. He delights in each step they take. If they fall it isn't fatal, for the Lord holds them with His hand. I have been young and now I am old. And in all my years I have never seen the Lord forsake a man who loves Him; nor have I seen the children of the godly go hungry. Instead, the godly are able to be generous with their gifts and loans to others, and their children are a blessing. So if you want an eternal home, leave your evil, low-down ways and live good lives. For the Lord loves justice and fairness; He will never abandon His people. They will be kept safe forever; but all who love wickedness shall perish. The godly shall be firmly planted in the land and live there forever. The godly man is a good counselor because he is just and fair and knows right from wrong.

Don't be impatient for the Lord to act! Keep steadily along His pathway and in due season He will honor you with every blessing, and you will see the wicked destroyed. I myself have seen it happen: a proud and evil man towering like a cedar of Lebanon, but when I looked again, he was gone! I searched but could not find him! But the good man—what a different story! For the good man—the blameless, the upright, the man of peace—he has a wonderful future ahead of him. For him there is a happy ending. The Lord saves the godly! He is their salvation and their refuge when trouble comes. Because they trust in Him, He helps them and delivers them from the plots of evil men.

23. A Prayer for Recovery

O Lord, Your arrows have struck deep; Your blows are crushing me. Because of Your anger my body is sick, my health is broken beneath my sins. They are like a flood, higher than my head; they are a burden too heavy to bear. I am exhausted and crushed; I groan in despair. Lord, You know how I long for my health once more. You hear my every sigh.

I said to myself, I'm going to quit complaining! I'll keep quiet, especially when the ungodly are around me. But as I stood there silently, the turmoil within me grew to the bursting point. The more I mused, the hotter the fires inside. Then at last I spoke, and pled with God: Lord, help me to realize how brief my time on earth will be! Help me to know that I am here for but a moment more. My life is no longer than my hand! My whole lifetime is but a moment to You. Proud man! Frail as breath! A shadow! And all his busy rushing ends in nothing. He heaps up riches for someone else to spend. When You punish a man for his sins, he is destroyed; for he is as fragile as a moth-infested cloth; yes, man is frail as breath.

Hear my prayer, O Lord; listen to my cry! Don't sit back, unmindful of my tears! For I am Your guest! I am a traveler passing through the earth as all my fathers were! Spare me, Lord! Let me recover and be filled with happiness again. I am poor and needy, yet the Lord is thinking about me right now! O my God, You are my helper; You are my Saviour; come quickly and save me. Please don't delay!

24. Good News

I waited patiently for God to help me; then He listened and heard my cry. He lifted me out of the pit of despair, out from the bog and the mire and set my feet on a hard, firm path and steadied me as I walked along. He has given me a new song to sing, of praises to our God. Now many will hear of the glorious things He did for me, stand in awe before the Lord and put their trust in Him. Many blessings are given to those who trust the Lord and have no confidence in those who are proud or who trust in idols. O Lord my God, many and many a time You have done great miracles for us, and we are ever in Your thoughts. Who else can do such glorious things? No one else can be compared with You. There isn't time to tell of all Your wonderful deeds.

It isn't sacrifices and offerings which You really want from Your people. Burnt animals bring no special joy to Your heart. But You have accepted the offer of my lifelong service. Then I said, "See, I have come, just as all the prophets foretold. And I delight to do Your will, my God; for Your law is written upon My heart!" I have told everyone the good news that You forgive men's sins. I have not been timid about it, as You well know, O Lord. I have not kept this good news hidden in my heart, but have proclaimed Your loving-kindness and truth to all the congregation.

O Lord, don't hold back Your tender mercies from me! My only hope is in Your love and faithfulness! May the joy of the Lord be given to everyone who loves Him and His salvation. May they constantly exclaim, "How great God is!"

25. Thirsting for God

As the deer pants for water, so I long for You, O God. I thirst for God, the living God. Where can I find Him to come and stand before Him? Day and night I weep for His help, while my enemies taunt me. "Where is this God of yours?" they scoff. Take courage, my soul! Do you remember those times (but how could you ever forget them!) when you led a great procession to the Temple on festival days, singing with joy, praising the Lord? Why then be downcast? Why be discouraged and sad? Hope in God! I shall yet praise Him again! Yes, I shall again praise Him for His help.

Yet I am standing here depressed and gloomy; but I will meditate upon Your kindness to this lovely land where the Jordan River flows and where Mount Hermon and Mount Mizar stand. All your waves and billows have gone over me, and floods of sorrow pour upon me like a thundering cataract. Yet day by day the Lord also pours out His steadfast love upon me, and through the night I sing His songs and pray to God who gives me life.

O my soul, don't be discouraged! Don't be upset! Expect God to act! For I know that I shall again have plenty of reason to praise Him for all that He will do! He is my help! He is my God! Oh, send out Your light and Your truth—let them lead me. Let them lead me to Your Temple on Your holy mountain, Zion. There I will go to the altar of God my exceeding joy, and praise Him with my harp. O God—my God! O my soul, why be so gloomy and discouraged? Trust in God! I shall again praise Him for His wondrous help; He will make me smile again, *for He is my God!*

26. God Our Refuge and Strength

God is our refuge and strength, a tested help in times of trouble. And so we need not fear even if the world blows up and the mountains crumble into the sea. Let the oceans roar and foam; let the mountains tremble! There is a river of joy flowing through the city of our God—the sacred home of the God above all gods. God Himself is living in that city; therefore it stands unmoved despite the turmoil everywhere. He will not delay His help. The nations rant and rave in anger—but when God speaks, the earth melts in submission and kingdoms totter into ruin. The commander of the armies of heaven is here among us. He, the God of Jacob, has come to rescue us.

Come, see the glorious things that our God does, how He brings ruin upon the world, and causes wars to end throughout the earth, breaking and burning every weapon. "Stand silent! Know that I am God! I shall be honored by every nation in the world!" The commander of the heavenly armies is here among *us!* He, the God of Jacob, has come to rescue *us!*

27. Trusting in Riches

Listen, everyone! High and low, rich and poor, all around the world—listen to my words, for they are wise and filled with insight. I will tell in song accompanied by harps the answer to one of life's most perplexing problems: *There is no need to fear when times of trouble come,* even though surrounded by enemies! For they trust in their wealth and boast about how rich they are! Yet not one of them, though rich as kings, can ransom his own brother from the penalty of sin! For God's forgiveness does not come that way! For a soul is far too precious to be ransomed by mere earthly wealth. There is not enough of it in all the earth to buy eternal life for just one soul, to keep it out of hell.

Rich man! Proud man! Wise man! You must die like all the rest! You have no greater lease on life than foolish, stupid men. You must leave your wealth to others! You name your estates after yourselves as though your lands could be yours forever, and you could live on them eternally! But man with all his pomp must die like any animal! Such is the folly of these men, though after they die they will be quoted as having great wisdom!

But as for me, God will redeem my soul from the power of death, for He will receive me. So do not be dismayed when evil men grow rich and build their lovely homes. For when they die they carry nothing with them! Their honors will not follow them. Though a man calls himself happy all through his life— and the world loudly applauds success—yet in the end he dies like everyone else and enters eternal darkness. For man with all his pomp must die—death is the shepherd of all mankind.

28. True Worship

The mighty God, the Lord, has summoned all mankind from east to west! God's glory-light shines from the beautiful Temple on Mount Zion. He has come to judge His people. To heaven and earth He shouts, "Gather together My own people who by their sacrifice upon My altar have promised to obey Me."

O My people, listen! For I am your God. Listen! Here are My charges against you: I have no complaint about the sacrifices you bring to My altar, for you bring them regularly. But it isn't sacrificial bullocks and goats that I really want from you! For all the animals of field and forest are Mine! The cattle on a thousand hills! And all the birds upon the mountains! If I were hungry, I would not mention it to you—for all the world is Mine and everything in it. No, I don't need your sacrifices of flesh and blood! What I want from you is your true thanks; I want your promises fulfilled. *I want you to trust Me in your times of trouble so I can rescue you, and you can give Me glory!* True praise is a worthy sacrifice; this really honors Me. Those who walk My paths will receive salvation from the Lord.

29. Prayer for Pardon and Restoration

O loving and kind God, have mercy. Have pity upon me and take away the awful stain of my transgressions. Oh, wash me, cleanse me from this guilt. Let me be pure again. For I admit my shameful deed—it haunts me day and night. It is against You and You alone I sinned and did this terrible thing. You saw it all, and Your sentence against me is just. But I was born a sinner, yes, from the moment my mother conceived me. You deserve honesty from the heart; yes, utter sincerity and truthfulness. Oh, give me this wisdom.

Sprinkle me with the cleansing blood and I shall be clean again. Wash me and I shall be whiter than snow. And after You have punished me, give me back my joy again. Don't keep looking at my sins—erase them from Your sight.

Create in me a new, clean heart, O God, filled with clean thoughts and right desires. Don't toss me aside, banished forever from Your presence. Don't take Your Holy Spirit from me. Restore to me again the joy of Your salvation, and make me willing to obey You. Then I will teach Your ways to other sinners, and they—guilty like me—will repent and return to You.

Don't sentence me to death, O my God, You alone can rescue me. Then I will sing of Your forgiveness, for my lips will be unsealed—oh, how I will praise You. You don't want penance. If You did, how gladly I would do it! You aren't interested in offerings burned before You on the altar. It is a broken spirit You want—remorse and penitence. A broken and a contrite heart, O God, You will not ignore.

30. Under His Wings

O God, have pity, for I am trusting You! I will hide beneath the shadow of Your wings until this storm is past. I will cry to the God of heaven who does such wonders for me. He will send down help from heaven to save me because of His love and His faithfulness. O God, my heart is quiet and confident. No wonder I can sing Your praises! Rouse yourself, my soul! Arise, O harp and lyre! Let us greet the dawn with song! I will thank You publicly throughout the land. I will sing Your praises among the nations. Your kindness and love are as vast as the heavens. Your faithfulness is higher than the skies. Yes, be exalted, O God, above the heavens. May Your glory shine throughout the earth.

I will surely do what I have promised, Lord, and thank You for Your help. You have seen me tossing and turning through the night. You have collected all my tears and preserved them in Your bottle! You have recorded every one in Your book. You have saved me from death and my feet from slipping so that I can walk before the Lord in the land of the living. Blessed be God who didn't turn away when I was praying and didn't refuse me His kindness and love.

31. Rock of Ages

I stand silently before the Lord, waiting for Him to rescue me. For salvation comes from Him alone. Yes, He alone is my rock, my rescuer, defense and fortress. Why then should I be tense with fear when troubles come?

O God, listen to me! Hear my prayer! For wherever I am, though far away at the ends of the earth, I will cry to You for help. When my heart is faint and overwhelmed, lead me to the mighty, towering rock of safety. For You are my refuge, a high tower where my enemies can never reach me. I shall live forever in Your tabernacle; oh, to be safe beneath the shelter of Your wings. For You have heard my vows, O God, to praise You every day, and You have given me the blessings You reserve for those who reverence Your name. You will give me added years of life as rich and full as those of many generations all packed into one! And I shall live before the Lord forever. Oh, send Your loving-kindness and truth to guard and watch over me, and I will praise Your name continually, fulfilling my vow of praising You each day.

Blessed be God who didn't turn away when I was praying and didn't refuse me His kindness and love. Yes, He alone is my rock, my rescuer, defense and fortress—why then should I be tense with fear when troubles come? My protection and success come from God alone. He is my refuge, a rock where no enemy can reach me. Give your burdens to the Lord. He will carry them. He will not permit the godly to slip or fall.

32. Longing for God

O God, *my* God! How I search for You! How I thirst for You in this parched and weary land where there is no water! How I long to find You! How I wish I could go into Your sanctuary to see Your strength and glory! For Your love and kindness are better to me than life itself. How I praise You! I will bless You as long as I live, lifting up my hands to You in prayer. At last I shall be fully satisfied; I will praise You with great joy! I lie awake at night thinking of You—Oh, how much You have helped me—and how I rejoice through the night beneath the protecting shadow of Your wings!

33. With God in His Sanctuary

O God in Zion, we wait before You in silent praise and thus fulfill our vow. And because You answer prayer, all mankind will come to You with their requests. Though sins fill our hearts, You forgive them all. How greatly to be envied are those You have chosen to come and live with You within the holy tabernacle courts! What joys await us among all the good things there. With dread deeds and awesome power You will defend us. You are the only hope of all mankind throughout the world and far away upon the sea. What awe we feel, kneeling here before Him in the sanctuary. The God of Israel gives strength and mighty power to His people. Blessed be God!

34. Harvest Song

Sing to the Lord, all the earth! Sing of His glorious name! Tell the world how wonderful He is. How awe-inspiring are Your deeds, O God! How great Your power! All the earth shall worship You and sing of Your glories. Come, see the glorious things God has done. What marvelous miracles happen to His people!

He formed the mountains by His mighty strength. He quiets the raging oceans and all the world's clamor. In the farthest corners of the earth the glorious acts of God shall startle everyone. The dawn and sunset shout for joy! He waters the earth to make it fertile. The rivers of God will not run dry! He prepares the earth for His people and sends them rich harvests of grain. He waters the furrows with abundant rain. Showers soften the earth, melting the clods and causing seeds to sprout across the land. Then He crowns it all with green, lush pastures in the wilderness; hillsides blossom with joy. The pastures are filled with flocks of sheep, and the valleys are carpeted with grain. All the world shouts and sings with joy.

O God, in mercy bless us; let Your face beam with joy as You look down at us. Send us around the world with the news of Your saving power and Your eternal plan for all mankind. How everyone throughout the earth will praise the Lord! How glad the nations will be, singing for joy because You are their King and will give true justice to their people! Praise God, O world! May all the peoples of the earth give thanks to You. For the earth has yielded abundant harvests. God, even our own God, will bless us. And peoples from remotest lands will worship Him.

35. In Old Age

Lord, You are my refuge! Don't let me down! Rescue me! Bend down Your ear and listen to my plea and save me. Be to me a great protecting rock, where I am always welcome. O Lord, You alone are my hope; I've trusted You from childhood. Yes, You have been with me from birth and have helped me constantly—no wonder I am always praising You!

All day long I'll praise and honor You, O God, for all that You have done for me. And now, in my old age, don't set me aside! Don't forsake me now when my strength is failing! Pull me out of this mire. Don't let me sink in. Rescue me from those who hate me and from these deep waters I am in. Don't let the floods overwhelm me or the ocean swallow me; save me from the pit that threatens me. O Jehovah, answer my prayers, for Your loving-kindness is wonderful; Your mercy is so plentiful, so tender and so kind.

O God, You have helped me from my earliest childhood— and I have constantly testified to others of the wonderful things You do. And now that I am old and gray, don't forsake me. Give me time to tell this new generation (and their children too) about all Your mighty miracles. Your power and goodness, Lord, reach to the highest heavens. You have done such wonderful things. Where is there another God like You?

You have let me sink down deep in desperate problems. But You will bring me back to life again, up from the depths of the earth. You will give me greater honor than before. And You will turn again and comfort me. I will praise You with music, telling of Your faithfulness to all Your promises, O Holy One of Israel. I will shout and sing Your praises for redeeming me. I will talk to others all day long about Your justice and Your goodness.

36. When the Wicked Prosper

How good God is to Israel—to those whose hearts are pure. But as for me, I came *so* close to the edge of the cliff! My feet were slipping and I was almost gone. For I was envious of the prosperity of the proud and wicked. Yes, all through life their road is smooth! They grow sleek and fat. They aren't always in trouble and plagued with problems like everyone else, so their pride sparkles like a jeweled necklace, and their clothing is woven of cruelty! These fat cats have everything their hearts could ever wish for! They scoff at God and threaten His people. How proudly they speak! They boast against the very heavens, and their words strut through the earth. And so God's people are dismayed and confused and drink it all in.

"Does God realize what is going on?" they ask. "Look at these men of arrogance; they never have to lift a finger—theirs is a life of ease; and all the time their riches multiply."

It is so hard to explain it—this prosperity of those who hate the Lord. Then one day I went into God's sanctuary to meditate and thought about the future of these evil men. What a slippery path they are on—suddenly God will send them sliding over the edge of the cliff and down to their destruction: an instant end to all their happiness, an eternity of terror. Their present life is only a dream! They will awaken to the truth as one awakens from a dream of things that never really were!

When I saw this, what turmoil filled my heart! I saw myself so stupid and so ignorant; I must seem like an animal to You, O God. But even so, You love me! You are holding my right hand! You will keep on guiding me all my life with Your wisdom and counsel; and afterwards receive me into the glories of heaven! Whom have I in heaven but You? And I desire no one on earth as much as You! My health fails; my spirits droop, yet God remains! He is the strength of my heart; He is mine forever! I get as close to Him as I can! I have chosen Him and I will tell everyone about the wonderful ways He rescues me.

37. Too Troubled to Sleep

I cry to the Lord; I call and call to Him. Oh, that He would listen. I am in deep trouble and I need His help so badly. All night long I pray, lifting my hands to heaven, pleading. There can be no joy for me until He acts. I think of God and moan, overwhelmed with longing for His help. I cannot sleep until You act. I am too distressed even to pray! I keep thinking of the good old days of the past, long since ended.

Then my nights were filled with joyous songs. I search my soul and meditate upon the difference now. Has the Lord rejected me forever? Will He never again be favorable? Is His loving-kindness gone forever? Has His promise failed? Has He forgotten to be kind to one so undeserving? Has He slammed the door in anger on His love? I recall the many miracles He did for me so long ago. Those wonderful deeds are constantly in my thoughts. I cannot stop thinking about them.

O God, Your ways are holy. Where is there any other as mighty as You? You are the God of miracles and wonders! You still demonstrate Your awesome power. Let those who love Your salvation exclaim, "What a wonderful God He is!" But I am in deep trouble. Rush to my aid, for only You can help and save me. O Lord, don't delay.

38. Prayer for the Nation

O shepherd of Israel who leads Israel like a flock; O God enthroned above the cherubim, bend down Your ear and listen as I plead. Display Your power and radiant glory. O Jehovah, God of heaven's armies, how long will You be angry and reject our prayers? You have fed us with sorrow and tears, and have made us the scorn of the neighboring nations. They laugh among themselves.

Turn us again to Yourself, O God of Hosts. Look down on us in joy and love; only then shall we be saved. You brought us from Egypt as though we were a tender vine and drove away the heathen from Your land and planted us. You cleared the ground and tilled the soil and we took root and filled the land.

Come back, we beg of You, O God of the armies of heaven, and bless us. Look down from heaven and see our plight and care for this Your vine! Protect what You Yourself have planted, and we will never forsake You again. Revive us to trust in You. Turn us again to Yourself, O God of the armies of heaven. Look down on us, Your face aglow with joy and love— only then shall we be saved.

39. Listen, My People!

The Lord makes us strong! Sing praises! Sing to Israel's God! Sing, accompanied by drums; pluck the sweet lyre and harp. Sound the trumpet! Come to the joyous celebrations at full moon, new moon and all the other holidays! For God has given us these times of joy; they are scheduled in the laws of Israel. He gave them as reminders of His war against Egypt where we were slaves on foreign soil. I heard an unknown voice that said, "Now I will relieve your shoulder of its burden; I will free your hands from their heavy tasks."

He said, "You cried to Me in trouble and I saved you; I answered from Mount Horeb where the thunder hides. I tested your faith at Meribah when you complained there was no water. Listen to Me, O My people, while I give you stern warnings. O Israel, if you will only listen! *You must never worship any other god,* nor ever have an idol in your home. For it was I Jehovah your God, who brought you out of the land of Egypt. Only test Me! Open your mouth wide and see if I won't fill it! You will receive every blessing you can use! But no, My people won't listen. Israel doesn't want Me around. So I am letting them go their blind and stubborn way, living according to their own desires. But, oh that My people would listen to Me! Oh that Israel would follow Me."

40. How Lovely Is Your Temple!

How lovely is Your Temple, O Lord of the armies of heaven. I long, yes, faint with longing to be able to enter Your courtyard and come near to the Living God. Even the sparrows and swallows are welcome to come and nest among Your altars and there have their young, O Lord of heaven's armies, my King and my God! How happy are Your priests who can always be in Your Temple, singing Your praises. Happy are those who are strong in the Lord, who want above all else to follow Your steps.

When they walk through the Valley of Weeping it will become a place of springs where pools of blessing and refreshment collect after rains! They will grow constantly in strength and each of them is invited to meet with the Lord in Zion! O Jehovah, God of the heavenly armies, hear my prayer! Listen, God of Israel. O God, our defender and our shield, have mercy.

A single day spent in Your Temple is better than a thousand anywhere else! I would rather be a doorman of the Temple of my God than live in palaces of wickedness. For Jehovah God is our light and our protector. He gives us grace and glory. No good thing will He withhold from those who walk along His paths. O Lord of the armies of heaven, blessed are those who trust in You.

Hallelujah! Yes, let His people praise Him, as they stand in His Temple courts. Praise the Lord because He is so good; sing to His wonderful name.

41. Prayer for Revival

Lord, You have poured out amazing blessings on this land! You have restored the fortunes of Israel, and forgiven the sins of Your people—yes, covered over each one. Now bring us back to loving You, O Lord, so that Your anger will never need rise against us again.

I am listening carefully to all the Lord is saying—for He speaks peace to His people, His saints, if they will only stop their sinning. Surely His salvation is near to those who reverence Him; our land will be filled with His glory! Mercy and truth have met together. Grim justice and peace have kissed! Truth rises from the earth and righteousness smiles down from heaven. Yes, the Lord pours down His blessings on the land and it yields its bountiful crops.

Oh, revive us! Then Your people can rejoice in You again. Pour out Your love and kindness on us, Lord, and grant us Your salvation.

42. In Deep Trouble

Bend down and hear my prayer, O Lord, and answer me, for I am deep in trouble. Protect me from death, for I try to follow all Your laws. Save me, for I am serving You and trusting You. Be merciful, O Lord, for I am looking up to You in constant hope. Give me happiness, O Lord, for I worship only You. O Lord, You are so good and kind, so ready to forgive; so full of mercy for all who ask Your aid. Listen closely to my prayer, O God. Hear my urgent cry.

I will call to You whenever trouble strikes, and You will help me. For You are great and do great miracles. You alone are God. Tell me where You want me to go and I will go there. May every fiber of my being unite in reverence to Your name. With all my heart I will praise You. I will give glory to Your name forever, for You love me so much! And You are constantly so kind! And You have rescued me from deepest hell. You are merciful and gentle, Lord, slow in getting angry, full of constant loving-kindness and of truth; so look down in pity and grant strength to Your servant and save me.

43. At Death's Door

O Jehovah, God of my salvation, I have wept before You day and night. Now hear my prayers; oh, listen to my cry, for my life is full of troubles, and death draws near. They say my life is ebbing out—a hopeless case.

Lord, hear my prayer! Listen to my plea! Don't turn away

from me in this time of my distress. Bend down Your ear and give me speedy answers, for my days disappear like smoke. My health is broken and my heart is sick; it is trampled like grass and is withered. My food is tasteless, and I have lost my appetite. I am reduced to skin and bones because of all my groaning and despair. I am like a vulture in a far-off wilderness or like an owl alone in the desert. I lie awake, lonely as a solitary sparrow on the roof.

My eyes grow dim with weeping. Each day I beg Your help; O Lord, I reach my pleading hands to You for mercy. Soon it will be too late! Of what use are Your miracles when I am in the grave? How can I praise You then? Can those in the grave declare Your loving-kindness? Can they proclaim Your faithfulness? Can the darkness speak of Your miracles? Can anyone in the Land of Forgetfulness talk about Your help? O Lord, I plead for my life and shall keep on pleading day by day.

44. Numbering Our Days

Lord, through all the generations You have been our home! Before the mountains were created, before the earth was formed, You are God without beginning or end. You speak, and man turns back to dust. A thousand years are but as yesterday to You! They are like a single hour! We glide along the tides of time as swiftly as a racing river and vanish as quickly as a dream. We are like grass that is green in the morning but mowed down and withered before the evening shadows fall. You spread out our sins before You—our secret sins—and see them all.

No wonder the years are long and heavy here beneath Your wrath. All our days are filled with sighing. Seventy years are given us! And some may even live to eighty. But even the best of these years are often emptiness and pain; soon they disappear, and we are gone. Teach us to number our days and recognize how few they are; help us to spend them as we should.

O Jehovah, come and bless us! How long will You delay? Satisfy us every morning with Your loving-kindness, giving us constant joy to the end of our lives. Give us gladness in proportion to our former misery! Replace the evil years with good. Let us see Your miracles again; let our children see glorious things, the kind You used to do, and let the Lord our God favor us and give us success.

45. Shielded by His Wings

We live within the shadow of the Almighty, sheltered by the God who is above all gods. This I declare, that He alone is my refuge, my place of safety; He is my God, and I am trusting Him. For He rescues you from every trap and protects you from the fatal plague. He will shield you with His wings! They will shelter you. His faithful promises are your armor.

Now you don't need to be afraid of the dark any more, nor fear the dangers of the day; nor dread the plagues of darkness, nor disasters in the morning, for He orders His angels to protect you wherever you go. They will steady you with their hands to keep you from stumbling against the rocks on the trail. You can safely meet a lion or step on poisonous snakes; yes, even trample them beneath your feet!

For the Lord says, "Because he loves Me, I will rescue him; I will make him great because he trusts in My name. When he calls on Me I will answer; I will be with him in trouble, rescue him and honor him. I will satisfy him with a full life and give him My salvation."

Jehovah is my refuge! I choose the God above all gods to shelter me.

46. Thanksgiving Every Morning

It is good to say, "Thank You" to the Lord, to sing praises to the God who is above all gods. Every morning tell Him, "Thank You for Your kindness," and every evening rejoice in all His faithfulness. Sing His praises, accompanied by music from the harp and lute and lyre. You have done so much for me, O Lord. No wonder I am glad! I sing for joy. O Lord, what miracles you do! And how deep are Your thoughts!

The godly shall flourish like palm trees and grow tall as the cedars of Lebanon. For they are transplanted into the Lord's own garden and are under His personal care. Even in old age they will still produce fruit and be vital and green. This honors the Lord and exhibits His faithful care. He is my shelter. There is nothing but goodness in Him! The Lord continues forever, exalted in the heavens.

47. Come, Let Us Worship

Oh, come, let us sing to the Lord! Give a joyous shout in honor of the rock of our salvation! Come before Him with thankful hearts. Let us sing Him psalms of praise. For the Lord is a great God, the great King of all gods. He controls the formation of the depths of the earth and the mightiest mountains; all are His. He made the sea and formed the land; they too are His. Come, kneel before the Lord our Maker, for He is our God. We are His sheep and He is our shepherd! Oh, that you would hear Him calling you today and come to Him!

Sing a new song to the Lord! Sing it everywhere around the world! Sing out His praises! Bless His name. Each day tell someone that He saves. Publish His glorious acts throughout the earth. Tell everyone about the amazing things He does. For the Lord is great and greatly to be praised. Worship only Him. Worship the Lord with the beauty of holy lives. Let the earth tremble before Him.

Tell the nations that Jehovah reigns! He rules the world. His power can never be overthrown. He will judge all nations fairly. Let the heavens be glad, the earth rejoice; let the vastness of the roaring seas demonstrate His glory. Praise Him for the growing fields, for they display His greatness. Let the trees of the forest rustle with praise. For the Lord is coming to judge the earth; He will judge the nations fairly and with truth! The Lord loves those who hate evil; He protects the lives of His people, and rescues them from the wicked. Light is sown for the godly and joy for the good. May all who are godly be happy in the Lord and crown Him our holy God.

48. Lord of All!

Jehovah is King! Let all the earth rejoice! Tell the farthest islands to be glad. Sing a new song to the Lord telling about His mighty deeds! For He has won a mighty victory by His power and holiness. He has announced this victory and revealed it to every nation by fulfilling His promise to be kind to Israel. The whole earth has seen God's salvation of His people. That is why the earth breaks out in praise to God and sings for utter joy!

Sing your praise accompanied by music from the harp. Let the cornets and trumpets shout! Make a joyful symphony before the Lord the King! Let the sea in all its vastness roar with praise! Let the earth and all those living on it shout, "Glory to the Lord." Let the waves clap their hands in glee and the hills sing out their songs of joy before the Lord, for He is coming to judge the world with perfect justice.

Jehovah sits in majesty in Zion, supreme above all rulers of the earth. Let them reverence Your great and holy name. This mighty King is determined to give justice. Fairness is the touchstone of everything He does. He gives justice throughout Israel. Exalt the Lord our holy God! Bow low before His feet. When Moses and Aaron and Samuel, His prophets, cried to Him for help, He answered them. He spoke to them from the pillar of cloud and they followed His instructions. Exalt the Lord our God and worship at His holy mountain in Jerusalem, for He is holy.

49. Entering His Courts

Shout with joy before the Lord, O earth! Obey Him gladly; come before Him singing with joy. Try to realize what this means—the Lord is God! He made us—we are His people, the sheep of His pasture. Go through His open gates with great thanksgiving; enter His courts with praise. Give thanks to Him and bless His name. For the Lord is always good. He is always loving and kind, and His faithfulness goes on and on to each succeeding generation.

50. A Blameless Path

I will sing about Your lovingkindness and Your justice, Lord. I will sing Your praises! I will try to walk a blameless path, but how I need Your help—especially in my own home where I long to act as I should. Help me to refuse the low and vulgar things; help me to abhor all crooked deals of every kind, to have no part in them. I will reject all selfishness and stay away from every evil. I will not tolerate any slander of my neighbors; I will not permit conceit and pride.

I will make the godly of the land my heroes and invite them to my home. Those who are truly good shall be my examples.

51. Bless the Lord!

I bless the holy name of God with all my heart. Yes, I will bless the Lord and not forget the glorious things He does for me.

He forgives all my sins! He heals me!

He ransoms me from hell! He surrounds me with loving-kindness and tender mercies!

He fills my life with good things! My youth is renewed like the eagle's!

He gives justice to all who are treated unfairly.

He revealed His will and nature to Moses and the people of Israel. He is merciful and tender toward those who don't deserve it; He is slow to get angry and full of kindness and love! He never bears a grudge, nor remains angry forever. He has not punished us as we deserve for all our sins, for His mercy towards those who fear and honor Him is as great as the height of the heavens above the earth. He has removed our sins as far away from us as the east is from the west. He is like a father to us, tender and sympathetic to those who reverence Him.

For He knows we are but dust, and that our days are few and brief, like grass, like flowers, blown by the wind and gone forever. But the loving-kindness of the Lord is from everlasting to everlasting to those who reverence Him; His salvation is to children's children of those who are faithful to His covenant and remember to obey Him!

The Lord has made the heavens His throne; from there He rules over everything there is. Bless the Lord, you mighty angels of His who carry out His orders, listening for each of His commands. Yes, bless the Lord, you armies of His angels who serve Him constantly. Let everything everywhere bless the Lord. And how I bless Him too!

52. The Lord of Creation

I bless the Lord: O Lord my God, how great You are! You are robed with honor and with majesty and light! You stretched out the starry curtain of the heavens, and hollowed out the surface of the earth to form the seas. The clouds are His chariots! He rides upon the wings of the wind! You bound the world together so that it would never fall apart. You clothed the earth with floods of waters covering up the mountains. You spoke, and at the sound of Your shout the water collected into its vast ocean beds. Mountains rose and valleys sank to the levels You decreed. And then You set a boundary for the seas, so that they would never again cover the earth. There before me lies the mighty ocean, teeming with life of every kind, both great and small. And look! See the ships! And over there, the whale You made to play in the sea! Every one of these depends on You to give them daily food. You supply it, and they gather it! You open wide Your hand to feed them and they are satisfied with all Your bountiful provision.

He placed springs in the valleys and streams that gush from the mountains. They give water for all the animals to drink. There the wild donkeys quench their thirst, and the birds nest beside the streams and sing among the branches of the trees. He sends rain upon the mountains and fills the earth with fruit. The tender grass grows up at His command to feed the cattle, and there are fruit trees, vegetables and grain for man to cultivate, and wine to make him glad, and olive oil as lotion for his skin, and bread to give him strength. The Lord planted the cedars of Lebanon. They are tall and flourishing. There the birds make their nests, the storks in the firs. High in the mountains are pastures for the wild goats; and rock-badgers burrow in among the rocks and find protection there.

O Lord, what a variety You have made! And in wisdom You have made them all! The earth is full of Your riches. Praise God forever! How He must rejoice in all His work! I will sing to the Lord as long as I live! I will praise God to my last breath! May He be pleased by all these thoughts about Him, for He is the source of all my joy. I will praise Him. Hallelujah!

53. The Lord of History

Thank the Lord for all the glorious things He does; proclaim them to the nations. Sing His praises and tell everyone about His miracles. Glory in the Lord; O worshipers of God, rejoice. Search for Him and for His strength, and keep on searching! Think of the mighty deeds He did for us, His chosen ones—descendants of God's servant Abraham, and of Jacob. Remember how He destroyed our enemies. He is the Lord our God. His goodness is seen everywhere throughout the land. Though a thousand generations pass He never forgets His promise, His covenant with Abraham and Isaac and confirmed with Jacob. This is His never-ending treaty with the people of Israel: *"I will give you the land of Canaan as your inheritance."* He said this when they were but a few in number, very few, and were only visitors in Canaan. He called for a famine on the land of Canaan, cutting off its food supply.

Then He sent Joseph as a slave to Egypt to save His people from starvation. There in prison they hurt his feet with fetters and placed his neck in an iron collar until God's time finally came—how God tested his patience! Then the king sent for him and set him free. He was put in charge of all the king's possessions. At his pleasure he could imprison the king's aides and teach the king's advisers. Then Jacob (Israel) arrived in Egypt and lived there with his sons. In the years that followed, the people of Israel multiplied explosively until they were a greater nation than their rulers.

At that point God turned the Egyptians against the Israeli; they hated and enslaved them. But God sent Moses as His representative, and Aaron with him, and brought His people safely out from Egypt, loaded with silver and gold; there were no sick and feeble folk among them then. Egypt was glad when they were gone, for the dread of them was great.

He spread out a cloud above them to shield them from the burning sun and gave them a pillar of flame at night to give them light. They asked for meat and He sent them quail and gave them manna—bread from heaven. He opened up a rock, and water gushed out to form a river through the dry and barren land; for He remembered His sacred promises to Abraham His servant.

So He brought His chosen ones singing into the Promised Land. He gave them the lands of the Gentiles, complete with their growing crops; they ate what others planted. This was done to make them faithful and obedient to His laws. Hallelujah! Thank You, Lord! How good You are! Your love for us continues on forever. Who can ever list the glorious miracles of God? Who can ever praise Him half enough? Blessed be the Lord, the God of Israel, from everlasting to everlasting. Let all the people say, "Amen!" Hallelujah!

54. Thanksgiving for God's Loving-Kindness

Say "Thank You" to the Lord for being so good, for always being so loving and kind. Has the Lord redeemed you? Then speak out! Tell others He has saved you from your enemies.

He brought the exiles back from the farthest corners of the earth. They were wandering homeless in the desert, hungry and thirsty and faint. "Lord, help!" they cried, and He did! He led them straight to safety and a place to live. *Oh, that these men would praise the Lord for His loving-kindness, and for all of His wonderful deeds!* For He satisfies the thirsty soul and fills the hungry soul with good.

Who are these who sit in darkness, in the shadow of death,

crushed by misery and slavery? They cried to the Lord in their troubles, and He rescued them! He led them from the darkness and shadow of death and snapped their chains! *Oh, that these men would praise the Lord for His loving-kindness and for all of His wonderful deeds!* For He broke down their prison gates of brass and cut apart their iron bars.

And then there are the sailors sailing the seven seas, plying the trade routes of the world. They too observe the power of God in action. He calls to the storm winds; the waves rise high. Their ships are tossed to the heavens and sink again to the depths; the sailors cringe in terror. They reel and stagger like drunkards and are at their wit's end. Then they cry to the Lord in their trouble, and He saves them! He calms the storm and stills the waves. What a blessing is that stillness, as He brings them safely into harbor! *Oh, that these men would praise the Lord for His loving-kindness and all of His wonderful deeds!* Let them praise Him publicly before the congregation and before the leaders of the nation.

O God, my heart is ready to praise You! I will sing and rejoice before You. Wake up, O harp and lyre! We will meet the dawn with song. I will praise You everywhere around the world, in every nation. For Your loving-kindness is great beyond measure, high as the heavens! Your faithfulness reaches the skies! Listen, if you are wise, to what I am saying. Think about the loving-kindness of the Lord!

55. Thanksgiving for His Mighty Miracles

Hallelujah! I want to express publicly before His people my heartfelt thanks to God for His mighty miracles! All who are thankful should ponder them with me. For His miracles demonstrate His honor, majesty and eternal goodness. Who can forget the wonders He performs—deeds of mercy and of grace? He gives food to those who trust Him; He never forgets His promises!

All He does is just and good, and all His laws are right, for they are formed from truth and goodness. They stand firm forever. He has paid a full ransom for His people; now they are always free to come to God (what a holy, awe-inspiring name that is). How can men be wise? The only way to begin is by reverence for God. For growth in wisdom comes from obeying His laws. Praise His name forever. For all who fear God and trust in Him are blessed beyond expression. Yes, happy is the man who delights in doing His commands.

56. Thanksgiving for Deliverance from Death

I love the Lord because He hears my prayers and answers them. Because He bends down and listens, I will pray as long as I breathe! Death stared me in the face—I was frightened and sad. Then I cried, "Lord, save me!"

How kind He is! How good He is! So merciful, this God of ours! The Lord protects the simple and the childlike: I was facing death and then He saved me. Now I can relax. For the Lord has done this wonderful miracle for me. He has saved me from death, my eyes from tears, my feet from stumbling. I shall live! Yes, in His presence—here on earth! In my discouragement I thought, "They are lying when they say I will recover."

But now what can I offer Jehovah for all He has done for me? I will bring Him an offering and praise His name. I will publicly bring Him the sacrifice I vowed I would. His loved ones are very precious to Him and He does not lightly let them die. O Lord, You have freed me from my bonds and I will serve you forever. I will worship You and offer You a sacrifice of thanksgiving. Here in the courts of the Temple in Jerusalem, before all the people, I will pay everything I vowed to the Lord. Praise the Lord.

57. Thanksgiving for Steadfast Love

This is the day the Lord has made. We will rejoice and be

glad in it. Oh, thank the Lord, for He's so good! His loving-kindness is forever. Praise the Lord, all nations everywhere. Laud Him, all the peoples of the earth. For He loves us very dearly, and His truth endures. Praise the Lord.

In my distress I prayed to the Lord and He answered me and rescued me. He is for me! How can I be afraid? What can mere man to do me? The Lord is on my side, He will help me. Let those who hate me beware. It is better to trust the Lord than to put confidence in men. It is better to take refuge in Him than in the mightiest king!

Open the gates of the Temple—I will go in and give Him my thanks. Those gates are the way into the presence of the Lord. The godly enter there. O Lord, thank you so much for answering my prayer and saving me. The stone rejected by the builders has now become the capstone of the arch! This is the Lord's doing, and it is marvelous to see!

Jehovah God is our light. I present to Him my sacrifice upon the altar, for You are my God, and I shall give You this thanks and this praise. Oh, give thanks to the Lord, for He is so good! For His loving-kindness is forever.

58. Pathway to Happiness

Happy are all who perfectly follow the laws of God. Happy are all who search for God and always do His will, rejecting compromise with evil and walking only in His paths. You have given us Your laws to obey—Oh, how I want to follow them consistently. Then I will not be disgraced, for I will have a clean record. After You have corrected me I will thank You by living as I should! I *will* obey! Oh, don't forsake me and let me slip back into sin again.

How can a young man stay pure? By reading Your word and following its rules. I have tried my best to find You— don't let me wander off from Your instructions. I have thought much about Your words, and stored them in my heart so that they would hold me back from sin. Blessed Lord, teach me Your rules. Open my eyes to see wonderful things in Your word. I am but a pilgrim here on earth: how I need a map—and Your commands are my chart and guide.

Never forget Your promises to me Your servant; for they are my only hope. They give me strength in all my troubles; how they refresh and revive me! Forever, O Lord, Your Word stands firm in heaven. Your faithfulness extends to every generation, like the earth You created; it endures by Your decree, for everything serves Your plans. I would have despaired and perished unless Your laws had been my deepest delight. I will never lay aside Your laws, for You have used them to restore my joy and health. Oh, how I love them. I think about them all day long.

Lord, deal with me in loving-kindness, and teach me, Your servant, to obey; for I am Your servant, therefore give me common sense to apply Your rules to everything I do. I praise You for letting me learn Your laws. I will sing about their wonder, for each of them is just. Stand ready to help me because I have chosen to follow Your will. O Lord, I have longed for Your salvation and Your law is my delight. If You will let me live, I will praise You; let Your laws assist me. I have wandered away like a lost sheep; come and find me for I have not turned away from Your commandments.

59. Day and Night Guardian

Shall I look to the mountains for help? No! My help is from Jehovah who made the mountains! And the heavens too! O God enthroned in heaven, I lift my eyes to You. We look to Jehovah our God for His mercy and kindness just as a servant keeps his eyes upon his master or a slave girl watches her mistress for the slightest signal.

He will never let you stumble, slip or fall. For He is always watching, never sleeping. Jehovah Himself is caring for you! He is your defender. He protects you day and night. He keeps you from all evil and preserves your life. He keeps His eye upon you as you come and go and always guards you. Our help is from the Lord who made heaven and earth!

60. When God's People Worship

I was glad for the suggestion of going to Jerusalem to the Temple of the Lord. Now we are standing here inside the crowded city. All Israel—Jehovah's people—have come to worship as the law requires, to thank and praise the Lord. Those who trust in the Lord are steady as Mount Zion, unmoved by any circumstance. Just as the mountains surround and protect Jerusalem, so the Lord surrounds and protects His people.

Pray for the peace of Jerusalem. May all who love this city prosper. O Jerusalem, may there be peace within your walls and prosperity in your palaces. This I ask for the sake of all my brothers and my friends who live here; and may there be peace as a protection to the Temple of the Lord.

Oh, bless the Lord, you who serve Him as watchmen in the Temple every night. Lift your hands in holiness and bless the Lord. The Lord bless you from Zion—the Lord who made heaven and earth.

61. Homesick

Weeping, we sat beside the rivers of Babylon thinking of Jerusalem. We have put away our lyres, hanging them upon the branches of the willow trees, for how can we sing? Yet our captors, our tormentors, demand that we sing for them the happy songs of Zion! If I forget you, O Jerusalem, let my right hand forget her skill upon the harp. If I fail to love her more than my highest joy, let me never sing again.

When Jehovah brought back His exiles to Jerusalem, it was like a dream! How we laughed and sang for joy. And the other nations said, "What amazing things the Lord has done for them." Yes, glorious things! What wonder! What joy! May we be refreshed as by streams in the desert. Those who sow tears shall reap joy. Yes, they go out weeping, carrying seed for sowing and return singing, carrying their sheaves.

62. Family Joys

Blessings on all who reverence and trust the Lord—on all who obey Him! Their reward shall be prosperity and happiness. Your wife shall be contented in your home. And look at all those children! There they sit around the dinner table as vigorous and healthy as young olive trees.

Children are a gift from God; they are His reward. Children born to a young man are like sharp arrows to defend him. Happy is the man who has his quiver full of them. That man shall have the help he needs. That is God's reward to those who reverence and trust Him. May the Lord continually bless you with heaven's blessings as well as with human joys. May you live to enjoy your grandchildren! And may God bless Israel!

63. Waiting in Expectation

O Lord, from the depths of despair I cry for Your help: "Hear me! Answer! Help me!" Lord, if You keep in mind our sins then who can ever get an answer to his prayers? But You forgive! What an awesome thing this is! That is why I wait expectantly, trusting God to help, for He has promised. I long for Him more than sentinels long for the dawn. O Israel, hope in the Lord; for He is loving and kind, and comes to us with armloads of salvation.

64. Brotherly Harmony

How wonderful it is, how pleasant, when brothers live in harmony! For harmony is as precious as the fragrant anointing oil that was poured over Aaron's head and ran down onto his beard and onto the border of his robe. Harmony is as refreshing as the dew on Mount Hermon on the mountains of Israel. And God has pronounced this eternal blessing on Jerusalem, even life forevermore.

I am quiet now before the Lord, just as a child who is

weaned from the breast. Yes, my begging has been stilled.
You too should quietly trust in the Lord—now, and always.

65. God's Unfailing Loving-Kindness

Oh, give thanks to the Lord, for He is good; His loving-kindness continues forever. Give thanks to the God of gods, for His loving-kindness continues forever. Give thanks to the Lord of lords, for His loving-kindness continues forever. Praise Him who alone does mighty miracles, for His loving-kindness continues forever. Praise Him who made the heavens, for His loving-kindness continues forever. Praise Him who planted the water within the earth, for His loving-kindness continues forever. Praise Him who made the heavenly lights, for His loving-kindness continues forever: the sun to rule the day, for His loving-kindness continues forever; and the moon and stars at night, for His loving-kindness continues forever.

He remembered our utter weakness, for His loving-kindness continues forever. He gives food to every living thing, for His loving-kindness continues forever. Oh, give thanks to the God of heaven, for His loving-kindness continues forever.

Lord, with all my heart I thank You. I will sing Your praises before the armies of angels in heaven. I face Your Temple as I worship, giving thanks to You for all Your loving-kindness and Your faithfulness, for Your promises are backed by all the honor of Your name. When I pray, You answer me and encourage me by giving me the strength I need. Though I am surrounded by troubles, You will bring me safely through them. Your power will save me. The Lord will work out His plans for my life—for Your loving-kindness, Lord, continues forever. Don't abandon me—for You made me.

66. The All-Knowing and the All-Loving

O Lord, You have examined my heart and know everything about me. You know when I sit or stand. When far away You know my every thought. You chart the path ahead of me, and tell me where to stop and rest! Every moment, You know where I am! You know what I am going to say before I even say it. You both precede and follow me and place Your hand of blessing on my head. This is too glorious, too wonderful to believe!

I can *never* be lost to Your Spirit! I can *never* get away from God! If I go up to heaven You are there; if I go down to the place of the dead, You are there. If I ride the morning winds to the farthest oceans, even there Your hand will guide me, Your strength will support me. If I try to hide in the darkness, the night becomes light around me! For even darkness cannot hide from God; to You the night shines as bright as day. Darkness and light are both alike to You.

You made all the delicate, inner parts of my body and knit them together in my mother's womb. Thank You for making me so wonderfully complex! It is amazing to think about. Your workmanship is marvelous—and how well I know it. You were there while I was being formed in utter seclusion! You saw me before I was born and scheduled each day of my life before I began to breathe. Every day was recorded in Your book!

How precious it is, Lord, to realize that You are thinking about me constantly! I can't even count how many times a day Your thoughts turn towards me! And when I waken in the morning, You are still thinking of me! Search me, O God, and know my heart. Test my thoughts. Point out anything You find in me that makes You sad and lead me along the path of everlasting life.

67. From Behind Prison Bars

How I plead with God, how I implore His mercy, pouring out my troubles before Him. For I am overwhelmed and desperate, and You alone know which way I ought to turn to miss the traps my enemies have set for me. I am losing all hope; I am paralyzed with fear. I remember the glorious miracles You did in days of long ago. I reach out for You. I thirst for You as parched land thirsts for rain. Come quickly, Lord, and answer me, for my depression deepens; don't turn away from me or I shall die.

Hear my cry, for I am very low. Rescue me from my persecutors, for they are too strong for me. Bring me out of prison so that I can thank You. The godly will rejoice with me for all Your help. Hear my prayer, O Lord; answer my plea, because You are faithful to Your promises.

68. Gloria in Excelsis

I will praise You, my God and King, and bless Your name each day and forever. Great is Jehovah! Greatly praise Him! His greatness is beyond discovery! Let each generation tell its children what glorious things He does. I will meditate about Your glory, splendor, majesty and miracles. Your awe-inspiring deeds shall be on every tongue; I will proclaim Your greatness. Everyone will tell about how good You are and sing about Your righteousness.

Jehovah is kind and merciful, slow to get angry, full of love. He is good to everyone, and His compassion is intertwined with everything He does. All living things shall thank You, Lord, and Your people will bless You. They will talk together about the glory of Your kingdom and mention examples of Your power. They will tell about Your miracles and about the majesty and glory of Your reign. For Your kingdom never ends. You rule generation after generation. The Lord lifts the fallen and those bent beneath their loads.

The eyes of all mankind look up to You for help; You give them their food as they need it. You constantly satisfy the hunger and thirst of every living thing. The Lord is fair in everything He does and full of kindness. He is close to all who call on Him sincerely. He fulfills the desires of those who reverence and trust Him; He hears their cries for help and rescues them. He protects all those who love Him. I shall praise the Lord and call on all men everywhere to bless His holy name forever and forever.

69. Praise the Lord

Hallelujah! Yes, praise the Lord! How good it is to sing His praises! How delightful and how right! He is rebuilding Jerusalem and bringing back the exiles. He heals the brokenhearted, binding up their wounds. He counts the stars and calls them all by name. How great He is! His power is absolute! His understanding in unlimited. The Lord supports the humble, but brings the wicked into the dust. Sing out your thanks to Him; sing praises to our God, accompanied by harps.

He sends His orders to the world. How swiftly His word flies. He sends the snow in all its lovely whiteness, scatters the frost upon the ground and hurls the hail upon the earth. Who can stand before His freezing cold? But then He calls for warmer weather, and the spring winds blow and all the river ice is broken. He covers the heavens with clouds, sends down the showers and makes the green grass grow in mountain pastures. He feeds the wild animals and the young ravens cry to Him for food. The speed of a horse is nothing to Him. How puny in His sight is the strength of a man. But His joy is in those who reverence Him; those who expect Him to be loving and kind.

Praise Him, O Jerusalem! Praise Your God, O Zion! For He has fortified your gates against all enemies and blessed your children. He sends peace across your nation and fills your barns with plenty of the finest wheat. Praise the Lord! Yes, really praise Him! I will praise Him as long as I live, yes, even with my dying breath. Hallelujah! Yes, praise the Lord!

70. Hallelujah Chorus

Hallelujah! Yes, praise the Lord! Sing Him a new song. Sing His praises, all His people. Praise the Lord, O heavens! Praise Him from the skies! Praise Him, all His angels, all the armies of heaven. Praise Him, sun and moon and all you twinkling stars. Praise Him, skies above. Praise Him, vapors high above the clouds. Let everything He has made give praise to Him!

For He issued His command and they came into being; He established them forever and forever. His orders will never be revoked.

And praise Him down there on earth, you creatures of the ocean depths. Let fire and hail, snow, rain, wind and weather, all obey. Let the mountains and hills, the fruit trees and cedars, the wild animals and cattle, the snakes and birds, the kings and all the people with their rulers and their judges, young men and maidens, old men and children—all praise the Lord together. For He alone is worthy. His glory is far greater than all of earth and heaven.

Hallelujah! Yes, praise the Lord! Praise Him in His Temple and in the heavens He made with mighty power. Praise Him for His mighty works. Praise His unequalled greatness. Praise Him with the trumpet and with lute and harp. Praise Him with the timbrels and processional. Praise Him with stringed instruments and horns. Praise Him with the cymbals, yes, loud clanging cymbals. Let everything alive give praises to the Lord! *You* praise Him! Hallelujah!

PROVERBS

A distillation of the wisdom of ancient sages—that is the book of Proverbs. In this condensation, not only has the best of the Proverbs been selected and preserved, but they have been classified under appropriate headings. Here is a new, practical presentation for those who like an orderly arrangement of these short, pithy sayings.

1. The Voice of Wisdom

How does a man become wise? The first step is to trust and reverence the Lord! *For the reverence and fear of God are basic to all wisdom. Knowing God results in every other kind of understanding.*

Wisdom shouts in the streets for a hearing. She calls out to the crowds along Main Street, to the judges in their courts and to everyone in all the land: "You simpletons!" she cries, "how long will you go on being fools? How long will you scoff at wisdom and fight the facts? Come here and listen to me! I'll pour out the spirit of Wisdom upon you and make you wise. I have called you so often but still you won't come. I have pleaded, but all in vain."

Can't you hear the voice of wisdom? She is standing at the city gates and at every fork in the road, and at the door of every house. Listen to what she says: "Listen, men!" she calls. "How foolish and naive you are! Let me give you understanding. O foolish ones, let me show you common sense! Listen to me! For I have important information for you. Everything I say is right and true, for I hate lies and every kind of deception. My advice is wholesome and good. There is nothing of evil in it. My words are plain and clear to anyone with half a mind—if it is only open! My instruction is far more valuable than silver or gold. For the value of wisdom is far above rubies; nothing can be compared with it. Wisdom and good judgment live together, for wisdom knows where to discover knowledge and understanding. If anyone respects and fears God, he will hate evil. For wisdom hates pride, arrogance, corruption and deceit of every kind.

"I, Wisdom, give good advice and common sense. Because of my strength, kings reign in power. I show the judges who is right and who is wrong. I, Wisdom, will make the hours of your day more profitable and the years of your life more fruitful. Wisdom is its own reward, and if you scorn her, you hurt only yourself. Rulers rule well with my help. I love all who love me. Those who search for me shall surely find me. Unending riches, honor, justice and righteousness are mine to distribute. My gifts are better than the purest gold or sterling silver! My paths are those of justice and right. Those who love and follow me are indeed wealthy. I fill their treasuries.

"The Lord formed me in the beginning, before He created anything else. From ages past, I am. I existed before the earth began. I lived before the oceans were created, before the springs bubbled forth their waters onto the earth; before the mountains and the hills were made. Yes, I was born before God made the earth and fields and high plateaus. I was there when He established the heavens and formed the great springs in the depths of the oceans. I was there when He set the limits of the seas and gave them His instructions not to spread beyond their boundaries. I was there when He made the blueprint for the earth and oceans. I was always at His side like a little child. I was His constant delight, laughing and playing in His presence. And how happy I was with what He created— His wide world and all His family of mankind!

"And so, young men, listen to me, for how happy are all who follow my instructions. Listen to my counsel—oh, don't refuse it—and be wise. Happy is the man who is so anxious to be with me that he watches for me daily at my gates or waits for me outside my home! For whoever finds me finds life and wins approval from the Lord. But the one who misses me has injured himself irreparably. Those who refuse me show that they love death.

"Yes, if you want better insight and discernment and are searching for them as you would for lost money or hidden treasure, then wisdom will be given you and knowledge of God Himself; you will soon learn the importance of reverence for the Lord and of trusting Him. For the Lord grants wisdom! His every word is a treasure of knowledge and understanding. He grants good sense to the godly—His saints. He is their shield, protecting them and guarding their pathway. He shows how to distinguish right from wrong, how to find the right decision every time. For wisdom and truth will enter the very center of your being, filling your life with joy."

2. The Wise Man and the Fool

If you rebuke a mocker, you will only get a smart retort; yes, he will snarl at you. So don't bother with him; he will only hate you for trying to help him. But a wise man, when rebuked, will love you all the more. Teach a wise man, and he will be the wiser; teach a good man, and he will learn more; the wise man is glad to be instructed, but a self-sufficient fool falls flat on his face. A wise man holds his tongue. Only a fool blurts out everything he knows; that only leads to sorrow and trouble. A fool's fun is being bad; a wise man's fun is being wise! A fool thinks he needs no advice, but a wise man listens to others. A fool is quick-tempered; a wise man stays cool when insulted.

The advice of a wise man refreshes like water from a mountain spring. Those accepting it become aware of the pitfalls on ahead. A man with good sense is appreciated. A treacherous man must walk a rocky road. A wise man thinks ahead; a fool doesn't, and even brags about it! Be with wise men and become wise. Be with evil men and become evil. If you are looking for advice, stay away from fools.

The wise man looks ahead. The fool attempts to fool himself and won't face facts. A wise man is cautious and avoids danger;

a fool plunges ahead with great confidence.

A short-tempered man is a fool. He hates the man who is patient. The simpleton is crowned with folly; the wise man is crowned with knowledge. The wise man saves for the future, but the foolish man spends whatever he gets. A prudent man foresees the difficulties ahead and prepares for them; the simpleton goes blindly on and suffers the consequences. A wise man is mightier than a strong man. Wisdom is mightier than strength. Fools start fights everywhere while wise men try to keep peace. There's no use arguing with a fool. He only rages and scoffs, and tempers flare.

3. The Good Man and the Evil Man

Let me describe for you a worthless and a wicked man; first, he is a constant liar; he signals his true intentions to his friends with eyes and feet and fingers. Next, his heart is full of rebellion. And he spends his time thinking of all the evil he can do, stirring up discontent. But he will be destroyed suddenly, broken beyond hope of healing. For there are six things the Lord hates—no, seven:

> haughtiness,
> lying,
> murdering,
> plotting evil,
> eagerness to do wrong,
> a false witness and
> sowing discord among brothers.

The good man's earnings advance the cause of righteousness. The evil man squanders his on sin. A good man is guided by his honesty; the evil man is destroyed by his dishonesty. The evil man gets rich for the moment, but the good man's reward lasts forever. The good man finds life; the evil man, death. The Lord hates the stubborn but delights in those who are good. You can be very sure that the evil man will not go unpunished forever. And you can also be very sure that God will rescue the children of the godly. The good man can look forward to happiness while the wicked can expect only wrath.

A good man's mind is filled with honest thoughts; an evil man's mind is crammed with lies.

The wicked accuse; the godly defend. The wicked shall perish; the godly shall stand. A good man is concerned for the welfare of his animals, but even the kindness of godless men is cruel. A good man hates lies; wicked men lie constantly and come to shame. The good man's life is full of light. The sinner's road is dark and gloomy. Be with wise men and become wise. Be with evil men and become evil. Curses chase sinners while blessings chase the righteous! When a good man dies, he leaves an inheritance to his grandchildren; but when a sinner dies, his wealth is stored up for the godly. There is treasure in being good, but trouble dogs the wicked.

The common bond of rebels is their guilt. The common bond of godly people is good will. The backslider gets bored with himself; the godly man's life is exciting. An evil man is stubborn, but a godly man will reconsider. O evil man, leave the upright man alone, and quit trying to cheat him out of his rights. Don't you know that this good man, though you trip him up seven times, will each time rise again? But one calamity is enough to lay you low. The wicked flee when no one is chasing them! But the godly are bold as lions! When the godly are successful, everyone is glad. When the wicked succeed, everyone is sad. The good man knows the poor man's rights; the godless don't care.

Don't do as the wicked do. Avoid their haunts—turn away, go somewhere else, for evil men don't sleep until they've done their evil deed for the day. They can't rest unless they cause someone to stumble and fall. They eat and drink wickedness and violence! But the good man walks along in the ever brightening light of God's favor; the dawn gives way to morning splendor while the evil man gropes and stumbles in the dark. The godly have a refuge when they die, but the wicked are crushed by their sins.

4. Honor Thy Father and Thy Mother

Young man, obey your father and your mother. Tie their

instructions around your finger so you won't forget. Take to heart all of their advice. Every day and all night long their counsel will lead you and save you from harm. When you wake up in the morning, let their instructions guide you into the new day. For their advice is a beam of light directed into the dark corners of your mind to warn you of danger and to give you a good life. Only fools refuse to be taught. Listen to your father and mother. What you learn from them will stand you in good stead; it will gain you many honors. If young toughs tell you, "Come and join us"—turn your back on them!

Happy is the man with a level-headed son; sad the mother of a rebel. It is a wonderful heritage to have an honest father. Only a fool despises his father's advice; a wise son considers each suggestion. A son who mistreats his father or mother is a public disgrace. God puts out the light of the man who curses his father or mother.

My son, how I will rejoice if you become a man of common sense. Yes, my heart will thrill to your thoughtful, wise words. Don't envy evil men but continue to reverence the Lord all the time, for surely you have a wonderful future ahead of you. O my son, be wise and stay in God's paths; don't carouse with drunkards and gluttons, for they are on their way to poverty. And remember that too much sleep clothes a man with rags. Listen to your father's advice and don't despise an old mother's experience. The father of a godly man has cause for joy—what pleasure a wise son is! So give your parents joy!

5. On Honor to God

My son, never forget the things I've taught you. If you want a long and satisfying life, closely follow my instructions. Never forget to be truthful and kind. Hold these virtues tightly. Write them deep within your heart. If you want favor with both God and man and a reputation for good judgment and common sense, then trust the Lord completely; don't ever trust yourself. In everything you do put God first, and He will direct you and crown your efforts with success. Don't be conceited, sure of your own wisdom. Instead, trust and reverence the Lord and turn your back on evil; when you do that, you will be given renewed health and vitality. Honor the Lord by giving Him the first part of all your income, and He will fill your barns with wheat and barley and overflow your wine vats with the finest wines.

Young man, do not resent it when God chastens and corrects you, for His punishment is proof of His love. Just as a father punishes a son he delights in to make him better, so the Lord corrects you. The man who knows right from wrong and has good judgment and common sense is happier than the man who is immensely rich! For such wisdom is far more valuable than precious jewels. Nothing else compares with it. Wisdom gives: a long, good life, riches, honor, pleasure and peace. Wisdom is a tree of life to those who eat her fruit; happy is the man who keeps on eating it. The Lord's wisdom founded the earth; His understanding established all the universe and space. The deep fountains of the earth were broken open by His knowledge, and the skies poured down rain.

Have two goals: wisdom—that is, knowing and doing right —and common sense. Don't let them slip away, for they fill you with living energy and are a feather in your cap. They keep you safe from defeat and disaster and from stumbling off the trail. With them on guard you can sleep without fear; and you need not be afraid of disaster or the plots of wicked men; for the Lord is with you: He protects you.

6. On Living Wisely

Young men, listen to me as you would to your father. Listen and grow wise, for I speak the truth—don't turn away. For I, too, was once a son, tenderly loved by my mother as an only child and the companion of my father. He told me never to forget his words. "If you follow them," he said, "you will have a long and happy life. *Learn to be wise,"* he said, *"and develop good judgment and common sense! I cannot overemphasize this point."* Cling to wisdom—she will protect you. Love her—she will guard you. Determination to be wise is the first step toward becoming wise! And with your wisdom, develop common sense and good judgment. If you exalt wisdom she will exalt you. Hold her fast and she will lead you to great honor; she will place a beautiful crown upon your head.

My son, listen to me and do as I say, and you will have a long, good life. I would have you learn this great fact: that a life of doing right is the wisest life there is. Listen, son of mine, to what I say. Listen carefully. Keep these thoughts ever in mind; let them penetrate deep within your heart.

7. A Good Wife—God's Gift

Can a man hold fire against his chest and not be burned? Can he walk on hot coals and not blister his feet? So it is with the man who commits adultery with another's wife. He shall not go unpunished for this sin. He is an utter fool, for he destroys his own soul. Wounds and constant disgrace are his lot.

Drink from your own well, my son—be faithful and true to your wife. Let your manhood be a blessing; rejoice in the wife of your youth. Let her charms and tender embrace satisfy you. Let her love alone fill you with delight. *For God is closely watching you,* and He weighs carefully everything you do.

A worthy wife is her husband's joy and crown; if you can find a truly good wife, she is worth more than precious gems! Her husband can trust her, and she will richly satisfy his needs. She will not hinder him, but help him all her life. She finds wool and flax and busily spins it. She buys imported foods, brought by ship from distant ports. She gets up before dawn to prepare breakfast for her household and plans the day's work for her servant girls. She goes out to inspect a field and buys it; with her own hands she plants a vineyard. She is energetic, a hard worker, and watches for bargains. She works far into the night!

She sews for the poor and generously gives to the needy. She has no fear of winter for her household, for she has made warm clothes for all of them. She also upholsters with finest tapestry; her own clothing is beautifully made—a purple gown of pure linen. Her husband is well known, for he sits in the council chamber with the other civic leaders. She makes belted linen garments to sell to the merchants. She is a woman of strength and dignity and has no fear of old age. When she speaks her words are wise, and kindness is the rule for everything she says. She watches carefully all that goes on throughout her household and is never lazy.

Her children stand and bless her; so does her husband. He praises her with these words: "There are many fine women in the world, but you are the best of them all!" Charm can be deceptive and beauty doesn't last, but a woman who fears and reverences God shall be greatly praised. Praise her for the many fine things she does. These good deeds of hers shall bring her honor and recognition from even the leaders of the nation. The man who finds a wife finds a good thing; she is a blessing to him from the Lord.

8. On Alcohol

Wine gives false courage; hard liquor leads to brawls; what fools men are to let it master them, making them reel drunkenly down the street! Whose heart is filled with anguish and sorrow? Who is always fighting and quarreling? Who is the man with bloodshot eyes and many wounds? It is the one who spends long hours in the taverns, trying out new mixtures.

Don't let the sparkle and the smooth taste of strong wine deceive you. For in the end it bites like a poisonous serpent; it stings like an adder. You will see hallucinations and have delirium tremens. You will say foolish, silly things that would embarrass you no end when sober. You will stagger like a sailor tossed at sea, clinging to a swaying mast, and afterwards you will say, "I didn't even know it when they beat me up . . . Let's go and have another drink!"

9. On Anger

A wise man controls his temper. He knows that anger causes mistakes. A relaxed attitude lengthens a man's life; jealousy rots it away. A short-tempered man is a fool. He hates the man who is patient. A soft answer turns away wrath, but harsh words cause quarrels. A quick-tempered man starts fights; a cool-tempered man tries to stop them. It is better to be slow-tempered than famous; it is better to have self-control than to control an army.

A dry crust eaten in peace is better than steak every day along with argument and strife. It is harder to win back the friendship of an offended brother than to capture a fortified city. His anger shuts you out like iron bars. A wise man restrains his anger and overlooks insults. This is to his credit. A short-tempered man must bear his own penalty; you can't do much to help him. If you try once you must try a dozen times! It is an honor for a man to stay out of a fight. Only fools insist on quarreling. Keep away from angry, short-tempered men, lest you learn to be like them and endanger your soul.

If your enemy is hungry, give him food! If he is thirsty, give him something to drink! This will make him feel ashamed of himself. God will reward you. A man without self-control is as defenseless as a city with broken-down walls. There is more hope for a fool than for a man of quick temper. As the churning of cream yields butter and a blow to the nose causes bleeding, so anger causes quarrels. It is hard to stop a quarrel once it starts, so don't let it begin.

10. On Discipline

You are a poor specimen if you can't stand the pressure of adversity. To learn, you must want to be taught. To refuse reproof is stupid. The man who is often reproved but refuses to accept criticism will suddenly be broken and never have another chance. If you refuse criticism you will end in poverty and disgrace; if you accept criticism you are on the road to fame. Anyone willing to be corrected is on the pathway to life. Anyone refusing has lost his chance. If you profit from constructive criticism you will be elected to the wise men's hall of fame. But to reject criticism is to harm yourself and your own best interests.

A rebellious son is a grief to his father and a bitter blow to his mother. A youngster's heart is filled with rebellion, but punishment will drive it out of him. Punishment that hurts chases evil from the heart. Discipline your son in his early years while there is hope. If you don't you will ruin his life. If you refuse to discipline your son, it proves you don't love him; for if you love him you will be prompt to punish him. Discipline your son and he will give you happiness and peace of mind. Teach a child to choose the right path, and when he is older he will remain upon it.

11. On Government

Without wise leadership, a nation is in trouble; but with good counselors there is safety. The good influence of godly citizens causes a city to prosper, but the moral decay of the wicked drives it downhill. When you remove dross from silver, you have sterling ready for the silversmith. When you remove corrupt men from the king's court, his reign will be just and fair. When there is moral rot within a nation, its government topples easily; but with honest, sensible leaders there is stability. With good men in authority the people rejoice; but with the wicked in power they groan. A wicked ruler will have wicked aides on his staff.

Where there is ignorance of God, the people run wild; but what a wonderful thing it is for a nation to know and keep His laws! Godliness exalts a nation, but sin is a reproach to any people.

12. On Honesty

The Lord hates cheating and delights in honesty. A good man is guided by his honesty; the evil man is destroyed by his dishonesty. The upright are directed by their honesty; the wicked shall fall beneath their load of sins. Lies will get any man into trouble, but honesty is its own defense. Telling the truth gives a man great satisfaction, and hard work returns many blessings to him. Some men enjoy cheating, but the cake they buy with such ill-gotten gain will turn to gravel in their mouths. Dishonest gain will never last, so why take the risk?

13. On Immorality

O my son, trust my advice—stay away from prostitutes. For a prostitute is a deep and narrow grave. Like a robber she waits for her victims. Stay far from her. Look straight ahead; don't even turn your head to look. Watch your step. Stick to the path and be safe. Don't sidetrack; pull back your foot from danger. For the lips of a prostitute are as sweet as honey and smooth flattery is her stock in trade. But afterwards only a bitter conscience is left to you, sharp as a double-edged sword. She leads you down to death and hell. For she does not know the path to life. She staggers down a crooked trail and doesn't even realize where it leads.

Young men, listen to me, and never forget what I'm about to say: *Run from her! Don't go near her house,* lest you fall to her temptation, lose your honor and give the remainder of your life to the cruel and merciless; lest strangers obtain your wealth, and you become a slave of foreigners. Lest afterwards you groan in anguish and in shame, when syphilis consumes your body, and you say, "Oh, if only I had listened! If only I had not demanded my own way! Oh, why wouldn't I take advice? Why was I so stupid? For now I must face public disgrace."

A prostitute is loud and brash and never has enough of lust and shame. She sits at the door of her house or stands at the street corners of the city, whispering to men going by and to those minding their own business. "Come home with me," she urges simpletons, "stolen melons are the sweetest; stolen apples taste the best!" But they don't realize that her former guests are now citizens of hell.

I was looking out the window of my house one day and saw a simple-minded lad, a young man lacking common sense, walking at twilight down the street to the house of this wayward girl, a prostitute. She approached him, saucy and pert, and dressed seductively. She was the brash, coarse type seen often in the streets and markets, soliciting at every corner for men to be her lovers. She put her arms around him and kissed him. With a saucy look she said, "I've decided to forget our quarrel! I was just coming to look for you and here you are! My bed is spread with lovely, colored sheets of finest linen imported from Egypt, perfumed with myrrh, aloes and cinnamon. Come on, let's take our fill of love until morning, for my husband is away on a long trip. He has taken a wallet full of money with him and won't return for several days."

So she seduced him with her pretty speech, her coaxing and her wheedling, until he yielded to her. He couldn't resist her flattery. He followed her as an ox going to the butcher or as a stag that is trapped, waiting to be killed with an arrow through its heart. He was as a bird flying into a snare, not knowing the fate awaiting it there.

Listen to me, young men, and not only listen but obey; don't let your desires get out of hand; don't let yourself think about her; don't go near her; stay away from where she walks, lest she tempt you and seduce you. For she has been the ruin of multitudes—a vast host of men have been her victims. If you want to find the road to hell, look for her house.

14. On Laziness

The lazy man is full of excuses. "I can't go to work!" he says. "If I go outside I might meet a lion in the street and be killed!" He sticks to his bed like a door to its hinges! He is too tired even to lift his food from his dish to his mouth! Yet in his own opinion he is smarter than seven wise men. A wise youth makes hay while the sun shines, but what a shame to see a lad who sleeps away his hour of opportunity. A lazy fellow is a pain to his employers—like smoke in their eyes or vinegar that sets the teeth on edge.

It is better to get your hands dirty—and eat, than to be too proud to work—and starve. Hard work means prosperity; only a fool idles away his time. Work hard and become a leader; be lazy and never succeed. A lazy man won't even dress the game he gets while hunting, but the diligent man makes good use of everything he finds. Hunger is good—if it makes you work to satisfy it! Idle hands are the devil's workshop; idle lips are his mouthpiece. If you won't plow in the cold you won't eat at the harvest. Do you know a hardworking man? He shall be successful and stand before kings!

I walked by the field of a certain lazy fellow and saw that it was overgrown with thorns and covered with weeds; and its walls were broken down. As I looked, I learned this lesson:

"A little extra sleep,
A little more slumber,
A little folding of the hands to rest,"

means that poverty will break in upon you suddenly like a robber and violently like a bandit.

Take a lesson from the ants, you lazy fellow. Learn from their ways and be wise! For though they have no king to make them work, yet they labor hard all summer, gathering food for the winter. But you—all you do is sleep. When will you wake up? "Let me sleep a little longer!" Sure, just a little more! And as you sleep, poverty creeps upon you like a robber and destroys you; want attacks you in full armor.

15. On Pride

Pride disgusts the Lord. Take my word for it—*proud men shall be punished.* Proud men end in shame, but the meek become wise. Pride leads to arguments; be humble, take advice and become wise. Pride goes before destruction and haughtiness before a fall. Better poor and humble than proud and rich. Pride ends in destruction; humility ends in honor. Pride, lust and evil actions are all sin. Just as it is harmful to eat too much honey, so also it is bad for men to think about all the honors they deserve! There is one thing worse than a fool, and that is a man who is conceited.

Don't brag about your plans for tomorrow—wait and see what happens. Don't praise yourself; let others do it! A man who refuses to admit his mistakes can never be successful. But if he confesses and forsakes them, he gets another chance. If you have been a fool by being proud or plotting evil, don't brag about it—cover your mouth with your hand in shame. The purity of silver and gold can be tested in a crucible, but a man is tested by his reaction to men's praise.

16. On Reverence

Reverence for God gives a man deep strength; his children have a place of refuge and security. Reverence for the Lord is a fountain of life; its waters keep a man from death. Better a little with reverence for God than great treasure and trouble with it. The road of the godly leads upward, leaving hell behind. Humility and reverence for the Lord will make you both wise and honored.

We can make our plans but the final outcome is in God's hands. We can always prove that we are right, but is the Lord convinced? Commit your work to the Lord, then it will succeed. We can justify our every deed but God looks at our motives. God is more pleased when we are just and fair than when we give Him gifts. God loathes the gifts of evil men, especially if they are trying to bribe Him! True humility and respect for the Lord lead a man to riches, honor and long life.

Who else but God goes back and forth to heaven? Who else holds the wind in His fists and wraps up the oceans in his cloak? Who but God has created the world? If there is any other, what is his name—and his son's name—if you know it? Every word of God proves true. He defends all who come to Him for protection. Listen to this wise advice; follow it closely, for it will do you good, and you can pass it on to others: *Trust in the Lord.*

17. On Riches

If you must choose, take a good name rather than great riches; for to be held in loving esteem is better than silver and gold. Don't weary yourself trying to get rich. Why waste your time? For riches can disappear as though they had the wings of a bird! The rich man's wealth is his only strength. The poor man's poverty is his only curse. Your riches won't help you on Judgment Day; only righteousness counts then. It is possible to give away and become richer! It is also possible to hold on too tightly and lose everything. Yes, the liberal man shall be rich! By watering others, he waters himself.

Trust in your money and down you go! Trust in God and flourish as a tree! Even his own neighbors despise the poor man, while the rich have many "friends." To despise the poor is to sin. Blessed are those who pity them. Anyone who oppresses the poor is insulting God who made them. To help the poor is to honor God. He who shuts his ears to the cries of the poor will be ignored in his own time of need. When you help the poor you are lending to the Lord—and He pays wonderful interest on your loan!

The rich man thinks of his wealth as an impregnable defense, a high wall of safety. What a dreamer! A man who loves pleasure becomes poor; wine and luxury are not the way to riches! Just as the rich rule the poor, so the borrower is servant to the lender. He who gains by oppressing the poor or by bribing the rich shall end in poverty. Hard work brings prosperity; playing around brings poverty. The man who wants to do right will get a rich reward. But the man who wants to get rich quick will quickly fail. Rich and poor are alike in this: each depends on God for light. When a poor man oppresses those even poorer, he is like an unexpected flood sweeping away their last hope.

Riches can disappear fast. And the king's crown doesn't stay in his family forever—so watch your business interests closely. Know the state of your flocks and your herds; then there will be lamb's wool enough for clothing, and goat's milk enough for food for all your household after the hay is harvested, the new crop appears and the mountain grasses are gathered in.

O God, I beg two favors from you before I die: first, help me never to tell a lie. Second, give me neither poverty nor riches! Give me just enough to satisfy my needs! For if I grow rich I may become content without God. And if I am too poor I may steal and thus insult God's holy name.

18. On the Tongue

Self-control means controlling the tongue! A quick retort can ruin everything. The man of few words and settled mind is wise; therefore even a fool is thought to be wise when he is silent. It pays him to keep his mouth shut. Don't talk so much. You keep putting your foot in your mouth. Be sensible and turn off the flow! When a good man speaks, he is worth listening to, but the words of fools are a dime a dozen. To quarrel with a neighbor is foolish; a man with good sense holds his tongue. A gossip goes around spreading rumors, while a trustworthy man tries to quiet them.

A good man is known by his truthfulness; a false man by deceit and lies. Some people like to make cutting remarks, but the words of the wise soothe and heal. Lies will get any man into trouble, but honesty is its own defense. Telling the truth gives a man great satisfaction.

Anxious hearts are very heavy but a word of encouragement does wonders! A good man thinks before he speaks; the evil man pours out his evil words without a thought. From a wise mind comes careful and persuasive speech. Kind words are like honey—enjoyable and healthful. An evil man sows strife; gossip separates the best of friends.

Love forgets mistakes; nagging about them parts the best of friends. A rebuke to a man of common sense is more effective than a hundred lashes on the back of a rebel. A fool gets into constant fights. His mouth is his undoing! His words endanger him. What dainty morsels rumors are. They are eaten with great relish! Any story sounds true until someone tells the other side and sets the record straight. Those who love to talk will suffer the consequences. Men have died for saying the wrong thing! Don't tell your secrets to a gossip unless you want them broadcast to the world.

Timely advice is as lovely as golden apples in a silver basket. It is a badge of honor to accept valid criticism. Telling lies about someone is as harmful as hitting him with an axe, wounding him with a sword or shooting him with a sharp arrow. Yanking a dog's ears is no more foolish than interfering in an argument that isn't any of your business.

Fire goes out for lack of fuel, and tensions disappear when gossip stops. A quarrelsome man starts fights as easily as a match sets fire to paper. Gossip is a dainty morsel eaten with great relish. Pretty words may hide a wicked heart, just as a pretty glaze covers a common clay pot. A man with hate in his heart may sound pleasant enough, but don't believe him; for he is cursing you in his heart. Though he pretends to be so kind his hatred will finally come to light for all to see.

19. On Violence

If young toughs tell you, "Come and join us"—turn your back on them! "We'll hide and rob and kill," they say; "good or bad, we'll treat them all alike! And the loot we'll get! All kinds of stuff! Come on, throw in your lot with us; we'll split with you in equal shares." Don't do it, son! Stay far from men like that, for crime is their way of life, and murder is their specialty. When a bird sees a trap being set, it stays away. But not these men; they trap themselves! They lay a booby trap for their own lives. Such is the fate of all who live by violence and murder. They will die a violent death.

Don't get into needless fights. Don't envy violent men. Don't copy their ways. For such men are an abomination to the Lord, but He gives His friendship to the godly. Don't envy godless men; don't even enjoy their company, for they spend their days plotting violence and cheating.

My son, watch your step before the Lord and the king and don't associate with radicals. For you will go down with them to sudden disaster and who knows where it all will end? To complain about the law is to praise wickedness. To obey the law is to fight evil. Evil men don't understand the importance of justice, but those who follow the Lord are much concerned about it. You will be given the sense to stay away from evil men who want you to be their partners in crime—men who turn from God's ways to walk down dark and evil paths, and exult in doing wrong, for they thoroughly enjoy their sins. Everything they do is crooked and wrong.

Winking at sin leads to sorrow; bold reproof leads to peace. A beautiful woman lacking discretion and modesty is like a fine gold ring in a pig's snout. Hope deferred makes the heart sick; but when dreams come true at last, there is life and joy. Only the person involved can know his own bitterness or joy—no one else can really share it. Laughter cannot mask a heavy heart. When the laughter ends, the grief remains. A happy face means a glad heart; a sad face means a breaking heart. A wise man is hungry for truth while the mocker feeds on trash. When a man is gloomy everything seems to go wrong; when he is cheerful everything seems right!

It is better to eat soup with someone you love than steak with someone you hate. How much better is wisdom than gold, and understanding than silver! The path of the godly leads away from evil; he who follows that path is safe. A true friend is always loyal, and a brother is born to help in time of need. An evil man is suspicious of everyone and tumbles into constant trouble. It's no fun to be a rebel's father. A cheerful heart does good like medicine, but a broken spirit makes one sick. A man's courage can sustain his broken body, but when courage dies, what hope is left?

Some people are friends in name only. Others are closer than brothers. A man may ruin his chances by his own foolishness and then blame it on the Lord! A rebellious son is a calamity to his father, and a nagging wife annoys like constant dripping. A father can give his sons homes and riches, but only the Lord can give them understanding wives. "Utterly worthless!" says the buyer as he haggles over the price. But afterwards he brags about his bargain! Since the Lord is directing our steps, why try to understand everything that happens along the way? A man's conscience is the Lord's searchlight exposing his hidden motives.

It is better to live in the corner of an attic than with a crabby woman in a lovely home. Better to live in the desert than with a quarrelsome, complaining woman. To plan evil is as wrong as doing it. Don't visit your neighbor too often or you will outwear your welcome! Putting confidence in an unreliable man is like chewing with a sore tooth or trying to run on a broken foot. Being happy-go-lucky around a person whose heart is heavy is as bad as stealing his jacket in cold weather or rubbing salt in his wounds. Honor doesn't go with fools any more than snow with summertime or rain with harvesttime!

The man who sets a trap for others will get caught in it himself. Roll a boulder down on someone and it will roll back and crush you. Wounds from a friend are better than kisses from an enemy! A constant dripping on a rainy day and a cranky woman are much alike! You can no more stop her complaints than you can stop the wind or hold onto anything with oil-slick hands. A friendly discussion is as stimulating as the sparks that fly when iron strikes iron. A mirror reflects a man's face, but what he is really like is shown by the kind of friends he chooses. Ambition and death are alike in this: neither is ever satisfied. Giving preferred treatment to rich people is a clear case of selling one's soul for a piece of bread.

Enjoy prosperity whenever you can, and when hard times strike, realize that God gives one as well as the other—so that everyone will realize that nothing is certain in this life. The wise man is turned into a fool by a bribe; it destroys his understanding. It is better to be a poor but wise youth than to be an old and foolish king who refuses all advice. He who loves money shall never have enough. The foolishness of thinking that wealth brings happiness! Everything is appropriate in its own time. But though God has planted eternity in the hearts of men, even so, man cannot see the whole scope of God's work from beginning to end. And I found that though God has made men upright, each has turned away to follow his own downward road. To be wise is as good as being rich; in fact, it is better. Don't long for "the good old days," for you don't know whether they were any better than these!

ECCLESIASTES

"Ecclesiastes," or "the Preacher," says that a search for happiness and satisfaction apart from God is useless: it is "a chasing after the wind." Reverence for God and obedience to His commandments are the only things that count in the end.

1. Introducing the Preacher

Because the Preacher was wise, he went on teaching the people all he knew; and he collected proverbs and classified them. For the Preacher was not only a wise man, but a good teacher; he not only taught what he knew to the people, but taught them in an interesting manner. The wise man's words are like goads that spur to action. They nail down important truths. Students are wise who master what their teachers tell them.

The author was King David's son "the Preacher":

I, the Preacher, was king of Israel, living in Jerusalem. And I applied myself to search for understanding about everything in the universe. I discovered that the lot of man which God has dealt to him is not a happy one. It is all foolishness, chasing the wind. What is wrong cannot be righted; it is water over the dam; and there is no use thinking of what might have been.

All is futile, says the Preacher; utterly futile. In my opinion, nothing is worthwhile; for what does a man get for all his hard work? Generations come and go but it makes no difference. The sun rises and sets and hurries around to rise again. The wind blows south and north, here and there, twisting back and forth, getting nowhere. The rivers run into the sea but the sea is never full, and the water returns again to the rivers and flows again to the sea. Everything is unutterably weary and tiresome. No matter how much we see, we are never satisfied; no matter how much we hear, we are not content.

History merely repeats itself. Nothing is truly new; it has all been done or said before. What can you point to that is new? How do you know it didn't exist long ages ago? We don't remember what happened in those former times, and in the future generations no one will remember what we have done back here.

2. Search for Pleasure

I said to myself, "Come now, be merry; enjoy yourself to the full." But I found that this too was futile. For it is silly to be laughing all the time; what good does it do? So after a lot of thinking, I decided to try the road of drink, while still holding steadily to my course of seeking wisdom. Then I tried to find fulfillment by inaugurating a great public works program: homes, vineyards, gardens, parks and orchards for myself and reservoirs to hold the water to irrigate my plantations.

Next I bought slaves, both men and women, and others were born within my household. I also bred great herds and flocks, more than any of the kings before me. I collected silver and gold as taxes from many kings and provinces. Anything I wanted I took and did not restrain myself from any joy. I even found great pleasure in hard work. This pleasure was, indeed, my only reward for all my labors. But as I looked at everything I had tried, it was all so useless, a chasing of the wind, and there was nothing really worthwhile anywhere.

So I decided that there was nothing better for a man to do than to enjoy his food and drink and his job. Then I realized that even this pleasure is from the hand of God. For who can eat or enjoy apart from Him? So I conclude that, first, there is nothing better for a man than to be happy and to enjoy himself as long as he can; and second, that he should eat and drink and enjoy the fruits of his labors, for these are gifts from God.

3. Search for Contentment

Next I observed all the oppression and sadness throughout the earth—the tears of the oppressed and no one helping them, while on the side of their oppressors were powerful allies. So I felt that the dead were better off than the living. And most fortunate of all are those who have never been born and have never seen all the evil and crime throughout the earth. Then I observed that the basic motive for success is the driving force of envy and jealousy! But this too is foolishness, chasing the wind. I also observed another piece of foolishness around the earth. This is the case of a man who is quite alone, without a son or brother, yet he works hard to keep gaining more and more riches, and to whom will he leave it all? And why is he giving up so much now? It is all so pointless and depressing.

He who loves money shall never have enough. The foolishness of thinking that wealth brings happiness! The more you have, the more you spend right up to the limits of your income, so what is the advantage of wealth—except perhaps to watch it as it runs through your fingers! The man who speculates is soon back to where he began—with nothing. This, as I said, is a very serious problem. For all his hard work has been for nothing; he has been working for the wind. It is all swept away. All the rest of his life he is under a cloud—gloomy, discouraged, frustrated and angry. The man who works hard sleeps well whether he eats little or much, but the rich must worry and suffer insomnia.

To enjoy your work and to accept your lot in life—that is indeed a gift from God. The person who does that will not need to look back with sorrow on his past, for God gives him joy. Though a man lives a thousand years twice over, but doesn't find contentment—well, what's the use?

4. A Time for Everything

There is a right time for everything:
>   A time to be born;
>   A time to die;

A time to plant;
A time to harvest;

A time to kill;
A time to heal;

A time to destroy;
A time to rebuild;

A time to cry;
A time to laugh;

A time to grieve;
A time to dance;

A time for scattering stones;
A time for gathering stones;

A time to find;
A time to lose;

A time for keeping;
A time for throwing away;

A time to tear;
A time to repair;

A time to be quiet;
A time to speak up;

A time for loving;
A time for hating;

A time for war;
A time for peace.

5. Various Nuggets of Wisdom

A bird in the hand is worth two in the bush: mere dreaming of nice things is foolish; it's chasing the wind.

A good reputation is more valuable than the most expensive perfume.

It is better to be criticized by a wise man than to be praised by a fool! For a fool's compliment is as quickly gone as paper in fire, and it is silly to be impressed by it.

Finishing is better than starting! Patience is better than

pride! Don't be quick-tempered—that is being a fool.

Because God does not punish sinners instantly, people feel it is safe to do wrong.

But though a man sins a hundred times and still lives, I know very well that those who fear God will be better off.

See the way God does things and fall into line. Don't fight the facts of nature. Enjoy prosperity whenever you can, and when hard times strike, realize that God gives one as well as the other—so that everyone will realize that nothing is certain in this life.

No one can hold back his spirit from departing; no one has the power to prevent his day of death, for there is no discharge from that obligation and that dark battle. Certainly a man's wickedness is not going to help him then.

There is hope only for the living. "It is better to be a live dog than a dead lion!"

Live happily with the woman you love through the fleeting days of life, for the wife God gives you is your best reward down here for all your earthly toil.

If the boss is angry with you, don't quit! A quiet spirit will quiet his bad temper.

A dull axe requires great strength; be wise and sharpen the blade.

When the horse is stolen, it is too late to lock the barn.

Laziness lets the roof leak, and soon the rafters begin to rot.

Never curse the king, not even in your thoughts; nor the rich man either; for a little bird will tell them what you've said.

6. When Silence Is Golden

As you enter the Temple, keep your ears open and your mouth shut! Don't be a fool who doesn't even realize it is sinful to make rash promises to God, for He is in heaven and you are only here on earth, so let your words be few. Just as being too busy gives you nightmares, so being a fool makes you a blabbermouth. So when you talk to God and vow to Him that you will do something, don't delay in doing it, for God has no pleasure in fools. Keep your promise to Him. It is far better not to say you'll do something than to say you will and then not do it. In that case, your mouth is making you sin. Dreaming instead of doing is foolishness, and there is ruin in a flood of empty words; fear God instead.

7. Long-Term Investing

Give generously, for your gifts will return to you later. Divide your gifts among many, for in the days ahead you yourself may need much help. When the clouds are heavy, the rains come down; when a tree falls, whether south or north, the die is cast, for there it lies. If you wait for perfect conditions, you will never get anything done.

God's ways are as mysterious as the pathway of the wind and as the manner in which a human spirit is infused into the little body of a baby while it is yet in its mother's womb. Keep on sowing your seed, for you never know which will grow—perhaps it all will. It is a wonderful thing to be alive! If a person lives to be very old, let him rejoice in every day of life, but let him also remember that eternity is far longer and that everything down here is futile in comparison.

8. To Youth

Young man, it's wonderful to be young! Enjoy every minute of it! Do all you want to; take in everything, but realize that you must account to God for everything you do. Don't let the excitement of being young cause you to forget about your Creator. Honor Him in your youth before the evil years come—when you'll no longer enjoy living. It will be too late then to try to remember Him, when the sun and light and moon and stars are dim to your old eyes and there is no silver lining left among your clouds. For there will come a time when your limbs will tremble with age, your strong legs will become weak and your teeth will be too few to do their work. And there will be blindness too. Then let your lips be tightly closed while eating, when your teeth are gone! And you will waken at dawn with the first note of the birds; but you yourself will be deaf and tuneless with quavering voice. You will be afraid of heights and of falling—a white-haired, withered old man, dragging himself along: without sexual desire, standing at death's door and nearing his everlasting home as the mourners go along the streets.

Yes, remember your Creator now while you are young before the silver cord of life snaps, the golden bowl is broken, the pitcher is broken at the fountain and the wheel is broken at the cistern; and the dust returns to the earth as it was, and the spirit returns to God who gave it. Here is my final conclusion: fear God and obey His commandments, for this is the entire duty of man. For God will judge us for everything we do, including every hidden thing, good or bad.

THE SONG OF SOLOMON

The Song of Solomon is rich in oriental imagery and vivid descriptions of nature. Accepted in its best sense, it is an idyll of courtship and betrothal between two devoted lovers.

1. The Bridegroom

"My beloved is a bouquet of flowers in the gardens of Enge-di. How beautiful you are, my love, how beautiful! Your eyes are soft as doves'. What a lovely, pleasant thing you are, lying here upon the grass, shaded by the cedar trees and firs.

"Your teeth are white as sheep's wool, newly shorn and washed; perfectly matched, without one missing. Your lips are like a thread of scarlet—and how beautiful your mouth. Your cheeks are matched loveliness behind your locks. How lovely your cheeks are with your hair falling down upon them. How stately your neck with that long string of jewels. You are so beautiful, my love, every part of you. Yes, a lily among thorns, so is my beloved as compared with any other girls."

2. The Bride

"My beloved one is tanned and handsome, better than ten thousand others! His head is purest gold! And he has wavy, raven hair. His eyes are like doves' beside the water brooks, deep and quiet. His cheeks are like sweetly scented beds of spices. His lips are perfumed lilies, his breath like myrrh. His arms are round bars of gold set with topaz; his body is bright ivory encrusted with jewels. His legs are as pillars of marble set in sockets of finest gold, like cedars of Lebanon; none can rival him. His mouth is altogether sweet, lovable in every way. Such is my beloved, my friend."

3. The Bridegroom's Song

"How beautiful you are, my love, how beautiful! You have ravished my heart, my lovely one, my bride; I am overcome by one glance of your eyes. How sweet is your love, my darling, my bride. How much better it is than mere wine. The perfume of your love is more fragrant than all the richest spices. Your lips, my dear, are made of honey. Yes, honey and cream are under your tongue, and the scent of your garments is like the scent of the mountains and cedars of Lebanon.

"My darling bride is like a private garden, a spring that no one else can have, a fountain of my own. You are like a lovely orchard bearing precious fruit, with the rarest of perfumes: nard and saffron, calamus and cinnamon, and perfume from every other incense tree; as well as myrrh and aloes and every other lovely spice. You are a garden fountain, a well of living water, refreshing as the streams from the Lebanon Mountains."

4. The Bride's Song

"Come, north wind, awaken; come, south wind, blow upon my garden and waft its lovely perfume to my beloved. For the winter is past, the rain is over and gone. The flowers are springing up and the time of the singing of birds has come. Yes, spring is here. The leaves are coming out and the grapevines are in blossom. How delicious they smell!

"My lover is an apple tree, the finest in the orchard as compared with any of the other youths. I am seated in his much-desired shade and his fruit is lovely to eat. He brings me to the banquet hall and everyone can see how much he loves me. My beloved is mine and I am his.

"Seal me in your heart with permanent betrothal, for love is strong as death and jealousy is as cruel as Sheol. It flashes fire, the very flame of Jehovah. Many waters cannot quench the flame of love, neither can the floods drown it. If a man tried to buy it with everything he owned, he couldn't do it."

INDEX